Gorgias Reprint Series

Volume 19

AMURATH TO AMURATH

THE MONASTERY OF RABBÂN HORMUZD.

AMURATH TO AMURATH

BY

GERTRUDE LOWTHIAN BELL

Author of "The Desert and the Sown," &c.

GORGIAS PRESS

2002

First Gorgias Press Edition.

ISBN 0-9715986-9-X

GORGIAS PRESS
46 Orris Ave., Piscataway, NJ 08854 USA
www.gorgiaspress.com

Printed in the United States of America

قال لَبيد بن رَبيعَة

بَلِينَا وَمَا تَبْلَى النُّجُومُ الطَّوَالِعُ . وَتَبْقَى الْجِبَالُ بَعْدَنَا وَالْمَصَانِعُ

We wither away but they wane not, the stars that above us rise;
The mountains remain after us, and the strong towers when we are gone.

Labîd ibn Rabî'ah.

PREFACE

DEAR LORD CROMER,

When I was pursuing along the banks of the Euphrates the leisurely course of oriental travel, I would sometimes wonder, sitting at night before my tent door, whether it would be possible to cast into shape the experiences that assailed me. And in that spacious hour, when the silence of the embracing wilderness was enhanced rather than broken by the murmur of the river, and by the sounds, scarcely less primeval, that wavered round the camp fire of my nomad hosts, the task broadened out into a shape which was in keeping with the surroundings. Not only would I set myself to trace the story that was scored upon the face of the earth by mouldering wall or half-choked dyke, by the thousand vestiges of former culture which were scattered about my path, but I would attempt to record the daily life and speech of those who had inherited the empty ground whereon empires had risen and expired. Even there, where the mind ranged out unhindered over the whole wide desert, and thought flowed as smoothly as the flowing stream—even there I would realize the difficulty of such an undertaking, and it was there that I conceived the desire to invoke your aid by setting your name upon the first page of my book. To you, so I promised myself, I could make clear the intention when accomplishment lagged far behind it. To you the very landscape would be familiar, though you had never set eyes upon it: the river and the waste which determined, as in your country of the Nile, the direction of mortal energies. And you, with your profound experience of the East, have learnt to reckon with the unbroken continuity of its history. Conqueror follows upon the heels of conqueror, nations are overthrown and cities topple down into the dust, but the conditions of existence are unaltered and irresistibly they fashion the new age in the likeness of the old. "Amurath an Amurath succeeds" and the tale is told again.

Where past and present are woven so closely together, the habitual appreciation of the divisions of time slips insensibly away. Yesterday's raid and an expedition of Shalmaneser fall into the same plane; and indeed what essential difference lies between them? But the reverberation of ancient fame sounds more richly in the ears than the voice of modern achievement. The banks of the Euphrates echo with ghostly alarums; the Mesopotamian deserts are full of the rumour of phantom armies; you will not blame me if I passed among them "trattando l'ombre come cosa salda."

And yet there was a new note. For the first time in all the turbulent centuries to which those desolate regions bear witness, a potent word had gone forth, and those who had caught it listened in amazement, asking one another for an explanation of its meaning. Liberty—what is liberty? I think the question that ran so perplexingly through the black tents would have received no better a solution in the royal pavilions which had once spread their glories over the plain. Idly though it fell from the lips of the Bedouin, it foretold change. That sense of change, uneasy and bewildered, hung over the whole of the Ottoman Empire. It was rarely unalloyed with anxiety; there was, it must be admitted, little to encourage an unqualified confidence in the immediate future. But one thing was certain: the moving Finger had inscribed a fresh title upon the page. I cannot pretend to a judicial indifference in this matter. I have drawn too heavily upon the good-will of the inhabitants of Asiatic Turkey to regard their fortunes with an impartial detachment. I am eager to seize upon promise and slow to be overmastered by disappointment. But I should be doing an equivocal service to a people who have given me so full a measure of hospitality and fellowship if I were to underestimate the problems that lie before them. The victories of peace are more laborious than those of war. They demand a higher integrity than that which has been practised hitherto in Turkey, and a finer conception of citizenship than any which has been current there. The old tyranny has lifted, but it has left its shadow over the land.

The five months of journeying which are recounted in this book were months of suspense and even of terror. Constitutional government trembled in the balance and was like to be outweighted by the forces of disorder, by fanaticism, massacre and civil strife. I saw the latest Amurath succeed to Amurath and rejoiced with all those who love justice and freedom to hear him proclaimed. For 'Abdu'l Ḥamîd, helpless as he may then have been in the hands of the weavers of intrigue, was the symbol for retrogression, and the triumph of his faction must have extinguished the faint light that had dawned upon his empire.

The confused beginnings which I witnessed were the translation of a generous ideal into the terms of human imperfection. Nowhere was the character of the Young Turkish movement recognized more fully than in England, and nowhere did it receive a more disinterested sympathy. Our approval was not confined to words. We have never been slow to welcome and to encourage the advancement of Turkey, and I am glad to remember that we were the first to hold out a helping hand when we saw her struggling to throw off long-established evils. If she can win a place, with a strong and orderly government, among civilized states, turning her face from martial adventure and striving after the reward that waits upon good administration and sober industry, the peace of the world will be set upon a surer basis, and therein lies our greatest advantage as well as her own. That day may yet be far off, but when it comes, as I hope it will, perhaps some one will take down this book from the shelf and look back, not without satisfaction, upon the months of revolution which it chronicles. And remembering that the return of prosperity to the peoples of the Near East began with your administration in Egypt, he will understand why I should have ventured to offer it, with respectful admiration, to you.

GERTRUDE LOWTHIAN BELL.

Rounton, Oct. 1910.

NOTE

THE greater part of Chapter IV appeared in the *Quarterly Review*, and half of Chapter VIII in *Blackwood's Magazine;* I have to thank the editors of these journals for giving me permission to reprint my contributions to them. I am indebted also to the editor of the *Times* for allowing me to use, in describing the excavations at Babylon and at Asshur, two articles written by me which were published in the *Times*. The Geographical Society has printed in its journal a paper in which I have resumed the topographical results of my journey down the Euphrates. The map which accompanies this book is based upon the map of Asiatic Turkey, recently published by that society, and upon a map of the Euphrates from Tell Aḥmar to Hît which was drafted to illustrate my paper.

Mr. David Hogarth, Mr. L. W. King, Mr. O. M. Dalton and Professor Max van Berchem have furnished me with valuable notes. To Sir Charles Lyall, who has been at the pains to help me with the correcting of the proofs, I tender here my grateful thanks for this and many another kindness.

CONTENTS

LIST OF ILLUSTRATIONS

AMURATH TO AMURATH

CHAPTER I

ALEPPO TO TELL AḤMAR

Feb. 3—Feb. 21

A SMALL crowd had gathered round one of the booths in the saddlery bazaar, and sounds of controversy echoed down the vaulted ways. I love to follow the tortuous arts of Oriental commerce, and moreover at the end of the dark gallery the February sun was shining upon the steep mound of the citadel; therefore I turned into the saddlers' street, for I had no other business that afternoon than to find the road back into Asia, back into the familiar enchantment of the East. The group of men round the booth swayed and parted, and out of it shouldered the tall figure of Fattûḥ.

"May God be exalted!" said he, stopping short as he caught sight of me. "It is well that your Excellency should witness the dealings of the saddlers of Aleppo. Without shame are they. Thirty years and more have I lived in Aleppo, and until this day no man has asked me to give two piastres for a hank of string." He cast a withering glance, charged with concentrated animosity, upon the long-robed figure that stood, string in hand, upon the counter.

"Allah!" said I warily, for I did not wish to parade my ignorance of the market value of string. "Two piastres?"

"It is good string," said the saddler ingratiatingly, holding out what looked like a tangled bundle of black wool.

"Eh wah!" intervened a friend. "'Abdullah sells nought but the best string."

I took a seat upon a corner of the counter and Fattûḥ

came slowly back, shaking his head mournfully, as one who recognizes but cannot amend the shortcomings of mankind. The whole company closed in behind him, anxious to witness the upshot of the important transaction upon which we were engaged. On the outskirts stood one of my muleteers like a man plunged in grief; even the donkey beside him—a recent purchase, though acquired at what cost of eloquence only Fattûḥ can know—drooped its ears. It was plain that we were to be mulcted of a farthing over that hank of string.

Fattûḥ drew a cotton bag out of his capacious trousers.

"Take the mother of eight," said he, extracting a small coin.

"He gives you the mother of eight," whispered one of the company encouragingly to the saddler.

"By God and the Prophet, it cost me more! Wallah, it did, oh my uncle!" expostulated the saddler, enforcing his argument with imaginary bonds of kinship.

Fattûḥ threw up his eyes to the vault as though he would search heaven for a sign to confound this impious statement; with averted head he gazed hopelessly down the long alley. But the vault was dumb, and in all the bazaar there was no promise of Divine vengeance. A man touched his elbow.

"Oh father," he said, "give him the mother of ten."

The lines of resolution deepened in Fattûḥ's face. "Sir, we would finish!" he cried, and fumbled once more in the cotton bag. The suspense was over; satisfaction beamed from the countenances of the bystanders.

"Take it, oh father, take it!" said they, nudging the saddler into recognition of his unexampled opportunity.

The hank of string was handed over to Ḥâjj 'Amr, who packed it gloomily into the donkey's saddle bags, already crammed to overflowing with the miscellaneous objects essential to any well-ordered caravan on a long journey. Fattûḥ and Ḥâjj 'Amr had been shopping since dawn, and it was now close upon sunset.

I climbed down from the counter. "With your leave," said I, saluting the saddler.

"Go in peace," he returned amicably. "And if you want more string Fattûḥ knows where to get it. He always deals with me."

The crowd melted back to its avocations, if it had any, and the excitement caused by our commercial dealings died away.

"Oh Fattûḥ," said I, as we strolled down the bazaar with the donkey. "There is great labour in buying all we need."

Fattûḥ mopped his brow with a red handkerchief. "And the outlay!" he sighed. "But we got that string cheap." And with this he settled his tarbush more jauntily, kicked the donkey, and "Yallah, father!" said he.

If there be a better gate to Asia than Aleppo, I do not know it. A virile population, a splendid architecture, the quickening sense of a fine Arab tradition have combined to give the town an individuality sharply cut, and more than any other Syrian city she seems instinct with an inherent vitality. The princes who drew the line of massive masonry about her flanks and led her armies against the emperors of the West, the merchants who gathered the wealth of inner Asia into her bazaars and bartered it against the riches of the Levant Company have handed down the spirit of enterprise to the latest of her sons. They drive her caravans south to Baghdâd, and east to Vân, and north to Konia, and in the remotest cities of the Turkish empire I have seldom failed to find a native of Aleppo eager to provide me with a local delicacy and to gossip over local politics. "Here is one who heard we were from Aleppo," says Fattûḥ with an affected indifference. "His brother lives in the next street to mine, and he has brought your Excellency some apples. But they are not like the apples of Aleppo." Then we exchange a greeting warm with fellow-citizenship and the apples are flavoured with good-will, even if they cannot be expected to vie with the fruit of our own countryside.

It was at Aleppo that I made acquaintance with the Turkey which had come into being on July 24, 1908. Even among those whose sympathies were deeply engaged on behalf of the new order, there were not many Europeans who, in

January 1909, had any clue to public opinion outside Constantinople and Salonica. The events of the six stirring months that had just elapsed had yet to be heard and apprehended, and no sooner had I landed in Beyrout than I began to shed European formulas and to look for the Asiatic value of the great catchwords of revolution. In Aleppo, sitting at the feet of many masters, who ranged down all the social grades from the high official to the humblest labourer for hire, I learnt something of the hopes and fears, the satisfaction, the bewilderment, and the indifference of Asia. The populace had shared in the outburst of enthusiasm which had greeted the granting of the constitution—a moment of unbridled expectation when, in the brief transport of universal benevolence, it seemed as if the age-long problems of the Turkish empire had been solved with a stroke of the pen; they had journeyed back from that Utopia to find that human nature remained much as it had been before. The public mind was unhinged; men were obsessed with a sense of change, perplexed because change was slow to come, and alarmed lest it should spring upon them unawares. The relaxation of the rule of fear had worked in certain directions with immediate effect, but not invariably to the increase of security. True, there was a definite gain of personal liberty. The spies had disappeared from official quarters, and with them the exiles, who had been condemned by 'Abdu'l Ḥamîd, on known or unknown pretexts, to languish helplessly in the provincial capitals. Everywhere a daily press had sprung into existence and foreign books and papers passed unhindered through the post. The childish and exasperating restrictions with which the Sultan had fettered his Christian subjects had fallen away. The Armenians were no longer tied to the spot whereon they dwelt; they could, and did, travel where they pleased. The nâmûsîyeh, the identification certificate, had received the annual government stamp without delay, and without need of bribes. In every company, Christian and Moslem, tongues were unloosed in outspoken criticism of official dealings, but it was extremely rare to find in these freely vented opinions anything of a constructive nature. The government was still, to the bulk of the population, a higher power, disconnected from those upon whom it exercised its will. You might complain of its lack of understanding just as you cursed the hailstorm that destroyed your crops, but you were in no way answerable for it, nor would you attempt to control or advise it, any more than you would offer advice to the hail cloud. Many a time have I searched for some trace of the Anglo-Saxon acceptance of a common responsibility in the problems that beset the State, a sense the germs of which exist in the Turkish village community and in the tribal system of the Arab and the Kurd; it never went beyond an embryonic application to small local matters, and the answers I received resembled, *mutatis mutandis*, that of Fattûḥ when I questioned him as to the part he had played in the recent general election. "Your Excellency knows that I am a carriage-driver, what have I to do with government? But I can tell you that the new government is no better than the old. Look now at Aleppo; have we a juster law? wallah, no!"

In some respects they had indeed a yet more laggard justice than in "the days of tyranny"—so we spoke of the years that were past—or perhaps it would be truer to say a yet more laggard administration. The dislocation of the old order was a fact considerably more salient than the substitution for it of another system. The officials shared to the full the general sense of impermanence that is inevitable to revolution, however soberly it may be conducted; they were uncertain of the limits of their own authority, and as far as possible each one would shuffle out of definite action lest it might prove that he had overstepped the mark. In the old days a person of influence would occasionally rectify by processes superlegal a miscarriage of the law; the miscarriages continued, but intervention was curtailed by doubts and misgivings. The spies had been in part replaced by the agents of the Committee, who wielded a varying but practically irresponsible power. How far the supremacy of the local committees extended it was difficult to judge, nor would a conclusion based upon evidence from one province have been applicable to another; but my impression is that nowhere were they of much account, and that the further the district was removed from the coast, that is, from contact with the European centres of the new movement, the less influential did they become. Possibly in the remoter provinces the local committee was itself reactionary, as I have heard it affirmed, or at best an object of ridicule, but in Syria, at any rate, the committees existed in more than the name. Their inner organization was at that time secret, as was the organization of the parent society. They had taken form at the moment when the constitution was proclaimed, and had undergone a subsequent reconstruction at the hands of delegates from Salonica, who were sent to instruct them in their duties. I came across one case where these delegates, having been unwisely selected, left the committee less well qualified to cope with local conditions than they found it, but usually they discharged their functions with discretion. The committees opened clubs of Union and Progress, the members of which numbered in the bigger towns several hundreds. The club of Aleppo was a flourishing institution lodged in a large bare room in the centre of the town. It offered no luxuries to the members, military and civilian, who gathered round its tables of an evening, but it supplied them with a good stock of newspapers, which they read gravely under the shadow of a life-sized portrait of Midhat Pasha, the hero and the victim of the first constitution. The night of my visit the newly formed sub-committee for commerce was holding its first deliberations on a subject which is of the utmost importance to the prosperity of Aleppo: the railway connection with the port of Alexandretta. To this discussion I was admitted, but the proceedings after I had taken my seat at the board were of an emotional rather than of a practical character, and I left with cries of "Yasha Inghilterra!" ("Long live England!") in my ears. I carried away with me the impression that whatever might be the future scope of its activities, the committee could not fail, in these early days, to be of some educational value. It brought men together to debate on matters that touched the common good and invited them to bear a part in their promotion. The controlling authority of the executive body was of much more questionable advantage. Its members, whose names were kept profoundly secret, were supposed to keep watch over the conduct of affairs and to forward reports to the central committee: I say *supposed*, because I have no means of knowing whether they actually carried out what they stated to be their duties. They justified their position by declaring that it was a temporary expedient which would lapse as soon as the leaders of the new movement were assured of official loyalty to the constitution, and arbitrary as their functions may appear it would have been impossible to assert that Asiatic Turkey was fit to run without leading-strings. But I do not believe that the enterprise of the committees was sufficient to hamper a strong governor; and so far as my observation went, the welfare of each province depended, and must depend for many a year to come, upon the rectitude and the determination of the man who is placed in authority over it.

Underlying all Turkish politics are the closely interwoven problems of race and religion, which had been stirred to fresh activity by exuberant promises. Fraternity and equality are dangerous words to scatter broadcast across an empire composed of many nationalities and controlled by a dominant race. Under conditions such as these equality in its most rigid sense can scarcely be said to exist, while fraternity is complicated by the fact that the ruling race professes Islâm, whereas many of the subordinate elements are Christian. The Christian population of Aleppo was bitterly disheartened at having failed to return one of their own creed out of the six deputies who represent the vilayet. I met, in the house of a common friend, a distinguished member of the Christian community who threw a great deal of light on this subject. He began by observing that even in the vilayet of Beyrout, though so large a proportion of the inhabitants are Christian, the appointment of a non-Moslem governor would be impossible; so much, he said, for the boast of equality. This is, of course, undeniable, though in the central government, where they are not brought into direct contact with a Moslem population, Christians are admitted to the highest office. He complained that when the Christians of Aleppo had urged that they should be permitted to return a representative to the Chamber, the Moslems had given them no assistance. "They replied," interposed our host, "that it was all one, since Christians and Moslems are merged in Ottoman." I turned to my original interlocutor and inquired whether the various communions had agreed upon a common candidate.

"No," he answered with some heat. "They brought forward as many candidates as there are sects. Thus it is in our unhappy country; even the Christians are not brothers, and one church will not trust the other."

I said that this regrettable want of confidence was not confined to Turkey, and asked whether, if they could have commanded a united vote, they would have carried their candidate. He admitted with reluctance that he thought it would have been possible, and this view was confirmed by an independent witness who said that a Christian candidate, carefully chosen and well supported, would have received in addition the Jewish vote, since that community was too small to return a separate representative.

As for administrative reform, it hangs upon the urgent problem of finance. From men who are overworked and underpaid neither efficiency nor honesty can be expected, but to increase their number or their salary is an expensive business, and money is not to be had. How small are the local resources may be judged from the fact that Aleppo, a town of at least 120,000 inhabitants, possesses a municipal income of from £3,000 to £4,000 a year. Judges who enjoy an annual salary of from £60 to £90 are not likely to prove incorruptible, and it is difficult to see how a mounted policeman can support existence on less than £12 a year, though one of my zaptiehs assured me that the pay was sufficient if it had been regular. In the vilayet of Aleppo and the mutesarriflik of Deir all the zaptiehs who accompanied me had received the arrears due to them as well as their weekly wage, but this fortunate condition did not extend to other parts of the empire.

The plain man of Aleppo did not trouble his head with fiscal problems; he judged the new government by immediate results and found it wanting. I rode one sunny afternoon with the boy, Fattûḥ's brother-in-law, who was to accompany us on our journey, to the spring of 'Ain Tell, a mile or two north of the town. Jûsef—his name, as Fattûḥ was careful to point out, is French: "I thought your Excellency knew French," he said severely, in answer to my tactless inquiry—Jûṣef conducted me across wet meadows, where in spring the citizens of Aleppo take the air, and past a small mound, no doubt artificial, a relic perhaps of the constructions of Seif ed Dauleh, whose palace once occupied these fields. Close to the spring stands a mill with a pair of stone lions carved on the slab above the door, the heraldic supporters of some prince of Aleppo. They had been dug out of the mound together with a fine basalt door, like those which are found among the fourth and fifth century ruins in the neighbouring hills; the miller dusted it with his sleeve and observed that it was an antîca. A party of dyers, who were engaged in spreading their striped cotton cloths upon the sward, did me the honours of their drying-ground—merry fellows they were, the typical sturdy Christians of Aleppo, who hold their own with their Moslem brothers and reckon little of distinctions of creed.

"Christian and Moslem," said one, "see how we labour! If the constitution were worth anything, the poor would not work for such small rewards."

"At any rate," said I, "you got your nâmûsîyeh cheaper this year."

"Eh true!" he replied, "but who can tell how long that will last?"

"Please God, it will endure," said I.

"Please God," he answered. "But we should have been better satisfied to see the soldiers govern. A strong hand we need here in Aleppo, that the poor may enjoy the fruits of their toil."

"Eh wah!" said another, "and a government that we know."

Between them they had summed up popular opinion, which is ever blind to the difficulties of reform and impatient because progress is necessarily slow footed.

We passed on our return the tekîyeh of Abu Bekr, a beautiful Mamlûk shrine with cypresses in its courtyard, which lift their black spires proudly over that treeless land. The brother of the hereditary sheikh showed me the mosque; it contains an exquisite miḥrâb of laced stone work, and windows that are protected by carved wooden shutters and filled with old coloured glass. Near the mosque is the square hall of a bath, now fallen into disrepair. Four pendentives convert the square into an octagon, and eight more hold the circle of the dome—as fine a piece of massive construction as you would wish to see. The sheikh and his family occupied some small adjoining rooms, and the young wife of my guide made me welcome with smiles and lemon sherbet. From the deep embrasure of her window I looked out upon Aleppo citadel and congratulated her upon her secluded house set in the thickness of ancient walls.

"Yes," she replied, eagerly detailing the benefits of providence, "and we have a carpet for winter time, and there is no mother-in-law."

Aleppo is the Greek Berœa, but the town must have played a part in the earlier civilizations of North Syria. It lies midway between two Hittite capitals, Carchemish on the Euphrates, and Cadesh on the Orontes, in the heart of a fertile country strewn with mounds and with modern mud-built villages. The chief town of this district was Chalcis, the modern Kinnesrîn, a day's journey to the south of Aleppo, but with the development of the great Seleucid trade-route between Seleucia on the Tigris and Antioch on the Orontes, which Strabo describes as passing through Hierapolis, Aleppo, being on the direct line to Antioch, must have gained in importance, and it was perhaps for this reason that the little Syrian village saw the Seleucid foundations of Berœa. The Arabic name, Ḥaleb, retains a reminis-

FIG. 1.—ALEPPO, THE CITADEL.

FIG. 2.—ALEPPO, HITTITE LION IN CITADEL.

FIG. 3.—BASALT EAGLE IN THE FRENCH CONSULATE.

FIG. 4.—ALEPPO, JÂMI' ESH SHAIBÎYEH, CORNICE.

FIG. 5.—FIRDAUS, MEDRESSEH OF EL MALIK EẒ ẒÂHIR.

cence of the original local appellation, which never slipped out of memory and finally conquered the Greek Berœa. Mohammadan tradition recognizes the fact that Ḥaleb was the ancient name of the city in the foolish tale which connects it with the cows of Abraham, the root of the word Ḥaleb being the verb signifying to milk, and the Emperor Julian knew that Berœa was the same as Chaleb. Aleppo is not without evidences of a remote antiquity. Every archæologist in turn has tried his hand at the half obliterated Hittite inscription which is built, upside down, into the walls of the mosque of Ḳiḳân near the Antioch gate; among the ruins of the citadel are two roughly worked Hittite lions (Fig. 2; Mr. Hogarth was the first to identify them), and I found in the French Consulate a headless eagle carved in basalt which belongs to the same period (Fig. 3). The steep escarpment of the castle mound is akin to the ancient fortified sites of northern Mesopotamia. Julian mentions the acropolis of Berœa. It was protected in a later age by a revetment of stone slabs, most of which were stripped away by Tîmûr Leng when he overwhelmed the town in 1401 and laid it in ruins. I know of only one building in Aleppo the origin of which can be attributed with certainty to the pre-Mohammadan period, the Jâmi' el Ḥelâwîyeh near the Great Mosque (Fig. 6). It has been completely rebuilt; the present dome, resting on pendentives, with a tambour broken by six windows, belongs to one of the later reconstructions, but the beautiful acanthus capitals must be ascribed to the fifth century on account of their likeness to the capitals in the church of St. Simeon Stylites, a day's journey north-west of Aleppo. The great school of architecture which they represent affected the builders of Islâm through many a subsequent age, and you will find the Mamlûks still flinging the leaves of the wind-blown acanthus about the capitals in their mosques. In the tenth century Aleppo was the chief city of the Ḥamdânid prince Seif ed Dauleh, a notable patron of the arts. It was he who built the south gate in the walls, the Bâb Kinnesrîn, and rebuilt the Antioch Gate after its destruction by Nicephorus Phocas; he repaired the citadel, set the shrine of Ḥussein upon the hill-side west of the town, and erected his own splendid dwelling outside the walls to the north. His palace was ravaged before his death, his gates and mosques have been rebuilt, and there remains for the period before Saladin little or nothing but the mosque inside the citadel, built in 1160 by Nûr ed Dîn, the greatest of the Syrian atabegs, and the Jâmi' esh Shaibîyeh near the Antioch Gate, which, in spite of its ruined condition, is one of the loveliest monuments of the art of Islâm in the whole town of Aleppo (Fig. 4).[1] Along the top of the wall and carried uninterruptedly round the square minaret, runs a Cufic inscription, cut in a cavetto moulding. Below it is a band of interlacing rinceaux, unsurpassed in boldness and freedom of design, and above it a heavy cymatium, borne on modillions and adorned with rinceaux. The classical outline of the cornice, together with the exquisite Oriental decoration, give it a singular hybrid beauty. This mosque apart, the finest buildings are due to the Ayyûbids, and chiefly to El Malik eẓ Ẓâhir, the son of Saladin, who ruled in Aleppo at the end of the twelfth century. Beyond the walls to the south of the city, in the quarter of Firdaus, the descendants of Saladin held their court, and though their palaces have disappeared —how much more we should know of Mohammadan architecture if each successive conqueror had not ruined the house of his predecessor!—the suburb is still resplendent with mosques and tombs. Here stands the Medreseh of El Malik eẓ Ẓâhir, with an arcade borne on capitals that retain a reminiscence of classical form though they are hung with a garland of leaves that are closer to the Sasanian than to the Greek (Fig. 5).[2] Near it is the mosque of Firdaus built by the king's widow when she was regent for her son. Over the miḥrâb of this mosque is a bold entrelac decoration which is to be found also in the shrine of Ḥussein, a building that

[1] It is dated in the year 545 A.H., *i. e.* A.D. 1150.

[2] The Persian influence had probably filtered through Egypt, for similar leaf motives are to be found in Cairo, for example in a fine bit of woodwork in the Museum: Herz Bey, *Catalogue Raisonné*, fig. 24. The prototype must be looked for in the plaster decorations of Ibn Ṭûlûn.

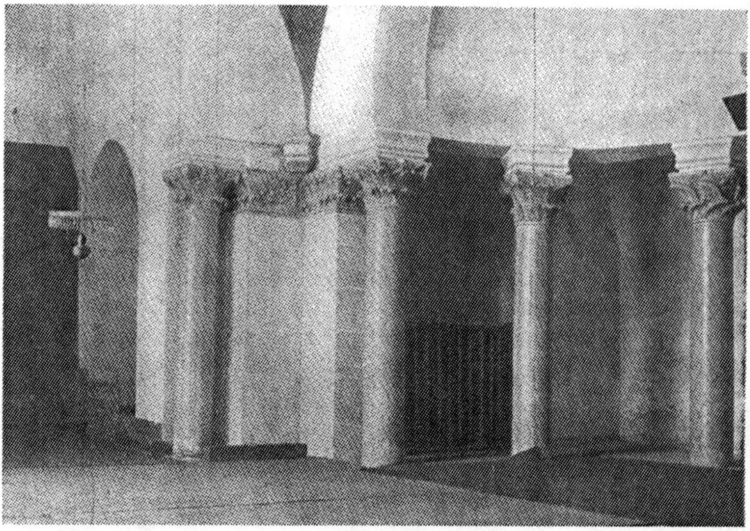

FIG. 6.—ALEPPO, JÂMI' EL ḤELAWÎYEH.

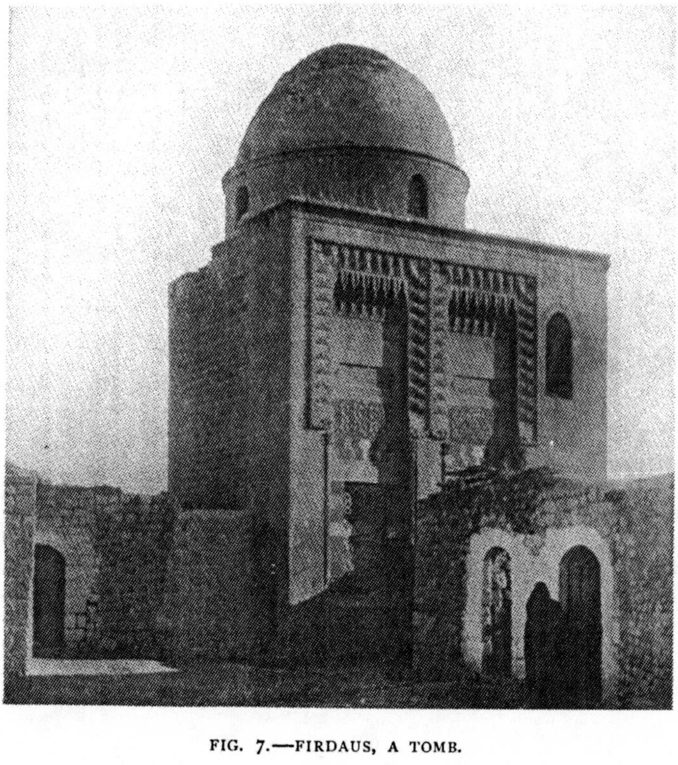

FIG. 7.—FIRDAUS, A TOMB.

FIG. 8.—ALEPPO, A MAMLÛK DOME.

FIG. 9.—ALEPPO, A MAMLÛK DOME.

owes its present form to El Malik eẓ Ẓâhir.[1] The mosque of Eṣ Ṣâliḥîn shelters a gigantic footprint of Abraham, and about it lie the tombs of the pious who sought a resting-place near the site sanctified by the patriarch—tombstones worthy of a museum, carved with Cufic inscriptions and with vine scrolls and bunches of grapes. And falling now into unheeded decay are other memorials of the dead, their walls covered with delicate tracery and their windows filled with an exquisite lacework of stone (Fig. 7). They were great builders these princes of Islâm, Ayyûbid and Mamlûk, and in nothing greater than in their mastery of structural difficulties. The problem of the dome, its thrust and its setting over a square substructure, received from them every possible solution; they bent the solid stone into airy forms of infinite variety (Figs. 8 and 9). Their splendid masonry satisfied the eye as does the wall of a Greek temple, and none knew better than they the value of discreet decoration. The restraint and beauty of such treatment of the wall surface as is to be found in the Khân el Wazîr (Fig. 10) or the Khân es Sabûn (Fig. 11) bear witness to a master hand. The grace and ordered symmetry of these façades are as devoid of monotony as are the palace walls of the early Venetian renaissance, to which they are closely related, and here as in Venice the crowning beauty of colour is added to that of form and proportion. But it is colour of the sun's own making; the sharp black outline of a window opening, the half tones of a carved panel lying upon the smooth brightness of the masonry soberly enhanced by the occasional use of a darker stone, either in courses or in alternate voussoirs. If you are so fortunate as to have many friends in Aleppo, you will find that the domestic architecture is no less admirable, and drinking your coffee under panelled ceilings rich with dull golds and soft deep reds, you will magnify once again the genius of the artificers of Asia.

The walls and gates of the city, though they are not so well preserved as those of Diyârbekr, are fine examples of

[1] M. Saladin believes this entrelac to be of Damascene origin. *Manuel d'Art Musulman*, i. p. 115.

mediæval fortification. To the north a prosperous quarter lies beyond the older circuit and the heraldic lions of the Mamlûks look down upon streets crowded with traffic. Armorial bearings played a large part in the decorative scheme of the Mohammadan builders. The type characteristic of Aleppo is a disk projecting slightly from the wall, carved with a cup from the base of which spring a pair of leaves. Upon the cup there are strange signs which are said to have been imitated from Egyptian hieroglyphs, a motive introduced by the Mamlûks; but I have noticed a variety of coats of the same period, such as the whorl which fills the disk upon the Bâb el Maḳâm, and the pair of upright pot-hooks, set back to back, upon the Jâmi' el Maḳâmât in the Firdaus quarter. These disks, together with bands of inscriptions, are the sole ornaments placed upon the city gates.

The sombre splendour of the architecture of Aleppo is displayed nowhere better than in the Bîmâristân of El Malik eẓ Ẓâhir, which was built as a place of confinement for criminal lunatics and is still used for that purpose. The central court terminates at the southern end in the lîwân of a mosque covered with an oval dome; before it lies the ceremonial water-tank, if any one should have the heart to wash or pray in that house of despair. A door from the court leads into a stone corridor, out of which open rectangular stone chambers with massive walls rising to a great height, and carrying round and oval domes. Through narrow window slits, feeble shafts of light fall into the dank well beneath and shiver through the iron bars that close the cells of the lunatics. They sit more like beasts than men, loaded with chains in their dark cages, and glower at each other through the bars; and one was sick and moaned upon his wisp of straw, and one rattled his chains and clawed at the bars as though he would cry for mercy, but had forgotten human speech. "They do not often recover," said the gaoler, gazing indifferently into the sick man's cell, and I wondered in my heart whether there were any terms in which to reckon up the misery that had accumulated for generations under El Malik eẓ Ẓâhir's domes.

FIG. 10.—KHÂN EL WAZÎR.

FIG. 11.—KHÂN ES SABÛN.

FIG. 12.—WINDOW OF A TURBEH, FIRDAUS.

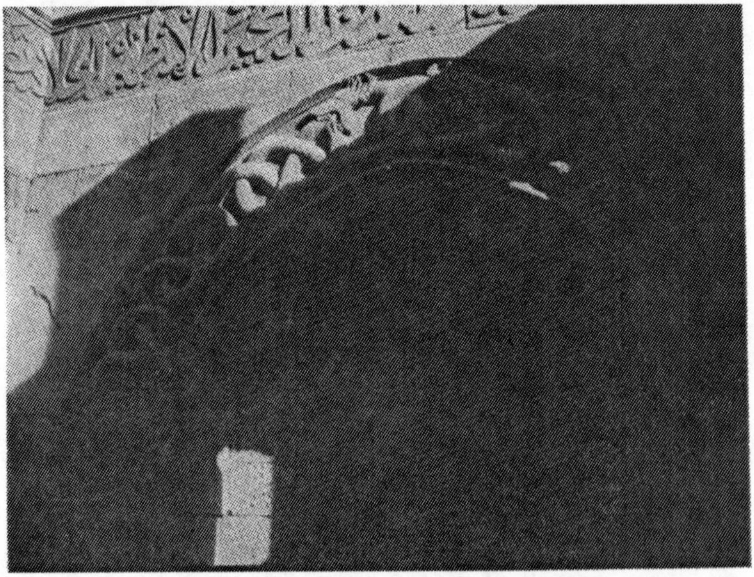

FIG. 13.—GATE OF CITADEL, ALEPPO.

Like the numismatic emblem of a city goddess, Aleppo wears a towered crown. The citadel lies immediately to the east of the bazaars. A masonry bridge resting on tall narrow arches spans the moat between a crenelated outpost and the great square block of the inner gatehouse. Through a worked iron door, dated in the reign of El Malik eẓ Ẓâhir, you pass into a vaulted corridor which turns at right angles under an arch decorated with interlaced dragons (Fig. 13), and ends at another arched doorway on which stand the leopards of Sultan Baybars, who rebuilt the castle in the thirteenth century. Above the entrance is a columned hall, grass-grown and ruined; passages lead down from it into vaulted chambers which would seem to have been repaired after Tîmûr had sacked Aleppo. Some of the blocks used in the walls here are Jewish tombstones dated by Hebrew inscriptions in the thirteenth century, and since it is scarcely possible that Baybars should have desecrated a cemetery of his own day, they must indicate a later period of reconstruction. The garrison was supplied with water from a well eighty metres deep which lies near the northern edge of the castle mound. Besides the well-hole, a stair goes down to the water level, near which point vaulted passages branch out to right and left. Tradition says that the whole mound is raised upon a substructure of masonry, but tradition is always ready with such tales, and the only inscription in the passages near the well is Cufic. At the northern limit of the enclosure stands a high square tower, up which, if you would know Aleppo, you must climb. From the muedhdhin's gallery the town lies revealed, a wide expanse of flat roof covering the bazaars, broken by dome and minaret, by the narrow clefts of streets and the courts of mosque and khân. The cypresses of Abu Bekr stand sentinel to the north; from that direction Tîmûr entered through the Bâb el Ḥadîd. In the low ground beyond the Antioch Gate, the armies of the Crusaders lay encamped; the railway, an invader more powerful than Baldwin, holds it now. Turn to the east, and as far as the eye can see, stretch rolling uplands, the granary of North Syria, and across them wind the caravan tracks that lead into inner Asia. There through the waste flows the Euphrates—you might almost from the tower catch the glint of its waters, so near to the western sea does its channel approach here.

I have never come to know an Oriental city without finding that it possesses a distinctive personality much more strongly accentuated than is usually the case in Europe, and this is essentially true of the Syrian towns. To compare Damascus, for example, with Aleppo, would be to set side by side two different conceptions of civilization. Damascus is the capital of the desert, Aleppo of the fertile plain. Damascus is the city of the Arab tribes who conquered her and set their stamp upon her; Aleppo, standing astride the trade routes of northern Mesopotamia, is a city of merchants quick to defend the wealth that they had gathered afar. So I read the history that is written upon her walls and impressed deep into the character of her adventurous sons.

At Aleppo the current of the imagination is tributary to the Euphrates. With Xenophon, with Julian, with all the armies captained by a dream of empire that dashed and broke against the Ancient East, the thoughts go marching down to the river which was the most famous of all frontier lines. So we turned east, and on a warm and misty February morning we passed under the cypresses of Abu Bekr and took the road to Hierapolis. It was a world of mud through which we journeyed, for the rains had been heavy, and occasionally a shower fell across our path; but rain and mud can neither damp nor clog the spirit of those who are once more upon the road, with faces turned towards the east. The corn was beginning to sprout and there were signs too of another crop, that of the locusts which had swarmed across the Euphrates the year before, and after ravaging the fields had laid their eggs in the shallow earth that lies upon the rocky crest of the ridges between cornland and cornland. Whenever the road climbed up to these low eminences we found a family of peasants engaged, in a desultory fashion, in digging out the eggs from among the stones. Where they lay the ground was pitted like a face scourged with smallpox, but for every square yard cleared a square mile was left undisturbed, and the peasants worked for the immediate small reward which the government paid for each load of eggs, and not with any hope of averting the plague that ultimately overwhelmed their crops. It comes and goes, for what reason no man can tell, lasting in a given district over a term of lean years, and disappearing as unaccountably as it came: perhaps a storm of rain kills the larvæ as they are hatching out, perhaps the breeding season is unfavourable—God knows, said Ḥâjj 'Alî, the zaptieh who accompanied me. The country is set thick with villages, of which Kiepert marks not the tenth part—and even those not always rightly placed. We passed his Sheikh Najar, and at Sheikh Ziyâd I went up to see the ziyârah, the little shrine upon the hill-top, but found there nothing but a small chamber containing the usual clay tomb. We left Serbes on the right—it was hidden behind a ridge—and took a track that passed through the village of Shammar. Not infrequently there were old rock-cut cisterns among the fields and round the mounds whereon villages had once stood. At Tell el Ḥâl, five hours from Aleppo, a modern village lies below the mound, and by the roadside I saw part of the shaft of a column, with a moulded base, while several more fragments of columns were set up as tombstones in the graveyard. An hour before we reached Bâb we caught sight of the high minaret of the ziyârah above it. It is a flourishing little place with a bazaar and several khâns, in one of which I lodged. The heavy rain-clouds that had hung about us all day were closing down as evening approached, but I had time to climb the steep hill to the west of the village, where a cluster of houses surrounds the ziyârah of Nebî Ḥâshil—so I heard the name, but Abu'l Fidâ calls it the Mashhad of 'Aḳil ibn Abî Ṭâlib, brother of the Khalif 'Alî[1]—an old shrine of which the lower part of the walls is built of rusticated stones. The tomb itself was closed, but I went to the top of the minaret and had a fine view of the shallow fruitful valley of the Deheb, which, taking its source near Bâb and the more northerly Tell Batnân, runs down to the salt marshes at the foot of Jebel

[1] Ed. Reinaud, p. 267. He wrote in A.D. 1321.

el Ḥaṣṣ. Across the valley there is a notable big mound with a village at its foot, the Buzâ'â of the Arab geographers, "smaller than a town and larger than a village," said Ibn Jubeir in the twelfth century. The ancient Bathnæ where Julian rested under "a pleasant grove of cypress trees" is represented by Buzâ'â and its "gate" Bâb. He compares its gardens with those of Daphne, the famous sanctuary of Apollo near Antioch, and though the gardens and cypresses have been replaced by cornfields, it is still regarded by the inhabitants of Aleppo as an agreeable and healthy resort during the hot months of summer. Perhaps we may carry back its history yet earlier and look here for the palace of Belesys, the Persian governor of Syria, at the source of the river Dardes, which Xenophon describes as having "a large and beautiful garden containing all that the seasons produce." [1] Cyrus laid it waste and burned the palace, after which he marched three days to Thapsacus on the Euphrates; but the Arab geographers place Bâlis (which some have conjectured to have occupied the site of the Persian palace) two days from Aleppo, and the position of Thapsacus has not been determined with any certainty. If it stood at Dibseh, as Moritz surmises,[2] Cyrus could well have reached it in three marches from Bâb, and I am inclined to think that Xenophon's account identifies the satrap's pleasaunce with the garden of Bathnæ. In Kiepert's map the relative distances between Aleppo and Bâb and Bâb and Manbij are not correct. I rode the two stages in almost exactly the same time (seven and a quarter hours), and the caravan took nine hours each day, whereas the map would have the march to Manbij a good two hours longer than the march to Bâb.[3]

A stormy wind, bringing with it splashes of rain, swept us next morning over the wet uplands. About an hour from Bâb we were joined by a Circassian wrapped in a thick black felt cloak, which, with the white woollen hood over an

[1] Anabasis, Bk. I. ch. iv, 10.

[2] *Zur antiken Topographie der Palmyrene,* p. 31.

[3] Mr. Hogarth also noticed that Bâb is marked out of its true place: *Annual of the British School at Athens,* XIV. p. 185.

astrachan cap, skirted coat with cartridges ranged across the breast, and high riding-boots, is the invariable costume of these emigrants from the north. His name was Maḥmûd Aghâ. His father had left the Caucasus after the Russians took the country and had gone with all his people to Roumelia, where they settled down and built houses. And then the Russians seized that land also, and again they left all and came to Manbij, and the Sultan gave them fields on his own estates. "But if the Russians were to come here too," he concluded, with the anxious air of one who faces an ever-present danger, "God knows where we should go."

"Their frontier is far," said I reassuringly.

"Please God," said he.

I asked him about the recent elections and found that he took a lively interest in the politics of the day. He knew the names of the deputies who had been returned for the vilayet of Aleppo, and said that a thousand people had given their votes in the Manbij district, though there should have been many more if all had been on the register. But they would not trouble to have their names placed upon it.

"Wallah, no," observed Ḥâjj 'Alî. "Do you think that the fellaḥîn of all these villages wish to vote? If they knew that their name was written down by the government, they would take to their heels and flee into the desert, leaving all that they have. So great would be their fear."

This was a new view of the duties and privileges of citizenship, and once more I had to shift my ground and look at representative institutions through the eyes of the Syrian peasant.

"Then none of the Arab vote?" I asked, when I had accomplished this revolution of the mind. The Arab are the Bedouin.

"God forbid!" replied Ḥâjj 'Alî. "Where is Aleppo and where their dwelling-place!"

"We are all equal now before the law," said Maḥmûd Aghâ inconsequently (but he was thinking of townsfolk, not of the Arab), "and all will be given an equal justice. We shall not wait for months at the door of the serâyah before we are given a hearing—and then only with bribes."

"I have heard that all are equal," said I, "and that Christian and Moslem will serve together in the army. What think you?"

"Without doubt the Christians may serve," he answered, "but they cannot command."

In three and a half hours we reached the village of Arîmeh, where there are two Roman milestones that have been copied by Mr. Hogarth. He dates them A.D. 197, in which year the Emperor Septimius Severus, whose name is inscribed upon them, probably completed the road. I suspect that it followed the Seleucid trade route mentioned by Strabo. There are not more than a dozen houses at Arîmeh, but the ancient settlement was more important. Cut stones lie about the modern hovels, and behind them are ruined foundations, among which we found the fragment of a bas-relief, a pair of shod feet and another foot beside them: I did not judge it to be earlier than the Roman period. A large stone block built into the wall of one of the courtyards bore a much worn foundation inscription of El Malik eẓ Ẓâhir, his name and the words "he built it" being alone decipherable. We rode on to Hierapolis across a hollow plain, all cultivated, the sacred domain of the Syrian goddess "whom some call Nature herself, the cause that produces the seed of all things."[1] When we passed over the ground it was still a chiflik, the private property of 'Abdu'l Ḥamîd, wrested by him bit by bit during the last thirty years from its owners, the half-settled Arabs. With all the rest of his landed estates it was appropriated after his deposition in April by the State, and if it is put up for sale there will be no lack of customers in Aleppo, for the merchants are eager to lay field to field, and I have heard them complain of the difficulty of buying land near home, since all was held by the Sultan. We rode between the air-holes of underground canals, of which there were a great number bringing water to Hierapolis. The old line of

[1] Plutarch: *In Crass.*

the city walls is clearly marked, though the Circassian colony, which grows in numbers and prosperity in spite of the antagonism of the neighbouring Arabs, is rapidly digging out the stones and using them in the construction of houses. Just within the walls, as we approached from the west, is a large pond, surrounded by masonry, the remains of the stairs by which the worshippers descended into the pool of Atargatis that they might swim to the altar in its midst. Lucian declares that the pool wherein were kept the sacred fish was over 200 cubits deep, but his informants must have exaggerated, inasmuch as Pocock, who visited Hierapolis in 1787, mentions that the pool was dry, and does not speak of so remarkable a hole as Lucian's estimate would imply. Maundrell, who saw it in 1699, describes it as a deep pit containing a little water, but choked by the walls and columns of great buildings that had stood all about it. East of the pool there is a modern mosque erected by 'Abdu'l Ḥamîd on the site of a foundation of El Malik eẓ Ẓâhir. Nothing remained of the earlier building, I was told, but a ruined minaret,[1] which has now gone. In the ṣaḥn, the court, I saw three inscriptions of El Malik eẓ Ẓâhir which had belonged to his mosque. Below the pavement of the ṣaḥn, said the guardian of the mosque, a second pavement had been found which he believed to have been that of a Christian church; there were one or two columns lying about here, and an acanthus capital which was certainly pre-Mohammadan and probably pre-Christian. Manbij was at one time a bishopric; the earlier travellers mention several ruined churches which have now vanished, and Ibn Khurdâdhbeh, one of the first of the Arab geographers, remarks that "there is no wooden building fairer than the church at Manbij, for it has arches of jujube wood"[2]—an observation which is repeated with wearisome iteration by many of his successors.

The pool and the mosque stand for the two periods of former splendour, the pagan and the Mohammadan. Bam-

[1] Sachau saw it: *Reise in Syrien und Mesopotamien*, p. 148.
[2] Ed. de Goeje, p. 162. He wrote in A.D. 864.

byce—to give it the classicized form of its ancient local name[1]—must have been a shrine of some importance when the Seleucids rechristened it Hierapolis, but, as at Aleppo, the older word was never forgotten, and Strabo in the first century calls it by both names. His account is suggestive of the conditions that prevailed in the Seleucid empire. "The road for merchants," says he, "going from Syria to Seleucia and Babylon, lies through the country of the Scenitæ and through the desert belonging to their territory. The Euphrates is crossed in the latitude of Anthemusia, a place in Mesopotamia.[2] Above the river, at a distance of four schœni, is Bambyce, where the Syrian goddess Atargatis is worshipped. After crossing the river the road runs through a desert country on the borders of Babylonia, to Scenæ. From the passage across the river to Scenæ is a journey of five-and-twenty days. There are on the road owners of camels who keep resting-places which are well supplied with water from cisterns, or transported from a distance. The Scenitæ exact a moderate tribute from merchants, but do not molest them: the merchants therefore avoid the country on the banks of the river and risk a journey through the desert, leaving the river on the right hand at a distance of nearly three days' march. For the chiefs of the tribes living on both sides of the river are settled in the midst of their own peculiar domains, and each exacts a tribute of no moderate amount for himself."[3] It is evident that the Alexandrids never succeeded in subduing the Arab tribes, who pushed up in a wedge along the Euphrates between their Mesopotamian and their Syrian provinces, and Strabo has here left us a description of the pre-Parthian line of traffic. Where it crossed the river it would be hazardous to pronounce. The two most famous passages of the middle Euphrates were at Birejik and at Thapsacus: at the former Seleucus Nicator

[1] Manbij is the name used in literary Arabic, but it is noticeable that in the colloquial the word approaches more nearly to the earliest form, being pronounced Bumbuj.

[2] Eskî Serûj according to Chapot: *La frontière de l'Euphrate*, p. 306.

[3] *Geography*, Bk. XVI. ch. i. 27.

built a bridge,[1] and Crassus, in the first century before Christ, found a bridge at Birejik and crossed with all the omens against him, even the eagle of the first standard turning its head backwards when it was brought down to the river. But between these two points the Euphrates can easily be crossed in boats at many places,[2] and in the numerous Roman expeditions against the Sasanians, when Hierapolis came to be used as a convenient starting-point for eastern campaigns, the passage seems usually to have been made lower down than Birejik, more nearly opposite Hierapolis, and the Mesopotamian road ran thence by Thilaticomum and through the desert to Bathnæ in Osrhœne.[3] Julian marching from Hierapolis presumably took this shorter road, for he was anxious to reach Mesopotamia before intelligence of his movements should have come to the enemy,[4] and it has been conjectured that he threw his bridge of boats across the river from Cæciliana, a place mentioned in the Peutinger Tables and identified tentatively with Ḳal'at en Nejm.[5] There is, however, a ferry just below the mouth of the Sajûr river which during the last few years has been used regularly by caravans and carriages going to Urfah, the ancient Edessa, in preference to the longer road by Birejik. This route had long been abandoned on account of the insecurity of the deserts through which it passes. Before the granting of the constitution some advance had been made towards order, and since the overthrow of Ibrahîm Pasha, the Kurd, in the autumn of 1908, it has become as safe as can reasonably be expected. The landing-place on the east bank is at Tell Aḥmar, a tiny hamlet which has inherited the site of a very ancient city. Here perhaps Strabo's road crossed the river;[6] here Julian may

[1] Ritter: *Erdkunde*, Vol. VII. p. 961.

[2] Procopius makes the same observation: *De Bell. Per.*, II. 20.

[3] It is so given in the Antonine Itinerary: Hierapoli—Thilaticomum—Bathnas—Edissa.

[4] Ammianus Marcellinus, Bk. XXIII. ch. ii. 7.

[5] Chapot, *op. cit.* p. 281.

[6] Chapot believes that the passage was effected at a point north of Cæciliana, which would fit in with Tell Aḥmar: *op. cit.* p. 254, note 5.

have constructed his pontoon bridge, and it is not improbable that for the first four or five hundred years of the Christian era it was the customary point of passage for travellers from Hierapolis to Edessa.[1] Thapsacus, which lies lower down than Cæciliana-Ḳal'at en Nejm, was of earlier importance. Xenophon crossed there, and nearly a hundred years later, Darius, fleeing headlong eastwards with his broken army after the battle of Issus, with Alexander headlong at his heels, passed over the river at Thapsacus.[2]

Julian saw Manbij in the last days of its pagan glory, and for him, as for Crassus before him, the omens of Hierapolis were unfavourable, for as he entered the gates of "that large city, a portico on the left fell suddenly while fifty soldiers were passing under it, and many were wounded, being crushed beneath the vast weight of the beams and tiles."[3] A couple of hundred years later its estate was so much diminished that no attempt was made to defend it against Chosroes,

[1] Mr. Hogarth suggests that the Abbess Ætheria crossed at Tell Aḥmar on her way to Edessa: *loc. cit.* p. 183.

[2] Birejik and the Tell Aḥmar passage (whatever may have been its ancient name) and Thapsacus do not exhaust the number of recorded routes, for Chosroes, in his first expedition against Justinian, crossed at Obbanes, somewhere about the modern Meskeneh, and on his third expedition he built a bridge of boats near Europus, which is perhaps the modern Jerâblus. (Mr. Hogarth doubts the accepted identification of Jerâblus with Europus: *Annals of Arch. and Anthrop.*, Vol. II. p. 169.) During the Mohammedan period other points are mentioned. Ibn Khurdâdhbeh, writing in the ninth century, makes the road from Aleppo to Babylon cross at Bâlis, the ancient Barbalissos (ed. de Goeje, p. 74), but Iṣṭakhrî, a hundred years later, says that Bâlis, though it was once the Syrian port on the Euphrates, had fallen into decay since the days of Seif ed Dauleh, and was little used by merchants (ed. de Goeje, p. 62). In the twelfth century, and perhaps earlier, its place had been taken by Ḳal'at en Nejm, where Nûr ed Dîn, who died in 1145, built a great fortress, famous during the wars against the Crusaders. The bridge there was called Jisr Manbij ("the bridge of Manbij"), but it cannot have been constructed by Nûr ed Dîn, for Ibn Jubeir, writing about the year 1185 a description of his journey from Ḥarrân (Carrhae) to Manbij, says that he "crossed the river in small boats, lying ready, to a new castle called Ḳal'at en Nejm" (Gibb Memorial edition, p. 248). In Yâḳût's day (circa 1225) the caravans from Ḥarrân to Syria always crossed here.

[3] Ammianus Marcellinus, Bk. XXIII. ch. ii. 6.

who held it to ransom, and then treacherously sacked it. Procopius says that the space enclosed by the wide circuit of the walls was at that time a desert, and since it was far too large to be defended by the scanty remnants of the population, Julian drew in the walls to a smaller compass.[1] After the Mohammadan conquest, Hârûn er Rashîd made Manbij one of the fortresses of his frontier province, el 'Awâṣim, the Strongholds; it passed from hand to hand in the wars carried on by the Greek emperors and the Crusaders against the khalifs, and finally remained in the possession of the latter. Under the house of Saladin it enjoyed a second period of prosperity, and the inscriptions near the mosque show that El Malik eẓ Ẓâhir, that great builder, must have expended some of his skill upon it. Ibn Jubeir found it rich and populous, with large bazaars and a strong castle. But its fortifications could not protect it against Hûlâkû, who took and sacked it in 1259, and sixty years later Abu'l Fidâ found most of its walls and houses in ruins. It never recovered from this disaster, but sank gradually into the featureless decay from which the Circassian colony is engaged in rescuing it.

The khânjî and all others interested in our arrival being happily engaged in receiving the news of the day from Fattûḥ, I slipped away alone and walked round the western and southern line of the ruined city wall. The space within is covered by shapeless heaps of earth, with cut stones and fragments of columns emerging from them. Towards the north-east corner, where the ground rises, the hollow of the theatre is clearly marked just inside the wall, and beyond it a large depression probably indicates the site of the stadium. The rain-clouds scudded past upon the wind; little and solitary, a Circassian shepherd boy came wandering in over the high downs, driving his flock of goats across the ruins of the wall and through the theatre, where they stopped to graze in shelter from the furious blast. I followed them half across the wasted city and turned aside to pay my respects to the tomb of a holy man, a crumbling mosque, with the graves of

[1] *The Buildings of Justinian* (Palest. Pilgrims' Text Society), p. 66.

the Faithful about it. The Circassian who has his dwelling in the courtyard hastened to open the shrine and to relate the story of Sheikh 'Aḳil. He lived in the days of Tîmûr Leng, and enjoyed so great a reputation that when the conqueror was preparing to besiege the town, he thought fit to warn the sheikh of his intentions. Sheikh 'Aḳil begged him to hold aloof for three days, and having obtained this respite, he counselled the inhabitants to destroy all that might tempt to pillage. They followed his advice, and Tîmûr, finding nothing but smoking ruins, passed the city by, while the populace escaped with their lives. So ran the Circassian's tale: I give it for what it is worth. Meantime the baggage had come in and the horses were being watered at the sacred pool, amid anxious cries from the muleteers, who had heard rumours of its fabulous depth: "Oh father, look to yourself! may God destroy your dwelling! no further!" Besides Ḥâjj 'Amr, who had travelled with me before, Fattûḥ had engaged two others, both Christians, Selîm and Ḥabîb, the latter a brother of his own. These three, with Jûsef, accompanied me during all the months of the journey, and I never heard a word of complaint from them, neither had I cause to complain.

I had intended to ride next day to Carchemish, sending the caravan across the ford to Tell Aḥmar, where I meant to join it in the evening, but the khânji and Maḥmûd Aghâ, who had dropped in to see that we were comfortably lodged, dissuaded me, saying that if the wind rose, as it had done that evening, the ferry boats would not come over from Tell Aḥmar and I should be left on the river bank with my camp on the opposite side. I was reluctant to give up my scheme, and Fattûḥ backed me with the observation that the passage was easy and need not be taken into account.

"Oh my brother," Maḥmûd admonished him, "it is the Euphrates!" And we were all silenced.

Early in the morning, I left Manbij with Jûsef and Ḥâjj 'Alî, and rode past a bewildering number of villages unmarked by Kiepert (I noted Mangâbeh and Wardâna on our left hand, and after them 'Ain Nakhîleh on our right) to the

FIG. 14.—ALEPPO, THE GREAT MOSQUE.

FIG. 15.—TELL AḤMAR FERRY.

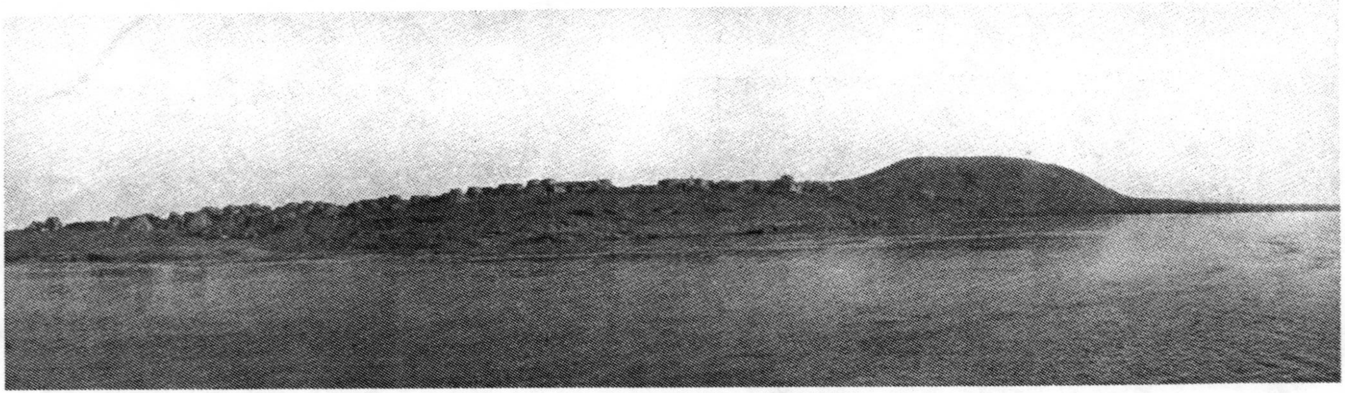

FIG. 16.—TELL AḤMAR.

FIG. 17.—CARCHEMISH FROM THE BIG MOUND.

Sajûr valley, which we reached near Chat. We had left the carriage track and now followed the windings of the Sajûr by a path narrow at best and none the better for the recent rains. A man on a donkey jogged along behind us, and I caught fragments of his conversation with Ḥâjj 'Alî. He asked the meaning of the word ḥurrîyeh (liberty), a question to which he received no very definite answer. He did not press the point, but remarked that for his part he knew nothing of the new government, but this he knew, that no one in these villages had done military service (I suppose on account of the exemption that was extended to all who dwelt upon the Sultan's domains) and no one was written down "'and el ḥukûmeh" (on the official register). He prayed God that this fortunate estate might not suffer change. In three hours from Manbij we reached Osherîyeh, turned a bit of rising ground and came in sight of the Euphrates, flowing beneath white cliffs. If I had been instructed in the proper ceremonies I should have wished to offer up a sacrifice or raise a bethel stone, but failing these I paid the only tribute that can be accorded in an ungracious age and photographed it. Ḥâjj 'Alî drew bridle and watched the proceeding.

"I see it for the first time," said I apologetically.

"Eh yes," he replied, "this is our Euphrates," and he turned an indulgent eye upon the rolling waters that are charged with the history of the ancient world.

The path dropped down into the valley and ran under cliffs which are honeycombed with chambered caves, made, or at least deepened, by the hand of man. The water was low at this season, and where we joined the river it was divided into two arms by a long island. Half-an-hour further down the arms met, and lower still another little island, which is covered after the snows begin to melt in the northern mountains, was set in the wide stream. Here was the ferry (Fig. 15). A company of bedraggled camels and camel-drivers waited on the sands while the cumbrous boats were dragged up from the point to which they had been washed by the current. The ferrymen had been weatherbound at Tell Aḥmar, and the caravans had spent a weary two days by the river's edge.

They had eaten misery, sighed the camel-drivers; wallah, no bread they had had, no fire and no tobacco; but with the patient deference of the East they stood aside when the first boat came lumbering up and observed that the Consul Effendi had best cross while the air was still. We drove our horses into the ferry boat, and by a most unnautical process, connected with long poles, our craft was run ashore upon the island, over which we ploughed our way and found a second boat ready to take us across the smaller channel. We landed in Mesopotamia at the village of Tell Aḥmar, which takes its name from the high mound, washed by Euphrates, under which it lies (Fig. 16). Jûsef spread out my lunch on the top of the tell, and we watched the caravan embark from the opposite bank and were well pleased to have accomplished the momentous passage in good order, with all our eagles pointing the right way.

I lingered on the mound, making acquaintance with a world which was new to me, but immeasurably old to fame. The beautiful empty desert stretched away east and north and south, bathed in the soft splendour of the February sun, long gentle slopes and low bare hills, and the noble curves of the Euphrates bordering the waste. Near the river and scattered over the first two or three miles of country to the east of it, there are a number of isolated mounds which represent the site of very ancient settlements.[1] Of these Tell Aḥmar is by far the most important. The ridge of silted earth which marks the line of the walls encloses three sides of a parallelogram, the river itself defending the fourth side. Strewn about the village are several stone slabs carved in relief with Hittite figures; outside one of the gates in the east wall are the broken remains of a Hittite stela, and before the second more southerly gate lie two roughly carved lions with inscrip-

[1] A few of these may have preserved a certain importance in a later age: Tell el Ghânah, directly to the east of Tell Aḥmar, has been conjectured to be Thilaticomum (possibly incorrectly: Regling, *Beiträge zur alten Geschichte,* 1902, Vol. I. p. 474) and Tell Bada'ah to be Aniana, the first being mentioned in the Antonine Itinerary and the second by Ptolemy.

tions of Shalmaneser II.[1] By the time I had finished lunch Ḥâjj 'Alî had selected a villager to serve me as guide to the wonders of Tell Aḥmar, and we set off together to inspect the written stones. My new friend's name was Ibrahîm. As we ran down to Shalmaneser's lions he confided to me that for some reason, wholly concealed from him, wallah, he was not beloved of the Ḳâimmaḳâm of Bumbuj, and added that he proposed to place himself under my protection, please God.

"Please God," said I, wondering to what misdeeds I might, in the name of my vassal, stand committed.

The fragments of the Hittite stela were half buried in the ground, and I sent Ibrahîm to the village, bidding him collect men with picks and spades to dig them out. The monument had been a four-sided block of stone with rounded corners, covered on three sides with an inscription and on the fourth with a king in low relief standing upon a bull (Fig. 18). When we had disengaged the bull from the earth the villagers fell to discussing what kind of animal it was, and Ibrahîm took upon himself to pronounce it a pig. But Ḥâjj 'Alî, who had been tempted forth from the tents to view the antîca, intervened decisively in the debate.

"In the ancient days," said he, "they made pictures of men and maidens, lions, horses, bulls and dogs; but they never made pictures of pigs."

This statement was received deferentially by all, and Ibrahîm, with the fervour of the newly convinced, hastened to corroborate it.

"No, wallah! They never made pictures of pigs."

The whole village turned out to help in the work of making moulds of the inscriptions, those who were not actively employed with brush and paste and paper sitting round in an attentive circle. There is little doing at Tell Aḥmar, and even the moulding of a Hittite inscription, which is not to the European an occupation fraught with interest, affords a wel-

[1] Mr. Hogarth (at whose request I visited Tell Aḥmar) has published the carved slabs and the stela in the *Annals of Archæology and Anthropology*, Vol. II. No. 4. He saw them when he was at Tell Aḥmar in 1908.

come diversion—to say nothing of the prospect of earning a piastre if you wait long enough. But on the third day, wind and rain called a halt, and guided by the sheikh of the neighbouring village of Ḳubbeh I explored the river-bank. Half-an-hour below Tell Aḥmar, among some insignificant ruins, we found a small Hittite inscription cut on a bit of basalt, and close to it a block of limestone carved with a much effaced relief. A few minutes further to the east a lion's head roughly worked in basalt lay upon a mound. The head is carved in the round, but we dug into the mound and uncovered a large block on which the legs were represented in relief. We rode on to Ḳubbeh, where the inhabitants are Arabic-speaking Kurds, and found in the graveyard the fragment of a Latin inscription in well-cut letters—

C O M F
L O N G
H F R
V I A S

We left the hamlet of Ja'deh a little to the right, and an hour further down passed the village of Mughârah, beyond which the eastern ridge of high ground draws in towards the river. In a small valley, just before we reached the slopes of the hill, I saw the remains of some construction that looked like a bridge built of finely squared stones, and on the further side a graveyard with a couple of broken stone sarcophagi in it. The sheikh said that after rain he had found glass and gold rings here. He insisted on my inspecting some caves by the water's edge where he was positive we should find writing, and I went reluctantly, for a series of disillusions has ended in destroying the romantic interest that once hung about caves. These were no better than I had expected, and the writing was a cross incised over one of the entrances. The rain had stopped and we rode on to the big mound of Ḳara Kazâk (Kiepert calls it Kyrk Kazâk), at the foot of which there is a considerable area covered with cut and moulded stones, and massive door-jambs still standing upright with half their height buried in the earth. I should say that it was the site of a town of the Byzantine period. When we returned to

FIG. 18.—TELL AḤMAR, HITTITE STELA.

FIG. 19 —TELL AḤMAR, EARTHENWARE JAR.

FIG. 21.—SERRÎN, NORTHERN TOWER TOMB.

FIG. 22.—SERRÎN, SOUTHERN TOWER TOMB.

camp Ibrahîm brought me two fragments of a large earthenware jar decorated round the top with a double line raised and notched in the clay (Fig. 19). In the band between were set alternately a head in high relief and a semi-circle of the notched clay. The heads were finely worked, the eyes rather prominent and the cheeks round and full—a type which recalled that of the stone heads carved upon the walls of the Parthian palace at Hatra. Whether it were Parthian or not, the jar was certainly pre-Mohammadan.

The night closed in cloudless and frosty, and I resolved to risk the caprices of the river and ride up next morning to Carchemish, for it is impossible to lie within half-a-day's journey of a great capital and yet make no effort to see it. Before dawn we sent a messenger up the river and charged him to bring us a boat to a point above the camp, that we might land on the west bank of the Euphrates above its junction with the Sajûr, a river which we were told was difficult to cross. In half-an-hour Fattûḥ and I reached Tell el 'Abr (the Mound of the Ford), where there is a small village, and on going down to the river found, to our surprise, that the boat was there before us—but not ready; that would have been too much to expect. I left Fattûḥ to bale out the water with which it was filled and went off to inspect Tell el Kumluk, a quarter of an hour away if you gallop. Here there was no village, but only a large graveyard with broken columns used as tombstones. By the time I returned to the river the boat had been made more or less seaworthy, but a sharp little wind had risen, the swift current of the Euphrates was ruffled, and the boatmen shook their heads and doubted whether they would dare to cross. We did not leave the decision to them, but hurried the horses into the leaking craft and pushed off. The stream swept us down and the wind held us close to the east bank, but with much labour and frequent invocation of God and the Prophet we sidled across and ran aground on the opposite shore. Our troubles were not yet over, for our landing-place turned out to be a big island, and there was still an arm of the river before us. The stream had risen during the rain of the previous day and was racing angrily through the second channel, but we plunged in and, with the water swirling round the shoulders of our horses, succeeded in making the passage. We shook ourselves dry and turned our faces to Carchemish. The road under the bluffs by the river-side was impassable, and we climbed up a gorge into the rocky country that lies along the top of the cliff. At one point we saw a mass of ruins, door-jambs and squared stones, which Kiepert—I know not on what ground—calls Kloster Ruine. In that bare land we met a cheerful old man driving a donkey and carrying a rifle. "Whither going in peace?" said he. "To Carchemish," we answered (only we called it Jerâblus), and I fell to considering how often the same question had met with the same answer when the stony path was full of people from the Tell Aḥmar city going up and down to learn the news of the capital and bring back word of the movements of Assyrian armies and the market price of corn. Fattûḥ, elated by the conquest of the river, bubbled over with talk, simple tales of his beloved Aleppo, of the ways of its inhabitants great and small, and of his many journeys to Killîz and 'Ain Tâb, Urfah, Diyârbekr, and Baghdâd.

"Your Excellency knows that I was the first man to take a carriage to Baghdâd, for there was no road then, but afterwards they made it. And as for my carriage, Zekîyeh has lined it inside and filled it with cushions, so that the gentry may lie at ease while I drive them. And have I told you how I got Zekîyeh?"

"No," said I mendaciously; I have travelled with Fattûḥ before, and have not been left unaware of the episodes that led to his betrothal, but reminiscences that take the listener into the heart of Eastern life bear repetition. The lady of Fattûḥ's choice was fourteen when he first set eyes on her; he went straight to her father and made a bid for her hand, but the girl was very fair and the father asked a larger dowry than Fattûḥ could give. "Fortunately," continued Fattûḥ ingenuously, "he had an illness of the eyes, and I said to him: 'There is in Aleppo a doctor who loves me, and will cure you for my sake.' But he answered: 'God give you wisdom! none can cure me save only God.' And I mounted him in my carriage, and drove him to that doctor, and look you, he healed him so that he saw like a youth. Then he said, 'There is none like Fattûḥ, and I will give him my daughter even without a dowry.' So I bought her clothes and a gold chain and all that she desired, for I said, 'She shall have nought but what I give her.' And since we married I have given her gold ornaments and dresses of silk, and when we return from this journey I will take her on a pilgrimage to Jerusalem. And indeed she loves me mightily, and I her," said Fattûḥ, bringing his idyll to a satisfactory conclusion. I have seen Zekîyeh in all the bravery of her silk gowns and gold ornaments, and I do not think she has ever had cause to regret the day when Fattûḥ mounted her father in his carriage.

We rode fast, and in a couple of hours came down to the Euphrates again, and so over the low ground for another hour till we reached a tell by the river with a village close to it. This village and tell, as well as the large mound half-an-hour away to the north-west, and the farm near it, are all called Jerâblus,[1] and probably local tradition is right in drawing no distinction between the widely separated mounds, the whole area between them having been, in all likelihood, occupied by the houses and gardens of the Hittite capital. Until you come to Babylon there is no site on the Euphrates so imposing as the northern mound of Carchemish (Fig. 17). It was the acropolis, the strongly fortified dwelling-place of king and god. At its north-eastern end it rises to a high ridge enclosed on two sides in a majestic sweep of the river. From the top of this ridge you may see the middle parts of the strategic line drawn by the Euphrates from Samosata to Thapsacus, strung with battlefields whereon the claims of Europe and Asia were fought out; while to the west stretch the rich plains that gave wealth to Carchemish, to Europus,

[1] Jerâblus or Jerâbîs, the names are used indiscriminately. The former is thought by Nöldeke to be an Arabic plural of Jirbâs (mentioned by Yâḳût as opposite Ḳinnesrin, Dictionary, Vol. II. p. 688) and the latter as Arabicized from Europus.

and to Hierapolis. They are now coming back into cultivation as the merchants of Aleppo acquire and till them, or enter into an agricultural partnership with their Arab proprietors, and if the Baghdâd railway is brought this way, as was confidently expected, the returns from them will be doubled or trebled in value. The northern mound is covered with the ruins of the Roman and Byzantine city, columns and moulded bases, foundations of walls set round paved courtyards, and the line of a colonnaded street running across the ruin field from the high ridge to a breach that indicates the place of a gate in the southern face of the enclosing wall. A couple of carved Hittite slabs, uncovered during Henderson's excavations and left exposed at the mercy of the weather, bear witness to the antiquity of the site. It has long been desolate, but there is no mistaking the greatness of the city that was protected by that splendid mound.

Fattûḥ had ordered the boatmen to pull or punt the boat over to the west bank during our absence; the river was rising and the arm that we had crossed with difficulty in the morning might have been impassable by nightfall. The boat was surrounded when we arrived by every one in the district who happened to have business on the opposite bank, and recognized in our passage an unusually favourable opportunity for getting over for nothing. As soon as we had embarked, some twenty persons and four donkeys hustled in after us and were like to swamp us, but Fattûḥ rose up in anger and ejected half of them, pitching the lean and slender Arab peasants over the gunwales and into the water at haphazard until we judged the boat to be sufficiently lightened. Those who were allowed to remain earned their passage, for when we presently ran aground on the head of the island—as it was obvious to the most inexperienced eye that we must—they leapt out and wading waist high in the stream, pushed us off. So we galloped home beside the swiftly-flowing river, aglint with the sunset, and found the camp fire lighted and the cooking pots a-simmer, and Tell Aḥmar settling down to its evening meal and to rest.

CHAPTER II

TELL AḤMAR TO BUSEIRAH

Feb. 21—March 7

THE water of the Euphrates is much esteemed by the inhabitants of its banks. It is, I think, an acquired taste; the newcomer will be apt to look askance at the turgid liquid that issues from the spout of his teapot and to question whether a decoction of ancient dust can be beneficial to the European constitution. Fattûḥ, being acquainted with my idiosyncrasies in the matter of drinking water, accepted without a murmur the sacrilegious decree that that which was destined for my flask must be boiled; whereby, though we did not succeed in removing all solid bodies, we reduced them to a comparative harmlessness. But if it cannot be described as a good table river, the Euphrates is the best of travelling companions, and the revolution of the seasons will never again bring me to the last week of February without setting loose a desire for the wide reaches of the stream and the open levels of the desert through which it flows, the sharp cold of nightfall, the hoar frost of the dawn, and the first long ray of the sun striking a dismantled camp. "There is no road," said Fattûḥ, "like the road to Baghdâd: the desert on one hand and the water on the other."

Our way next morning took us past Ḳubbeh to Mughârah, which we reached in three hours. Here we left the river and climbing the low, rocky hill to the east, found ourselves in a stony and thinly populated country bounded by another ridge of eastern hill. After twenty-five minutes' riding we saw the hamlet of Ḳayyik Debû about half-a-mile to the left of the track, and in another quarter of an hour we reached a few deserted houses. Four hours from Tell Aḥmar we pitched camp on the further bank of a small stream near the village of Serrîn, for I wished to examine two towers which stand upon the crest of a high ridge about half-an-hour to the east. They are called by the Arabs the Windmills, but in reality they are tower tombs. The more northerly, which is the best preserved, is 4·20 m. square and two storeys high (Fig. 20). The walls of the lower storey rise in solid masonry to a height of about six metres and are crowned by a plain course of projecting stones, which serves

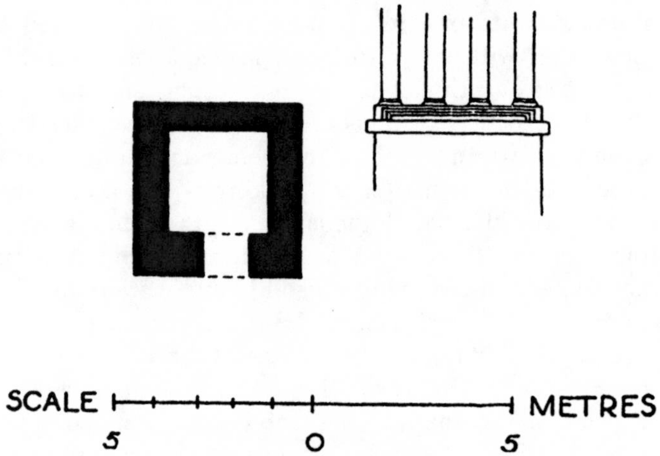

FIG. 20.—SERRÎN, NORTH TOWER TOMB, PLAN AND ELEVATION SHOWING MOULDINGS.

as cornice (Fig. 21). On the east and west sides, just below the cornice, there is a pair of gargoyles, much weathered. They represent the head and fore-quarters of lions. A little below the pair of heads on the west side is a Syriac inscription, dated in the year 385 of the Seleucid era, *i. e.* A.D. 74, which states that the tomb was built by one Manu for himself and his sons.[1] The second storey is decorated with fluted engaged columns, four on either side, the outer pair forming

[1] The inscription is given by Pognon : *Inscriptions de la Mésopotamie*, p. 17. The tomb was visited by Oppenheim, and is mentioned by him in *Tell Halaf* (1st number, 10th year of Der alte Orient), and in his *Griechische und lateinische Inschriften.* (*Byzantinische Zeitschrift*, 1905, p. 7.)

the angles. The bases of these columns rest upon a course of masonry adorned with three fasciæ: it is to be noted that the mouldings are not carried straight through to the angles, but are returned one within the other like the mouldings of a door lintel. The Ionic capitals carry a plain Ionic entablature consisting of an architrave with fasciæ, which are here taken through to the corners, a narrow frieze and a cyma of considerable projection. Probably the whole was surmounted by a stone pyramid. There are two burial chambers, one in each storey. The lower chamber can be entered by a door in the east wall which was originally closed by a large block of stone. The entrance to the upper chamber, high up in the east wall between the columns, was closed in the same fashion, and the block of porphyry which sealed it is still intact.[1] Pognon, who has given the best description and illustrations of the monument, mentions five other examples of tower tombs crowned with pyramids, one of them being the southern tower at Serrîn. The well-known tower tombs of Palmyra and the Ḥaurân are not capped by a pyramid, nor is the face of their walls broken at any point by engaged columns. I believe the type illustrated at Serrîn to be compounded of the simple tower tomb and the canopy, or cyborium, tomb.[2] The cyborium tomb exists in an infinite number of variations in Syria, in the mountain district near Birejik (whence M. Cumont has supplied me with four examples, three of them as yet unpublished[3]), in Asia Minor and in the African Tripoli. Sometimes the columns stand free,[4] sometimes they are engaged in the walls,[5] some-

[1] Oppenheim thought it was the end of a sarcophagus, but Pognon's guide climbed into the upper chamber and found it to be nothing but a block of stone closing the entrance.

[2] For the cyborium tomb, see Heisenburg: *Grabeskirche und Apostelkirche*, Vol. I. ch. xvi.

[3] A photograph of the fourth, the Ziareh of Khoros at Cyrrhus, was published by Chapot in *Le Tour du Monde*, April 8, 1905, p. 162.

[4] Mylasa: published by the Dilettanti Society; Tripoli: *Nouvelles Archives des Missions*, Tome XII. fas. 1; Dana: De Vogüé, *La Syrie Centrale*, plate 78.

[5] Tomb of Absalom, Jerusalem.

times they are represented only by engaged angle piers,[1] sometimes by free standing angle piers,[2] and occasionally column and pier have dropped away and the plain wall alone remains,[3] but the pyramidal roof is an almost constant feature, which, even in the simplest of these tombs, recalls the original canopy type. In the hill side near the tower I noticed several rock-cut mausoleums, now half-choked with stones and earth, and the hill was no doubt the necropolis of a town lying in the low ground that stretches down to the modern village by the stream.[4] The second tower, of which only the south wall remains, is situated on the southern end of the ridge, half-an-hour's ride from the first (Fig. 22). It differs slightly in detail from the other. In the lower storey a shallow engaged pier stands at either angle, while in the upper storey, in place of the porphyry block, there is an arched niche between the two central engaged columns. The fasciæ returned at the corners reappear, but the columns are not fluted. The hill top commands a wide view over country which appears to be entirely desert. My guide, who was a Christian from Aleppo, an agent of the Liquorice Trust for the Serrîn district, said that there was no settled population to the east of us, and that the few Arab encampments which were visible upon the rolling steppe were those of the Benî Sa'îd, a subdivision of the Benî Faḥl. As we sat in the sunshine under the tower, Jirjî related tales of his neighbours, the Arab sheikhs, for whom he entertained, as the townsman will, feelings that ranged between contempt and fear—contempt for their choice of a black tent in the desert as a dwelling-place, and fear inspired by the authority

[1] Gereme: Rott, *Kleinasiatische Denkmäler*, p. 171; El Bârah: De Vogüé, *op. cit.* pl. 75.

[2] M. Cumont's monuments are of this type and I have seen a fine example at Barâd in N. Syria, also as yet unpublished except for a photograph given by me in *The Desert and the Sown*, p. 287.

[3] Maden Sheher: published by Sir W. Ramsay and myself in *The Thousand and One Churches*, p. 230.

[4] The name which has been suggested for the site is Baisampse, a place mentioned by Ptolemy. There are a considerable number of cut stones on the mound near the village.

which they wielded from that humble abode. But chiefly his simple soul was exercised by the swift downfall of Ibrahîm Pasha, who for so many years had been, as the fancy prompted him, the scourge or the mighty protector of all the inhabitants of northern Mesopotamia, a man with whom the government had to make terms, while the great tribes stood in awe of him and the lesser tribes fled at the whisper of his name. Jirjî, like many another, refused to believe that he was dead, and entertained us with wild surmises as to the manner of his possible return from the unknown refuge where he lay in hiding. "God knows he was a brave man," said he. "Oh lady, do you see Ḳal'at en Nejm yonder?" And he pointed west, where across the Euphrates the walls and bastions of the fortress crowned the precipitous bank. "There be forded, he and eight hundred men with him, when he hastened back from Damascus to his own country, hearing that the government was against him. They swam the river with their horses and rested that night at Serrîn. But the Pasha was grave and silent: God's mercy upon him, for he befriended us Christians." Ḥâjj 'Alî shook his head. "He wrecked the world," said he. "Praise God he is dead." Somewhere between the two opinions lies the truth. I suspect that though the way in which his overthrow was accomplished left much to be desired, the Millî Kurds, of whom he was the chief, had gained under his bold leadership a pre-eminence in lawlessness which no government was justified in countenancing. But since he is dead, peace to his memory, for he knew no fear.

We could not see the river from Serrîn, but next morning I rode down to it and looked across to the splendid walls of Ḳal'at en Nejm. The castle, seated upon a rocky spur, encloses the steep slopes with its masonry until it seems like a massive buttress of the hill, as ageless and no less imperishable than the rock itself. We turned away from this stern ghost of ancient wars and rode from the Euphrates up a bare valley wherein we came upon a great cave, inhabited by a few Arabs. It contained three large chambers, the opening of which had been fenced in by the latest inhabitants with screens made of rushes. Upon one of the walls I found a curious inscription written in characters not unlike those seen by Sachau in a cave near Urfah [1] (Fig. 23).

FIG. 23.—INSCRIPTION IN CAVE NEAR SERRÎN.

The Arab women with their children in their arms clamoured round me, and I distributed among them what small coins I had with me, without satisfying the claims of all. One scolding wench ran after us up the valley vociferating her demand that ten paras should be given to her swaddled babe. We had not ridden far before Jûsef's horse slipped and fell upon a smooth stone, dismounting his rider, who was at no time too certain of his seat. "Allah!" ejaculated Ḥâjj 'Alî; "it was the woman's curse that brought him down." But the malediction had missed fire, or perhaps it was only ten paras' worth of damnation, for Jûsef and his horse scrambled up together unhurt. At the head of the valley we came out on to a green sward. The rains on this side of the river had been scanty and the grass had scarcely begun to grow, but already there were a few encampments of the Faḥl in sheltered places which later in the season would be set thick with the black tents of the 'Anazeh, who do not come down to the river until the rain pools are exhausted in their winter quarters. The thin blue smoke of the morning camp fires rose out of the hollows and my heart rose with it, for here was the life of the desert, in open spaces under the open sky, and when once you have known it, the eternal savage in your breast rejoices at the return to it. As we rode near the tents a man galloped up to us and begged for a pinch of tobacco. He was clothed in a ragged cotton shirt and a yet more ragged woollen cloak, but Ḥâjj

[1] It was re-copied by Pognon and published by him in *Inscrip. de la Mésopotamie*, p. 82. The similarity between some of the characters in the two inscriptions is striking.

'Alî looked after him as he turned away and observed, "His mare is worth £200."

In three hours from Serrîn we caught up the baggage animals at the last village we were to see until we reached Raḳḳah. Mas'ûdîyeh is its name. On a mound close to the river Oppenheim found three mosaic pavements, parts of which are still visible, but the most beautiful of the three has been almost destroyed and nothing remains of it but a simple geometrical border of diagonal intersecting lines.[1] Beyond Mas'ûdîyeh we crossed a long belt of sand, lying in a bend of the river; we left a small mound (Tell el Banât) a mile to the east, climbed a ridge of bare hill and dropped down into a wide stretch of grass country, empty, peaceful and most beautiful. It was enclosed in a semicircle of hills that stood back from the river, and from out of the midst of it rose an isolated peak known to the Arabs as Ḳuleib. This land is the home of the Weldeh tribe, and not far from the Euphrates we found a group of their tents pitched between green slopes and the broad reaches of sand which give the spot its name, Rumeileh, the Little Sands. It was the encampment of Sheikh Ṣallâl, and no sooner had we arrived than the sheikh's son, Muḥammad, came out to bid us welcome and invite us to his father's tent. The two zaptiehs and I took our places round the hearth while Muḥammad roasted and pounded the coffee beans, telling us the while of the movements of the great tribes, where Ḥâkim Beg of the 'Anazeh was lying, and where Ibn Hudhdhâl of the Amarât, and similar matters of absorbing interest. Sheikh Ṣallâl was in reduced circumstances by reason of a recent difference of opinion with the government. His brother had been enlisted as a soldier and had subsequently deserted, whereupon the government had seized Ṣallâl's flocks and clapped the sheikh into gaol, and finally he had sold "the best mare left to us, wallah!" for £T37 and with the money procured his own release.

[1] It appears in the extreme right-hand top corner of his Fig. 22, *Inschrif. aus Syrien und Mesopot.*

"Eh billah!" said Ḥâjj 'Alî, shaking his head over the confused tale in which, as is usual in these episodes, the wrongdoing seemed to be shared impartially by all concerned. "Such is the government!"

"And now, oh lady," pursued the sheikh, "we have neither camels nor sheep, for the government has eaten all."

"How do you live?" said I, looking round the circle of dark, bearded faces by the camp fire.

"God knows!" sighed the sheikh, and turning to Ḥâjj 'Alî he asked him what was this new government of which he heard, and liberty, what was that?

"Liberty?" said Ḥâjj 'Alî, evading the question; "how should there be liberty in these lands? Look you, they talk of liberty, but there is no change in the world. In Aleppo many men are murdered every week, and who knows what they are doing, those envoys whom we sent to Constantinople?"

In spite of his misfortunes Sheikh Ṣallâl designed to entertain me at dinner and had set aside for that purpose an ancient goat. My attention was attracted to it by the sound of bleating in the women's quarters and I was just in time to save its life, expending myself, however, in protestations of gratitude. Muḥammad ibn Ṣallâl took me round the encampment before the light failed and pointed out the foundations of a number of stone-built houses. Behind my tents the summits of some grassy mounds were ringed round with circles of great stones, of the origin of which he knew nothing. I counted five of them; in the largest lay foundations of small rectangular chambers.

As we walked back to the tents Muḥammad said reproachfully:

"Oh lady, you have not laughed once, not when I showed you the ruins, nor when I told you the name of the hills."

I hastened to amend my ways, and thus encouraged he enumerated a string of ruined sites in the neighbourhood and accepted an invitation to serve us as guide next morning. He prepared himself for the journey by slipping on four cartridge belts, one over the other, although our whole road lay in the Weldeh country, and the worst enemy we encountered was a raging wind which sent the Euphrates sands whirling about us and obscured the landscape near the river. In about an hour we climbed up on to the higher ground of the grass plain at a point called Shems ed Dîn, where among a heap of cut stones I found fragments of an entablature carved with dentils and palmettes. Perhaps the ruins were the remains of a tower tomb. At Tell eẓ Ẓâher, an hour further south, we saw heaps of unsquared building-stones. Above this site stood Sheikh Sîn, a steep hill which we ascended, but found no trace of construction on it. I sent my zaptieh down to stop the baggage and bid Fattûḥ camp at the mound of Munbayah near the river, and with Muḥammad turned inland to a hill called by him Jernîyeh, some five miles to the east. Muḥammad rode across the downs at a hand gallop in the teeth of the wind, and I behind him, too much buffeted by the storm to call a halt. The immediate reason for our haste, as I presently discovered, was a couple of pedlars from whom he desired to buy soap, a commodity of which he stood in great need. The two men were Turks; they greeted me with effusion as a fellow alien in those wastes, and at parting pressed upon me a handful of raisins with their blessings. We galloped on faster than before and arrived breathless at Jernîyeh which lifts its solitary head a hundred feet or more above the surrounding plain. On the summit are three large mounds into which the Arabs had dug and uncovered fine cut stones; I conjecture that there may have been here watch towers or tower tombs belonging to the town of which the ruins lie below, to the south of the hill. These ruins comprise a large low mound ringed round with a wall and a ditch, and a considerable area covered with remains of buildings made of unsquared stones. Occasionally the plan of house or court was marked out upon the grass and Muhammad showed me several deep cisterns—altogether a very remarkable ruin field though it is not named on Kiepert's map. On our way back to the river we climbed Tell el Ga'rah and found the foundations of a fort on the top of it. Here we picked up a much-weathered Byzantine coin and a quantity of sherds of glazed Arab pottery, blue and green and purple. Munbayah, where my tents were pitched—the Arabic name means only an elevated spot—has been conjectured to be the Bersiba of Ptolemy's catalogue of place names. It is an irregularly-shaped double enclosure, resting on one side on the river (Fig. 25). The line of the walls is marked by high grass mounds, but here and there a bit of massive polygonal masonry, large stones laid without mortar, crops out of the soil. The outer enclosing wall is not continued along the north side, but ends in a heap of earth and stones which looks like the ruins of a tower or bastion. To the south there is a clearly-marked gate in the outer wall, corresponding with a narrower opening in the inner line of fortification; another gate leads out to the north, and facing the river there are traces of a broad water gate, protected on either side by a wall that drops down the slope towards the stream (Fig. 26). Twenty minutes further down the bank lies another mound, Tell Sheikh Ḥassan. There are vestiges of construction by the water's edge between the two mounds, and south of Tell Sheikh Ḥassan the ground is broken by a large stretch of ruin mounds, among which I saw a rude capital. In another half-hour down stream, at 'Anâb, there is again an enclosure of grassy heaps strewn with stones. For a distance of about three miles, therefore, the left bank of the river would seem to have been inhabited and guarded, though possibly at different dates. Jernîyeh and Munbayah are by far the most interesting sites which I saw on the little-known stretch of the river between Tell Aḥmar and Ḳal'at Ja'bar; it is useless to conjecture in what way, if at all, they were connected with each other, but in both places I should like to clear away the earth and see what lies beneath.

If it had been possible to cross the Euphrates I would have examined the high tell of Sheikh 'Arûd which had been all day the fixed point for my compass, but though there was a boat to be had, the intolerable wind continued till nightfall and made the passage impracticable. The mental exasperation produced by wind when you are living and

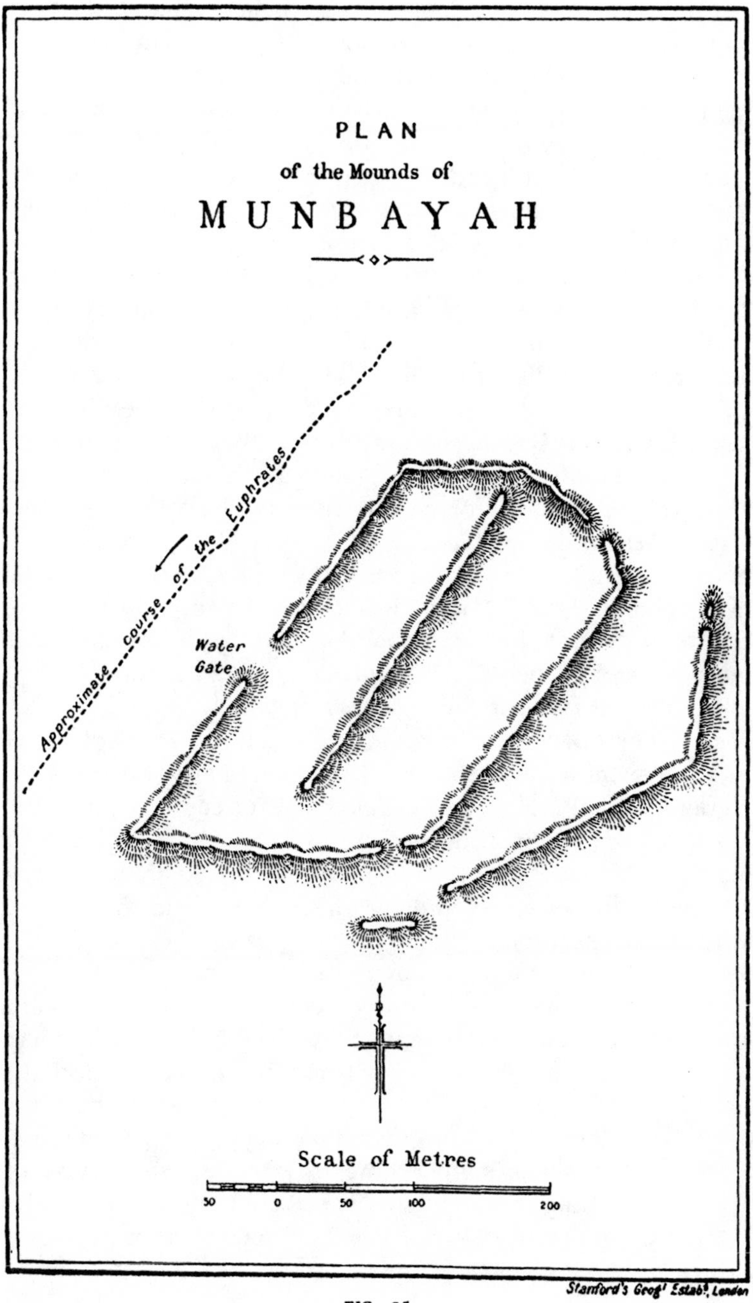
PLAN
of the Mounds of
MUNBAYAH
Approximate course of the Euphrates
Water Gate
Scale of Metres
50
0
50
100
200
Stanford's Geog! Estab! London

FIG. 25.

trying to work out of doors, passes belief. The blast seizes you by the hand as you would hold your compass steady, dances jigs with your camera and elopes with your measuring tape, and when after an exhausting struggle you return vanquished to your tent, it is only to find your books and papers buried in sand. Moreover, commissariat arrangements were complicated by the interruption of communications with the opposite side of the river. Fortunately I had foreseen that there would be little food for man or beast on the left bank, where no travellers pass, and contrary to my habits had laid in a provision of tinned meats, for which we had reason to be thankful. The baggage animals were lightly loaded and could carry four days' corn besides their packs; when this ran short Fattûḥ went foraging in every Arab encampment, but occasionally the horses were without their full allowance, for at this time of the year the Arabs themselves are very scantily supplied. We soon learnt to place no reliance on assurances, however emphatic, that the next sheikh down the river would be well furnished, and as our road led us into regions that had suffered more and more severely from the lack of rain, we gave up all hope of ekeing out our corn with the grass which never grew that year. The corn, too, became dearer, until at Baghdâd it touched famine prices. On the upper parts of the river there is no fuel and we carried charcoal for cooking purposes; but when the tamarisk bushes began to appear, about a day's march north of Raḳḳah, the muleteers boiled their big rice pot over a fire of sticks and the zaptiehs warmed their hands in the sharp chill of the early morning at the heap of embers that had been kept alive all night. The zaptiehs are supposed to feed themselves, but except on the rare occasions when we were on a high road, they shared the meals of my servants. I would find them sitting in the dark round the steaming dish served up by Ḥâjj 'Amr, and with them the Arab who had been our guide that day, or one who had dropped in towards supper time to give us information of the road, or any aged person considered by Fattûḥ to be worthy of our hospitality. We held many a frugal feast

FIG. 24.—WIFE AND CHILDREN OF A WELDEH SHEIKH

FIG. 26.—MUNBAYAH, WATER GATE.

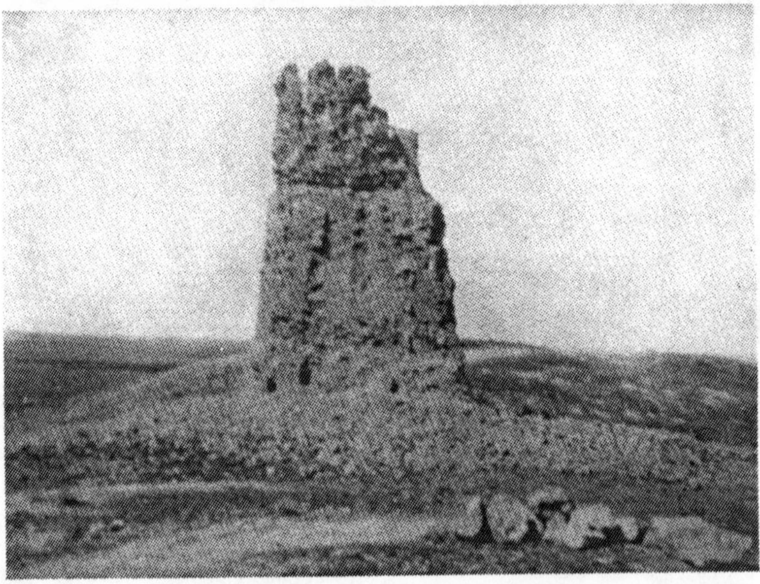

FIG. 28.—NESHABAH, TOWER TOMB.

under the stars where the waters of the Euphrates roll through the wild.

During the next day's ride we followed the course of the river closely, save where the grassy edge of the desert was separated from the water by a tract of sand and stones covered in time of flood, and therefore devoid of all trace of settled habitation. The tents of the Weldeh were scattered along the banks and occasionally a small bit of ground had been scratched with the plough and sown with corn. At one point we saw the white canvas tent of a man from Aleppo who was engaged in negotiating an amicable partnership with the Weldeh sheikhs. The majestic presence of the river in the midst of uncultivated lands, which, with the help of its waters, would need so little labour to make them productive, takes a singular hold on the imagination. I do not believe that the east bank has always been so thinly peopled, and though the present condition may date from very early times, it is probable that there was once a continuous belt of villages by the stream, their sites being still marked by mounds. Half-an-hour from 'Anâb we passed Tell Jifneh, with remains of buildings about it; in another hour and a half there were ruins at Ḥaliâweh, and forty minutes further we came to a big mound called Tell Muraibet. From this point the grass lands retreated from the Euphrates, leaving place for a wide stretch of sand and scrub opposite Old Meskeneh. Kiepert marks two towers on some high ground to the east, but they must have fallen into ruin since Chesney's survey, for I could not see them. Six hours from Bersiba we reached in heavy rain the tents of Sheikh Mabrûk and pitched our camp by his, so that we might find shelter for our horses under his wide roof. We were about opposite Dibseh, which was perhaps the famous ford of Thapsacus. Mabrûk told me that in summer, when the water is low, camels can cross the river just above Dibseh; at Meskeneh a ferry boat is to be had, but at no other point until you come to Raḳḳah.

Next morning a young man from the sheikh's tent, cousin to Mabrûk (all the unmarried youths of the sheikh's family are lodged in his great house of hair) rode with us to Ḳal'at Ja'bar. He told me of a ruin called Mudawwarah (the Circle), an hour and a half away to the east: it may represent one of Kiepert's towers, but according to Ibrahîm's account nothing is now to be seen but a heap of stones. We rode out of the camp with a troop of women and children driving donkeys into the hills, where they collect brushwood.

"Last year," said my companion, "they dared not stray from the tents, lest the horsemen of Ibrahîm Pasha should attack them and seize the donkeys. Wallah! the children could not drive out the goats to pasture, and every man sat with his loaded rifle across his knees and watched for the coming of raiders. For indeed he took all, oh lady; he robbed rich and poor; he held up caravans and killed the solitary traveller."

"Eh wah!" said the zaptieh, "and the soldiers of the government he killed also. He was sultan in the waste."

"But now that he is gone," continued Ibrahîm, "we are at rest. And as soon as we heard of his death we blessed the government, and all the men of the Weldeh rode out and seized the flocks that he had captured from us, and more besides. And behold, there they pasture by the river." And he pointed to some sheep grazing under the care of a couple of small boys.

"Then all the desert is safe now?" said I.

"Praise God!" he answered, "for the 'Anazeh are our friends. We have no foes but the Shammar, and their lands are far from us."

Before we reached Ḳal'at Ja'bar we galloped up into the low hills to see a rock-cut tomb. Through a hole in the ground we let ourselves down into a chamber 5·10 m. × 7·00 m., with nine arcosolia set round it, each containing from four to six loculi (Fig. 27). On one of the long sides there was a small rectangular niche between the arcosolia. Ibrahîm called the place Maḥall es Ṣafṣâf and assured me that it was the only cavern known to him in these hills. From here he took me down to a mound named Tell el Afrai, which lies about a quarter of a mile from the river. On the landward side it is protected by a dyke forming a loop from the Euphrates. At one time the water must have filled this moat, but the upper end has silted up and the channel is now dry. Out of the mound, which is unusually large, the rains had washed a number of big stones, some of them squared. We were now close to the two towers of Ḳal'at Ja'bar, one being a minaret that rises from the centre of the fortress, while the other, known to the Arabs as Neshabah, stands upon an isolated hill to the north-west [1] (Fig. 28). Of the Neshabah tower nothing remains but a rectangular core of masonry (unworked stones set in thick mortar) containing a winding stair which can be approached by a doorway about four metres from the ground. Below the door there is a vaulted niche which looks like the remains of a sepulchral chamber. All the facing stones have fallen away, but the core is ridged in a manner that suggests the former existence of engaged columns, and I believe that Neshabah is a tower tomb older than the castle, rather than the outlying watch-tower of an Arab fort.[2] The buildings at Ḳal'at Ja'bar are mainly of brick, though some stone is used in the walls and bastions that surround the hill-top (Fig. 29). The entrance is strongly guarded; from the outer gate-house a long narrow passage, hewn out of the rock, leads into the interior of the

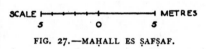

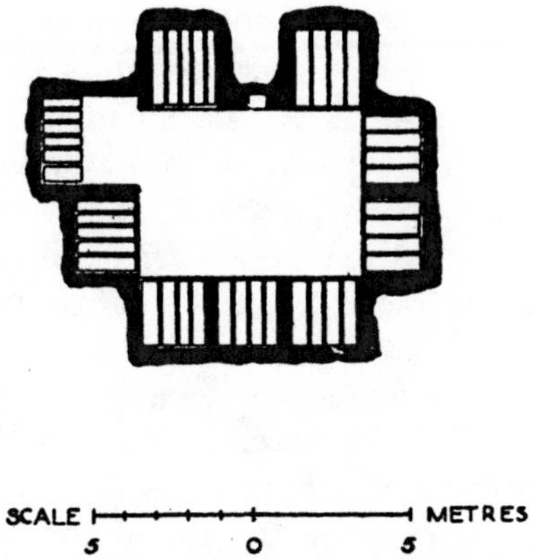

FIG. 27.—MAḤALL ES ṢAFṢAF.

[1] I could not reconcile the topography here with Kiepert's map. He marks a northern tower, which he calls Nesheib (doubtless my Neshabah) and places there the Mazâr of Sultan 'Abdullah. He has a second tower further to the south-east, and finally the castle itself. The second tower is non-existent, or else it represents the minaret in the castle. The only mazâr which I saw or heard mentioned is that of Sultan Selîm, a small modern building between Neshabah and the castle.

[2] It resembles the tower tombs at Irzî, which will be described later,

castle. Among the ruins within the walls are a vaulted hall and parts of a palace composed of a number of small vaulted chambers. The construction of the small vaults struck me as having stronger affinities with Byzantine than with the typical Mesopotamian systems, and I should not assign to them a very early date. The palace had also contained a hall of some size, but only the south wall is standing (Fig. 31). It is broken by a deep recess, possibly a miḥrâb, with a doorway on either side, and the upper part is decorated with a row of flat trifoliate niches. In the centre of the castle a round minaret rises from a massive square base (Fig. 30). Towards the top of the minaret there is a double band of ornamental brickwork with a brick inscription between. I could not decipher the inscription, owing to its great height, but the characters were not Cufic, and the round shape of the minaret makes it improbable that it should be earlier than the twelfth century. Beyond the minaret is a vaulted cistern. The shelving northwest side of the hill is defended by a double ring of brick towers, but on the south-east side, where the rocks are precipitous, there is little or no fortification. The brick walls of the buildings above the gate-way are decorated with string courses and bands of diamond-shaped motives, the diamonds set point to point or enclosed in hollow squares (Fig. 32).

The history of the castle is not easy to disentangle from the accounts left by the Arab geographers. An earlier name for it was Dausar, but even this does not seem to have been applied before the seventh century, though Idrîsî, writing in the twelfth century, ascribes its foundation to Alexander. He is the first author who mentions Dausar and he gives no authority for his statement as to its origin. Opposite Dausar, on the right bank of the Euphrates, stretches the battlefield of Ṣiffîn, where in A.D. 657 the Khalif 'Alî met the forces of the Umayyad Mu'âwiyah. Tradition has it that 'Alî entrusted his ally Nu'mân, a prince of the house of Mundhir, with the defence of these reaches of the Euphrates, and that a servant of the latter, Dausar by name, built the castle which was called after him. It took its present name from an Arab of the Ḳusheir, from whose sons it was wrested (in A.D. 1087)

FIG. 29.—ḲAL'AT JA'BAR.

FIG. 30.—ḲAL'AT JA'BAR, MINARET.

FIG. 31.—ḲAL'AT JA'BAR, HALL OF PALACE.

FIG. 32.—ḲAL'AT JA'BAR, BRICK WALL ABOVE GATEWAY.

by the Sultan Malek Shah, the Seljuk.[1] It was held by the Franks of Edessa during the first Crusade and captured by the Atabeg Nûr ed Dîn towards the middle of the twelfth century. It passed into the hands of the Ayyûbids, and in Yâḳût's time (1225) was held by Ḥâfiẓ, the nephew of Saladin. Benjamin of Tudela says that he found a colony of 2,000 Jews settled at Ja'bar, which was then a much-frequented ferry.[2] I did not observe any signs of habitation outside the castle, except a few caves in the rocks to the south; but half-an-hour further down the river, on a bluff called Kahf (Chahf in the Bedouin speech) ez Zaḳḳ, there are traces of houses which may represent the Jewish settlement. In Abu'l Fidâ's day (fourteenth century) the castle of Ja'bar was ruined and abandoned. The greater part of the existing buildings might well have been erected by Nûr ed Dîn, and failing further evidence it is to him that I should ascribe them.

Under Kahf ez Zaḳḳ we found the tents of Ḥamrî, one of the principal sheikhs of the Weldeh, a sturdy white-bearded man in the prime of age, with the fine free bearing of one long used to command. He sat in the sunshine and watched the pitching of our camp, ordering the young men of the tribe to bestir themselves in our service, one to gather brushwood, another to show the muleteers the best watering-place on the muddy river-bank, a third to fetch eggs and sour curds, and when he had seen to our welfare, he strode back to his tent and bade me follow. The coffee was ready when I arrived, and with the cups the talk went round of desert politics and the relation of this sheikh with that all through the Weldeh camps. The glow of sunset faded, night closed down about the flickering fire of thorns, a crescent moon looked in upon us and heard us speaking of new things. Even into this primeval world a rumour had penetrated, borne on the word Liberty, and the men round the hearth fell to discussing the meaning of those famous syllables, which have no meaning save to those who have lost that for which they stand. But

[1] This is Abu'l Fidâ's account, ed. Reinaud, p. 277. He wrote in A.D. 1321. Yâḳût, a century earlier, gives the same story.

[2] Quoted by Ritter, *Erdkunde*, Vol. X. p. 241.

Sheikh Ḥamrî interposed with the air of one whose years and experience gave him the right to decide in matters that passed the common understanding.

"How can there be liberty under Islâm?" said he. "Shall I take a wife contrary to the laws of Islâm, and call it liberty? God forbid." And we recognized in his words the oldest of the restrictions to which the human race has submitted. "God forbid," we murmured, and bowed our heads before the authority of the social code.

On the following day a dense mist hung over the valley. An hour from Kahf ez Zaḳḳ the path left the Euphrates at a spot called Maḥârîz where there are said to be ruins, but owing to the fog I could see nothing of them.[1] Three-quarters of an hour later we returned to the river and rode under low cliffs in which there were caves; my guide called the place Ḳdirân, which is, I suppose, Kiepert's Ghirân. Here again we left the water's edge, and half-an-hour later the fog melted away and revealed a monotonous green plain with the camels of the Weldeh pasturing over it. In summer it is a favourite camping-ground of the 'Anazeh. At Billânî, three and a half hours from our starting-point, we rejoined the Euphrates. Billânî is visible from afar by reason of a number of bare tree-trunks set in the ground to mark the Arab graves which are grouped about the resting-place of some holy man. The ancient sanctity of the place is still attested by numerous shafts of columns among the graves, but seventy years ago Chesney could make out a small octagonal temple.[2] It was a fine site for temple or for tomb. The river comes down towards it through many channels in the shape of a great fan, gathers itself into a single stream, broad and deep, and so sweeps under the high bank on which the fragments of the shrine are scattered, and beyond it round a wide bend clothed with thickets of tamarisk and thorn and blackberry. Through these thickets we rode for two hours and a half, and

[1] Ainsworth believed this to be the site of Benjamin of Tudela's Jewish settlement (*Euphrates Expedition*, Vol. I. p. 269), and he speaks of a monastic ruin here.

[2] It is so described in his map.

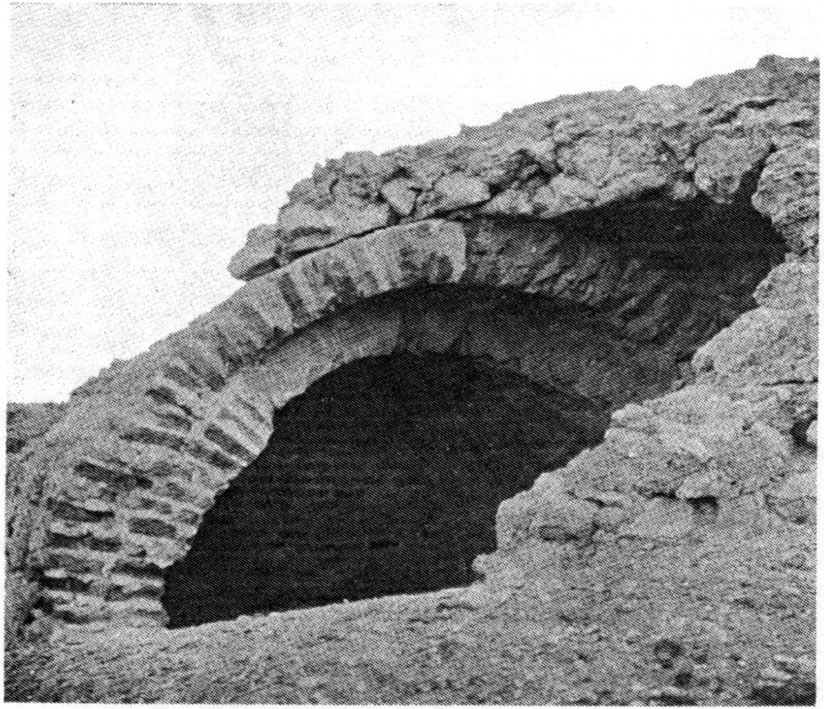

FIG. 34.—ḤARAGLAH, VAULT.

FIG. 35.—RAḲḲAH, EASTERN MINARET.

FIG. 37.—RAḲḲAH, MOSQUE FROM EAST.

FIG. 38.—RAḲḲAH, ARCADE OF MOSQUE, FROM NORTH.

then camped under a mound called Tell 'Abd 'Alî, not far from a couple of very poor tents of the Afâḍleh, with the river a mile away. The night was exquisitely still, but from time to time an owl cried with a shrill note like that of a shepherd-boy calling to his flocks.

Our camp proved to be but two hours' ride from Raḳḳah. A little more than half-way between the two places we reached the enigmatic ruin which is known to the Arabs as Ḥaraglah, a name which may be a corruption of Heraclea. It consists of a rectangular fortress, almost square, with a series of small vaulted chambers forming the outer parts of the block and, as far as I could judge, larger vaulted chambers filling up the centre (Fig. 33). At the four angles there are round towers. The building as it now stands is merely a substructure, a platform resting on vaults, on which stood an upper storey that has disappeared. The masonry is mostly of unsquared stones laid in a bed of very coarse mortar mixed with small stones, but the vaults are of brick tiles, and it is noticeable that these tiles are not laid in the true Mesopotamian fashion, whereby centering could be dispensed with (*i. e.* in narrow slices leaning back against the head-wall), but that the double ring of tiles is treated like the voussoirs of a stone arch and must have been built on a centering (Fig. 34). This structure would be enough to show that the work does not belong to the Mohammadan period. The fortress is ringed round by an outer wall, now completely ruined. Beyond it to the south runs a dyke, and beyond the dyke, some 500 m. south-east of the central fort, there is another mound on which I saw cut stones larger than the stones used at Ḥaraglah. Still further

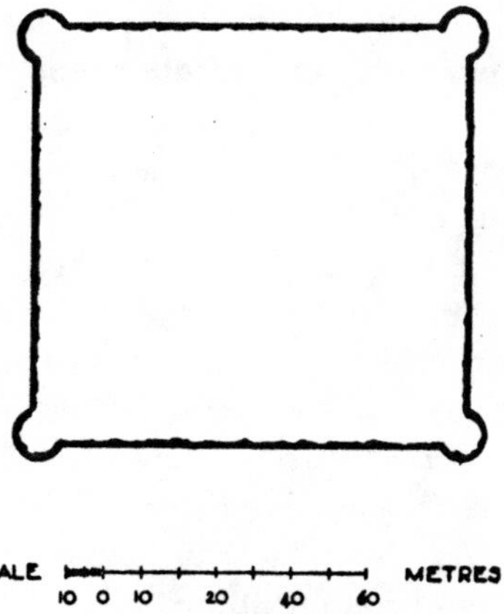

FIG. 33.—ḤARAGLAH.

to the south lies a third mound, Tell Meraish, with a second dyke to the south of it. The two dykes appeared to be loop canals from the Euphrates and must therefore have formed part of an extensive system of irrigation; probaby there had once been a considerable area of cultivation under the protection of the fortress.[1]

So we came to Raḳḳah and there joined forces with the army of Julian, who had marched down from Carrhæ and the head waters of the Belîkh 1,500 years ago and more—the account of the march given by Ammianus Marcellinus is, however, irreconcilable with the facts of geography, for he says that Julian reached Callinicum in one day from the source of the river Belias, whereas it is at least a two days' journey. Callinicum was not the earliest town upon the site of Raḳḳah, though the record of history does not go back further than to its immediate predecessor, Nicephorium, which some say was founded by Alexander and others by Seleucus Nicator. When Julian stopped there to perform the sacrifice due at that season to Cybele, Callinicum was a strong fortress and an important market. Chosroes, a couple of hundred years later, finding it insufficiently guarded, seized and sacked it. Justinian rebuilt the fortifications, but in A.D. 633, according to Abu'l Fidâ, it fell to the Mohammadan invaders. In A.D. 772 the Khalif Manṣûr strengthened the position with a second fortified city, Râfiḳah (the Comrade), built, it is said, upon the same round plan as Baghdâd, which was another city of his founding. Hârûn er Rashîd built himself a palace either in Raḳḳah or in Râfiḳah, and used the place as his summer capital. In the subsequent centuries the older foundations fell into ruin and the Comrade, which continued to be a flourishing town, usurped its name, so that in Yâkût's day (1225) the original Raḳḳah had disappeared, but Râfiḳah was known as Raḳḳah. Here is fine matter for confusion among the Arab geographers, and they do not fail to make the most of it. White Raḳḳah, Black Raḳḳah, Burnt Raḳḳah, and no

[1] Sachau thought that Ḥaraglah was of Hellenistic origin (*Reise in Syrien und Mesopotamien*, p. 245); Sarre believes that it may be Parthian, and the circular outer fortification gives colour to the suggestion (*Zeitschr. der Gesell. für Erdkunde zu Berlin*, 1909, No. 7).

less than two Middle Raḳḳahs figure upon their pages, and it is impossible to determine whether any or none of these titles stands for Râfiḳah, or which of them denotes the old Raḳḳah. But by 1321 when Abu'l Fidâ wrote, all the Raḳḳahs were reduced to uninhabited ruin (perhaps by the Mongol hordes of Hûlâgû), and it only remains for the traveller to collect the names of sites, which his Arab guide will furnish with an alacrity that runs ahead of accuracy, and apply them as he thinks best to the list of recorded towns. And lest I should fail to add my quota to the tangled nomenclature, I will hasten to state that at a distance of an hour and ten minutes east of the ruins that lie about the modern village, I rode over a large stretch of ground on which there were traces of habitation and was told that its name was Brown Raḳḳah—(Raḳḳat es Samrâ)—and on further inquiry I learnt that nearer to the Euphrates there was a similar area called Red Raḳḳah—(Raḳḳat el Ḥamrâ)—but as I neglected to visit the spot I need not do more than mention that Kiepert marks Black Raḳḳah—(Raḳḳat es Saudâ)—at about the place where it must be.

To come to matters less controvertible, the modern Raḳḳah consists of two villages, of which the westernmost has recently been erected by a Circassian colony upon high broken ground that certainly indicates the existence of an older settlement. Beyond it to the east there is a large semi-circular enclosure, the straight side turned towards the Euphrates and lying at a distance of about a mile from that river. The walls are built of sun-dried brick alternating with bands of burnt brick, and set at regular intervals with round bastions. There are clear traces of a moat or ditch and of a second, less important, wall beyond it. The Arab village lies in the south-west corner of this enclosure, near the centre are the ruins of a mosque with a round minaret, on the east side the remains of a large building, probably a palace, and at the south-east corner part of a gate called the Baghdâd gate. Still further east there is yet another ruin field. Towards the middle of it rises a square minaret standing in a rectangular space which has been enclosed by walls of sun-dried brick, no doubt a mosque (Fig. 35). The minaret is of brick, but it rests upon a square base formed of large blocks of marble. The brickwork is broken by six horizontal notched rings, the uppermost surmounting a wide band of ornamental brick. The notches in the brick were obviously intended to contain some other material, possibly wood, which has now perished. There are numerous fragments of columns in the neighbourhood of the minaret. The only other buildings are, north of the minaret, a small domed ziyârah, which local tradition would have to be the tomb of Yaḥyâ el Barmakî, who, as well as his more famous son Ja'far, was vizir to Hârûn er Rashîd, and not far from the Baghdâd gate a similar shrine, known as the Ziyârah of Uweis el Ḳaranî. Uweis fell in A.D. 657 in one of the engagements fought on the Euphrates between 'Alî and Mu'âwiyah, but his tomb is of no great interest except in so far as it is composed of older materials. Over the doorway is an inscription which states that "this fortress and shrine were repaired by Sultan Suleimân, son of Selîm Khân," who reigned from 1526–1574.[1] It is obvious that the stone must have been brought from elsewhere, since the inscription cannot refer to the insignificant structure on which it is placed. In the adjoining graveyard there are many fragments of columns, presumably taken from the mosque, and some much battered capitals, one of them worked with acanthus leaves. I saw, too, a small marble double column of the type so common in the early Christian churches of Asia Minor.

It is tempting to suppose that in the eastern ruin field we have the site of the oldest city, Nicephorium-Callinicum-Raḳḳah, that the columns were derived from Hellenistic or Byzantine buildings and re-used in a mosque of which nothing now remains but the square minaret.[2] I think it not

[1] Sachau (*op. cit.* p. 243) gives the inscription, and my copy tallied with his.

[2] Just as the first mosque in Cairo, that of 'Amr, was built entirely on columns taken from earlier buildings, Muḳaddasî describes one of the Raḳḳah mosques as معلق على عمود; it would be satisfactory to imagine that he referred to the columned arcades of the mosque round the square minaret, but the phrase cannot reasonably be twisted into that or any other meaning. The square minaret is the ancient Syrian tower type; Thiersch has recently published an exhaustive study of it in his *Pharos*.

FIG. 39.—RAḲḲAH, CAPITALS OF ENGAGED COLUMNS, MOSQUE.

FIG. 40.—RAḲḲAH, PALACE.

FIG. 41.—RAḲḲAH, DETAIL OF STUCCO ORNAMENT, PALACE.

FIG. 42.—RAḲḲAH, DOMED CHAMBER IN PALACE.

improbable that the semi-circular enclosure represents Manṣûr's foundation, Râfiḳah, though it does not follow that any of the existing ruins, except perhaps parts of the wall, belong

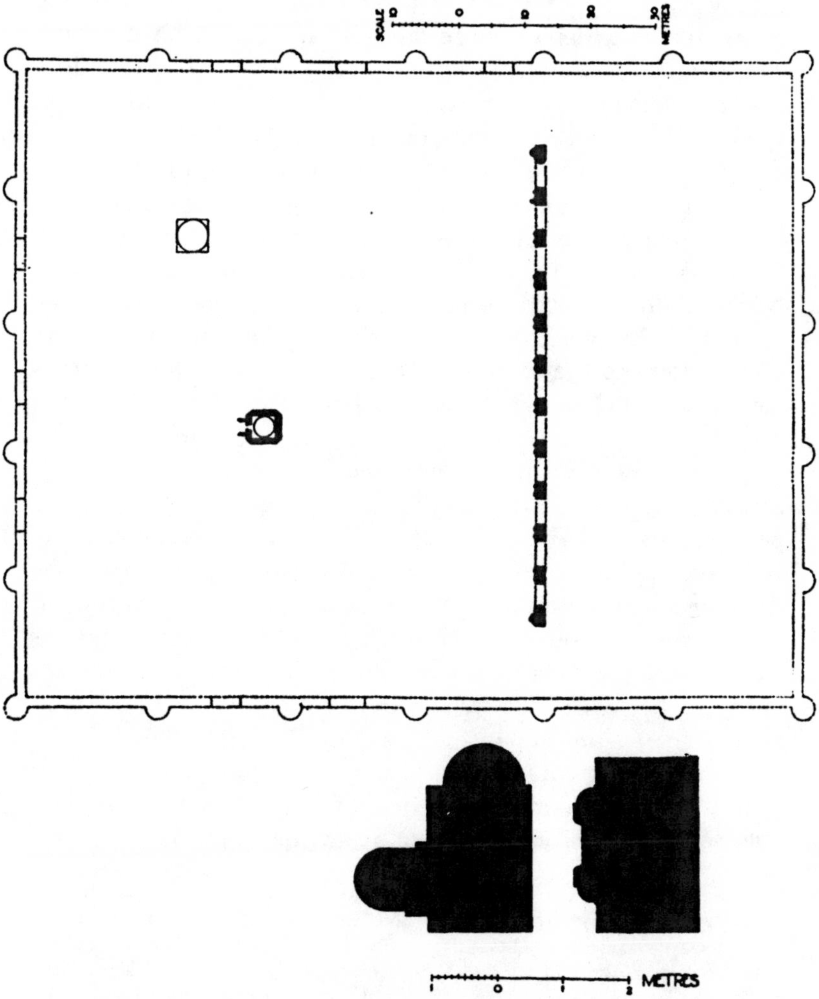

FIG. 36.—RAḲḲAH, PLAN OF MOSQUE AND SECTIONS OF PIERS.

to his time. They are nevertheless of great importance in the history of Mohammadan art. The mosque is surrounded by a wall of sun-dried brick broken by round bastions (Fig. 36). In the centre of the ṣaḥn, or court, there is a small ziyârah recently rebuilt, and in the north-east corner the round brick minaret springs from a square stone base composed of ancient materials (Fig. 37). The upper part of the minaret is decorated with bands of brick dog-tooth ornament. One of the great arcades which enclosed the ṣaḥn still stands on the south side (Fig. 38).[1] An inscription over the central arch states that the mosque was repaired by the Atabeg Nûr ed Dîn in 1166, and I conjecture that the minaret is of his building.[2] The mosque is of the true Mesopotamian type, of which the most famous examples are the two mosques at Sâmarrâ and the mosque of Ibn Ṭûlûn at Cairo. With all these it shows the closest structural affinities, and it may be assumed that Nûr ed Dîn retained the original plan when he repaired the building. The stucco capitals of the engaged columns on the piers belong to the same family as the elaborate stucco ornaments of Ibn Ṭûlûn, which date from the latter half of the ninth century, and in both cases the decorative motives employed are probably Mesopotamian in origin (Fig. 39). Stucco decorations are also the main feature of the group of palace ruins near the east wall. The most noticeable of these is a rectangular tower-like structure (Fig. 40), where the chamber on the ground-floor shows bold stucco ornament on which are traces of colour (Fig. 41). On the walls of another chamber of the palace, which was covered with a dome set upon squinch arches, there is a row of arched niches, the arch being cusped on the inside. Below the niches is a brick dog-tooth string-course (Fig. 42). The squinches contain a primitive stalactite motive. There are two other small rooms, both of which are roofed with an oval dome (3·87 m. × 3·32 m.

[1] I saw traces of two such arcades on the E., N. and W. sides of the court, and, judging from the vestiges that remain, the arcades must have been three deep to the south. The bricks of the vanished arcades have been dug out and carried away for building purposes. The outer walls are so much ruined that I could not determine the position of the gates with certainty.

[2] Professor van Berchem has published the inscription in his *Arabische Inschriften*, a chapter appended to the work of Professor Sarre and Dr. Herzfeld entitled *Reise in Euphrat- und Tigris-Gebiet*. But the publication has appeared too late for me to do more than refer to it.

FIG. 43.—RAḲḲAH, BAGHDÂD GATE FROM EAST.

FIG. 44.—RAḲḲAH, INTERIOR OF BAGHDÂD GATE.

FIG. 46.—ḤALEBÎYEH.

and 4·02 m. × 2·03 m.); in both cases the dome is very shallow and the rectangular substructure is adapted to the oval by means of wooden beams laid across the angles. Everywhere wooden beams were used in conjunction with brick, and it is to be borne in mind that though the country round Raḳḳah is now entirely devoid of trees, all the Arab geographers speak of the well-wooded gardens and groves of fruit-trees that surrounded the town. In the tower-like building and in the Baghdâd gate bands of wood were laid in the face of the wall, but the wood has perished, leaving the space it occupied to tell of its former presence, as in the eastern minaret. The cusp motive can be seen in the blind arcade on the exterior of the Baghdâd gate (Fig. 43). In the interior there is a bay to the south which appears to have been covered by a barrel vault, and may have been balanced by a similar bay to the north of the doorway, for the blind arcade on the outside of the gatehouse breaks off abruptly at the northern end and must certainly have been carried further (Fig. 44). This would allow for a northern bay corresponding to the bay that still appears south of the door. The vaulting of the gate has fallen, but from the indications that are left it appears certain that while the south bay was covered by a barrel vault the central space was occupied by a groin (Fig. 45).[1]

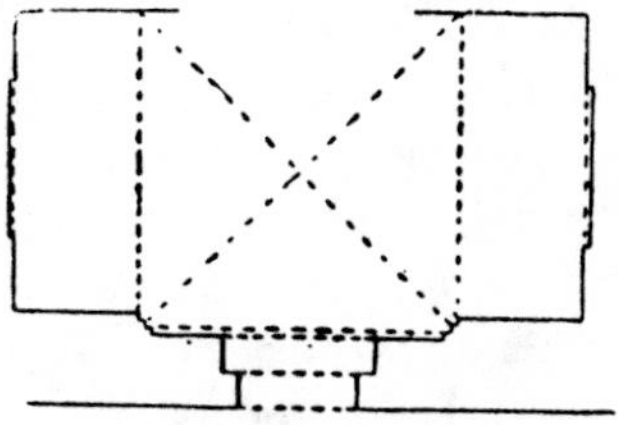

FIG. 45.—RAḲḲAH, BAGHDÂD GATE, RECONSTRUCTED.

The whole of the two areas of ruin are strewn with potsherds of the Mohammadan period, and over the greater part of the walled city the ground is honeycombed with irregular holes and trenches, the excavations of peasants in search of the now celebrated Raḳḳah ware. A few years ago their labours were rewarded by a large find of unbroken pieces, many of which made their way through the hands of Aleppo

[1] M. Viollet has published a short description of these ruins (*Publications de l'Académie des Inscrip. et Belles-Lettres*, 1909, Vol. XII. part 2). He believes the palace to have been erected by Hârûn er Rashîd.

dealers to Europe, and though such a stroke of good fortune is rare, perfect specimens are occasionally unearthed, and I saw a considerable number, together with one or two fragments of exquisite glass embossed with gold, during the two days I spent at Raḳḳah. In some instances the original factories and kilns have been brought to light, and it is not unusual to see bowls or jars which have been spoilt in the baking and thrown away by the potter. No exhaustive study of Raḳḳah ware has as yet been made, though it is of the utmost importance in the history of the arts of Islâm. The fabrication of it must have reached a high state of perfection during the twelfth and thirteenth centuries, to which period the pieces which have been preserved are usually assigned.

At Raḳḳah matters fell out in a way which, if they had not been handled firmly, might well have wrecked my plans, for a telegram arrived from the Vâlî of Aleppo directing all whom it might concern to put a stop to my progress down the left bank of the Euphrates, on account of the disturbed condition of the desert. The Vâlî commanded that I should be turned back across the river and conveyed carefully from guardhouse to guardhouse along the high road. It was the Mudîr of Raḳḳah who was ultimately responsible for the execution of these orders, and he, honest man, was much perplexed when he discovered that one side of the Euphrates was not the same to me as the other, nor was he helped to a better understanding when I explained that I preferred the Jezîreh, the Mesopotamian bank, because no one travelled there. The Shâmîyeh, the Syrian bank, he hastened to assure me, was also chôl (wilderness), if that was what I desired, and he begged me to believe that I should find the guardhouses most commodious. Thereupon I took up the question on a different issue, and called his attention to the fact that the Vâlî, who was newly appointed to Aleppo, could not have heard how peaceful the desert had become since the death of Ibrahîm Pasha. The Mudîr admitted the truth of this observation, and we compromised by sending a telegram to the Vâlî, asking him to reconsider his decision. But the telegraphic system of the Turkish empire leaves an ample margin for the exercise of individual discretion in emergencies, and since upon the third day no reply had been received, I was spared from showing a direct disregard of official dictates, while the Mudîr, seeing my caravan set out towards the Belîkh, wisely made the best of a bad business and sent a couple of zaptiehs with me. One of them was a Circassian who had little Arabic, but the other, Maḥmûd by name, proved an agreeable and intelligent fellow-traveller, well informed, and a keen politician.

It is exactly two hours' ride from Raḳḳah to the Belîkh. Our path lay between stretches of marsh, which must always have existed hereabout, for the word Raḳḳah means a swamp. Where we crossed the Belîkh it was a muddy brook, almost all the water having been drawn off for irrigation purposes, and the bridge was merely a few bundles of brushwood laid upon some poles. I sent the caravan down the bank of the Euphrates and taking one of my zaptiehs with me, turned slightly inland towards a group of hills called Jebel Munâkhir, the Nebs. In about two hours we reached a small outlying limestone tell on the top of which there were traces of masonry. Jebel Munâkhir, a mile or so from the tell, is an extinct volcano, and the lava beds extend almost to the tell. We climbed to the summit of the mountain and found the crater to be a distinctly marked basin with broken sides. On one of the peaks there is a ziyârah, a square enclosure made of undressed stones piled together without mortar, and a small tomb-chamber of the same construction. I looked carefully for any trace of ancient work, but my search was rewarded only by finding clumps of pale blue irises growing among the rocks. The west massif of Jebel Munâkhir, on which we were standing, rises several hundred feet above the level of the plain, and we had an extensive view over the unknown desert to the north. About three miles to the east lay another but smaller block of hill called Jebel Munkhar esh Sharḳî, the Eastern Neb, and on the horizon, almost due north, we could see some rising ground which my guide, an Arab of those parts, stated to be Jebel 'Uḳala.[1] Below it there are

[1] I expect that this is Sachau's Bergland Tulaba—see Kiepert's map.

wells, and another well, Abu Tuṭah, lies between it and the Belîkh. Between Jebel Munâkhir and Jebel 'Abdu'l 'Azîz (which I could not see) there is a low ridge of hill, Jebel Beiḍâ. All through this desert country there are small wells of water (jubb is the Arabic word) sufficient to supply the 'Anazeh, who pasture their flocks here during the spring; I saw a few of their encampments, but the greater part of the tribe was still in winter quarters further to the east and south. The tents along the river were those of the 'Afaḍleh—'Ajeil el Ḥamrî is the chief sheikh of the tribe, but I did not happen to meet him. An hour's ride from the hills we reached a large encampment at a spot called Ḳubûr ej Jebel, near the Euphrates. The name means the Graves of the Mountain, but I could not hear of any tombs in the neighbourhood. Our own tents were pitched an hour further down on some grassy mounds by the river far from any Arabs; Meiḍa, my guide called the place. In the low ground between Ḳubûr ej Jebel and Meiḍa, but above flood-water level, we crossed an area ringed round with a notable deep ditch. Somewhere near my camp Julian must have received his Arab reinforcements. On leaving Nicephorium, he marched along the bank of the Euphrates, "and at night he rested in a tent, where some princes of the Saracen tribes came as suppliants bringing him a golden crown and adoring him as master of the world, and of their own nations. . . . While he was addressing them," pursues Ammianus Marcellinus,[1] "a fleet arrived as large as that of the mighty lord Xerxes; . . . they threw a bridge over the broadest part of the Euphrates. The fleet consisted of one thousand transports bringing provisions and arms, and fifty ships of war, and fifty more for the construction of bridges. . . ." At this point a hubbub arose in the servants' tents; the golden crowns and the battleships went tumbling on to the grass, and I ran out just in time to see a troop of little shadowy forms hurrying in the moonlight across the sands by the water's edge. They were wild pig, the only herd we encountered.

It is essential to have a local man by you if you would

[1] Bk. XXIII. ch. iii. 8.

ascertain local names (even then the nomenclature is apt to be confusing), and accordingly I took an Arab with me next morning. We rode in five minutes to a grassy mound by the river, Khirbet Hadâwî, in another quarter of an hour to Khirbet ed Dukhîyeh, and in twenty minutes more to Jedeideh. At none of these places did I see any trace of construction, but at Abu Sa'îd, ten minutes further, there is an 'Anazeh mazâr with graves round it marked by fragments of columns and small basalt mills for grinding corn. It would be interesting to know from what period these mills date; I saw quantities of them in the burial-grounds between Munbayah and Tell Murraibet, but none of the Arabs know what they are, and when they find them they use them as tombstones. At Abu Sa'îd we turned away from the river and rode inland in a north-easterly direction. The great bare levels were more than usually enchanting that morning; the hot sun beat upon them, a sharp little wind, the very breath of life, swept across them, and all the plain was aromatic with sweet-scented plants. Presently we passed a few 'Anazeh tents, and I stopped and gave the aristocracy of the desert a respectful salutation. An inmate of the tents, hearing my greeting, picked up his spear, mounted his mare and bore us company for a mile or two; I do not know what dangers he expected to encounter or whether the spear was merely for sheref (honour), but when time hangs as heavy as it does in an Arab tent, you may as well put in the hours by carrying a spear about the countryside as in any other manner. We engaged in an exceedingly desultory conversation, in the course of which he called out to me:

"Lady, my mare is sick."

"God cure her," said I.

"Please God!" he returned. "It is her mind—her mind is sick." But I could suggest no remedy for that complaint, whether in man or beast.

When he left us, the zaptieh and I began to talk of the prospects of good administration under the new order. Maḥmûd was by birth a Turk, a native of Kars, whence he had migrated when it fell into the hands of the Russians.

His long acquaintance with the Arabs had only served to enhance in his estimation the Turkish capacity for government, and the granting of the constitution had raised it yet higher. "The Turks understand politics," said he, "and look you, the constitution was from them. But as for the Arabs, what do they know of government?" He placed great confidence in the Young Turks, and said that every one except the effendis was in favour of the dastûr (the constitution). "The effendis fear liberty and justice, for these are to the advantage of the poor. But they, being corrupt and oppressors of the poor, set themselves in secret against the dastûr, and because of this we have confusion everywhere. And if one of them is sent to Constantinople as a deputy his work will not be good, for he will work only for himself. And in the vilayets there will be no justice unless the English will send into each province an overseer (mufattish) who will look to it that the dastûr is carried out. Effendim, do you see my clothes?" I examined his ragged nondescript attire; save for the torn and faded jacket it would have been difficult to recognize in it a military uniform. "Twice a year the government gives us clothes, but they never reach us at Raḳḳah. The officers in Aleppo eat them, and with my own money I bought what I wear now."

"Are you paid?" I inquired.

"The government owes me twenty-four months' pay," he answered.

I asked what he thought of the scheme for enlisting Christians.

"Why not?" said he. "The Christians should help the Moslems to bear the burden of military service." And then he added, "If there be no treachery."

There was no need to ask him what he meant by the last phrase. I had heard too often from the lips of Christians the expression of a helpless fear that the new régime must founder in blood and anarchy, after which the nations of Europe would step in, please God, and take Turkey for themselves. This forecast was not by any means confined to the Christians, but they, of all others, should have refrained from putting it into words, for it did not encourage patriots like Maḥmûd to believe in their loyalty.

We reached our goal, Tell esh Sha'îr, in two hours and forty minutes from Abu Sa'îd, but the time in this case represents about twelve miles, since we were not riding at caravan pace. There were no buildings on the tell, but a number of large stones had been dug out of it and set up as a landmark—rijm, the Arabs call such guiding stone heaps. Two shepherds of the 'Anazeh joined us while we were at lunch, much to their material advantage, for we shared our provisions with them; from them I learnt that there had once been a well here, but that it was now choked up. They knew of no ruins in the desert beyond, and my impression is that there has never been any settled population in this region, away from the Euphrates. We struck back to the river in a south-easterly direction, and in three hours came to our camp, pitched by some Afaḍleh tents on a mound of which I have not recorded the name. It is the boundary between the kazas of Raḳḳah and of Deir, and lies about an hour's march below a site called by Kiepert the Khân. From our camp we rode in an hour to the ruins of Khmeiḍah, where there were vestiges of a considerable town, squared stones, baked brick walls and a stone sarcophagus. An Arab on a broken-down mare joined us here, and as we rode together Maḥmûd described to me the nature of the authority exercised by the government over the tribes, and particularly the incidence of the sheep-tax.

"Effendim," said he, "you must know that the government levies the sheep-tax from each sheikh." Four piastres per head of sheep is the amount. "And the scribe having computed the number of sheep that belong to those tents, he calls upon the sheikh to make good the sum due, and perhaps the sheikh will have to pay 2,000 piastres. Then he levies from the men of his tents 3,000 piastres, and to the government he gives 1,800."

"True, true," said the Arab beside us. "Wallah, so it is."

"And then," pursued Maḥmûd, "another man is sent out by the government, with his clerk and half-a-dozen of us zaptiehs. And all this costs much money. And the sheikh levies another 500 piastres, and pays 150 piastres; and so it goes on till the sum is found, but the expenses of collection are heavy. And as for the tax on cultivated land, the owner gives a bribe to him who is sent to value it, and he estimates the produce at less than half the real amount. And so it is with the sheep-tax. Effendim, do you think that all the sheep are counted? No, wallah! Last year the cornlands of the Shâmîyeh between Raḳḳah and Deir paid only £800, and the sheep-tax in the Jezîreh was no more than £2,000."

"Eh yes," said the Arab, "but the government takes much."

"The sheikhs take much," returned Maḥmûd. "Oh Ma'lûl, is it not true that they levy a tax for themselves on every tent?"

"Eh wallah!" said the Arab.

"But if the men of the tents make complaint, the sheikh attacks them and slays them."

"Allah, Allah! he knows the truth," cried Ma'lûl in vociferous approval.

"And they have no protection," concluded Maḥmûd.

"Eh wah!" responded the Arab, "who is there to protect us?"

So the ancient tyrannies bear sway even in the open wilderness.

Three-quarters of an hour from Khmeiḍah we passed another mound strewn with potsherds, and thirty-five minutes further down we came upon the ruins of Abu 'Atîḳ. They lie upon high rocky ground that drops steeply into an old bed of the Euphrates from which the river has retreated into a new bed a few hundred yards away. The whole area is covered with stone and brick foundations, some of them built of great blocks of hewn basalt, and the site must represent a city of no small importance. Below it the river is forced into a narrow defile where it flows between steep hills. A little valley, Wâdî Mâliḥ, joins the main stream half-an-hour from the ancient town, and it was here that we were overtaken by a breathless zaptieh from Raḳḳah who was the bearer of the answer to my telegram to the Vâlî of Aleppo. It was a refusal, politely worded, to my request that I should be permitted to travel down the left bank of the Euphrates, and with it came a covering letter from the Mudîr of Raḳḳah saying that if I did not return he would be obliged to recall the zaptiehs he had sent with me. I fear that even those who cannot properly be numbered among the criminal classes catch an infection from the lawless air of the desert, but whatever may be the true explanation of our conduct, we never contemplated for a moment the alternative of obedience, and bidding a regretful farewell to friend Maḥmûd, we went on down the defile. Maḥmûd came galloping back to give us a final word of advice. "Ride," said he, "to Umm Rejeibah, where you will find a ḳishlâ (a guardhouse), but do not camp to-night in a solitary place, for this is the country of the Baggârah, and they are all rogues and thieves."

The Euphrates, gathered into a single channel, flows very grandly through the narrow gorge. At first the hills slope down almost to the water's edge, but afterwards they draw back and leave room for a tract of level ground by the stream. An hour and a half from Wâdî Mâliḥ the valley widens still more, and on the opposite bank the great castle of Ḥalebîyeh lifts its walls from the river almost to the summit of the hill, a towered triangle of which the apex is the citadel that dominates all the defile (Fig. 46).[1] Twenty minutes lower down, the Mesopotamian bank is crowned by the sister fortress of Zelebîyeh. It is a much less important building. The walls, set with rectangular towers, enclose three sides of an oblong court; the fourth side—that towards the river—must also have been walled, and it is probable that the castle approached more nearly to a square than at present appears, for the current has undermined the precipitous bank and the western part of the fortifications has fallen away. The masonry is of large blocks of stone, faced on the interior and on the exterior of the walls, while the core is mainly of rubble

[1] It was visited and planned by Sarre and Herzfeld in 1907; Sarre, *Reise in Mesopotamien*, in the *Zeitschrift der Gesch. für Erdkunde zu Berlin*, 1909, No. 7, p. 429. Sarre pronounces the greater part of the ruins to date from the time of Justinian.

and mortar. There are six towers, including the corner bastions, in the length of the east wall, and between the two central towers is an arched gate. On the north and south sides there is now but one tower beyond the corner. Each tower contains a small rectangular chamber approached by an arched doorway. The court is covered with ruins, and on either side of the gate there is a deep arched recess. Under the north side of the castle hill there are foundations of buildings in hewn stone, but the area of these ruins is not large.

The name Zelebîyeh carries with it the memory of an older title; in the heyday of Palmyrene prosperity a fortress called after Zenobia guarded the trade route from her capital into Persia, and all authorities are agreed that the fortress of Zenobia described by Procopius is identical with Ḥalebîyeh. Procopius states further that Justinian, who rebuilt Zenobia and Circesium, refortified the next castle to Circesium, which he calls Annouca. The Arab geographers make mention of a small town, Khânûḥah, midway between Ḳarḳîsîyâ (Circesium) and Raḳḳah,[1] and the probable identity of Annouca and Khânûḳah has already been observed by Moritz.[2] But I think it likely that the flourishing mediæval Arab town was situated not in the confined valley below Zelebîyeh but at Abu 'Atîḳ, where the ruin field is much larger. It may be that there was a yet older settlement at Abu 'Atîḳ, and that the stone foundations there belonged to the town of Annouca which stood at the head of the defile, while the castle of the same name guarded the lower end.

We struck across the barren hills and so came down in an hour and half to Ḳubrâ, a ziyârah lying about a quarter of a mile from the river. There were no tents to be seen, whether of the Baggârah or of any other tribe, and no man from whom we could ask the way; by misfortune we happened to be that day without an Arab guide, and mindful of Maḥmûd's parting injunctions, we began to look eagerly

[1] Ibn Ḥauḳal is, I think, the first to speak of it. Idrîsî says that it had busy markets and that much traffic went through it. They wrote respectively in the tenth and twelfth centuries.

[2] *Zur antiken Topographie der Palmyrene*, p. 39.

ahead for the ḳishlâ. Some way lower down, the Euphrates swept close under a low ridge which we were obliged to climb, and once on the top we espied Ḳishlâ el Munga'rah nestling under the further side of the slope. It had taken us two and a half hours to reach it from Zelebîyeh. The ḳishlâ, which was built ten years ago and is already falling into ruin, was garrisoned by eight soldiers. They gave us an enthusiastic welcome and helped us to pitch our tents under the mud walls of the guardhouse; visitors are scarce, and the monotony of existence is broken only by episodes connected with the lawless habits of the Baggârah. I never came into contact with the tribe, but I was told that, alone among the river Arabs, they had been the allies of Ibrahîm Pasha and were consequently gôm (foes) of the 'Anazeh and their group. Enmities of this kind are usually accompanied by overt acts, and the Baggârah had their hand against every man.

It would be difficult to exaggerate the isolation of the guardhouses which are scattered through remote parts of the Turkish empire. The garrisons receive but a scanty allowance of their pay, and a still scantier of clothing; frequently they are left unchanged for years in the midst of an ungrateful desert where the task assigned to them is too heavy for them to perform—eight men, as the soldiers at Munga'rah observed, cannot keep a whole tribe in check—and where there is no alternative occupation. Often enough I have contemplated with amazement, in some lonely ḳishlâ or karâghôl, the patient Oriental acceptance of whatever fate may be allotted by the immediate or the ultimate authority; and many an hour has passed, far from unprofitably for the understanding of the East, while a marooned garrison has shown me, with a pitiful and childlike eagerness, its poor little efforts to while away the weary days—here a patch of garden snatched from the wilderness, where only a hand-to-hand struggle with the drifting sand can keep the rows of wizened onions from total extinction; there a desultory excavation in a neighbouring mound, in which if you dig far enough a glittering treasure must surely lie; a captive quail for snaring, warmly pressed upon me for my evening meal, or the small achievements in what may, for want of an exacter term, be called carpentry, with which the living-room is adorned. If you will reckon up the volume of unquestioning, if uninstructed, obedience upon which floats the ship of the Turkish State, you will wonder that it should ever run aground.

The relaxation of the men of Munga'rah was taken among the ruins that covered the top of the hill. Umm Rejeibah is a large area enclosed in a wall, clearly marked by mounds, with a ditch beyond it. On the north side an old channel of the river sweeps under the hill, and before the water left this course, it had carried away a part of the ground on which the city stood. The walls break off abruptly where the hill has fallen away, and it is therefore difficult to determine the exact shape of the enclosure. It appears to have been an irregular octagon. Towards its northern extremity the hill-top is seamed by the deep bed of a torrent draining down to the present channel of the Euphrates; it cuts through the ruins and reveals in section what is elsewhere hidden by an accumulation of soil. On the slope of its bank the soldiers had observed traces of masonry, and by digging a little way into the hill had disclosed a small circular chamber with brick walls and a white tesselated pavement. Just above the ḳishlâ, in an Arab graveyard, there are fragments of columns and basalt flour mills.

The oldest, raggedest and most one-eyed of the garrison accompanied us to Deir: I had not the heart to refuse his proffered escort, since it would enable him to spend a night in the local metropolis. The road was entirely without interest. About an hour from Deir cultivation began on the river bank in patches of cornland irrigated by rude waterwheels; jird is the Arabic word for them. We reached the ferry in six hours. The road from Aleppo to Môṣul crosses the Euphrates at Deir, and some ten years ago it was proposed to replace the ferry by a bridge. The work was actually put in hand and has advanced at the rate of one pier a year, according to my calculations; but it can scarcely be expected that this rate of progress will be maintained, since the point has been reached where the piers must be built in the bed of the stream, and construction will necessarily be slower than it was when the masons were still upon dry ground. We pitched our camp upon the left bank and there spent thirty-six hours, resting the horses and laying in provisions. The bazaars are well supplied, but Deir is not in other respects remarkable. It is first mentioned by Abu'l Fidâ, in A.D. 1331,[1] and contains, so far as I know, no vestiges of older habitation. It is built partly upon an island; the gardens of this quarter, exactly opposite my camp, were rosy with flowering fruit-trees. None but the richer sort, and such as have flocks to bring over, cross the river in the ferry boats; more modest persons are content with an inflated goat-skin. I had not seen this entertaining process, except on the Assyrian reliefs in the British Museum, and I watched it with unabated zest during the greater part of an afternoon. You blow out your goat-skin by the river's edge, roll up your cloak and place it upon your head, tuck your shirt into your waistcloth and so embark, with your arms resting upon the skin and your legs swimming in the water. The current carries you down, and you make what progress you can athwart it. On the further side you have only to wring out your shirt, don your cloak and deflate your goat-skin, and all is done.

The Mutesarrif of Deir had recently been removed and the new man had not yet arrived, but I paid my respects to his vicegerent, the Ḳâḍî, a white-bearded old Turk, who did not regard my visit as an honour, though he promised me all I wanted in the matter of ẓaptiehs. The interview took place while he was sitting in the seat of judgment and was presently interrupted by a case. It was a dispute concerning a debt between a merchant and an Arab Sheikh. The sheikh came in dressed in the full panoply of the desert, black-and-gold cloak, black kerchief and white under-robe; his skin was darkened by the sun, his beard coal-black. The

[1] The reference is not, however, certain: Moritz, *op. cit.* p. 35.

merchant was a shaven, white-faced townsman in a European coat. The pair were, to my fancy, symbolic of the East and the advancing West, and I backed the West, if only because the merchant had the advantage of speaking Turkish, and the Ḳâḍî was anything but proficient in Arabic. After a few moments of angry recrimination they were both dismissed to gather further evidence; but the Ḳâḍî called the sheikh back and shook his finger at him. "Open your eyes, oh sheikh," said he. Asia, open your eyes!

I have some friends in Deir, Mohammadan gentlemen of good birth and education; to them I went for information as to passing events, no news from the outer world having reached me for a fortnight. They told me that the Grand Vizir, Kiamil Pasha, had fallen, which was true; and that the Mejlis had quarrelled with the Sultan and were about to depose him, which was only prophetic. They made me realize how different an aspect the new-born hopes of Turkey wore on the Bosphorus, or even on the Mediterranean, from that which they presented to the dwellers on the Euphrates: I had already passed beyond the zone that had been quickened by the enthusiasm of European Turkey into some real belief in the advent of a just rule. One of my friends had received an invitation to join the local committee, but he had refused to do so. "I am lord over much business," said he, "but they are the fathers of idle talk." All thinking men in Deir were persuaded that a universal anarchy lay before them; the old rule was dead, the new was powerless, and the forces of disorder were lifting their heads. "Yes," said another, "revolution means the shedding of blood—and the land of the Ottomans will not escape. Then perhaps the nations of Europe will come to our aid and we shall all have peace." I replied that the only substantial peace would be one of their own making, and that good government takes long to establish. "What benefit have I," he protested, "if my children's children see it?" I asked whether they had heard any rumours of an Arab movement, and they answered that there was much wild writing in the newspapers of a separate Arab assembly, and that words like these might stir up trouble and revolt. "But where is unity? Aleppo hates Deir, and Deir hates Damascus, and we have no Arab nation." The financial position, both public and private, they pronounced to be hopeless. "I know a man," said one, "who has land on the Euphrates that might be worth £15,000 and is worth as many piastres. He dares not put money into irrigation because he could not get protection against the tribes and his capital would bring him no return. But indeed there is not enough capital in all Deir to develop the land." He complained that the best land was chiflik, the private property of the Sultan, and this I mention because it is a grievance that has already been remedied—may it be of good omen! The conversation left me profoundly discouraged, there was so much truth in all that I had heard, together with so complete an absence of political initiative. Thus it is through all the Asiatic provinces, and the further I went the more convinced did I become that European Turkey is the head and brains of the empire, and that if the difficult task of reform is to be carried out in Asia it can only be done from western Turkey. I believe that this has been recognized in Constantinople, for the provincial governors appointed under the new régime have been almost invariably well chosen.

On March 6 we took the road again, still following the left bank of the Euphrates. The country down these reaches of the river is, as Xenophon says, exceptionally dull: "the ground was a plain as level as the sea." Below Deir the Euphrates has left its original channel and now runs further to the west, and there was generally a stretch of low ground, an older bed, between our road and the stream. This alluvial land is thinly populated and partly irrigated by water-wheels. Along the higher ground, which had once been the bank but is now touched only by the extreme points of the river loops, there were occasional mounds representing the villages of an earlier age. The baggage animals travelled in six and three-quarter hours to Buseirah, which lies in the angle formed by the Khâbûr and the Euphrates. The site is very ancient. Xenophon when he arrived at the Araxes (the Khâbûr) found there a number of villages stored with corn and wine, and the army rested for three days collecting provisions. Diocletian made Circesium the frontier station of the Roman empire. He fortified it with a wall, says Procopius, terminating at either end on the Euphrates in a tower, but he did not protect the side of the town along the Euphrates. The stream sapped one of the towers, the walls were allowed to fall into decay, and Chosroes in his first expedition had no difficulty in taking possession of the fortress. Justinian repaired the ruined tower with large blocks of stone, built a wall along the Euphrates, and added an outer wall to that which already existed, besides improving the baths in the town. Under the name of Ḳarḳîsîyâ, Circesium continued to be a place of some importance during the Middle Ages. Iṣṭakhrî (tenth century) praises its gardens and fruit-trees, but the later geographers describe it as being smaller than its neighbour Raḥbah, on the opposite side of the Euphrates, and with this it fades out of history.

Extensive though not very scientific excavations were being carried on when I was at Buseirah. The peasants were engaged in digging out bricks from the old walls, ostensibly to provide materials for a bridge over the Khâbûr. I was therefore able to see more of the ruins than was revealed to former travellers, and my conviction is that I saw nothing that was older than the time of Justinian, while most of the work belonged to the Arab period. The excavations were so unsystematic that it was never possible to make out a ground plan, but in one place the peasants had dug down at least 5 m. below the upper level of the ruin heaps, and had cleared some small chambers near the northern fortification wall. The materials used in these buildings were square tiles in two sizes (42 × 45 × 3 cm. and 21 × 21 × 3 cm.) laid in mortar as wide as the tiles themselves, and small roughly-squared stones also laid in thick mortar. The lower parts of the chambers were of large tiles, the upper parts of stone. From the traces left upon the walls, the rooms would seem to have been roofed over with barrel vaults, and there were some remains of brick arched niches below the stonework. Above these rooms, which were possibly only a vaulted substructure, there were foundations of upper rooms constructed of the smaller tiles. The face of the tile walls had been covered with plaster. There were simple patterns moulded in the broad sides of tiles:    At the south-east angle of the enclosing wall stands a tower, round and domed and built entirely of the smaller tiles. The dome is slightly flattened and I believe the structure to be Mohammadan work. The Euphrates flows at a distance of about a mile from the city enclosure, but in all probability its course was once immediately under the wall, and the bed has made the same change here as it has done immediately above Circesium. The modern Buseirah must be the site of the ancient city, and I conclude that in Diocletian's time the Euphrates flowed under the mound and that this was the side which was not fortified until Justinian's day.

In the Arab village, which has sprung up near the south-west corner of the ruins, there are portions of a large building which the natives call the church. It is surrounded on three sides by a very thick wall, roughly built of brick and rubble, with round towers at the angles. Within the wall there are remains of a niched structure which, so far as I could judge, consisted of two domed octagonal chambers. The masonry is of brick and rubble, plastered over, and both this ruin and the outer wall seem to have been built out of older materials pillaged from other parts of the town and mixed indiscriminately together. Finally there is a substructure of brick, octagonal in plan and covered by a much flattened brick dome. The flattened dome is typically Mohammadan: I do not remember any instance where it can be assigned with certainty to an earlier period, and I am therefore led to the conclusion that the whole building cannot be older than the time of the khalifs. The area of the city is strewn with potsherds, by far the greater proportion being unmistakably Arab and closely related to the coarser sorts of Raḳḳah ware. Almost all the coins that were brought to me were Arab.

My tents were pitched outside the city wall, at the extreme limit of the Roman empire, a frontier line which you must travel far to find. Did Julian, with the ominous news from Gaul in his hand, feel any misgiving when he ordered the building of the bridge over which his army was to pass to the irrevocable destruction that Sallust predicted in his letters? "No human power or virtue," says Ammianus Marcellinus, "can prevent that which is prescribed by Fate." Impending disaster, long since fallen, leapt again from his pages and stood spectral upon the banks of the Khâbûr.

CHAPTER III

BUSEIRAH TO HÎT

March 7—March 18

At Buseirah we were confronted with one of the difficulties that awaits the traveller in the Jezîreh. Since there is no traffic along the left bank of the river, there are no zaptiehs to serve as escort; my two zaptiehs from Deir were to have been relieved at Buseirah, but there was only one available man there, and he feared the return journey alone, and was therefore extremely reluctant to come with us. We solved the question by carrying off Muṣṭafâ, one of the men from Deir, whereupon Ḥmeidî, the Buseirah zaptieh, consented to bear him company. Both were to return from Abu Kemâl, three days' journey lower down. This plan suited Ḥmeidî well, for he was a doubly married man, and while one of his wives remained at Buseirah, the other dwelt at Abu Kemâl. His beat was between the two places. "And so," he explained, "I find a wife and children to welcome me at either end."

"That is very convenient," said I.

"Yes," he replied gravely.

We crossed the Khâbûr in a ferry-boat so badly constructed that loaded animals could not enter it, and in consequence all the packs had to be carried down to the river and re-loaded on the other side. I pitied Cyrus from the bottom of my heart, and regarded Julian's bridge with feelings very different from those that had been conjured up by the moon of the previous night. The level ground on the opposite side was covered with potsherds, most of them blue and green glazed wares, and all, so far as I saw, Mohammadan. An hour later we passed over another small area strewn thickly with the same pottery, and while I was acquainting Ḥmeidî with the nature of the evidence it supplied, I took occasion to confide to him my belief that the ruin at Buseirah which they call the church dates from the Mohammadan period.

"Effendim," he replied, "what you have honoured us by observing is quite correct. The origin of that church is Arab. It was doubtless built by Nimrod, who lived some years before Hârûn er Rashîd."

"That is true," said I, with a mental reservation as to parts of the statement.

Between the Khâbûr and the Euphrates, Kiepert marks an ancient canal and names it the Daurîn. According to the map it leaves the Khâbûr at a point opposite to the village of Ḥöjneh and joins the Euphrates opposite Ṣâliḥîyeh.[1] The existence of the canal cutting is well known to all the inhabitants of these parts (they call it the Nahr Dawwarîn), but they affirm that its course is much longer than is represented by Kiepert, and that it touches the Euphrates at Werdî. My route on the first day lay between the canal and the Euphrates, at a distance that varied from an hour to half-an-hour from the river, and though I did not see the Dawwarîn, its presence was clearly indicated by the line of Ḳanâts (underground water conduits) running in a general southerly direction—NNW. to SSE. to be more accurate—across ground that was almost absolutely level. The whole of this region must once have been cultivated, and it had also been thickly populated.[2] Twenty-five minutes' ride beyond the potsherds where Ḥmeidî had sketched for me the history of Buseirah, we passed some foundations constructed out of the smaller sort of tiles which I had observed in the town. A quarter of an hour further there was a low mound called Tell el Kraḥ, covered with tiles and coloured pottery—indeed the pottery was continuous between the one patch of broken tiles and the other, and Nimrod had evidently been very busy here. The villages

[1] Sachau travelled up the left bank of the Khâbûr, and should therefore have crossed the course of the canal, but he makes no mention of it.

[2] I should conjecture that on the Euphrates as on the Tigris the disappearance of the settled population dates from the terrible disaster of the Mongol invasion.

represented by these remains had been supplied with water from the Dawwarîn. In another hour and five minutes we reached a considerable mound, Tell Buseyiḥ; it formed three sides of a hollow square, the side turned towards the river being open. We were now close to the Euphrates and could see, about half-a-mile away, a long tract of cultivation and the village of Tiyâna on the water's edge. We turned slightly inland from Buseyiḥ and in fifty minutes came to the mounds of Jemmah where, so far as identification is possible on a hasty survey, I would place Zeitha. "Here," says Ammianus Marcellinus, "we saw the tomb of the Emperor Gordian, which is visible for a long way off." Jemmah consists of a large area surrounded by a wall and a deep ditch; beyond the ditch lies broken ground where, at one point, the Arabs had scratched the surface and revealed what looked like a pavement of solid asphalt; still further away there is an Arab graveyard strewn with fragments of the smaller tiles. Except in the graveyard there are no tiles and very little pottery, none of it characteristically mediæval Mohammadan. The ditch had been fed by a water channel coming from the north-east, no doubt an arm of the Dawwarîn if it were not the canal itself. We rode from Jemmah to the Euphrates in an hour and ten minutes and found the camp pitched immediately below the village of Bustân. The baggage animals had been six hours on the march from the Khâbûr. The climate was changing rapidly as we journeyed south. The last cold day we experienced was March 2, when I had ridden out to Tell esh Sha'îr; on March 7 when we camped at Bustân the temperature at three o'clock in the afternoon was 70° in the shade, but the nights were still cold.

A strip of irrigated land and numerous villages lay along the river for the first two hours of the succeeding day's march. We were forced to ride outside the cornfields that we might avoid the water conduits, but I do not think we missed anything of importance, for every twenty or thirty years the Euphrates rises high enough to submerge the cultivation, and the floods must have destroyed all vestiges of an older civilization. The low-lying fields cannot have been, within historic times, a former bed of the stream, as was the case above Buseirah; an occasional mound near the river showed that the bank had long been inhabited. We passed on the high ground a tell that looked like the site of an ancient village which had received its water from the Nahr Dawwarîn. An enormous amount of labour is expended upon the irrigation of the cornfields; sometimes there is a double system of jirds, those nearest the river watering the lowest fields and filling deep channels whence the water is again lifted by another series of jirds to the higher level. In the lower ground the peasants grow a little corn and clover for early pasture and sow a second crop when the spring floods have retreated. After two hours' riding we entered a long stretch of sand heaped up into little hills which were held together by tamarisk thickets; it is apt to be submerged when the river is high, and we saw more than one overflow channel filled with pools of stagnant water. On the Syrian side the Euphrates is hemmed in here by hills whereon stands the castle of Ṣâliḥîyeh. In this wilderness we came upon some Arabs who were ploughing up a desolate spot in search of locusts' eggs.

"Are there many locusts here?" said I, for locusts are not accustomed to lay their eggs in sand.

"No," they answered, "there are none here; but, as God is exalted! there are thousands lower down."

"Then why do you plough here?" I asked, with the tiresome persistence of the European.

"The government ordered it," said they, and resumed their task.

In another hour we reached Tell ech Cha'bî (el Ka'bî?) where there is an Arab cemetery, the graves covered with unglazed potsherds. Ḥmeidî told me that when the Arabs bury their dead in such places they dig into the mound and extract broken pottery to strew upon the graves; the Bedouin use no pottery, their water-vessels being of copper or of skin. While we sat upon the top of the tell lunching and waiting for the caravan, which was delayed for nearly an hour in the loose sand, Ḥmeidî gave me his views on politics.

"Effendim," said he, "we do not care what sultan we have so long as he is a just ruler. But as for 'Abdu'l Ḥamîd, he keeps three hundred women in his palace, and, look you, they have eaten our money." Wherein he wronged the poor ladies; it was not they who scattered the revenues of the State.

In thirty minutes we came to Tell Simbal, a small sandy mound; in one hour and fifteen minutes more to Tell el Hajîn, with a village by the river, and after another hour and twenty minutes to Tell Abu'l Ḥassan, where we camped, seven and a quarter hours from Bustân. Abu'l Ḥassan is marked in Chesney's map as "mound." It is a very striking tell rising fifty feet above the river; upon the summit are Arab graves strewn with coarse pottery and with undressed stones dug out of the hill, and for a distance of a quarter of an hour's walk to the north and east there are fragments of brick upon the ground. The graves are those of the Jebbûr, who, said Ḥmeidî, left this district thirty years ago and migrated to the Tigris, where I subsequently saw them. Nearly all the Silmân have also gone away, and though their camping grounds are marked by Kiepert on the Euphrates, their present quarters are on the Khâbûr. The Deleim and the Ageidât, a base-born tribe, together with the Bu Kemâl, now occupy the Euphrates' banks, and the 'Anazeh come down to the river in the summer. There was no living thing near our camp except an enormous pelican, who was floating contentedly on the broad bosom of the stream. Our advent roused in him the profoundest interest, and as he floated he cast backward glances at us, to see what we were doing in his wilderness.

A pleasant four hours' march, mostly through tamarisk thickets that were full of ducks, pigeons and jays, brought us to the ferry opposite Abu Kemâl. When we had pitched our tents near the reed- and mud-built village of Werdî, Fattûḥ and Selîm went across to buy corn and Ḥmeidî to report our arrival and ask for fresh zaptiehs. The village of Abu Kemâl has recently been removed to a distance of about a mile from the right bank, because the current has undermined the foundations of the original village, which now stands deserted and in ruin. But it is chiefly on the left bank that the river has played tricks with the land. Within the circuit of a great bend in the channel, the ground for three miles or so is extremely low, and is partially submerged when the stream comes down in flood. The low ground is bounded on its eastern side by a rocky ridge which crosses the desert from a point a little to the south of the Khâbûr, passes behind what I suppose to be the course of the Dawwarîn, and terminates in the bold bluffs of Irzî above the Euphrates, at the lower limit of the Werdî bend. When the river is exceptionally high it covers the whole area up to the hills; my informant, one 'Isâ, an Arab of the Bu Kemâl, remembered having once seen this occur; but in ordinary seasons it merely overflows a narrow belt and fills a canal that lies immediately under the eastern hills. The canal is fed by two branch canals from the river and joins the Euphrates under the bluff of Irzî. The river rises "at the time of the flowering of pomegranates," said 'Isâ, "for unto all things is their season," that is, about the middle of April; but the big canal under the hills was still half full of water when I saw it in March, and the crops were irrigated from it by jirds. It is known locally as the Werdîyeh, but I was informed that it was in fact the lower end of the Dawwarîn which joins the Euphrates here and not at Ṣâliḥîyeh.[1] The site of Werdî is generally believed to be that of Xenophon's Corsote, "a large deserted city which was entirely surrounded by the Mascas." The river Mascas was a plethron (100 ft.) in breadth; the army of Cyrus stayed there three days and the soldiers furnished themselves with provisions.[2] By the Mascas, Xenophon is understood to have meant a loop canal, and I think it probable that the canal was not merely a small loop enclosing the bend of the river, but that it is represented to this day by the Dawwarîn and the irrigation system connected with it.

[1] I looked carefully for any trace of a big canal opposite Ṣâliḥîyeh and saw none.

[2] *Anabasis*, Bk. I. ch. 5, 9.

But if Werdî be the descendant of Corsote, at least one other town must be placed between these two in the genealogical table. The bluff at the lower end of the river bend is covered with the ruins of Irzî, which have been remarked by every traveller who has passed by, either on the river or on the west bank. Balbi, who descended the Euphrates in 1579, says that the ruins occupied a site larger than Cairo and appeared to be the massive walls and towers of a great city. So far as I know no one has examined them closely, and when I climbed up the hill I found, not the bastioned walls that I had expected, but a number of isolated tower tombs. They stand in various stages of decay round the edge of the bluff and over the whole extent of a high rocky plateau which cannot be seen from below. There are no traces of houses, nor any means of obtaining water from the river, nor any cisterns for the storage of rain. Balbi's city is a city of the dead; it is the necropolis of a town that stood, presumably, in the irrigated country below. The towers were all alike (Fig. 47). They are built of irregular slabs of stone, the shining gypsum of which the hill is formed, laid in beds of mortar. Each tower rests upon a square substructure, about 1·70 m. high; in this substructure are the tombs, hollowed out of the solid masonry, irregular in number and in position. In the best preserved of the towers I could see but one tunnel-like grave opening on the west side (Fig. 48), while there were two or three to the north and east. The tombs are covered by a small vault made of two stones leaning against one another. Above the substructure the walls are broken by corner piers of small projection, with two engaged columns between them. The columns are crowned by capitals made of a single projecting slab, above which a slightly projecting band of plaster forms an entabla-

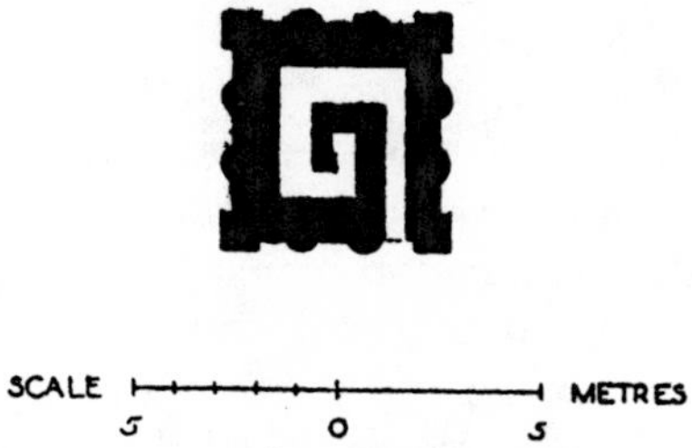

FIG. 47.—IRZÎ, TOWER TOMB.

ture. Then follows a plain piece of wall about a metre high upon which stands an upper order of engaged columns, half as large as those below, so that there was place for five between the corner piers, if these were repeated on the upper part of the tower. A door between the corner pier and one of the engaged columns opens on to a winding stair which leads to the top of the tower. No rule was observed as to the direction of the compass in which the doors were placed. The towers cannot be as old as Xenophon's time; they are more likely to date from the first or second century of the Christian era; therefore the town to which they belonged must have been later than Corsote, and Corsote, it will be remembered, was deserted when he saw it. It is easy to understand that a city lying in the low ground might have been destroyed by inundations, and to imagine that a region so favourably situated for purposes of cultivation, and provided with an elaborate system of irrigation, should have been repopulated in a later age. And this is the explanation which I offer.[1]

The practice of burying the dead above "the common crofts, the vulgar thorpes," is still observed by the Arabs. All their graves lie loftily upon the nearest height, even if it should be only a mound by the river. From my camp I watched one of their funeral processions making its slow way from the village of Abu Kemâl towards some barren hills. Three or four miles the dead man was carried across the desert to find his resting-place among the graves of his ancestors, and no tribesman would have been content to lay him at the village gates, like a Turk or a town dweller. They carried him to the hills and so performed, as in the days of the Irzî city, their final service.

Fattûḥ and Selîm returned after nightfall, and reported the zaptieh problem to be still unsolved. Even at Abu Kemâl there was but one man, and we were forced once again to commandeer Muṣṭafâ, who saw himself dragged further and

[1] With the doubtful contribution made by Ammianus Marcellinus to the question, I have dealt in the Appendix to this chapter.

FIG. 48.—IRZÎ, TOWER TOMB.

FIG. 49.—NAQURA OF 'AIMÎYEH.

FIG. 50.—THE INHABITANTS OF RAWÂ.

further from his home at Deir. We promised that he should return from Ḳâyim with 'Abdullah, the zaptieh from Abu Kemâl, and Muṣṭafâ agreed with alacrity to this arrangement. All zaptiehs of my acquaintance enjoy travelling, with its contingent advantage of a regular daily fee from the effendi whom they escort. But neither he nor 'Abdullah knew the way along the left bank. "We have never heard of any one who wished to go by this road, wallah!" Moreover, they stood in considerable fear of the tribes whom we might encounter. I therefore engaged as guide 'Isâ, the affable, ragged person who had conducted me to Irzî, but since we were fully loaded with corn, we could not mount him and he marched smilingly for seven hours through a temperature of 83° in the shade. We rode over the Irzî bluffs and dropped by a steep and rocky path into the plain on the farther side, between the hills and the meandering river. To the right the village of Rabâṭ, with a long stretch of corn, lay near the water's edge, and though our path lay only through tamarisk thickets, traces of numerous irrigation canals showed that the ground must once have been under cultivation. The plain is known as the Ḳâ'at ed Deleim, the land of the Deleim, and the tents of that tribe were to be seen on the banks of the Euphrates. It did not take me long to discover that we should reach Ḳâyim, or rather the point opposite to it, for it lies on the right bank, in about five hours from Werdî, and my heart sank to contemplate another long delay while we crossed and changed zaptiehs; therefore I refused to go down to the Euphrates and cut straight across a bend over high stony ground. So it happened that we never went near Ḳâyim, and the two kidnapped zaptiehs were embarked before they knew it on the road to 'Anah. We touched the river again seven hours from Werdî, where we found an encampment of the Jerâif, and since we were completely ignorant of what lay ahead, we pitched our tents there, opposite an island which Kiepert calls Ninmala. I found it almost impossible to get at any names for the numerous islands in these reaches of the Euphrates. The generic word for them is khawîjeh, and they bear no other title in the local speech.

The Jerâif or Jerîfeh is a tribe which belongs properly to the right bank, but a few tents had come over on account of the terrible drought, there being always more pasture in the Jezîreh than in the Shâmîyeh. They are usually, so 'Isa explained, gôm to his tribe, the Bu Kemâl, but a truce had recently been patched up and he was received as hospitably as any of us.

There lies below 'Ânah and to the west of the Euphrates a region of desert through which few travellers have passed. The track of Chesney's journey of 1857 skirts it to the west; Thielmann crossed it nearly forty years later a little further to the east; Huber, following the Damascus post-road, touched its northern edge. So said Kiepert, and with this meagre information as a base I questioned that night the Arabs gathered round Fattûḥ's cooking fire as to the north-west corner of the Sasanian Empire. Among them was an aged man who had been to Nejd, in Central Arabia, and had brought back thence a bullet which was still lodged in his cheek; he knew that country, and if I would give him a horse he would take me to all the castles therein, Khubbâz, 'Amej, Themail, Kheiḍir. . . .

"Where is Kheiḍir?" said I, for the name was unknown to me or to Kiepert.

"Beyond Shetâteh," answered a lean and ragged youth. "I too know it, wallah!"

"Is it large?" I asked.

"It is a castle," he replied vaguely, and one after another the men of the Jerâif chimed in with descriptions of the road. The sum total of the information offered by them seemed to be that water was scarce and raids frequent, but there were certainly castles; yes, in the land of Fahd Beg ibn Hudhdhâl, the great sheikh of the Amarât, there was Kheiḍir. I made a mental note of the name.

The region which we had now entered is particularly lawless. The government makes no attempt to control the Bedouin, and according to their custom they are occupied exclusively in raiding one another and in harrying the outlying property of the inhabitants of Rawâ, the town opposite to 'Ânah. In addition to the depredations of the local tribes, the country is swept by armed bands of the Shammar from far away to the east, and of the Yezîdis, whom the Mohammadans call Devil Worshippers, from the Jebel Sinjâr. Accordingly when we asked for a guide, we were told that there was no one who would come with us alone, lest he should be attacked on his solitary return by blood enemies from half the world away. We took with us, therefore, two horsemen, 'Affân, of the sheikhly house, and Murawwaḥ, the one armed with a rifle and the other with a rusty sword, and for the better part of the day we discussed the observance of blood feud. The old man with the bullet in his cheek, who was on his way to Baghdâd and proposed to travel with us as far as possible, served as an illustration of the text. It had a purely objective interest, for in spite of the fears exhibited by the Jerâif, there was very small risk of our meeting with a foe; the season for raiding is the summer, but the spring is a close time. 'Affân was eloquent in describing the long rides across the desert in the burning heat: "Lady, I have ridden four days with no water but what I could carry; that was when we bore off cattle and mules from the Jebel Sinjâr."

"Eh billah!" asseverated Murawwaḥ, and felt for the hilt of his rusty sword.

We had not gone far before my mare shied out of the path and there swung up beside us a jovial personage mounted on a blood camel with his serving-man clinging behind him. He proved to be a sheikh of the Amarât, who are a branch of the 'Anazeh, and indeed he was own brother to Fahd ibn Hudhdhâl. His appearance suited his high birth. He was wrapped in a gold-bordered cloak, a fine silk kerchief was bound about his head, and his feet were shod with scarlet leather boots; he was tall and well liking, as are few but the great sheikhs among the half-fed Bedouin. He related to me the business which had brought him so far from his own people. One of the Jerâif had murdered a man of the Amarât, and the two tribes being on friendly terms, Sheikh Jid'ân (such was his name) had crossed the river to demand the summary execution of the murderer or the payment of blood money. He was hunting the man down through the Jerâif tents.

"Shall you find him?" I asked.

"Eh wah!" he affirmed and laughed over his task.

Him too I questioned concerning Kheiḍir. "Go forward to 'Ânah," he said, "and there any man will take you to Kheiḍir. And if you come to my tents, welcome and kinship." So we parted.

In thirty-five minutes from the camp we passed the mound of Balîjah with Arab graves upon it; then for three hours we saw nothing of interest until we came to the mazâr of Sultan 'Abdullah, a small modern shrine. Somewhere near it are the ruins of Jabarîyeh, but they must lie closer to the mazâr than Kiepert would have them. I rode on looking for them for half-an-hour, and when I questioned 'Affân he replied: "Jebarîyeh? It is under the mazâr. When you turned away I thought you did not wish to see those ruins." It was too hot to go back. We were now opposite Ḳal'at Râfiḍah, a splendid pile upon the right bank of the Euphrates, and here we left the caravan with Murawwaḥ to guide it and followed the course of the river to Ḳal'at Bulâḳ, which the Arabs call Retâjah, an hour and a quarter's ride in blazing sun. We found there a small square fort with round towers at the angles, the whole built of sun-dried brick. Though it is in complete ruin, I believe it to be modern, probably a Turkish ḳishlâ, but I saw some fragments of stone and mortar building which are, at any rate, older than the mud fort, and the site is so magnificent that it can scarcely have been neglected in ancient times. The hill on which the ruins stand is all but converted into an island by an abrupt turn of the river, which washes the precipitous rock on three sides. The current is gradually undermining the high seat of Retâjah and the greater part of the older stone building has fallen into the stream. We had a hard gallop to catch up the caravan, and a long pull over rocky ground before we sighted the river again, flowing in wide and tranquil curves under the sunset. On either side the banks were lined with naouras, the Persian water-wheels. The quiet air was full of the rumble and grumble of them, a pleasant sound telling of green fields and clover pastures, but there were no villages or any other sign of man. As I looked, I knew that we had passed over an unseen frontier; whether the geographers admitted it or no, this was Babylonia.

We rode down wearily to the first naoura and there threw ourselves from our horses. The river turned the wheel, the wheel lifted the water, the water raced down the conduit and spread itself out over a patch of corn and round the roots of a solitary palm-tree, and all happened as if it were a part of the processes of nature, like the springing of the palm tree and the swelling of the ears of corn. But it was nature in leading-strings, and the lords of creation, in a very unassuming guise, surged up from a hole in the ground roofed with palm fronds and bade us welcome to their domain—two men and a little boy who watched over the crops on behalf of a Rawâ merchant. The place has a name, 'Ajmîyeh, and a history, if only I could have deciphered it in the cut stones and fragments of wall which the river slowly washed bare and then washed away. But the immediate present was of greater importance. Before the moon was up, supper was spread by the naoura, and the watchmen, the boy, the Arabs and the old man with the bullet were sharing with my servants and zaptiehs an ample meal of rice. We had marched ten hours.

In the morning I saw that quantities of pottery were washed out of the bank together with the stones. Much of it was glazed with black upon the inside, some was the usual coloured Mohammadan stuff, and there were pieces of the big pointed jars, unglazed, which belong to every age. Beyond the corn lay masses of similar potsherds; the river bank must once have been strewn with small villages. When we had ridden for half-an-hour we met three horsemen of the Jerâif, and 'Affân declared that he would return with them to his tents, and as for Murawwaḥ he might cross with us to 'Ânah and go home along the right bank. I had no objection to raise, and as Murawwaḥ did not demur to the scheme 'Affân was allowed to leave us. Murawwaḥ was a small man and a lean, mounted on a half-starved mare, himself half starved, with naked feet, a ragged cotton cloak thrown over his head to protect him from the sun, and a rusty sword by his side to defend him from his enemies. We had struck up a wordless friendship and now that 'Affân was gone we fell into talk. I asked him whether he had heard of liberty.

"Eh wah!" he answered, "but we know not what it means."

"It means to obey a just law," said I, seeking for some didactic definition. But Murawwaḥ knew nothing of obedience nor yet of just rule.

The zaptieh 'Abdullah took up my word. "Oh Murawwaḥ," said he, "when there is liberty in this land, there will be no more raiding and the Arabs will serve as soldiers."

"No wallah!" returned Murawwaḥ firmly.

'Abdullah laughed. "Slowly, slowly," he said, "the government will lay hands on the desert, and the Arabs will be brought in, for they are all thieves."

Murawwaḥ drew himself up on his hungry mare. "Thieves!" he cried. "Thieves are dogs. How can you compare the Arabs with them? We will not bow our heads to any government. To the Arabs belongs command." And he slashed the air defiantly with his tamarisk switch as he proclaimed the liberties of the wilderness, the right of feud, the right of raid, the right of revenge—the only liberty the desert knows.

Three hours and a half from 'Ajmîyeh we stopped at a naoura, Natârîyeh, to water our horses, and just beyond it we were overtaken by half-a-dozen angry men from Rawâ, mounted and carrying rifles. The cause of their ride and of their anger they were not slow to make known to us. The watchman at their naoura had sent in word to Rawâ that the Deleim had come down and were pasturing their mares in the corn. "And we went to the Ḳâimmaḳâm and asked for soldiers to drive them off, and the Ḳâimmaḳâm answered, 'Go ask the Vâlî of Baghdâd, for I have none.' As God is exalted! there were but two soldiers in the ḳishlâ of Rawâ. And we took our rifles and mounted our mares and rode out alone, and all last night we hunted them through the desert until we were so far from the river that we dared not go on. We are six men, look you, and the Deleim are counted by thousands. So we returned, and a curse upon the government that cannot protect our property, and may all Arabs burn in hell!"

At this point one of them perceived Murawwaḥ, who was riding in discreet silence by my side. "Listen, you! dog son of a dog," he cried. "We lay out our capital and you take the interest; we sow and you gather the harvest, yes, without reaping, and we may starve that you and your accursed brothers may fatten. I have a mind to take you as hostage to Rawâ and hold you till we get our due." Murawwaḥ, though for a free child of the desert he was unfortunately placed between zaptiehs and angry citizens, was not alarmed by the threat. We had changed parts as soon as we neared civilization, and he now edged nearer to me, knowing that he was safe under my protection, but for which he would not have ventured into Rawâ where there were too many reckonings scored up against the tribes.

We were not to escape without ourselves taking a lesson in the elements of raiding. Half-an-hour or so from Natârîyeh, Jûsef came riding up from the caravan, which was behind us, to ask if we had seen anything of the donkey, the unrivalled donkey purchased in Aleppo, and to our consternation we discovered that he was missing. There had been a few Arabs at Natârîyeh, and while we were engaged in watering the baggage animals, the donkey had strayed away to make acquaintance with some low-born Bedouin donkeys and had remained behind. Fattûḥ and 'Abdullah rode back and speedily found him (he was twice the size of the others), but his pack saddle and other trappings were gone. Thereupon Fattûḥ, like the merchants of Rawâ, took the law into his own hands, drove off an Arab donkey together with our own, and declared that unless the Arabs restored our property to us that night at 'Ânah he would sell theirs in the open market and keep the money. Thus it was that we turned raiders like every one else who lives in the desert. Fattûḥ caught me up two and a half hours later opposite the island of Ḳarâbileh, where I had stopped to lunch, and we sent Murawwaḥ back to reclaim the pack saddle, bidding him join us at 'Ânah. He was exceedingly loth to obey this order, saying that he dared not enter 'Ânah alone, and I never expected to see him again, in spite of the fact that he had not received his bakhshîsh. In another twenty minutes we were riding through the fruit gardens and palm groves of Rawâ—the fruit-trees were all in flower, a delectable sight for travellers in the wilderness. While the ferry-boats were being brought up I climbed the hill to the modern citadel (Rawâ, so far as I am aware, has no ancient history) and thence looked down upon the long thin line of 'Ânah, houses and palm-trees folded between the hills and the river, and afar the island that was ancient Anatho, floating upon the broad waters. The populátion of Rawâ swarmed up the hill after me, watching my every movement with strained attention, and before we were fairly embarked I registered a vow that no caravan of mine should ever again pass through the town, so exasperating it is to find two hundred people in your path whichever way you would turn (Fig. 50). When once we had crossed the river we fell into a merciful obscurity; the post-road runs through 'Ânah, and it matters not a para to anybody but the khânjî whether one European more or less comes down it. The khânjî, a friend of Fattûḥ's, was unfeignedly glad to see us, and his khân looked good, but better still the patch of ground behind that stretched down to the water's edge. Here with the consent of mine host we pitched our tents, in full view of an exquisite little island, green with corn and shaded by palm-trees; and whatever love you bear the desert there can be no doubt that green growing things are pleasant to the eye, and that the spirit rests comfortably upon the assurance that a good dinner, not tinned curry, will shortly be forthcoming. Just as it was ready, behold Murawwaḥ, obedient to the call of hunger—minus his sword indeed, for he had left it in pawn to the ferryman, but bringing with him the owner of the donkey we stole, together with the goods that had been stolen from us. And every one came to his own again. But the episode has never faded from Fattûḥ's memory, and in the hour of reminiscence he is wont to say, "Your Excellency remembers how we raided the Arabs? May God be exalted! We have travelled much in the desert, and the only raid we ever saw was one of our own making."

There was another arrival at our camp that night. Late in the evening Jûsef inquired whether I would receive a soldier, and thinking it was to-morrow's zaptieh, I consented. A grizzled man appeared at the tent door and sat down on his heels.

"Peace be upon you," said he.

"And upon you peace," I answered.

"Effendim," he said, "I am a man advancing in years." He made the gesture of one who strokes a venerable beard, although his chin was bare. "And for long I have prayed for a son. Praise be to God, this night God has granted my request."

"Praise be to God," said I.

"God give you the reward," he rejoined. "Effendim, in honour of this exceptional occasion, will you kindly help with the expenses?"

Now it happened somewhere about the year 1300 B.C. that Hattusil, King of the Hittites, wrote to the King of Babylon, and among other matters of international interest, he observed that the reason for the interruption of diplomatic relations with the court of Babylonia was the uncertainty of travel caused by the movements of the Bedouin. No other consideration, he said, should have prevented him from dispatching his ambassador to the son of so excellent a father. The conditions described in Hattusil's letter hold good until to-day. The Bedouin are still masters of the desert road, and established order is helpless before the lawless independence of the tribes. The truth is that nomad life and civilization are incompatible terms: the peaceful cultivator and the merchant cannot exist side by side with the sheikh, and either the settled population must drive the Bedouin from out their borders, or the Bedouin will put progress and the accumulation of wealth beyond the power of the most industrious. Until we drew near to 'Ânah, our road had led us through regions which the Arabs hold in undisturbed possession. No caravans pass down the east bank of the Euphrates; no towns are built there; save for the spasmodic labours of the half settled tribes, no fields are cultivated. But with the first naoura of the Rawâ townsmen the conditions were altered, and when we crossed the river we plunged into the struggle that has been waged for all time between the nomad and the State. For four days we followed the high road to Baghdâd—unwillingly enough, since I was ever looking for a door into the Syrian desert—and I had opportunity to study the oldest problem of government.

The town of 'Ânah has been lengthening steadily ever since the sixteenth century, for Rauwolff says that it is one hour long, and della Valle two, and I know that it is three. But it was and remains a single street wide, a Babylonish mud-built thoroughfare, green with palms, murmurous with naouras and lapped by the swift current of the Euphrates (Fig. 51). From the hilltop of Rawâ I had already caught sight of the only vestiges of antiquity that 'Ânah can boast, the ruined castle and tall minaret upon the island of Lubbâd at the lower end of the town. Here stood the fortress which, "like many others in that country, is surrounded by the Euphrates."[1] Julian, seeing the difficulties of a siege, came to terms with the inhabitants, who surrendered to him and were treated with all kindness. But the fortress he burnt. I was determined not to leave 'Ânah without visiting the island, and having settled with Fattûḥ the length of the day's march, I left him to buy provisions and load the caravan, and rode down to a ferry opposite the island. The boat was commonly used to transport stones from the castle, and when we arrived it was in course of being loaded on the other side. Much shouting at length attracted the attention of the ferryman, and we went into a neighbouring coffee-house to await his coming. A party of citizens had gathered together over the morning cup; we joined the circle and shared in the coffee and the

[1] *Amm. Mar.*, Bk. XXIV. ch. i. 6.

FIG. 51.—'ÂNAH FROM THE ISLAND OF LUBBÂD.

FIG. 52.—'ÂNAH, A FISHERMAN.

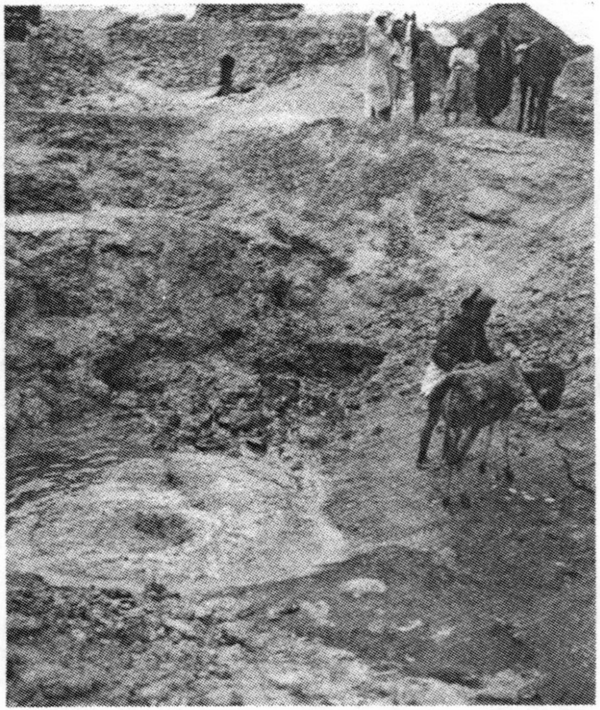

FIG. 53.—HÎT, PITCH-SPRING.

talk. The men in the coffee-house entertained no hope that the constitutional or any other government would succeed in establishing order.

"Ever since the days of the Benî Ghassân," said one (and I could have added "ever since the days of the Hittites"), "the Arabs have ravaged the land, and who shall stop them? The government does nothing and we can do nothing. We have no power and all of us are poor."

"In the last six years," said another, "we have had fourteen Ḳâimmaḳâms at 'Ânah. Not one of these gave a thought to the prosperity of the town, but he extorted what money he could before he was removed."

"There is a new Ḳâimmaḳâm on his way here," I observed.

"True," he replied. "When the telegram came last summer telling of liberty and equality, the people assembled before the serâyah, the government house, and bade the Ḳâimmaḳâm begone, for they would govern themselves. Thereat came orders from Baghdâd that the people must be dispersed; and the soldiers fired upon them, killing six men. And we do not know what the telegram about liberty and brotherhood can have meant, but at least the Ḳâimmaḳâm was dismissed."

My zaptieh broke in here. "Effendim," said he, "it fell out once that I was in Bombay—yes, I was sent from Baṣrah with horses for one of the kings of India. And there I saw a poor man whose passport had been stolen from him, and he carried his complaint to the judge. Now the judge was of the English, and he fined the thief and cut off two of his fingers. That is government; in India the poor are protected."

"Allah!" said one of the coffee-drinkers in undisguised admiration.

I knew better than to question the validity of the anecdote, and, with what modesty I could assume, I accepted the credit that accrued from it.

"But even the English," pursued another, "cannot hold the tribes. Effendim, have the Afghans submitted to you? Wallah, no."

He had laid his finger upon a knotty point, and I took up the question from a different side.

"Have not you men of 'Ânah sent a deputy to the mejlis?" I asked.

"Eh wallah!" they answered.

"Let him make known in Constantinople the evils under which you suffer, that the government may seek for a remedy."

The suggestion was received in silent perplexity.

"For what purpose did you pay the deputy to go to Stambûl?" I pursued.

"The order came," replied one of my interlocutors. "We do not know why the deputy was sent. Doubtless he has his own business in Stambûl and he is not concerned with 'Ânah."

"His business is yours," I said; "and if he will not see to it, at the next election you must choose a better man."

"Will there be another election?" said they, and I found all 'Ânah to be under the impression that their representative held a life appointment.

The island is a little paradise of fruit-trees, palms and corn, in the middle of which is a village of some thirty houses built in the heaped-up ruins of the castle. From among the houses springs a tall and beautiful minaret, octagonal in plan (Fig. 56). Its height is broken by eight rows of niches, each face of the octagon bearing in alternate storeys a double and single niche, all terminating in the cusped arch which is employed at Raḳḳah. Some of the niches are pierced with windows to light the winding stair. The tower rises yet another two storeys, but the upper part is of narrower diameter, and the windows and niches are covered with plain round arches. At the northern end of the island the walls and round bastions of the fortress stand in part, but they are not very ancient. Ibn Khurdâdhbeh, who is the first of the Mohammadan geographers to mention 'Ânah, says only that it is a small town on an island;[1] in Abu'l Fidâ's time it was still confined to the island;[2] Rauwolff (1564) notices the town on the island

[1] Ed. de Goeje, p. 233.
[2] Ed. Reinaud, p. 286.

and the town on the right bank;[1] Yâḳût (1225) speaks of the castle, but the walls which I saw cannot be as old as his day. The minaret may belong to a different period, and de Beylié places it in the earliest centuries of Islâm.[2] I think that there was probably a fortress on the island long before the first written record which has come down to us, but I was close upon a generation too late to see the remains of it. From two informants in 'Ânah I heard that there had been big stone slabs at the northern end of the island "with figures of men upon them and a writing like nails," but they had fallen into the water within the memory of the older inhabitants and had been washed away or covered by the stream. This tale of cuneiform inscriptions would not in itself be worth much, but while I was examining the minaret, a villager brought me a fragment of stone covered with carving in relief which was unmistakably Assyrian. I asked him whence it came, and he replied that it had formed part of a big stone picture which had fallen into the river. I bought from him a broken bowl inscribed with Jewish incantations of the well-known type.[3]

The island was once connected with both banks by bridges. There are some traces of the section that led across to the Jezîreh, and many piers of the Shâmîyeh bridge stand in the river. Though these piers no longer serve the purpose for which they were intended, they are still put to use, for the inhabitants of the island spread nets between them, and the fish swimming down with the current are entangled in the meshes and so caught (Fig. 52). We pulled up one of the nets as we passed, and it produced two large fish which I bought for a few pence. It is curious that the Bedouin neglect the ample supply of food with which the river would furnish them; in spite of frequent inquiries we had never found fish in their tents.

Just below the houses of 'Ânah on the Shâmîyeh bank

[1] Quoted by Ritter, Vol. XI. p. 717.

[2] De Beylié: *Prome et Samarra*, p. 68. See, too, Viollet's memoir presented to the Acad. des Inscrip. et B.-Lettres, quoted above. He, too, was shown the fragment of Assyrian relief and gives an illustration of it, for which reason I do not trouble to publish my photograph.

[3] Pognon: *Inscriptions mandaïtes des coupes de Khouabir.*

there were mounds by the river from which, said my zaptieh, the people get antîcas after rain, and sometimes small gold ornaments are washed out of them. On the opposite bank I could see ruins for a distance of an hour's ride from 'Ânah; they ended at a big mound called Tell Abu Thor, which appeared to be a natural outcrop of the rock, though there were many small, seemingly artificial, mounds about it.[1] An hour and a half from 'Ânah we passed another rocky hill, also called Tell Abu Thor, but I could see no traces of ruins round it. From the summit of the tell there was a fine view of the little fortified island of Tilbês, the island castle of Thilutha, whose inhabitants refused to surrender to Julian. I could see the bastions of masonry on the upper end of the island, together with the ruins of a castle on the Jezîreh bank, and if there had been any possibility of crossing the river I should have gone down to it; but there was no ferry nearer than 'Ânah. I did not follow the winding course of the Euphrates from 'Ânah to Hît. Many of the ruins marked in Chesney's map deserve a careful survey, but my mind was now set upon another matter, and we rode on from stage to stage hoping each day that the next would provide us with a guide into the western desert. My zaptieh, Muḥammad, lent a sympathetic ear to the scheme which I developed to him as we rode. The arm of the law, weak enough on the Euphrates, does not reach into the wilderness, and his duties had taken him but a little way west of the road; the main difficulty to be encountered was the lack of water, a difficulty much enhanced by the drought.

"God send us rain!" he sighed. "Effendim, at this time of the year I am used to stay my mare at such places as these" (he pointed to the hollows in the barren ground), "and while I smoke a cigarette she will have eaten her fill of grass. But this year there is no spring herbage, and in the season of the rains, forty days have passed without rain. All the water-pools in the Shâmîyeh are exhausted, and the Arabs are

[1] Chesney notices that the ruins of the old town lie on the left bank below the present 'Ânah. Quoted by Ritter, Vol. XI. p. 724.

crossing to the Jezîreh lest they die, for their flocks can give no milk."

Presently we met a train of thirsty immigrants driving their goats to the Euphrates. Muḥammad called to them and asked if they would give us a cup of leben, sour milk. A half-starved girl shouted back in answer:

"If we had leben we should not be crossing to the Jezîreh."

"God help you!" cried Muḥammad. "Cross in the peace of God."

A little further we passed through a number of newly-made graves, scattered thickly on either side of the road. "They are graves of the Deleim," said Muḥammad. "A year ago a bitter quarrel arose within the tribe, and here they fought together and seventy men were slain. They buried them where they fell, the one party on one side of the road, and the other on the other side."

We travelled fast and in five hours from 'Ânah came down to the river at Fḥemeh, where we found our tents pitched near a ḳishlâ. The guardhouse is the only building here, the village of Fḥemeh being in the Jezîreh about half-an-hour up stream. About the same distance lower down lies the island of Kuro, which is perhaps Julian's Akhaya Kala, but I saw it only from afar and do not know whether there are still ruins upon it. We had parted at 'Ânah from Cyrus and from Julian; they marched with their armies down the Jezîreh bank, and our road lost much of its charm in losing the shadowy pageants of their advance.

We were tormented during the next three days by an intolerable east wind. It blew from sunrise to sunset, and, for aught we could tell, it might have issued from the mouth of a furnace, so scorching was its dust-laden breath. I heard of ruins at Sûs, a place where the Jerâif own corn-fields; but it lay at the head of a peninsula formed by a great bend of the stream, and I had no heart to go so far out of the way.[1] We reached Ḥadîthah in six hours from

[1] It is, I suppose, Chesney's Sarifah, which has been conjectured to be the Kolosina of Ptolemy: Ritter, Vol. XI. p. 730.

Fḥemeh and camped there, partly because we were weary of the wind and dust, and partly because Muḥammad had advised me to seek there for a guide into the desert. The nearer we came to that adventure, the more formidable did it appear, and I was beginning to realize that it would be folly to take a caravan across the parched and stony waste, and to revolve plans for sending the muleteers to Kerbelâ and taking only Fattûḥ with me to Kheiḍir. At Ḥadîthah we met an aged corporal, who declared that nothing would be easier than to go straight thence to Ḳaṣr 'Amej, and for water we should find every night a pool of winter rain. He had crossed the desert two years ago and there had been no lack of water.

"But this year there has been no rain," I objected; "and all the Arabs are coming down to the river because of the great drought. Where, then, shall we find the pools?"

"God knows," he answered piously, and I put an end to the discussion and turned my attention to the ruins of Ḥadîthah.

The village, like all the villages in these parts, lies mainly upon an island, though a small modern suburb has sprung up upon the right bank. At the upper end of the island are the ruins of a castle, not unlike the ruins at 'Ânah. A bridge had been thrown over both arms of the river, and a straight causeway across the island had connected the two parts. Needless to say, the bridge has fallen. Still more remarkable, and quite unexpected, was a large area of ruins some way inland on the Shâmîyeh side, hidden from the river village by a ridge of high ground. It must have been the site of a big town. In one place I saw four columns lying upon the ground, no doubt pre-Mohammadan, though upon one of them were four lines of a much-defaced Arabic inscription of which I could read only a few words.[1] Nearer to the river, and visible from it, are a number of small mazârs, remarkable only because their pointed dome-like roofs show the same construction that is to be seen in the famous tomb of the Sitt Zobeideh at Baghdâd.

[1] These ruins give additional weight to Ritter's suggestion that Ḥadîthah was the Parthian station of Olabus: Vol. XI. p. 731. The Arab town of Ḥadîthah is first mentioned by Ibn Khurdâdhbeh, ed. de Goeje, p. 74.

From 'Ânah the river landscape is exceedingly monotonous: a few naouras and a patch or two of cultivation, each with its farmhouse, a small domestic mud fortress with a tower; an occasional village set in a grove of palm-trees on an island in midstream. The houses were of sun-dried brick, the walls sloping slightly inwards, and crowned with a low mud battlement—line for line a copy of their prototypes on the Assyrian reliefs. This world, which was already sufficiently dreary, was rendered unspeakably hideous by the east wind. River, sky and mud-built houses showed the universal dun colour of the desert, and even the palm-trees turned a sickly hue, their fronds dishevelled by the blast and steeped in dust.

An hour and a half from Ḥadîthah we crossed the Wâdî Ḥajlân, in which there is a brackish spring. Just opposite its mouth are the remains of a castle on an island, Abu Sa'îd, but the greater part of the island, and with it the castle, has been carried away by the stream. Below it is the palm-covered island of Berwân. Twenty minutes further we passed over a dry valley, Wâdî Fâḍîyeh, where I left the high road and crossed the desert to Alûs, which we reached in an hour and forty minutes. Kiepert, following Chesney, calls it Al' Uzz, but I doubt whether this spelling can be justified; the Arab geographers knew it as Alûs or Alûsah, and the name has not changed until this day. The village stands on an island, but there is also a ruined castle on the right bank of the river. We rode straight from Alûs to Jibbeh in two hours, though the zaptiehs reckon it three for a caravan. There was nothing to encourage us to loiter, inasmuch as our path lay over a horrible wilderness, stony, waterless and devoid of any growing thing. Rather more than half-way across we came to the 'Uglet Ḥaurân, a valley which is said to have its source in the Ḥaurân mountains south of Damascus. At the point where we crossed it, it was dry, but my zaptieh told me that there were springs higher up and that in wet years the water will flow down it from the Ḥaurân to the Euphrates. The wind was so strong that I could not row over to the village which stands on the island of Jibbeh.

though I was tempted by the tall round minaret that rises from among the palm-trees. As far as I could see through my glasses, it bears an inscription on its summit and a brick dog-tooth cornice. On the Jezîreh bank there is a large and well-preserved fortress. We reached the solitary khân of Baghdâdî a few minutes later; the caravan was there before us, having accomplished what is reckoned to be a nine-hours' stage in eight hours sixteen minutes. The village of Baghdâdî is an hour's march lower down, and the khân by which we camped was only four months old; "Before that," said Fattûḥ, "we used to sleep under the sky, and there was no one but us and the jackals." I had heard that Fadh Beg Ibn Hudhdhâl had a garden at Baghdâdî, and I cherished a hope that we might meet there one of his family who would help us on the way to Kheiḍir; but when we passed by the garden a solitary negro was in charge, and as the palms were not yet three feet high, I could not blame Fadh Beg for not having elected to dwell among them. There was nothing to be done but to ride on to Hît.[1]

From Baghdâdî the road climbs up into the barren hills. It is no better than a staircase cut out of the rock, and Fattûḥ admitted that carriage driving is not an easy matter here. He added that the stage from Baghdâdî to Hît is less secure than any other, by reason of its being infested by the Deleim who exact a toll from unguarded caravans. We had found two zaptiehs at the khân and had taken one on with us when we sent the Ḥadîthah man back, leaving the khân protected by a single zaptieh, so limited is the number of soldiers posted along the road. If you are not a person of sufficient consequence to claim an escort, you must wait until a body of travellers shall have collected at Baghdâd or Aleppo, as the case may be, and set forth in their company, since it is not

[1] Julian crossed the Euphrates at Parux Malkha, which cannot be far from Baghdâdî, and captured the castle of Diacira. This castle must have stood at the southern end of the great bend made by the Euphrates below Baghdâdî. Chesney saw the ruins of a fortress there. It is perhaps Ptolemy's Idicara and the Izannesopolis of Isidorus: Ritter, Vol. XI. p. 737.

safe to venture singly over the Sultan's highroad. We met that morning a large caravan of people driving, riding in panniers, and walking. No matter what their degree, all wore the singularly abandoned aspect to which only the Oriental on a journey can attain, and the shapelessness of their baggage enhanced their personal disqualifications. About half-an-hour after the caravan had passed, we came upon five or six ragged peasants, who stopped us and lifted their voices in lamentation. They had been held up by five Deleimîs in the valley below; their cloaks had been taken from them, and the bread that was to have sufficed them till they reached 'Ânah: "We are poor men," they wailed. "God curse those who rob the poor!"

"God curse all the Deleim!" cried Fattûḥ. "Why did you linger behind the caravan in this part of the road?"

"We were weary and one of us had fallen lame," they explained. "But have a care when you reach the valley bottom; five men with rifles are lurking among the sand-hills."

Their tale filled me with a futile anger, so that I desired nothing so much as to catch and punish the thieves, and without waiting to consider whether this lay within our power, I galloped on in the direction indicated by the peasants, with Fattûḥ, Jûsef and the zaptiehs at my heels. We were all armed and had nothing to fear from five robbers. The valley was a sandy depression with a sulphur stream running through it. We searched the sand-hills without success, but when we came down to the Euphrates, there were five armed men strolling unconcernedly along the bank as though they would take the air. Now, you do not wander with a rifle in your hand in unfrequented parts of the Euphrates' bank for any good purpose, and we were persuaded that these black-browed Arabs were the five we sought. Probably they had intended to reap a larger harvest, but finding the caravan too numerous they had contented themselves with the stragglers. Unfortunately we had no proof against them: the bread was eaten and the cloaks secreted among the stones, and though we spent some minutes in heaping curses upon them, we could take no steps of a more practical kind. The zaptieh, for his part, was in an agony of nervous anxiety lest we should propose to relieve them of their rifles. He looked forward to a return journey alone to Baghdâdî, and it is not good for a solitary man to have an outstanding quarrel with the Deleim. Finally I realized that we were wasting breath in useless bluster and called Fattûḥ away. If we were to concern ourselves with the catching of thieves, we might as well abandon all other pursuits in Turkey.

The town of Hît stands upon an ancient mound washed by the Euphrates (Fig. 54). Among the palm-trees at the river's edge rise columns of inky smoke from the primitive furnaces of the asphalt burners, for the place is surrounded by wells of bitumen, famous ever since the days when Babylon was a great city.[1] Heaps of rubbish and cinders strew the sulphur marshes to the north of the town, and a blinding dust-storm was stirring up the whole devil's cauldron when we arrived. It was impossible to camp and we took refuge in the khân, where we were so fortunate as to meet with an English traveller on his way back from India, the first European whom I had seen since we left Aleppo. The dust-storm rose yet higher towards evening, and though we closed the shutters of the khân—there was no glass in the windows—the sand blew in merrily through the chinks, and we ate a gritty supper in a temperature of ninety-three degrees.

Hît was the last possible starting-point for the Syrian desert, and no sooner had we arrived than I summoned Fattûḥ and presented him with an ultimatum. We had failed to get any but the most contradictory reports of wells upon the road to Kheiḍir and I would not expose the caravan to such uncertain chances, but if we went alone we could carry enough water for our needs. It only remained to dispatch

[1] Herodotus mentions the bitumen wells and calls the town Is. It has been identified with the Ihi of the Babylonian inscriptions, the Ahava of Ezra, and with the Ist from which a tribute of bitumen was brought to Thothmes III, according to an inscription at Karnak.

FIG. 54.—HÎT.

FIG. 55.—HÎT, THE SULPHUR MARSHES.

FIG. 56.— MINARET ON ISLAND OF LUBBÂD.

FIG. 57.—MINARET AT MA'MÛREH.

FIG. 59.—MADLÛBEH.

the muleteers along the highway and to find a guide for ourselves.

"Upon my head!" said Fattûḥ blandly. "Three guides wish to accompany your Excellency."

"Praise be to God," said I. "Bid them enter."

"It would be well to see each separately," observed Fattûḥ, "for they do not love one another."

We interviewed them one by one, with an elaborate show of secrecy, and each in turn spent his time in warning us against the other two. Upon these negative credentials I had to come to a decision, and I made my choice feeling that I might as logically have tossed up a piastre. It fell upon a man of the Deleim, a tribe to whom we were not well disposed, but since the country through which we were to pass was mainly occupied by their tents, it seemed wiser to take a guide who claimed cousinship with their sheikhs. He was to find an escort of five armed horsemen and to bring us to Kheiḍir in return for a handsome reward, but we undertook to engage our own baggage camels. One of the drawbacks to this arrangement was that no camels were to be got at Hît, and I felt the more persuaded that we had struck a bad bargain when Nâif came back and said:

"How do I know that you will keep your word? Perhaps to-morrow you will choose another guide."

"The English have but one word," said I; it is a principle that should never be abandoned in the East. We struck hands upon it and Nâif left us "in the peace of God."

Fattûḥ needed a day to complete his preparations, and I to see the pitch wells of Hît which lie some distance from the town. I did not see them all, but from the accounts I heard they would appear to be five in number. The largest is called the Marj (the Meadow); it is an hour and a quarter north-east of Hît and is said to be inexhaustible. The pitch is better in quality here than elsewhere, and the peasants can, when they choose, get 2,000 donkey-loads from it daily. The next in importance is at Ma'mûreh, but it is not worked. The pitch flows out over the desert and dries into an asphalt pavement about half-a-mile square. Further south is a small spring, Lteif, from which they get twenty loads a day, and near the town there is a fourth well which yields fifty loads a day (Fig. 53). The fifth well is on the other side of the Euphrates, at 'Atâ'ut; the average yield from it is twenty loads a day.

Near the asphalt beds of Ma'mûreh, about an hour south-west of Hît, lie the ruins of a village clustered round a minaret (Fig. 57). All the buildings were constructed of small unsquared stones set in mortar; the minaret was plastered on the outside and seemed to have been built of large blocks of stone and mortar, firmly welded together before they had been placed in position. The round tower, narrowing upwards and decorated at the top with a zigzag ornament, was placed upon a low octagonal structure which in turn rested upon a square base (Fig. 58). I climbed the winding stair that I might survey the country through which Nâif was to take us. It was incredibly desolate, empty of tent or village save where to the west the palm-groves of Kebeisah made a black splash upon the glaring earth. The heavy smoke of the pitch fires hung round Hît, and the sulphur marshes shone leprous under the sun—a malignant landscape that could not be redeemed by the little shrines which were scattered like propitiatory invocations among the gleaming salts.

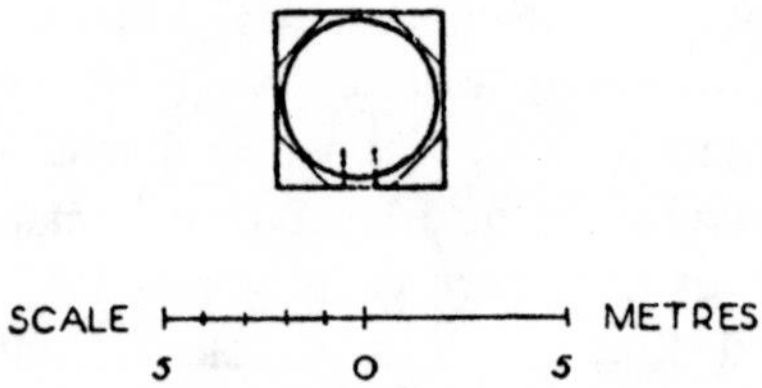

FIG. 58.—MA'MÛREH, MINARET.

About a mile from Ma'mûreh there is a still more remarkable ruin known as Madlûbeh. It is a large, irregularly shaped area marked off from the desert by heaps of stones half buried in sand. Standing among these heaps, and no doubt in their original position, there are a number of large monolithic slabs placed as if they were intended to form a wall (Fig. 59). Many of these must have fallen and been covered with the sand if the enclosure were at any time continuous, and perhaps the heaps are composed partly of buried slabs.

Two stand in line with a narrow space between like a door (one of them was 5 m. long × 1·3 m. thick, and it stood 2 m. out of the ground); in another there was a small rectangular cutting that suggested a window-hole on the upper edge (it was 10 m. long × 1·3 m. thick, and stood about 3 m. out of the ground). The stones were carefully dressed on all sides. They may have formed the lower part of a wall of which the upper part was of sun-dried brick or rubble, but at what age they were placed in those wilds a cursory survey would not reveal.

When I returned to the khân, Fattûḥ greeted me with the intelligence that the Deleimî had broken his engagement. Nâif admitted that for ordinary risks the money we had offered would have been sufficient, but Kheiḍir lay in the land of his blood enemies, the Benî Ḥassan, and he would not go. Perhaps he hoped to force us to a more liberal proposal, but in this he was disappointed. A bargain is a bargain, and we fell back upon my boast that the English have but one word. In this dilemma Fattûḥ suggested that he should see what could be done with the Mudîr, and having a lively confidence in Fattûḥ's diplomacy, I entrusted him with my passports and papers, of which I kept a varied store, and gave him plenipotentiary powers. He returned triumphant.

"Effendim," said he, "that Mudîr is a man." This is ever the highest praise that Fattûḥ can bestow, and my experience does not lead me to cavil at it. "When he had read your buyuruldehs he laid them upon his forehead and said, 'It is my duty to do all that the effendi wishes.' I told him," interpolated Fattûḥ, "that you were a consul in your own country. He will give you a zaptieh to take you to Kebeisah, and if you command, the zaptieh shall go with you to Ḳal'at Khubbâz, returning afterwards to Hît. And it cannot be that we shall fail to find a guide and camels at Kebeisah, which is a palm-grove in the desert; for all the dwellers in it know the way to Kheiḍir. As for the caravan, another zaptieh will take it to Baghdâd."

"Aferîn!" said I. "There is none like you, oh Fattûḥ."

"God forbid!" replied Fattûḥ modestly. "And now," he

proceeded, "let me bring your Excellency an omelet, for I am sure that you must be hungry." But I understood this exaggerated solicitude to be no more than a covert slur upon the culinary powers of Mr. X.'s servant, who had provided us with an abundant lunch during Fattûḥ's absence, and not even so voracious a consul as I could face a second meal. Fattûḥ retired in some displeasure to inform the muleteers that they would journey to Baghdâd and Kerbelâ and there rejoin us, please God.

We explored the village of Hît before nightfall, and a more malodorous little dirty spot I hope I may never see. "Why," says the poet, concerning some unknown wayfarer, "did he not halt that night at Hît?" and it is strange that Ibn Khurdâdhbeh, who quotes the question, should have been at a loss for the answer. Possibly he had no personal knowledge of Hît. On the top of the hill there is a round minaret, similar in construction to the minaret of Ma'mûreh, but I saw no other feature of interest. The sun was setting as we came down to the palm-groves by the river. The fires under the troughs of molten bitumen sent up their black smoke columns between the trees (Fig. 60); half-naked Arabs fed the flames with the same bitumen, and the Euphrates bore along the product of their labours as it had done for the Babylonians before them. So it must have looked, this strange factory under the palm-trees, for the last 5,000 years, and all the generations of Hît have not altered by a shade the processes taught them by their first forefathers.

THE PARTHIAN STATIONS OF ISIDORUS OF CHARAX

THE only modern record of the road along the left bank of the Euphrates from Raḳḳah to Deir is the rather meagre account given by Sachau; Moritz travelled down the left bank from Deir to Buseirah, but I know of no published description of the road from Buseirah to 'Ânah. It has not

FIG. 60.—HÎT, THE BITUMEN FURNACES.

FIG. 61.—THE EUPHRATES AT HÎT.

FIG. 62.—THE WELL AT KEBEISAH.

FIG. 63.—'AIN ZA'ZU.

therefore been possible hitherto to attempt to place in any continuous sequence the sites given by ancient authorities. Of these the fullest list is that of the Parthian stations furnished by Isidorus of Charax (*Geographi Græci Minores*, ed. by Müller, Vol. I. p. 244). It begins with the fixed point of Nicephorium (Raḳḳah) and ends with another fixed point, that of Anatho ('Ânah). Between these two lies Nabagath on the Aburas. The Aburas may safely be assumed to indicate the Khâbûr, and Nabagath is therefore Circesium-Buseirah. The following comparative table shows my suggestions for the remaining stations, combined with those which have already been made by Ritter and others. The times given are the rate of travel of my caravan; between Raḳḳah and Deir I had the advantage of comparing them with Sachau's time-table. No two caravans travel over any given distance at exactly the same pace, but the general average works out without any grave discrepancy. I have often tried to reckon the speed at which my caravan travels and have come to the conclusion that it is very little under three miles an hour, say about two and seven-eighths miles an hour. Isidorus computes his distances by the schœnus. According to Moritz 1 schœnus = 5·5 kilometres. From Buseirah to 'Ânah I travelled over Isidorus's road at the rate of 1 schœnus in 1 hr. 7 min., which would bring the schœnus down to 5·166 kilometres. The section from Raḳḳah to Buseirah is not so easy to calculate because Isidorus has in two places omitted to give the exact distance between the stations, but my rate of travel was not far different here from that noted in the other sections. So much for the average. The individual distances do not tally so exactly, and in attempting to determine the sites, the evidence that can be gathered from the country itself seems to me to weigh heavier in the scale than the measurements given by Isidorus, especially as his inexactitude is proved by the fact that the sum of the distances he allows from station to station do not coincide with the total distances, from the Zeugma (Birejik) to Seleucia, and from Phaliga to Seleucia, as he states them. In both cases the sum of the small distances comes to a larger figure than that which he allows for the totals—

Zeugma to Seleucia . . . . 171 sch.

total of distances between stations 174 sch., without the two omitted by him.

Phaliga to Seleucia . . . . 100 sch.

total of distances between stations 120 sch. without one omitted by him.

As regards the second section, Kiepert believed that a copyist's error of 10 sch. too much had been made in Isidorus's table between Izannesopolis and Aeipolis (the modern Hît), but even this correction will not bring the totals together (Ritter, Vol. XI. p. 738). The road from the Zeugma to Nicephorium does not follow the river, and I am therefore unable to control the statements of Isidorus above Raḳḳah; nor do I know the section between Hît and Seleucia. I need scarcely say that my table is of the most tentative character; it begins with the ninth station of Isidorus, Nicephorium.

The first remarkable site which I saw on the river below Raḳḳah was the large area surrounded by a ditch, half-an-hour above my camping-ground. Isidorus's tenth station from Zeugma is Galabatha. Ritter (Vol. XI. p. 687) observes that it must be above Abu Sa'îd, and the area enclosed by the ditch fulfils that condition. The eleventh station is Khubana which I put at Abu Sa'îd, where there are fragments of columns and other evidences of antiquity. The twelfth station is Thillada Mirrhada; I have placed it at Khmeiḍah (squared stones, brick walls, a broken sarcophagus), but the claims of Abu 'Atîḳ are considerable, the extent of the ruin field at the latter place being much larger than at Khmeiḍah. But Abu 'Atîḳ is 7 hrs. 5 min. from Abu Sa'îd, and the caravan time between Khmeiḍah and Abu Sa'îd (6 hrs. 5 min.) is already rather long for the 4 sch. allowed by Isidorus. The thirteenth station is Basilia with Semiramidis Fossa. Ritter long ago pointed to the probability of its having been situated at Zelebîyeh (Vol. XI.

Isidorus: Stations	Isidorus: Description	Schœni	Modern Sites	Time (hrs. min.)	Xenophon	Pliny	Ptolemy	Ammianus Marcellinus	Zosimos	Herodotus
9. Nicephorium . .	Greek town founded by Alexander	—	Raḳḳah	—	—	Nicephorium	Nicephorium	Callinicum	—	—
10. Galabatha . . .	Deserted village	4	Ditch	6 15	—	—	—	—	—	—
11. Khubana . . .	Village	1	Abu Sa'îd	1 30	—	—	—	—	—	—
12. Thillada Mirrhada	Royal station	4	Khmeiḍah	6 5	—	—	—	—	—	—
13. Basilia	Temple of Artemis built by Darius, village surrounded by wall	?	Zelebîyeh	3 40	—	—	—	—	—	—
Semiramidis Fossa	Euphrates dam									
14. Allan	Walled village	4	Umm Rejeibah	3	—	—	—	—	—	—
15. Biunan	Temple of Artemis	4	Near Deir	6	—	—	—	—	—	—
16. Phaliga	Village	6	?	—	—	Phaliscum	—	—	—	—
17. Nabagath . . .	Walled village on Aburas	Near Phaliga	Buseirah	7	Villages on Araxes	—	Khabura	Circesium	—	—
18. Asikha	Village	4	Jemmah	5 10	—	—	Zeitha	Zeitha	—	—
19. Dura Nicanoris .	Town founded by Macedonians, called Europus by Greeks	6	Abu'l Ḥassan	8 20	—	—	Thelda	—	—	—
20. Merrhan . . .	Castle and walled village	5	Irzî	6 30	Corsote	—	—	Dura	—	—
21. Giddan	Town	5	Jabariyeh ?	—	—	—	—	—	—	—
22. Belisibiblada . .	—	7	Ḳal'at Bulâḳ	9 25	—	—	Bonakhe	—	—	—
23. Island	—	6	Ḳarâbileh ?	—	—	—	—	—	—	—
24. Anatho	Island	4	Lubbâd, island opposite 'Ânah	11 50	—	—	Bethauna	Anatha	—	—
25. Olabus	Island, Parthian treasure-house	12	Ḥadithah	12	—	—	—	—	—	—
26. Izannesopolis . .	—	12	Chesney's Ḳaṣr	—	—	—	Idicara	—	—	—
27. Aeipolis . . .	Bitumen wells	16 (6 ?)	Hît	17 30	—	—	—	—	Sitha	Is

p. 687). Semiramidis Fossa was no doubt a canal; Chesney saw traces of an ancient canal below Zelebîyeh. The distance from Thillada to Basilia is not given by Isidorus. Ritter would allow 5 sch. and Herzfeld 7 sch. (*Memnon*, 1907, p. 92); according to my reckoning both these distances are too long. I marched from Khmeiḍah to Zelebîyeh in 3 hrs. 40 min., which implies a distance of not more than 3 sch. For the fourteenth station, Allan, Umm Rejeibah is the only possible site I saw. It is true that I reached it in 3 hrs. from Zelebîyeh, whereas Isidorus puts it 4 sch. from Basilia, but I cut straight across the hills, and if I had followed the river (*i. e.* from the mouth of the canal, Semiramidis Fossa) the time needed would have been considerably longer. The fifteenth station, Biunan, was conjectured by Ritter to lie opposite Deir. I saw no traces of ruins upon the left bank, though Sachau speaks of the remains of two bridges (*Reise*, p. 262), and I should be more inclined to look for Biunan at a nameless site mentioned by Moritz (*op. cit.*, p. 36). The difference is not in any case of importance, for the site seen by Moritz is immediately below Deir. He would have it to be Phaliga, which is doubtless Pliny's Phaliscum, but that suggestion is difficult to reconcile with Isidorus's 14 sch. from Basilia to Phaliga, which brings Phaliga much nearer to Circesium. Moreover, Isidorus states that Nabagath is near Phaliga—so near that he does not trouble to give any other indication of the distance between the two stations—and as Nabagath on the Aburas cannot be other than Buseirah, Phaliga too must be close to the Khâbûr mouth. I did not see the site mentioned by Moritz because I neglected to follow the river closely immediately below Deir; if it be, as I suppose, Biunan, I cannot attempt to identify the site of Phaliga. The seventeenth station, Nabagath, is, as has been said, Circesium-Ḳarḳîsîyâ-Buseirah. The eighteenth, Asikha, I would identify with the Zeitha of Ptolemy and Ammianus Marcellinus, and with the mounds I saw at Jemmah. For the nineteenth station, Dura, I know no other site than the very striking tell of Abu'l Ḥassan, the biggest mound upon this part of the river. Müller has suggested that the mound may represent Ptolemy's Thelda (in his edition of *Ptolemy's Geography*, p. 1003). Ammianus Marcellinus also mentions "a deserted town on the river" called Dura. The army of Julian reached it in two days' march from Zeitha, at which place the emperor had made an oration to his soldiers after sacrificing at Gordian's tomb. Now two days' march from Zeitha-Jemmah would bring the army to Werdî-Irzî, which is no doubt the place called by Xenophon Corsote and described by him as "a large deserted city." It is perhaps worthy of observation that, in spite of its being deserted, Cyrus provisioned his army at Corsote and that Julian's army found at Dura, though it too was deserted, "quantities of wild deer, so that the soldiers and sailors had plenty of food." My own impression on the spot was that Ammianus Marcellinus's Dura must be Irzî. The tower tombs were certainly erected before the middle of the fourth century, therefore they were in existence when Julian passed; moreover, they were far more numerous and conspicuous than they are at present, since almost all of them have now fallen into ruin. It is difficult to see how Irzî could have failed to attract the attention of Ammianus Marcellinus, and Dura is the one place mentioned by him between Zeitha and 'Ânah. But the Dura of Isidorus, the nineteenth station, has to be placed at Abu'l Ḥassan, not at Irzî, since his twentieth station, Merrhan, necessarily falls at Irzî, and I can only conjecture that, as in Julian's time both places were ruined and deserted, Ammianus Marcellinus made a confusion between them, or was wrongly informed, and transferred the name of Dura (Abu'l Ḥassan) to Merrhan (Irzî). For the twenty-first station, Giddan, I can offer no suggestion. Jabarîyeh will scarcely fit, as it is but 13 hrs. 15 min. from 'Ânah, and Giddan was 17 sch. from Anatho, but it must be admitted that all the distances between the stations from Merrhan to 'Ânah seem to be too long according to my caravan time. The twenty-second station, Belesibiblada, was placed by Chesney at Ḳal'at Bulâḳ, and I saw no better site for it, though I took only 9 hrs. and 25 min. to reach it from

Irzî, and the distance given by Isidorus is 12 sch. Ritter would place at Ḳal'at Bulâḳ Ptolemy's Bonakhe. I do not see any way of identifying with certainty the island station, the twenty-third, which was 4 sch. from 'Anah. There are many islands in the stream above 'Ânah. One of them, Ḳarâbileh, is reported to have ruins upon it; it was about four hours' journey from ancient 'Ânah, and may therefore be identical with the twenty-third station, which is placed at a distance of 4 sch. from Anatho. Anatho, the twenty-fourth station, Isidorus expressly states to be on an island; it was therefore the successor to the Assyrian fortress which I believe to have existed on the island of Lubbâd. Xenophon does not mention it; nor does Ptolemy, unless his Bethanna may be taken for 'Anah as Ritter believed (Vol. XI. p. 716). Rawâ may possibly be the Phathusa of Zosimos, but I would rather place Phathusa on the left bank, opposite and below the island of Lubbâd, where there are many mounds and ruins. I did not follow the river below 'Ânah very closely, but the ruins I saw near Ḥadîthah help to justify the presumption that Olabus was situated there. Chesney wished to identify Izannesopolis with the ruins of a castle between Baghdâdî and Hît. I did not go to the spot, and my caravan time between Ḥadîthah and Hît is therefore rather misleading, for if I had followed the river so as to visit the ḳaṣr, the journey would have taken more than the seventeen and a half hours which I have recorded. Isidorus's 16 sch. from Izannesopolis to Aeipolis can scarcely be correct, and Kiepert's emendation (6 instead of 16) may well be accepted.

CHAPTER IV

HÎT TO KERBELÂ

March 18—*March* 30

HISTORY in retrospect suffers an atmospheric distortion. We look upon a past civilization and see it, not as it was, but charged with the significance of that through which we gaze, as down the centuries shadow overlies shadow, some dim, some luminous, and some so strongly coloured that all the age behind is tinged with a borrowed hue. So it is that the great revolutions, "predestined unto us and we predestined," take on a double power; not only do they turn the current of human action, but to the later comer they seem to modify that which was irrevocably fixed and past. We lend to the dwellers of an earlier day something of our own knowledge; we watch them labouring towards the ineluctable hour, and credit them with a prescience of change not given to man. At no time does this sense of inevitable doom hang more darkly than over the years that preceded the rise of Islâm; yet no generation had less data for prophecy than the generation of Mohammad. The Greek and the Persian disputed the possession of western Asia in profitless and exhausting warfare, both harassed from time to time by the predatory expeditions of the nomads on their frontiers, both content to enter into alliance with this tribe or with that, and to set up an Arab satrap over the desert marshes. Thus it happened that the Benî Ghassân served the emperor of the Byzantines, and the Benî Lakhm fought in the ranks of the Sassanian armies. But neither to Justin II nor to Chosroes the Great came the news that in Mecca a child was born of the Ḳureish who was to found a military state as formidable as any that the world had seen, and nothing could have exceeded the fantastic improbability of such intelligence.

I had determined to journey back behind this great dividing line, to search through regions now desolate for evidences of a past that has left little historic record, calling upon the shades to take form again upon the very ground whereon, substantial, they had played their part. So on a brilliant morning Fattûḥ and I saw the caravan start out in the direction of Baghdâd, not without inner heart-searchings as to where and how we should meet it again, and having loaded three donkeys with all that was left to us of worldly goods, we turned our faces towards the wilderness. I looked back upon the ancient mound of Hît, the palm-groves, and the dense smoke of the pitch fires rising into the clear air, and as I looked our zaptieh came out to join us—a welcome sight, for the Mudîr might well have repented at the eleventh hour. Now no one rides into the desert, however uncertain the adventure, without a keen sense of exhilaration. The bright morning sun, the wide clean levels, the knowledge that the problems of existence are reduced on a sudden to their simplest expression, your own wit and endurance being the sole determining factors —all these things brace and quicken the spirit. The spell of the waste seized us as we passed beyond the sulphur marshes; Ḥussein Onbâshî held his head higher, and we gave each other the salaam anew, as if we had stepped out into another world that called for a fresh greeting.

"At Hît," said he, and his words went far to explain the lightness of his heart, "I have left three wives in the house."

"Mâshallah!" said Fattûḥ, "you must be deaf with the gir-gir-gir of them."

"Eh billah!" assented Ḥussein, "I shut my ears. Three wives, two sons and six daughters, of whom but two married. Twenty children I have had, and seven wives; three of these died and one left me and returned to her own people. But I shall take another bride this year, please God."

"We Christians," observed Fattûḥ, "find one enough."

"You may be right," answered Ḥussein politely; "yet I would take a new wife every year if I had the means."

"We will find you a bride in Kebeisah," said I.

Ḥussein weighed this suggestion.

"The maidens of Kebeisah are fair but wilful. There is one among them, her name is Shemsah—wallah, a picture! a picture she is!—she has had seven husbands."

"And the maidens of Hît?" I asked. "How are they?"

"Not so fair, but they are the better wives. That is why I choose to remain in Hît," explained Ḥussein. "The bimbâshî would have sent me to Baghdâd, but I said, 'No, let me stay here; the maidens of Hît do not expect much.' Your Excellency may laugh, but a poor man must think of these things."

We rode on through the aromatic scrub until the black masses of the Kebeisah palm-groves resolved into tall trunks and feathery fronds.[1] The sun stood high as we passed under the village gate and down the dusty street that led to the Mudîr's compound. We tied our mares to some mangers in his courtyard and were ourselves ushered into his reception-room, there to drink coffee and set forth our purpose. The leading citizens of Kebeisah dropped in one by one, and the talk was of the desert and of the dwellers therein. The men of Kebeisah are not 'Arab, Bedouin; they hold their mud-walled village and their 50,000 palm-trees against the tribes, but they know the laws of the desert as well as the nomads themselves, and carry on an uneasy commerce with them in dates and other commodities, with which even the wilderness cannot dispense, the accredited methods of the merchant alternating with those of the raider and the avenger of raids. There was no lack of guides to take me to Khubbâz, for the ruin is the first stage upon the post-road to Damascus, and half the male population was acquainted with that perilous way.

"It is the road of death," said Ḥussein Onbâshî, stuffing tobacco into the cup of his narghileh.

"Eh billah!" said one who laid the glowing charcoal atop.

[1] Yâḳût mentions Kebeisah as the oasis four miles from Hît upon the desert road. There are, he says, a number of villages there, the inhabitants of which live in the extreme of poverty and misery, by reason of the aridity of the surrounding waste.

"Eight days' ride, and the government, look you, pays no more than fifteen mejîdehs from Hît and back again."

An old man, wrapped in a brown cloak edged with gold, took up the tale.

"The government reckons fifteen mejîdehs to be the price of a man's life. Wallah! if the water-skins leak between water and water, or if the camel fall lame, the rider perishes."

"By the truth, it is the road of death," repeated Ḥussein. "Twice last year the Deleim robbed the mail and killed the bearer of it."

I had by this time spread out Kiepert.

"Inform me," said I, "concerning the water."

"Oh lady," said the old man, "I rode with the mail for twenty years. An hour and a half from Kebeisah there is water at 'Ain Za'zu', and in four hours more there is water in the tank of Khubbâz after the winter, but this year there is none, by reason of the lack of rain. Twelve hours from Khubbâz you shall reach Ḳaṣr 'Amej, which is another fortress like Khubbâz, but more ruined; and there is no water there. But eighteen hours farther you find water in the Wâdî Ḥaurân, at Muḥeiwir."

"Is there not a castle there?" I asked. Kiepert calls it the castle of 'Aiwir.

"There is nought but rijm," said he. (Rijm are the heaps of stones which the Arabs pile together for landmarks.) "And after nine hours more there is water at Ga'rah, and then no more till Dumeir, nine hours from Damascus."

If this account is exact, there must be four days of waterless desert on the road of death.

The springs in Kebeisah are strongly charged with sulphur, but half-way between the town and the shrine of Sheikh Khudr, that lifts a conical spire out of the wilderness, there is a well less bitter, to which come the fair and wilful maidens night and morning, bearing on their heads jars of plaited willow, pitched without and within (Fig. 62). We did not fill our water-skins there when we set out next day for Ḳaṣr Khubbâz, but rode on to 'Ain Za'zu', where the water is drinkable, though far from sweet (Fig. 63). There are

FIG. 64.—ḲAṢR KHUBBÂZ AND RUINS OF THE TANK.

FIG. 66.—ḲAṢR KHUBBÂZ, THE GATEWAY.

FIG. 67.—ḲAṢR KHUBBÂZ, A VAULTED CHAMBER.

FIG. 68.—THEMAIL.

two other sulphurous springs, one a little to the north and one to the south, round each of which, as at 'Ain Za'zu', the inhabitants of Kebeisah sow clover, the sole fodder of the oasis in rainless years like the spring of 1909; so said Fawwâz, the owner of the two camels on which we had placed our small packs. Fawwâz rode one of them and his nephew, Sfâga, the other, and they hung the dripping water-skins under the loads. We followed the course of a shallow valley westwards, and before we left it sighted a train of donkeys making to the north with an escort on foot—Arabs of the Deleim. They looked harmless enough, but I afterwards found that they had caused Fawwâz great uneasiness; indeed they kept him watchful all through the night, fearing that they might raid us while we slept. I was too busy observing the wide landscape to dwell on such matters. The desolate world stretched before us, lifting itself by shallow steps into long, bare ridges, on which the Arab rijm were visible for miles away. The first of these steps—it was not more than fifty feet high—was called the Jebel Muzâhir, and when we had gained its summit we saw the castle of Khubbâz lying out upon the plain. To the north the ground falls away into a wâdî, a shallow depression like all desert valleys, in which are traces of a large masonry tank that caught the trickle of the winter springs and held their water behind a massive dam (Fig. 64). The tank is now half full of soil and the dam leaks, so that as soon as the rains have ceased the water store vanishes. It had left behind it a scanty crop of grass and flowers, which seemed luxuriant to us in that dry season; we turned the mares and camels loose in what Fattûḥ called enthusiastically the rabî'ah (the herbage of spring), and pitched my light tent in the valley bottom, where my men could find shelter among the rocks against the chills of night. I left all these arrangements to Fattûḥ, and with Ḥussein and Fawwâz to hold the metre tape, measured and photographed the fort till the sun touched the western horizon.

The walls of Khubbâz are built of stones, either unworked or very roughly squared, set in a thick bed of coarse mortar,

In form the fort is a hollow square with round bastions at the angles, and except on the side facing towards Kebeisah, where the centre of the wall is occupied by a gate, there is also a round bastion midway between the angle towers (Fig. 65). All these bastions are much ruined and I may be wrong in representing them as if unequal size. Before the door there has been a vaulted porch, among the ruins of which lies a large block of stone which looks as if it had served

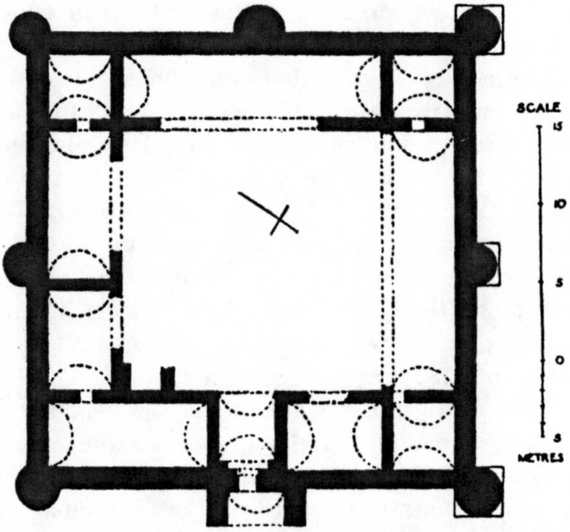

FIG. 65.—KHUBBÂZ.

as lintel to the outer door; I could see no moulding or inscription upon it (Fig. 66). The existing inner door is arched, the arch being set forward in a curious fashion. It opened into a vaulted entrance passage which communicated with an open court in the centre of the building. The court was surrounded by barrel-vaulted chambers, some of which showed traces of repair or reconstruction, though the old and the new work are now alike ruined.[1] All the vaults

[1] The central division wall in the long south chamber is a later addition.

are set forward about three centimetres beyond the face of the wall (Fig. 67). Above the outset the first few courses of stones are laid horizontally, inclining slightly inwards, but where the curve of the vault makes it impossible to continue this method without the aid of centering beams, the stone is cut into narrow slabs which are set upright so as to form slices of the vault, and each slice has an inclination backwards, the first resting against the head wall and every succeeding slice resting against the one behind it. This is the well-known Mesopotamian system of vaulting without a centering, which is as old as the Assyrians.[1] It is best adapted to brick, but it can be carried out in stone when the span of the vault is not large, provided that the stones be cut thin, so as to resemble as nearly as possible brick tiles. On the south side, which is the best preserved, there are traces of an upper storey, or possibly of an upper gallery or *chemin de ronde*. A doorway led from it into a small chamber hollowed out of the thickness of the central bastion: I imagine that there was a similar outlook chamber in the other bastions, but in all these the upper part is ruined. I could find no inscriptions; the Arab tribe marks (awâsim) were scratched upon the plaster with which the inner side of the walls had been coated. I do not doubt that Khubbâz belongs to the Mohammadan period, nor that it is a relic of the great days of the khalifate when the shortest road from Baghdâd to Damascus was guarded by little companies of soldiers stationed at Khubbâz and 'Amej, and perhaps at other points. The plan is that of many of the Roman and Byzantine lime fortresses upon the Syrian side of the desert,[2] of the Mohammadan forts and fortified khâns scattered over Syria and Mesopotamia,[3] and of the modern

[1] Described by Choisy: *L'Art de bâtir chez les Byzantins*, p. 31.

[2] For example Ḳasṭal (Brünnow and Domaszewski: *Provincia Arabia*, Vol. II. pl. xliv.); Ḳaṣr el Abyaḍ (de Vogüé: *La Syrie Centrale*, Vol. I. p. 69); Deir el Kahf, founded in A.D. 306 (Butler: *Ancient Architecture in Syria*, Section A, Part II. p. 146); Ḳuṣeir el Ḥallâbât, dated A.D. 213 (ditto, p. 72); barracks at Anderîn, dated A.D. 558 (ditto, Section B, Part II. pl. viii.).

[3] Ṭuba with a triple court (Musil: *Ḳuṣeir 'Amra*, Vol. I. p. 13); Kharânî (ditto, p. 97); Khân ez Zebîb (*Provincia Arabia*, Vol. II. p. 78).

Turkish guardhouse; the structural details are Mesopotamian, dictated by the conditions of the land.

At the pleasant hour of dusk I sat among the flowering weeds by my tent door while Fattûḥ cooked our dinner in his kitchen among the rocks, Sfâga gathered a fuel of desert scrub, Fawwâz stirred the rice-pot, and the bubbling of Ḥussein's narghileh gave a note of domesticity to our bivouac. My table was a big stone, the mares cropping the ragged grass round the tent were my dinner-party; one by one the stars shone out in a moonless heaven and our tiny encampment was wrapped in the immense silences of the desert, the vast and peaceful night. Next morning, as we rode back to Kebeisah, Fattûḥ and I, between intervals devoted to chasing gazelle, laid siege on our companions and persuaded them to accompany us in our further journey. Fawwâz avowed that he was satisfied with us and would come where we wished (and as for Sfâga he would do as he was told) as long as Ḥussein would give a semi-official sanction to the enterprise by his presence. It was more difficult to win over Ḥussein, who had received from the Mudîr no permission to absent himself so long from Hît; but Fattûḥ pointed out that, when you have three wives, with the prospect of a fourth, to say nothing of six daughters of whom but two are married, you cannot afford to neglect the opportunity of earning an extra bakhshîsh. This reasoning was conclusive, and before we reached 'Ain Za'zu' we had settled everything, down to the quantity of coffee-beans we would buy at Kebeisah for the trip. But when we got to Kebeisah we were greeted by news that went near to overturning our combinations. There had been alarums and excursions in our absence; the Deleim had attacked a party of fuel-gatherers two hours from the oasis, in the very plain we were to cross, and had made off with eight donkeys. One of the donkeys belonged to Fawwâz; he shook his head over the baleful activity of the tribe and murmured that we were a small party in the face of such perils. Moreover, in the Mudîr's courtyard there stood a half-starved mare which had been recaptured in a counter-raid from the seventh husband of the famous Shemsah. He too was of the Deleim. We gave the mare a feed of corn—her gentle, hungry eyes were turned appealingly on our full mangers; but to Shemsah I was harder hearted, though her eyes were more beautiful than those of the mare. She came suppliant as I sat dining on the Mudîr's roof at nightfall and begged me to recover her husband's rifle, which lay below in the hands of the government. Her straight brows were pencilled together with indigo and a short blue line marked the roundness of her white chin; a cloak slipping backwards from her head showed the rows of scarlet beads about her throat, and as she drew it together with slender fingers, Fattûḥ, Ḥussein and I gazed on her with unmixed approval, in spite of the irregular course of her domestic history. But I felt that to return his rifle to a Deleimî robber was not part of my varied occupations, though who knows whether Shemsah's grace, backed by what few mejîdehs she could scrape together, did not end by softening the purpose of Ḥussein and the Mudîr, "the Government," as in veiled terms we spoke of them?

With the exercise of some diplomacy we induced Fawwâz to hold to his engagement, but the Mudîr took fright when he heard of our intentions, and threatened our guides with dire retribution if they led us into the heart of the desert. I think the threat was only intended to relieve him of responsibility, for Ḥussein shrugged his shoulders, and said it would be enough if we rode an hour in the direction of Ramâdî, on the Euphrates, and then changed our course and made straight for Abu Jîr, an oasis where we expected to find Arab tents. We set off next morning in the clear sunlight which makes all projects seem entirely reasonable, and dropped, after three-quarters of an hour, into a little depression. When we had crossed the sulphur marsh which lay at the valley bottom, we altered our direction to the south-west and rode almost parallel to a long low ridge called the Ga'rat ej Jemâl, which lay about three miles to the west of us. Four hours from Kebeisah we reached a tiny mound out of which rose a spring of water, sulphurous but just drinkable. The top of the mound was lifted only a few feet above the surrounding level, but that was enough to give us a wide view, and since in all the world before us there was no shade or shelter from the sun, we sat down and lunched where we could be sure that a horseman would not approach us unawares. And as we rested, some one far away opened a bottle into which Solomon, Prophet of God, had sealed one of the Jinn. Up sprang a gigantic column of smoke that fanned outwards in the still air and hung menacingly over the naked, empty plain. I waited spellbound to see the great shoulders and huge horned head disengage themselves from the smoke-wreaths that rolled higher and—

"'Ain el 'Awâsil burns," said Fawwâz. "A shepherd has set it alight."

There was a small pitch-well an hour away to the south-east, and if springs that burn when the tinder touches them are more logical than spirits that issue from a bottle when the seal is broken, then the explanation of Fawwâz may be accepted. But at that moment I could not stay to think the problem out, for if it was hot riding, sitting still was intolerable, and we were not anxious to linger when every half-hour's march meant half-an-hour of dangerous country behind us. From noon to sunset the desert is stripped of beauty. Hour after hour we journeyed on, while the bare forbidding hills drew away from us on the right, and the plain ahead rolled out illimitable. We saw no living creature, man or beast, but an hour from 'Ain el 'Aṣfûrîyeh, where we had lunched, we came upon a deep still pool in an outcrop of rock, the water sufficiently sweet to drink. This spot is called Jelîb esh Sheikh; it contains several such pools, said Fawwâz, and he added that the water had appeared there of a sudden two years before, but that now it never diminished, nor rose higher in the rocky clefts. Just beyond the pool we crossed the Wâdî Muḥammadî, which stretched westwards to the receding ridges of the Gar'at ej Jemâl, and east to the Euphrates; it was dry and blotched with an evil-looking crust of sulphur. Fawwâz turned his camel's head a little to the east of south and began to look anxiously for landmarks. We hoped to find at Abu Jîr an encampment of the Deleim, and, eagerly as we wished to avoid the scattered horsemen of the tribe by day, it was essential that we should pass the night near their tents. The desert is governed by old and well-defined laws, and the first of these is the law of hospitality. If we slept within the circuit of a sheikh's encampment he would be "malzûm 'aleinâ" (responsible for us) and not one of his people would touch us; but if we lay out in the open we should court the attack of raiders and of thieves. Two hours from the Wâdî Muḥammadî we reached a little tell, from the top of which we sighted the 'alâmah (the landmarks) of Abu Jîr, a couple of high-piled mounds of stones. An hour later they lay to the east of us, and we saw still farther to the south-east the black line of tamarisk bushes that indicated the oasis. But it was another hour before we got up to it, and the sun was very low in the sky when we set foot on the hard black surface that gives the place its name. There was no time to lose, and we embarked recklessly on the "Father of Asphalt," only to be caught in the fresh pitch that had been spread out upon the wilderness by streams of sulphurous water. We dismounted and led our animals over the quaking expanse, coasting round the head-waters of the springs—there are, I believe, eight of them—and experimenting in our own persons on half-congealed lakes of pitch before we allowed the camels to venture across them. The light faded while we were thus engaged, and seeing that too much caution might well be our undoing, I shouted to Fattûḥ to follow, and struck out eastwards. Fattûḥ was half inclined to look upon our case as a result of premeditated treachery on the part of Fawwâz, but I had noted unmistakable signs of fear and bewilderment in the bearing of the latter, and at all hazards I was resolved not to sleep in a pool of tar. We made for a line of tamarisk bushes behind which lay a thin haze of smoke, and as we broke through the brushwood we beheld a black tent crouching in the hollow. We rode straight up to the door and gave the salaam.

"And upon you peace," returned the astonished owner.

"What Arabs are you, and where is your sheikh's tent?" said I, in an abrupt European manner.

He was taken aback at being asked so many questions and answered reluctantly, "We are the Deleim, and the tent of Muḥammad el 'Abdullah lies yonder."

We turned away, and I whispered to Fattûḥ not to hasten, and above all to approach the sheikh's tent from in front, lest we should be mistaken for such as come upon an evil errand. He fell behind me, and with as much dignity as a tired and dusty traveller can muster, I drew rein by the tent ropes and gave the salaam ceremoniously, with a hand lifted to breast and lip and brow. A group of men sitting by the hearth leapt to their feet and one came forward.

"Peace and kinship and welcome," said he, laying his hand on my bridle.

I looked into his frank and merry face and knew that all was well.

"Are you Muḥammad el 'Abdullah, for whom we seek?"

"Wallah, how is my name known to you?" said he. "Be pleased to enter."

Ḥussein Onbâshî, when he appeared with the camels a quarter of an hour later, found a large company round the coffee-pots, listening in breathless wonder (I no less amazed than the rest) while the sheikh related the exploits of—a motor!

"And then, oh lady, they wound a handle in front of the carriage, and lo, it moved without horses, eh billah! And it sped across the plain, we sitting on the cushions. And from behind there went forth semok." He brought out the English word triumphantly.

"Allah, Allah!" we murmured.

Ḥussein took from his lip the narghileh tube which was already between them and explained the mystery.

"It was the automobile of Misterr X. He journeyed from Aleppo to Baghdâd in four days, and the last day Muḥammad el 'Abdullah went with him, for the road was through the country of the Deleim."

"I saw them start," said Fattûḥ the Aleppine. "But the automobile lies now broken in Baghdâd."

Muḥammad paid no heed to this slur upon the reputation of the carriage.

"White!" said he. "It was all painted white. Wallah, the Arabs wondered as it fled past. And I was seated within upon the cushions."

That night Fattûḥ and I held a short council. We had won successfully through a hazardous day, but it seemed less than wisdom to go farther without an Arab guide, and I proposed to add Muḥammad el 'Abdullah to our party, if he would come.

"He will come," said Fattûḥ. "This sheikh is a man. And your Excellency is of the English."

Muḥammad neither demurred nor bargained. I think he would have accompanied me even if I had not belonged to the race that owned the carriage. Our adventure pleased him; he was one of those whose blood runs quicker than that of his fellows, whose fancy burns brighter, "whom thou, Melpomene, at birth" . . . upon many an unknown cradle the Muse sheds her clear beam.

"But if we were to meet the raiders of the Benî Ḥassan?" I asked, mindful of the unsuccessful parleyings at Hît.

"God is great!" replied Muḥammad, "and we are four men with rifles."

There was once a town at Abu Jîr, guarded by a little square fort with bastioned angles like Ḳaṣr Khubbâz. It was, however, much more ruined; of the interior buildings nothing remained, while the outer walls were little better than heaps of stones. But below this later work there were remains of older foundations, more careful masonry of larger materials, and outside the walls traces of a pavement, composed of big slabs of stone, accurately fitted together. All round the fort lay the foundations of houses, stone walls or crumbling mounds of sun-dried brick, not unlike the ruins of Ma'mûreh. There must have existed here a mediæval Mohammadan settlement, if there was nothing older, and the discovery was sufficiently surprising, for Abu Jîr now lies far beyond the limits of fixed habitation. The Deleim still turn the abundant water of the oasis to some profit, planting a few patches of corn and clover in the low ground below the ruins, but the insecurity of the desert forbids all permanent occupation. We had not gone far on our way next morning before Muḥammad stopped short in the ode he was singing and bent down from his saddle to examine some hoof-prints in the sandy ground. Two horsemen had travelled that way, riding in the same direction that we were taking.

"Those are the mares of our enemies," he observed.

"How do you know?" I asked.

"I heard that they had passed Abu Jîr in the night," he answered and resumed his song. When he had brought it to an end, he called out—

"Oh lady, I will sing the ode that I composed about the carriage."

At this the camel-riders and Ḥussein drew near and Muḥammad began the first ḳaṣîdah that has been written to a motor.

"I tell a marvel the like of which no man has known,
A glory of artifice born of English wit."

"True, true!" ejaculated Fawwâz ecstatically.

"Eh billah!" exclaimed Ḥussein.

"Her food and her drink are the breath from a smoke-cloud blown,
If her radiance fade bright fire shall reburnish it."

"Allah, Allah!" cried the enraptured Fawwâz.

"On the desert levels she darts like a bird of prey,
Her race puts to shame a mare of the purest breed;
As a hawk in the dusk that hovers and swoops to slay,
She swoops and turns with wondrous strength and speed."

"Wallah, the truth!" Ḥussein's enthusiasm was uncontrollable.

"Eh wallah!" echoed Fawwâz and Sfâga.

"He who mounts and rides her sits on the throne of a king . . ."

"A king in very truth!" cried Fawwâz.

"If the goal be far, to her the remote is near . . ."

"Near indeed!" burst from the audience.

> "More stealthy than stallions, more swift than the jinn a-wing,
> She turns the gazelle that hides from her blast in fear."

"Allah!" Fawwâz punctuated the stanza.

> "Not from idle lips was gathered the wisdom I sing . . ."

"God forbid!" exclaimed Fawwâz, leaning forward eagerly.

> "In the whole wide plain she has not met with her peer."

"Mâshallah! it is so! it is the truth, oh lady!" said Ḥussein.

"I did not quite understand it all," said I humbly, feeling rather like Alice in Wonderland when Humpty Dumpty recited his verses to her. "Perhaps you will help me to write it down this evening."

So that night, with the assistance of Fawwâz, who had a bowing acquaintance with letters, we committed it to paper, and I now know how the masterpieces of the great singers were received at the fair of 'Ukâẓ in the Days of Ignorance. "The truth! it is the truth!" shouted the tribes between each couplet. "Eh by Al Lât and by Al 'Uzzah!"

Three hours from Abu Jîr we cantered down to the Wâdî Themail and saw some black tents pitched by a tell on the farther side. Flocks of goats were scattered over the plain; the shepherds, when they perceived our party, drew them together and began to drive them towards the tents. At this Muḥammad pulled up, rose in his stirrups, and waved a long white cotton sleeve over his head—a flag of truce.

"They take us for raiders," said he, laughing. "Wallah, in a moment we should have had their rifles upon us."

The mound of Themail is crowned by a fort built of mud and unshaped stones (Fig. 68). It has a single door and round bastions at the angles of the wall, like Khubbâz, but the figure described by the walls is far from regular, and there is no trace of construction within. The existing building looked to me like rough Bedouin work, though I suspect that it has taken the place of older defences (Fig. 69). A copious sulphur spring rises below it and flows into the cornfields of the Deleim. With a supply of water so plentiful Themail must always have been a place worth holding. We stayed for an hour to lunch, Muḥammad's kinsmen supplementing our fare with a bowl of sour curds. Fawwâz was all for spending the night here, for there would be no tents at

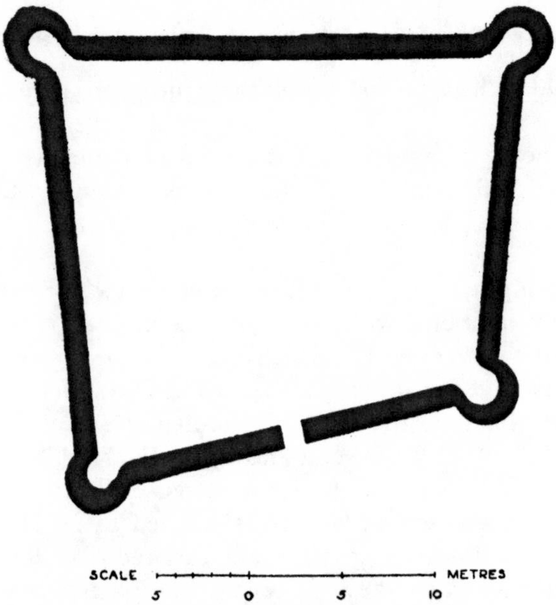

FIG. 69.—THEMAIL.

'Asîleh, where we meant to camp, and the noonday stillness was broken by a loud altercation between him and the indignant Fattûḥ. I paid no attention until the case was brought to me for decision—the final court of appeal should always be silent up to the moment when an opinion is requested—and then said that we should undoubtedly sleep at 'Asîleh.

"God guide us, God guard us, God protect us!" muttered Muḥammad as he settled himself into the saddle. He never took the road without this pious ejaculation.

Four hours of weary desert lie between Themail and 'Asîleh, but Muḥammad diversified the way by pointing out the places where he had attacked and slain his enemies. These historic sites were numerous. The Deleim have no friends except the great tribe of the 'Anazeh, represented in these regions by the Amarât under Ibn Hudhdhâl. To the 'Anazeh he always alluded as the Bedû, giving me their names for the different varieties of scanty desert scrub as well as the common titles. Even the place-names are not the same on the lips of the Bedû; for example El 'Asîleh is known to them as Er Radâf.

"Are not the Deleim also Bedû?" I asked.

"Eh wah," he assented. "The 'Anazeh intermarry with us. But we would not take a girl of the Afâḍleh; they are 'Agedât" (base born).

The friendship between the Amarât and the Deleim is intermittent at best, like all desert alliances. As we neared the Wâdî Burdân, Muḥammad called our attention to some tamarisk bushes where he and his raiding party had lain one night in ambush, and at dawn killed four men of the Amarât and taken their mares.

"Eh billah!" said he with a sigh of satisfaction.

The very rifle he carried had been taken in a raid from Ibn er Rashîd's people. He showed me with pride that the name of 'Abdu'l 'Azîz ibn er Rashîd, lately Lord of Nejd, was scratched upon it in large clear letters.

"I did not take it from them," he explained. "I found it in the hands of one of the Benî Ḥassan." I fell to wondering how many midnight attacks it had seen, and how many masters it had served since Ibn er Rashîd's agents brought it up from the Persian Gulf.

The Wâdî Burdân is one of three valleys that are reputed to stretch across the Syrian desert from the Jebel Ḥaurân to the Euphrates. The northernmost is the Wâdî Ḥaurân, which joins the river above Hît, and the southernmost the Wâdî Lebai'ah, on which stands Kheiḍir. When the snow melts in the Ḥaurân mountains water flows down all three, so I have heard, but later in the year there is no water in the

Wâdî Burdân, except at 'Asîleh, though Kiepert marks it "quellenreich." Muḥammad declared that there was no permanent water west of 'Asîleh save at Wîzeh, a spring which has often been described to me. It rises underground, and you approach it by a long passage through the rock, taking with you a lantern, my informants are careful to add. At the end of the passage you come to a shallow pool where the mud predominates, though it is always possible to quench your thirst at it. 'Asîleh is an autumn camping-ground of the 'Anazeh. The deep fine sand of the valley is bordered by a fringe of tamarisk bushes, covered, when we were there, with feathery white flower. Their roots strike down into the water, which rises into cup-shaped holes scooped out in the sand, and the deeper you dig the clearer and the colder it is. For four days we had found no water that was sweet, and the pools under the tamarisk bushes tasted like nectar. It was a delightful solitary camp. The setting sun threw a magic cloak of colour and soft shadows over the sandhills of the Wâdî Burdân, and under the starlight my companions lingered round the camp fire, smoking a narghileh and telling each other wondrous tales. When I joined them Fattûḥ was holding forth upon the evil eye, a favourite topic with him. I knew by heart the tragedy of his three horses who died in one day because an acquaintance had looked at them in their stable.

"And if your Excellency doubts," said Fattûḥ, "I can tell you that there is a man well known in Aleppo who has one good eye and one evil. And this he keeps bound under a kerchief. And one day when he was sitting in the house of friends they said to him, 'Why do you bind up the left eye?' He said, 'It is an evil eye.' Then they said, 'If you were to take off the kerchief and look at the lamp hanging from the roof, would it fall?' 'Without doubt,' said he; and with that he unbound the kerchief and looked, and the lamp fell to the ground."

"Allah!" said Fawwâz. "There is a man at Kebeisah who has never dared to look at his own son."

"At 'Ânah," observed Hussein, letting the narghileh

relapse into silence for a moment, "there is a sheikh who wears a charm against bullets."

But Muḥammad knew as much as most men about the ways of bullets, and he thought nothing of this expedient.

"Whether the bullet hits or misses," he remarked, "it is all from God." He poured me out a cup of coffee. "A double health, oh lady," said he.

The sun had not risen when we left 'Asîleh, but it fell upon us as we climbed the sandhills, and gave to every little thorny plant a long trail of shadow.

"God guide us, God guard us, God protect us!" murmured Muḥammad.

The desert was unbearably monotonous that morning. The ground rose gradually, level above level in an almost imperceptible slope which was just enough to prevent us from seeing more than a quarter of an hour ahead. A dozen times I marked a bush on the top of the rise and promised myself that when we reached it we should have a wider prospect; a dozen times the summit melted away into another slope as featureless as the last. We were journeying in a south-easterly direction, straight into the sun, and as I rode, with eyes downcast to avoid the glare, I noticed that the ground was strewn with yellow gourds larger than an orange.

"It is ḥanẓal," said Muḥammad. "It grows only where the plain is very dry, and best in rainless years. Wallah, so bitter is the fruit that, if you hold dates in your hand and crush the ḥanẓal with your foot, they say you cannot eat the dates for the flavour of the ḥanẓal. God knows."

His words set loose a host of memories, for though I had never before seen the bitter colocynth gourds, the great singers of the desert have drawn many an image from them, and I drifted back through their world of heroic loves and wars to where Imru'l Ḳais stood weeping, as though his eyelids were inflamed with the acrid juice.

Five hours from 'Asîleh we dipped into the Wâdî el 'Asibîyeh, where the marshy bottom still bore footprints of horses and camels that had come down to drink before the pools had vanished. A steep bank on the south side gave us a rim of shadow in which we stretched ourselves and lunched, and from the top of the bank we sighted the palm-trees of Raḥḥâlîyeh, an hour and a half to the south; we had seen them three hours earlier from the summit of a little mound and then lost them again. The oasis is surrounded by stagnant pools that lie rotting in the sun; at the end of the summer the evil vapours marry with the fresh dates, with which the inhabitants are surfeited, and breed a horrible fever that will kill a strong man in a few hours. The air was heavy with the rank smell of the marsh, and I warned my people to drink no water but that which we had brought with us from the clear pools of 'Asîleh. There are sixteen thousand palm-trees at Raḥḥâlîyeh and, buried in their midst, a village governed by a Mudîr, to whom I hastened to pay my respects. He gave me glasses of tea while my tent was being pitched—may God reward him! We camped that night in a palm garden, where we were entertained by a troop of musicians playing on drums and a double flute, to which music one of them danced between the sun and shade of the palm fronds. Their faces were those of negroes, though they had the clear yellow skin of the Arab, and I noticed that most of the population of Raḥḥâlîyeh was of this type. "They have always been here," said Ḥussein contemptuously, "they and the frogs." In spite of the flickering shade of the palm-trees it was stifling hot, and I looked with regret over the broken mud wall of our garden into the clean stretches of the open desert. But the splendours of the sunset glowed between the palm trunks; in matchless beauty a crescent moon hung among the dark fronds, and we lay down to sleep with the contentment of those who have come safely out of perilous ways.

The Mudîr had given me useful information concerning some ruins that lie between Raḥḥâlîyeh and Shetâteh. Next day I sent Fattûḥ and the camels direct to the second oasis, and, taking with me Ḥussein and Muḥammad, with a boy for guide, set out to explore the site of an ancient city. Fawwâz objected loudly to this arrangement, and on reflection I am inclined to think that we overrated the security

FIG. 70.—MUḤAMMAD EL 'ABDULLAH.

FIG. 71.—KHEIḌIR, MA'ASHÎ AND SHEIKH 'ALÎ.

FIG. 73.—BARDAWÎ FROM SOUTH-WEST.

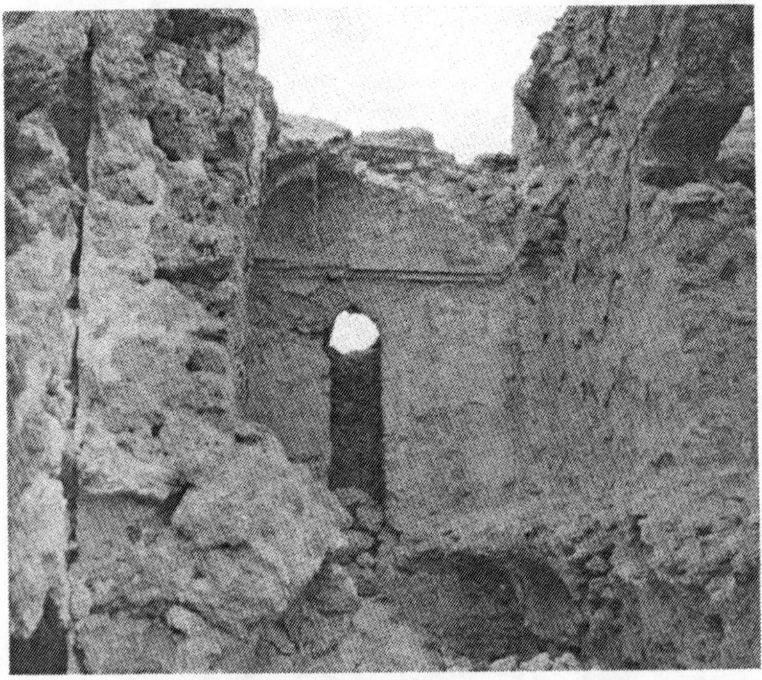

FIG. 74.—BARDAWÎ, EAST END OF VAULTED HALL.

of the road, though no harm came of it. About an hour to the south of Raḥḥâlîyeh, on the northern edge of low-lying marshy ground, rich in springs, stands the shrine of Sayyid Aḥmed ibn Hâshim, and near it to the north and west are vestiges of what must have been a large town. We followed for at least a quarter of a mile the foundations of a fine masonry wall 150 centimetres thick. Between this wall and the low ground the surface of the plain is broken by innumerable mounds and heaps of stone; here, said the boy, after rain, the women of the two oases find gold ornaments and pictured stones. I saw and bought some of the pictured stones at Shetâteh; they are Assyrian cylindrical seals; but without knowing in what quantities and with what other objects they appear, it would be rash to decide that the site is as old. There was undoubtedly a mediæval Arab city there; all the ground was strewn with fragments of Arab coloured pottery, and at the western limit of the ruin field there are remains of the usual four-square fort; Murrât is its present name.[1] It is built of uncut stone and unburnt brick; the doorway in the north wall is covered with a flattened pointed arch that suggests the thirteenth century or thereabouts.[2] My own belief is that the town to which this castle belonged stood on the site of an older city, and I place here 'Ain et Tamr, an oasis that was famous in the days of the Persian kings. Yâḳût describes it as having lain near Shetâteh, and observes that Khâlid ibn u'l Walîd took and sacked it in the year 12 A.H., but he says nothing about a later town on the same spot, to which the evidence of the ruins points. Perhaps it was absorbed in Shetâteh.

The interest of these speculations had caused me to forget that we were still in the desert. Our guide caught us up at Murrât, whither we had galloped recklessly, and explained that he had had some difficulty in allaying the suspicions of a small encampment of the Amarât half-hidden in the valley. The men, seeing us hurrying past, had taken us for robbers

[1] The whole area of ruins is known as Kherâb = ruin.

[2] It is not necessarily so late, for the Baghdâd Gate at Raḳḳah has the same arch, and it is certainly earlier.

and were preparing to shoot at us. At a soberer pace we turned back along the valley. It was marshy in places, intersected by little streams from the springs, and covered with a white crust of salts—sabkhah, the Arabs call such regions—on which nothing grew but a malignant-looking thorny shrub, thelleth, useless to man and beast. The water of the springs was "heavy," Muḥammad told me, like the water of Raḥḥâlîyeh. Half-an-hour's ride down the valley we crossed the Raḥḥâlîyeh-Shetâteh road at a point where there were traces of good masonry. Another half-hour ahead stood the mound of Bardawî, our objective. Being in good spirits we devoted the interval to song. Muḥammad gave us his ode to the motor, and I obliged with "God save the King," translated into indifferent Arabic for the benefit of the audience.

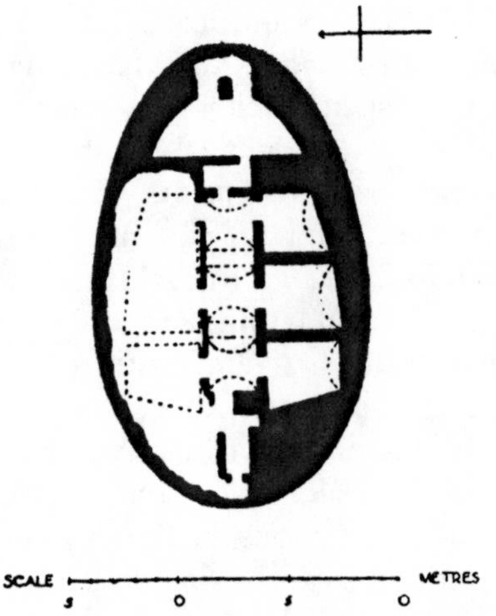

FIG. 72.—BARDAWÎ.

"The words are good," said Muḥammad politely, "but I do not care about the air."

So we came to Bardawî, a striking tell with an oval fortress standing upon it (Fig. 72). There had been at least three storeys of vaulted rooms lifting the strange tower-like structure high above the level of the desert (Fig. 73). It suggests a watch-tower guarding the eastern approaches to the city, but I am not prepared to affirm that the present edifice is earlier than the Mohammadan period. A substructure and the remains of an upper floor are standing, the ground plan of both being the same. A small vaulted hall, with three vaulted chambers on either side, occupied the centre of the building; the door, with traces of a porch or ante-room, lay to the west; while to the east there were two much-ruined chambers, which communicated with the hall by means of a narrow door. The masonry is of undressed stones laid in mortar. The vaults of the side chambers seem to have been built over a rude centering; they are much flattened and so irregularly constructed as to approach in form to a gable roof. These rooms were lighted by a small round hole in the outer wall, under the apex of the vault. The vault of the hall springs with a double outset from the wall and terminates at the eastern end (the west end is ruined) in a semi-dome which was adjusted to the rectangular corners by means of squinch arches (Fig. 74). The partition walls are carried up above the level of the upper vaults, apparently for another storey. The lower part of a strong facing of masonry is still in existence on the south side, and I conjecture that it was continued originally to the top of the tower. Having photographed and planned this singular building, we dismissed our guide, whose services we no longer needed, and set out over broken sabkhah in the direction of Shetâteh. We were jogging along between hummocks of thorn and scrub, Muḥammad as usual singing, when suddenly he broke off at the end of a couplet and said:

"I see a horseman riding in haste."

I looked up and saw a man galloping towards us along the top of a ridge; he was followed closely by another and yet another, and all three disappeared as they dipped down from the high ground. In the desert every newcomer is an enemy till you know him to be a friend. Muḥammad slipped a cartridge into his rifle, Ḥussein extracted his riding-stick from the barrel, where it commonly travelled, and I took a revolver out of my holster. This done, Muḥammad galloped forward to the top of a mound; I followed, and we watched together the advance of the three who were rapidly diminishing the space that lay between us. Muḥammad jumped to the ground and threw me his bridle.

"Dismount," said he, "and hold my mare."

I took the two mares in one hand and the revolver in the other. Ḥussein had lined up beside me, and we two stood perfectly still while Muhammad advanced, rifle in hand, his body bent forward in an attitude of strained watchfulness. He walked slowly, alert and cautious, like a prowling animal. The three were armed and our thoughts ran out to a possible encounter with the Benî Hassan, who were the blood enemies of our companion. If, when they reached the top of the ridge in front of us, they lifted their rifles, Ḥussein and I would have time to shoot first while they steadied their mares. The three riders topped the ridge, and as soon as we could see their faces Muḥammad gave the salaam; they returned it, and with one accord we all stood at ease. For if men give and take the salaam when they are near enough to see each other's faces, there cannot, according to the custom of the desert, be any danger of attack. The authors of this picturesque episode turned out to be three men from Raḥ-ḥâlîyeh. One of them had lent a rifle to the boy who had guided us and, repenting of his confidence, had come after him to make sure that he did not make off with it. We pointed out the direction in which he had gone and turned our horses' heads once more in the direction of Shetâteh.

"Lady," said Muḥammad reflectively, "in the day of raids I do not trust my mare to the son of my uncle and not to my own brother, lest they should see the foe and fear, and ride away. But to you I gave her because I know that the heart of the English is strong. They do not flee."

"God forbid!" said I, but my spirit leapt at the compliment paid to my race, however lightly it had been evoked.

The incident led to some curious talk concerning the rules that govern desert wars. You do not invariably raid to kill; on the contrary, you desire, as far as possible, to avoid bloodshed, with all its tiresome and dangerous consequences of feud.

"Many a day," explained Muḥammad, "we are out only to rob. Then if we meet a few horsemen who try to escape from us, we pursue, crying, 'Your mount, lad!' And if they surrender and deliver to us their mares, their lives are safe, even if they should prove to be blood enemies."

It is usual to hold in small esteem the courage called forth by Arab warfare, and I do not think that the mortality is,

FIG. 75.—SHETÂTEH, SULPHUR SPRING.

FIG. 76.—ḲAṢR SHAM'ÛN, OUTER WALL.

FIG. 77.—UKHEIḌIR FROM NORTH-WEST.

FIG. 78.—UKHEIḌIR, INTERIOR FROM SOUTH-EAST.

as a rule, high; but I have on one or two occasions found myself with an Arab guide under conditions that might have proved awkward, and I have never yet seen him give signs of fear. It is only to town-dwellers like Fawwâz that the wilderness is beset with terrors.

Shetâteh is an oasis of 160,000 palms. The number is rapidly diminishing, and on every side there are groups of headless trunks from which the water has been turned off. This is owing to the iniquitous exactions of the tax-gatherers, who levy three and four times in the year the moneys due from each tree, so that the profits on the fruit vanish and even turn to loss. The springs are sulphurous, but very abundant. The palm-trees rise from a bed of corn and clover; willows and pomegranates edge the irrigation streams, and birds nest and sing in the thickets. To us, who had dropped out of the deserts of the Euphrates, it seemed a paradise. The glimmering weirs, the sheen of up-turned willow leaves, the crinkled beauty of opening pomegranate buds were so many marvels, embraced in the recurring miracle of spring, that grows in wonder year by year.

Through these enchanted groves we rode from our camp to the castle of Sham'ûn, the citadel of the oasis. Its great walls, battered and very ancient, tower above the palm-trees, and within their circuit nestles a whole village of mud-built houses (Fig. 76). There is an arched gateway to the north, but the largest fragment of masonry lies to the east, a massive, shapeless wall of stone and unburnt bricks, seamed from top to bottom by a deep fissure, which the khalif, 'Alî ibn Abi Tâlib, said my guide, made with a single sword cut. Among the houses there are many vestiges of old foundations, and a few vaulted chambers, now considerably below the level of the soil. It was impossible to plan the place in its present state; I can only be sure that it was square with bastioned corners. My impression is that it is pre-Mohammadan, repaired by the conquerors, and local tradition, to which, however, it would be unwise to attach much value, bears out this view. Possibly Sham'ûn was the main fortress of 'Ain et Tamr before the Mohammadan invasion.

At Shetâteh I parted from Ḥussein, Muḥammad, and the camel riders. Kheiḍir was reported to be four hours away, a little to the south of the Kerbelâ road. The Ḳâimmaḳâm could supply me with two zaptiehs, and Fattûḥ had hired a couple of mules to carry our diminished packs. The four men intended to travel back together, making a long day from Raḥḥâlîyeh to Themail so as to avoid a night in the open desert. They started next morning in good heart, fortified by presents of quinine, a much-prized gift, and other more substantial rewards. Muḥammad would gladly have come with us to Kerbelâ, but we remembered the Benî Ḥassan and decided that it would be wiser for him to turn back, though before he left we had laid plans for a longer and a more adventurous journey to be undertaken another year, please God! We had not gone more than an hour from Shetâteh before we met a company of the Benî Ḥassan coming in to the oasis for dates, a troop of lean and ragged men driving donkeys. They asked us anxiously whether we had seen any of the Deleim at Shetâteh.

"No, wallah!" said Fattûḥ with perfect assurance, and I laughed, knowing that Muḥammad was well on his way to Raḥḥâlîyeh.

We had ridden to the south-east for about three hours, through a most uncompromising wilderness, when, in the glare ahead, we caught sight of a great mass which I took for a natural feature in the landscape. But as we approached, its shape became more and more definite, and I asked one of the zaptiehs what it was.

"It is Kheiḍir," said he.

"Yallah, Fattûḥ, bring on the mules," I shouted, and galloped forward.

Of all the wonderful experiences that have fallen my way, the first sight of Kheiḍir is the most memorable. It reared its mighty walls out of the sand, almost untouched by time, breaking the long lines of the waste with its huge towers, steadfast and massive, as though it were, as I had at first thought it, the work of nature, not of man. We approached it from the north, on which side a long low building runs out towards the sandy depression of the Wâdî Lebai'ah (Fig. 77). A zaptieth caught me up as I reached the first of the vaulted rooms, and out of the northern gateway a man in long robes of white and black came trailing down towards us through the hot silence.

"Peace be upon you," said he.

"And upon you peace, Sheikh 'Alî," returned the zaptieh. "This lady is of the English."

"Welcome, my lady Khân," said the sheikh; "be pleased to enter and to rest."

He led me through a short passage and under a tiny dome. I was aware of immense corridors opening on either hand, but we passed on into a great vaulted hall where the Arabs sat round the ashes of a fire.

"My lady Khân," said Sheikh 'Alî, "this is the castle of Nu'mân ibn Mundhir."

Whether it were a Lakhmid palace or no, it was the palace which I had set forth to seek. It belongs architecturally to the group of Sassanian buildings which are already known to us, and historically it is related to the palaces, famous in pre-Mohammadan tradition, whose splendours had filled with amazement the invading hordes of the Bedouin, and still shine with a legendary magnificence, from the pages of the chroniclers of the conquest. Even for the Mohammadan writers they had become nothing but a name. Khawarnaḳ, Sadîr, and the rest, fell into ruin with Ḥîrah, the capital of the small Arab principality that occupied the frontiers of the desert, and their site was a matter of hearsay or conjecture. "Think on the lord of Khawarnaḳ," sang 'Adî ibn Zaid prophetically—

"—— eyes guided of God see clear—
He rejoiced in his might and the strength of his hands, the encompassing wave and Sadîr;
And his heart stood still and he spake: 'What joy have the living to death addressed?
For the open cleft of the grave lies close upon pleasure and power and rest.
Like a withered leaf they fall, and the wind shall scatter them east and west.'"

But for all its total disappearance under the wave of Islâm, the Lakhmid state had played a notable part in the development of Arab culture. It was at Ḥirah that the desert came into contact with the highly organized civilization of the Persians, with the wealth of cultivated lands and the long-established order of a settled population; there, too, as among the Ghassânids on the Syrian side of the wilderness, they made acquaintance with the precepts of Christianity which exercised so marked an influence on the latest poets of the Age of Ignorance, some of whom, like 'Adî ibn Zaid himself, are known to have been Christians, and prepared the way for the Prophet's teaching.[1] So little have the eastern borders of the Syrian desert been explored that except for the ruin field of Ḥîrah, a town which was destroyed in order to furnish building materials for the Moslem city of Kûfah, and a cluster of mouldering vaults, said to represent the castle of Khawarnaḳ,[2] not one of the famous pre-Mohammadan sites has been identified, and it is possible that important vestiges of the Lakhmid age may lie unsuspected within a few days' journey from regions familiar to travellers and even to tourists. Meanwhile Kheiḍir (the name is the colloquial abbreviation of Ukheiḍir = a small green place) is the finest example of Sassanian architecture which has yet been discovered. Its wonderful state of preservation is probably due to the fact that it was some distance removed from the nearest inhabited spot. Shetâteh is separated from it by three hours of naked desert; the canals that feed Kerbelâ are yet further away, and the water supply of Ukheidir, derived from wells in the Wâdî Lebai'ah, is too small to have tempted the fellaḥîn to establish themselves there. Nowhere in the vicinity, so far as I could learn, are

[1] See Rothstein: *Die Dynastie der Lakhmiden in al Ḥîra*, p. 25. He gives reasons for believing that the art of writing Arabic was first practised at Ḥîrah. The population was largely Christian (the 'Ibad of the Arab historians); Ḥîrah was the seat of a bishopric, and frequent allusion is made to churches and monasteries in and near the town.

[2] Meissner: "Ḥîra und Khawarnaḳ" *Sendschriften der D. Orient Gesell.*, No. 2.

FIG. 86.—UKHEIḌIR, CHEMIN DE RONDE OF EAST WALL.

FIG. 87.—UKHEIḌIR, NORTH GATE, FROM OUTSIDE.

FIG. 83.—UKHEIḌIR, NORTH-EAST ANGLE TOWER.

FIG. 84.—UKHEIḌIR, STAIR AT SOUTH-EAST ANGLE.

FIG. 85.—UKHEIḌIR, INTERIOR OF SOUTH GATE.

there more abundant springs, and the palace has therefore been allowed to drop into a slow decay, forgotten in the midst of its wildernesses, save when a raiding expedition brings the Bedouin into the neighbourhood of Shetâteh.

Most of us who have had opportunity to become familiar with some site that has once been the theatre of a vanished civilization have passed through hours of vain imaginings during which the thoughts labour to recapture the aspect of street and market, church or temple enclosure, of which the evidences lie strewn over the surface of the earth. And ever, as a thousand unanswerable problems surge up against the realization of that empty hope, I have found myself longing for an hour out of a remote century, wherein I might look my fill upon the walls that have fallen and stamp the image of a dead world indelibly upon my mind. The dream seemed to have reached fulfilment at Ukheidir. There the architecture of a by-gone age presented itself in unexampled perfection to the eye. It was not necessary to guess at the structure of vaults or the decorative scheme of niched façades —the camera and the measuring-tape could register the methods of the builder and the results which he had achieved. But it was evident that no satisfactory record of Ukheidir could be made within the limits of the day which I had allowed myself for the expedition. We had exhausted our small stock of provisions, and the materials necessary for carrying out so large a piece of work as the planning of the palace were at Kerbelâ with the caravan. Fattûḥ disposed of these difficulties at once by declaring that he intended to ride into Kerbelâ that night and bring out the caravan next day. The truth was that he yearned for the sight of the baggage horses, and for my part I longed for a bed and for a table more than I could have thought it possible. I was weary of sleeping on the stony face of the desert, of sitting in the dust and eating my meals with a seasoning of sand—so infirm is feminine endurance. An Arab called Ghânim, clean-limbed and spare, like all his half-fed tribe, offered himself as guide, and 'Alî assured us that he knew every inch of the way. But when the zaptiehs heard that one of them was to accompany the expedition they turned white with fear. To ride through the desert at night, they declared, was a venture from which no man was likely to come out alive. I hesitated—it requires much courage to face risks for others—but Fattûḥ stood firm, 'Alî laughed, and the thought of the bed carried the day. They started at eight in the evening, and I watched them disappear across the sands with some sinking of heart. All next day I was too well occupied to give them much thought, but when six o'clock came and 'Alî set watchers upon the castle walls, I began to feel anxious. Half-an-hour later Ma'ashî, the sheikh's brother and my particular friend, came running down to my tent.

"Praise God! my lady Khân, they are here."

The Arabs gathered round to offer their congratulations, and Fattûḥ rode in, grey with fatigue and dust, with the caravan at his heels. He had reached Kerbelâ at five in the morning, found the muleteers, bought provisions, loaded the animals, and set off again about ten.

"And the oranges are good in Kerbelâ," he ended triumphantly. "I have brought your Excellency a whole bag of them."

It was a fine performance.

The Arabs who inhabited Kheiḍir had come there two years before from Jôf in Nejd: "Because we were vexed with the government of Ibn er Rashîd," explained 'Alî, and I readily understood that his could not be a soothing rule. The wooden howdahs in which the women had travelled blocked one of the long corridors, and some twenty families lodged upon the ground in the vaulted chambers of princes. They lived and starved and died in this most splendid memorial of their own civilization, and even in decay Kheiḍir offered a shelter more than sufficient for their needs to the race at whose command it had been reared. Their presence was an essential part of its proud decline. The sheikh and his brothers passed like ghosts along the passages, they trailed their white robes down the stairways that led to the high chambers where they lived with their women, and at night they gathered round the hearth in the great hall where their forefathers had beguiled the hours with tale and song in the same rolling tongue of Nejd. Then they would pile up the desert scrub till the embers glowed under the coffee-pots, while Ma'ashî handed round the delicious bitter draught which was the one luxury left to them. The thorns crackled, a couple of oil wicks placed in holes above the columns, which had been contrived for them by the men-at-arms of old, sent a feeble ray into the darkness, and Ghânim took the rebâbah and drew from its single string a wailing melody to which he chanted the stories of his race.

"My lady Khân, this is the song of 'Abdu'l 'Azîz ibn er Rashîd."

He sang of a prince great and powerful, patron of poets, leader of raids, and recently overwhelmed and slain in battle; but old or new, the songs were all pages out of the same chronicle, the undated chronicle of the nomad. The thin melancholy music rose up into the blackness of the vault; across the opening at the end of the hall, where the wall had fallen in part away, was spread the deep still night and the unchanging beauty of the stars.

"My lady Khân," said Ghânim, "I will sing you the song of Ukheiḍir."

But I said, "Listen to the verse of Ukheiḍir"—

> "We wither away but they wane not, the stars that above us rise;
> The mountains remain after us, and the strong towers when we are gone."

"Allah!" murmured Ma'ashî, as he swept noiselessly round the circle with the coffee cups, and once again Labîd's noble couplet held the company, as it had held those who sat in the banqueting-hall of the khalif.

One night I was provided with a different entertainment. I had worked from sunrise till dark and was too tired to sleep. The desert was as still as death; infinitely mysterious, it stretched away from my camp and I lay watching the empty sands as one who watches for a pageant. Suddenly a bullet whizzed over the tent and the crack of a rifle broke the silence. All my men jumped up; a couple more shots rang out, and Fattûḥ hastily disposed the muleteers round the tents and hurried off to join a band of Arabs who had streamed from the castle gate. I picked up a revolver and went out to see them go. In a minute or two they had vanished under the uncertain light of the moon, which seems so clear and yet discloses so little. A zaptieh joined me and we stood still listening. Far out in the desert the red flash of rifles cut through the white moonlight; again the quick flare and then again silence. At last through the night drifted the sound of a wild song, faint and far away, rhythmic, elemental as the night and the desert. I waited in complete uncertainty as to what was approaching, and it was not until they were close upon us that we recognized our own Arabs and Fattûḥ in their midst. They came on, still singing, with their rifles over their shoulders; their white garments gleamed under the moon; they wore no kerchiefs upon their heads, and their black hair fell in curls about their faces.

"Ma'ashî," I cried, "what happened?"

Ma'ashî shook his hair out of his eyes.

"There is nothing, my lady Khân. 'Alî saw some men lurking in the desert at the 'aṣr" (the hour of afternoon prayer), "and we watched after dark from the walls."

"They were raiders of the Benî Ḍafî'ah," said Ghânim, mentioning a particular lawless tribe.

"Fattûḥ," said I, "did you shoot?"

"We shot," replied Fattûḥ; "did not your Excellency hear?—and one man is wounded."

A wild-looking boy held out his hand, on which I detected a tiny scratch.

"There is no harm," said I. "Praise God!"

"Praise God!" they repeated, and I left them laughing and talking eagerly, and went to bed and to sleep.

Next morning I questioned Fattûḥ as to the events of the night, but he was exceptionally non-committal.

"My lady," said he, "God knows. 'Alî says that they

FIG. 88.—UKHEIḌIR, FLUTED DOME AT A.

FIG. 89.—UKHEIḌIR, FLUTED NICHE, SOUTH-EAST CORNER OF COURT D.

FIG. 90.—UKHEIḌIR, GREAT HALL.

were men of the Benî Ḍafî'ah." Then with a burst of confidence he added, "But I saw no one."

"At whom did you shoot?" said I in bewilderment.

"At the Benî Ḍafî'ah," answered Fattûḥ, surprised at the stupidity of the question.

I gave it up, neither do I know to this hour whether we were or were not raided in the night.

Two days later my plan was finished. I had turned one of the vaulted rooms of the stable into a workshop, and spreading a couple of waterproof sheets on the sand for table, had drawn it out to scale lying on the ground. Sometimes an Arab came in silently and stood watching my pencil, until the superior attractions of the next chamber, in which sat the muleteers and the zaptiehs, drew him away. As I added up metres and centimetres I could hear them spinning long yarns of city and desert. Occasionally Ma'ashî brought me coffee.

"God give you the reward," said I.

"And your reward," he answered gravely.

The day we left Kheiḍir, the desert was wrapped in the stifling dust of a west wind. I have no notion what the country is like through which we rode for seven hours to Kerbelâ, and no memory, save that of the castle walls fading like a dream into the haze, of a bare ridge of hill to our right hand and the bitter waves of a salt lake to our left, and of deep sand through which we were driven by a wind that was the very breath of the Pit. Then out of the mist loomed the golden dome of the shrine of Ḥussein, upon whom be peace, and few pious pilgrims were gladder than I when we stopped to drink a glass of tea at the first Persian tea-shop of the holy city.

THE PALACE OF UKHEIḌIR

I do not propose to enter here into a detailed account of the palace of Ukheiḍir, which must be reserved for a subsequent publication, but it is well to give a short elucidation of the plan, and to consider briefly the theories which have been formed with regard to the origin of the building.[1]

The palace consists of a rectangular fortification wall set with round bastions, with larger round bastions at the angles, and of an oblong building surrounded on three sides by a court, together with a small annex in the eastern part of the court (Fig. 79). That part of the oblong building which adjoins the northern fortification wall is three storeys high; the remainder of the palace is one storey high. Outside the enclosing fortification wall there is a structure composed of fourteen vaulted parallel chambers, with a small open court at the southern end. To the west of the small court and of the first five chambers lies a larger court with round bastions on its western side. Between each of these bastions there is a door and either one or two groups of windows, each group consisting of three narrow lights. I noticed foundations of masonry which ran down from near the northern end of this

[1] I have already published the plan in the *Hellenic Journal* for 1910, Part I., p. 69, in an article on the vaulting system of the palace. Ukheiḍir was visited in the year 1907 by M. Massignon, though this fact was unknown to me until I returned to England in July 1909. He has published an account of it, together with a sketch plan made under circumstances of great difficulty, in the *Bulletin de l'Acad. des Inscr. et Belles-Lettres* of March 1909, in the *Gazette des Beaux Arts* of April 1909, and in the *Mémoires de l'Institut français du Caire*, vol. xxviii. (The last named has not yet appeared, but he has been so kind as to let me see an advance copy.) Neither to M. Massignon nor to me belongs the honour of discovery; an unknown Englishman had visited the palace in the eighteenth century, and his brief report is given by Niebuhr (*Reisebeschreibung*, vol. ii., p. 225, note): "Ich habe in dem Tagebuch eines Engländers, der von Haleb nach Basra gereist war, gefunden, dass er 44 Stunden Südfost nach Osten von Hit, eine ganz verlassene Stadt in der Wüste angetroffen habe, wovon die Mauer 50 Fuss hoch und 40 Fuss dick war. Jede der vier Seiten hatte 700 Fuss, und in der Mauer waren Thürme. In dieser Stadt oder grossem Castell, findet man noch ein kleines Castell. Von eben dieser verlassenen Stadt hörte ich nachher, dass sie von den Arabern El Khader genannt werde, und nur 10 bis 12 Stunden von Meshed Ali entfernt sei." I cannot feel any doubt that the "forsaken town" referred to in the diary, the existence of which was confirmed by the Arabs, who spoke of it to Niebuhr under the name of Khader, is our Ukheiḍir. So far as I have been able to discover, the nameless Englishman was the first modern traveller to visit the site.

FIG. 91.—UKHEIḌIR, COURT D AND NICHED FAÇADE OF THREE-STOREYED BLOCK.

FIG. 92.—UKHEIḌIR, VAULT OF ROOM I.

FIG. 93.—UKHEIḌIR, ROOM I.

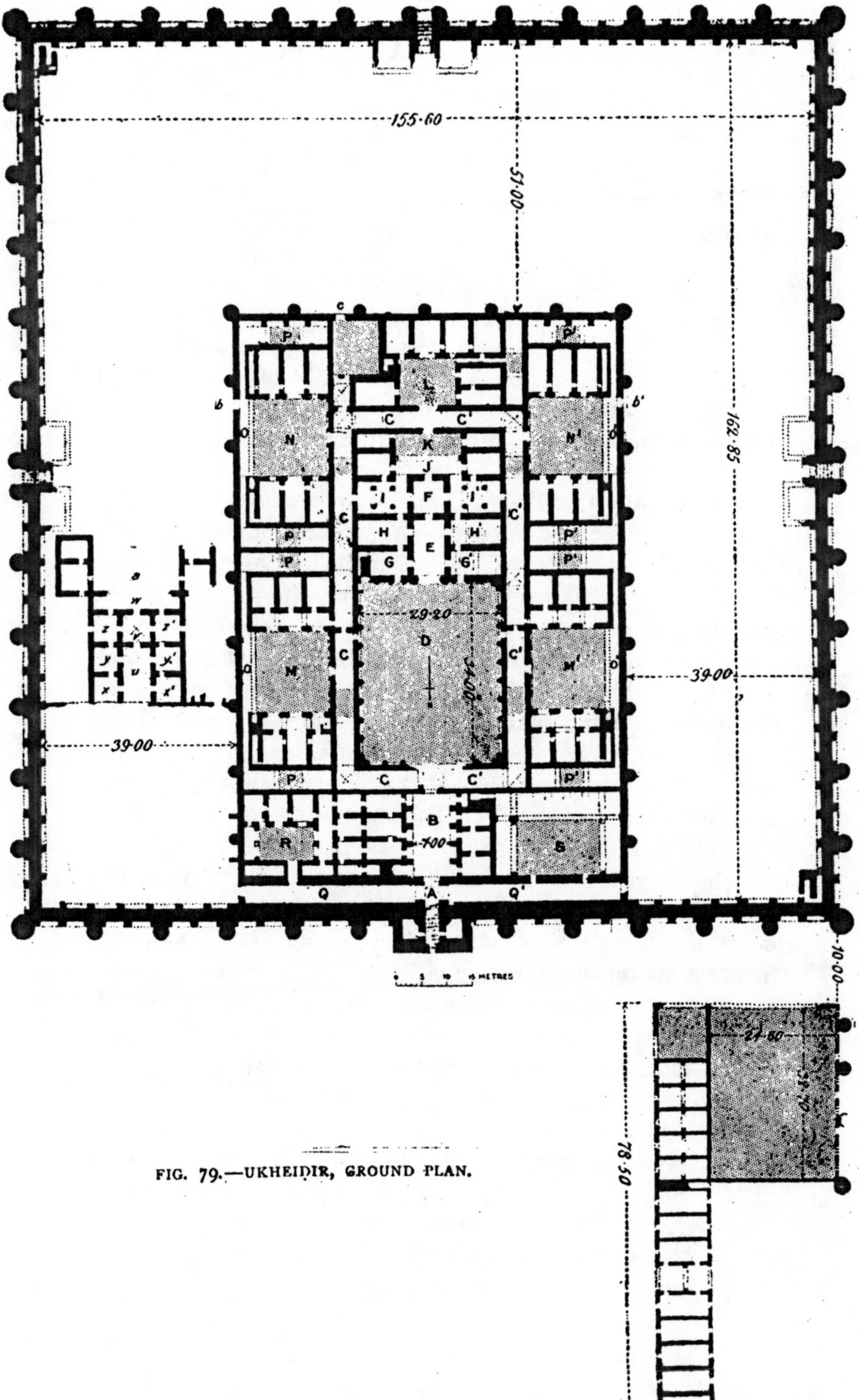

FIG. 79.—UKHEIDIR, GROUND PLAN.

out-building towards the valley. To the N.W. of the palace there is another small detached building called by the Arabs the Bath (Fig. 80). Near it the surface of the ground is broken by low mounds which may indicate the presence of ruins. The Arabs assured me that by digging here brackish water could be obtained; there is also a well of brackish water in the western part of the palace court, but it is not used for drinking purposes. The water supply of Ukheiḍir is derived from the Wâdî Lebai'ah. It is obtained by digging holes in the sandy bed of the valley.

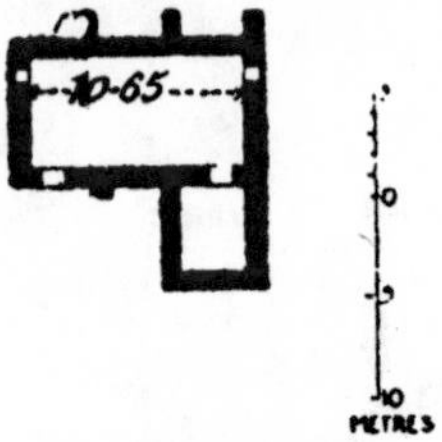

FIG. 80.—UKHEIḌIR, THE BATH.

The fortification wall is arcaded without and within up to two thirds of its height. These blind arcades support the walls of the *chemin de ronde*. The outer arcade serves the purpose of a machicoulis, a narrow space between its arches and the outer face of the main wall enabling the defenders in the *chemin de ronde* to protect with missiles the foot of the wall below them (Fig. 83). The *chemin de ronde* could be reached from the uppermost floor of the three-storeyed block of the palace, as well as by means of four staircases, one in each of the angles of the court (Fig. 84). Two of these staircases have now fallen completely. The *chemin de ronde* had been covered by a vault (Fig. 86). Arched doorways led into out-look chambers hollowed in the thickness of the bastions. Arched windows open on to the court. In the centre of each side of the fortification wall there is a gate (Fig. 85), that which stands on the northern side being the most important, since it communicates directly with the palace (Fig. 87). It opens into a passage with a guard-room on either side. The passage leads into a small rectangular chamber, A in the plan, covered with a fluted dome (Fig. 88). From this chamber an arched doorway communicates with a vaulted hall, B, which runs up to a height of two storeys and is the largest room in the palace (Fig. 90). The vault, borne on projecting engaged piers, spans seven metres. Beyond the hall vaulted corridors, C C C C, C′ C′ C′ C′, surround an open

FIG. 94.—UKHEIḌIR, CUSPED DOOR OF COURT S.

FIG. 95.—UKHEIḌIR, VAULTED END OF P, SHOWING TUBE.

FIG. 96.—UKHEIḌIR, CORRIDOR Q.

FIG. 97.—UKHEIḌIR, VAULTED CLOISTER O′.

FIG. 98.—UKHEIḌIR, GROIN IN CORRIDOR C.

FIG 99.—UKHEIḌIR, SQUINCH ARCH ON SECOND STOREY.

court, D, as well as a block of rooms lying to the south of the court. The court D is set round with engaged columns forming vaulted niches (Fig. 91). At the S.E. corner the vault of one of these niches is fluted (Fig. 89). The bracketed setting of these small semi-domes over the angles is to be noted. The block of chambers south of court D is more carefully built than any other part of the palace. It consists of an oblong antechamber, E, leading into a square room, F. On either side of the antechamber there are a pair of rooms, the walls and vaults of those lying to the west, G′ and H′, being finished with stucco decorations and small columned niches. On either side of the square chamber, F, is a room containing four masonry columns which support three parallel barrel vaults (Figs. 92 and 93). South of room F stretches a cloister, J, which was covered with a barrel vault, now fallen. It opens into an unroofed court, K. The corridor C C′ runs to the south of court K, and still further to the south is another open court, L, with vaulted rooms round it.

To east and west of the corridor C C, C′ C′, lie four courts, M M′ and N N′. To north and south of each of these courts there are three vaulted rooms, but in M and M′ small antechambers in the shape of a narthex separate the rooms from the court, whereas in N and N′ the rooms open directly on to the court. In every case there are traces of a vaulted cloister, O O and O′ O′, between the court and the outer wall (Fig. 97). Behind each block of rooms there is a rectangular space, P P P P and P′ P′ P′ P′, two-thirds of which are vaulted, while the central part is left open (Fig. 95). Similar open spaces are left in the corridor C C, C′ C′, which would otherwise be exceedingly dark.

To return to the north gate. On either side of the small domed chamber, A, long vaulted corridors, Q Q′, lead to the outer court (Fig. 96). A door on the south side of corridor Q communicates with a small court, R, with chambers to north and south of it and vaulted cloisters to east and west. A group of vaulted chambers is placed between court R and the great hall B. West of hall B there is a smaller group of vaulted chambers. In the south wall of corridor Q′, two doors lead into an open court surrounded on three sides by a vaulted cloister, the vault of which has now fallen except for fragments in the south-east and south-west corners. These fragments are adorned with stucco decorations. I have suggested (in the *Hellenic Journal*, loc. cit.) that this court may be a mosque of a primitive type. (See, too, *Der Islâm*,

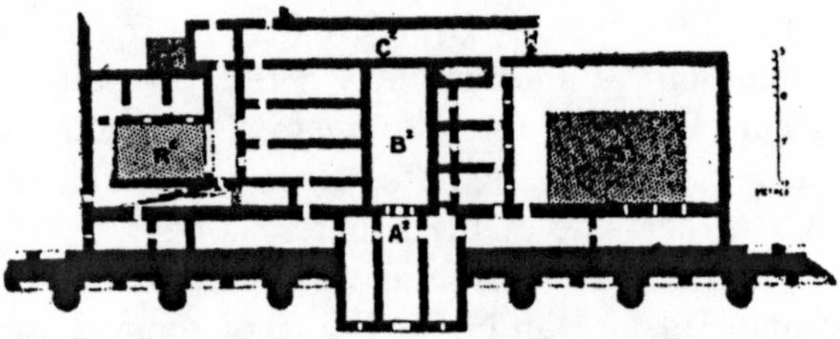

FIG. 81.—UKHEIḌIR, SECOND STOREY.

vol. i. part ii. p. 126, where Dr. Herzfeld points out that a chamber somewhat similarly placed in the palace of Mshatta may also be a mosque.)

No difficulty will be found in following on the plan the arrangement of the upper floors in the northern part of the palace. In the second storey, the space marked B^2 is occupied by the vault of the great hall B (Fig. 81). At A^2

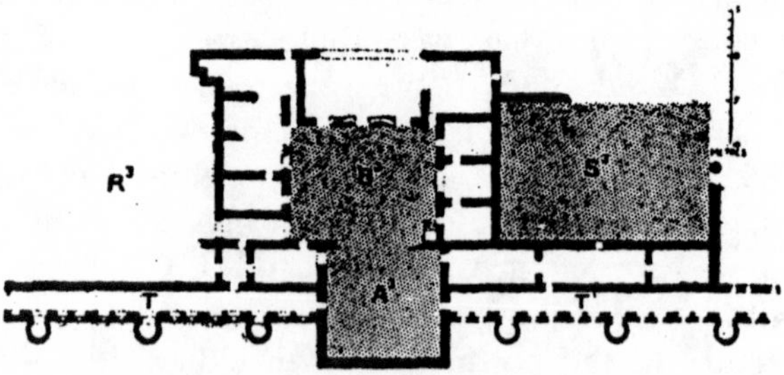

FIG. 82.—UKHEIḌIR, THIRD STOREY.

three windows open into the hall from the room in the second storey. R^2 and S^2 correspond with the two courts R and S. In the third storey the rectangular space A^3 is unroofed, and the space B^3, below which lies the vault of the great hall, is also unroofed (Fig. 82). The eastern part of this storey is completely ruined, but there would appear to have been rooms

FIG. 100.—UKHEIḌIR, NORTH SIDE OF COURT M.

FIG. 101.—UKHEIḌIR, SOUTH-EAST ANGLE OF COURT S.

FIG. 102.—UKHEIḌIR, WEST SIDE OF B^3.

FIG. 103.—UKHEIḌIR, DOOR LEADING FROM V TO W, SEEN FROM SOUTH.

round R^3 similar to the rooms round R^2. The *chemin de ronde*, T T′, is on a level with this storey.

Between the main palace block and the eastern fortification wall there lies a group of rooms which is clearly an addition to the original scheme. It is interesting to observe that these rooms are in all essentials of their plan a repetition of the group of rooms to the south of court D. Room U corresponds with the antechamber E; room V with the square room F; W with the cloister J; X, Y, and Z to G, H, and T. But the columns in I I′ are not repeated in the small rooms, Z Z′; room V is covered with a groined vault instead of the barrel vault of F, and the court A is not closed with a wall like the court K. I make no doubt that both these groups of rooms, which are so strikingly similar in arrangement, were intended for the same purposes, and I conjecture that they were ceremonial reception rooms. Herzfeld has compared E and F with the throne room of Mshatta (*Der Islâm*, loc. cit.).

All the rooms and corridors of the palace are vaulted. Some of the finer vaults are built of brick tiles (for example, over the great hall B and over rooms E, F, I, and I′), but as a rule the vaults are constructed with stones set in mortar, the stones being cut into thin slabs so as to resemble bricks as closely as possible. (*Cf.* the Sassanian palace of Firûzâbâd, Dieulafoy, *L'Art Ancien de la Perse*, vol. iv.) All the vaults, whether of brick or stone, are built without centering, and all are set forward slightly from the face of the wall. (The same construction is found at Ctesiphon, see below, Fig. 109.)[1] The groined vault occurs seven times in the corridor C C′ (Fig. 98), and it is also found in room V. (See my article in the *Hellenic Journal* above cited.) The fluted dome over room A is bracketed across the corners of the rectangular substructure (Fig. 88). In several cases where a barrel vault terminates not against a head wall but against another section of barrel vault, it is adjusted to the angles of the substructure

[1] I wish to call special attention to the presence of this construction at Ctesiphon because Dr. Herzfeld has stated erroneously that it does not exist in Sassanian buildings. (*Der Islâm*, vol. i. part ii. p. 111.)

by means of squinch arches (Fig. 99). A noticeable feature of the vault construction of Ukheiḍir is the presence of masonry tubes running between the parallel barrel vaults (Fig. 100). The structural purpose of these tubes is to diminish the mass of masonry between the barrel vaults. Whenever two barrel vaults lie parallel to one another, a tube will be found between them, and similar tubes exist between the vault of the cloister O O and O′ O′ and the outer wall. (See too Fig. 95, which shows a tube between a barrel vault and a straight wall.) Over the vaults of the rooms of the annex in the eastern part of the court, and also over the vaults of the fourteen parallel chambers outside the enclosing wall to the north, a false roof is laid (Fig. 103). It serves as a protection against the heat of the sun. Under the eastern annex there are some much-ruined subterranean chambers. A staircase at the south-eastern angle of court D leads down into similar cellars (serâdîb).

The arches over the doorways are usually of an ovoid shape, sometimes slightly pointed. When the door-jambs take the form of engaged columns, the capitals of the columns, roughly blocked out in masonry, carry an arch slightly narrower in width than the opening of the doorway beneath it. But when the door-jambs are formed merely by the straight section of the wall, the span of the arch is wider than the opening of the doorway (Fig. 102 illustrates both types). This set-back of the arch was doubtless employed in order to facilitate the placing of centering beams. Three wide doorways with round arches, b b′ and c, lead from the main block of the palace building into the surrounding court. The arches are usually characterized by double rings of voussoirs (*cf.* Ctesiphon and other buildings of the Sassanian and early Mohammadan period), the inner ring laid so as to show the broad face of the stones or tiles, while the narrow end shows in the outer ring. (See the arch in Fig. 102.) The arch construction in the eastern annex is, however, much rougher in style. The outer ring of voussoirs is omitted there, nor is it invariable in other parts of the palace.

The niche plays a large part in the decoration of Ukheiḍir. A row of narrow niches runs along the top of the outer face of the northern enclosing wall, but very little of it is now left (Fig. 87). The southern face of the three-storeyed block bears an elaborate niche decoration (Fig. 91). Here the lowest row of niches forms part of the series already mentioned which runs round court D. Above these, on the second storey, are remains of another row of arched niches, each of which contains three small niches. So far as I know, this feature of a large niche enclosing groups of smaller niches has not yet been observed in Sassanian architecture. It is found, however, in a certain well-known type of early Christian church (see, for instance, Ala Klisse, published by me in the *Thousand and One Churches*, p. 403). On the third storey of the palace the face of the wall has been left blank, but above the windows there are still traces of a third order of small niches. Pairs of niches flanked by engaged columns are to be seen in room G′. They are set high up in the wall between the transverse arches. On these transverse arches there is a plaster decoration, the same in character as that which occurs in the semi-domes at the ends of the vault in Court S (Fig. 101). The motives there used are the flute (in the squinch arch and in the conical segment of the semi-dome above it), and a pattern which resembles a tiny battlemented motive. Upon the transverse arches the battlemented motive is doubled so as to form diamond-shaped patterns. In the centre of each of these diamonds, and in the centre of the tiny arched niches at the bottom of the vault, and also between those niches, there are small funnel-shaped motives formed of concentric rings. Between the transverse arches there is a boldly worked ribbing. The arch round the eastern of the two doors that leads into corridor Q̤′ is surrounded by cusps (Fig. 94). (*Cf.* Ctesiphon, Dieulafoy, *op. cit.*, vol. v. plate 6.) A blind arcade, borne by pilasters, is to be seen in courts M M′ and N N′. In the antechamber U there are shallow niches on either side of the doors.

With regard to the date of Ukheiḍir there are three possible hypotheses. It may belong—

1. To the Sassanian or Lakhmid period prior to the Mohammadan conquest.

2. To the 150 years after the Mohammadan conquest.

3. To the Abbâsid period, *i. e.* after A.D. 750.

1. In defence of the first theory can be urged the close relationship between Ukheiḍir and other places of the Sassanian age, not only in plan (*cf.* Ḳaṣr-i-Shîrîn, de Morgan, *Mission Scientifique en Perse*, vol. iv., part 2), but also in the technique of brick and stone masonry and in the principles of vault construction (*cf.* Ctesiphon, Firûzâbâd, and Sarvistân, Dieulafoy, *op. cit.*). But since it is certain that the arts of the early Moslem era were dominated in Mesopotamia by Sassanian influence, these affinities do not offer a convincing proof of a pre-Mohammadan date. Even if Ukheiḍir belonged to the early Moslem age, it might, and probably would, have been built by Persian workmen. At the same time certain architectural features, such as the groined vault and the fluted dome, have not hitherto been observed in any Sassanian building. The earliest Mesopotamian example of the groined vault known to me, besides the groins of Ukheiḍir, is that of which fragments can be seen in the Baghdâd Gate at Raḳḳah.

There is, further, a passage in Yâḳût's Dictionary which might help to support the theory of a pre-Mohammadan origin (vol. ii., p. 626, under Dûmat ej Jandal). In the accounts given by the Arab historians of the invasion of Mesopotamia in 12 A.H. (A.D. 633-4), by Khâlid ibn u'l Walîd, frequent mention is made of 'Ain et Tamr, which Yâḳût expressly states to be the same as Shefâthâ (Shetâteh is the modern colloquial form of the name). When Khâlid ibn u'l Walîd had taken the oasis, which was inhabited by Christian Arabs, and appears to have been the one place that offered him serious resistance (Teano: *Annali dell' Islam*, vol. ii., p. 940), he is said to have marched on Dûmat ej Jandal, which he captured, putting to death its defender, Ukeidir 'Abdu'l Malik el Kindî.[1] It is generally admitted that the name Dûmat ej Jandal in this account is an error, and that the fortress which was taken by the Mohammadans in the

[1] The name Ukeidir can have no connection with the name Ukheiḍir. The two words are differently spelt in Arabic.

year 12 A.H. was Dûmat el Ḥîrah. (For the reasons for substituting Dûmat el Ḥîrah for Dûmat ej Jandal in Ṭabarî's text, see Teano, *op. cit.*, vol. ii., p. 991.) Now Yâḳût gives two conflicting traditions concerning the foundation of Dûmat el Ḥîrah, but he expresses no uncertainty as to its position. It was near to 'Ain et Tamr, and its ruins were known in Yâḳût's day (thirteenth century). According to the first tradition given by Yâḳût, the Prophet sent Khâlid ibn u'l Walîd in the year 9 A.H. against Ukeidir, who was lord of Dûmat ej Jandal. Khâlid captured Dûmat ej Jandal and made a treaty with Ukeidir, but after the death of Mohammad, Ukeidir broke the treaty, whereupon the Khalif 'Umar expelled him from Dûmat ej Jandal. He retired to Ḥîrah and built himself a palace near to 'Ain et Tamr, which he called Dûmah. This Dûmah, near 'Ain et Tamr, is no doubt Dûmat el Ḥîrah which Khâlid besieged and took in the year 12 A.H. The second tradition is substantially the same as the first as far as the Mohammadan invasion is concerned, but Yâḳût here implies that Ukeidir dwelt in the first instance at Dûmat el Ḥîrah, and was accustomed to resort to Dûmat ej Jandal for the purposes of the chase, and he adds that Ukeidir named Dûmat ej Jandal after Dûmat el Ḥîrah. Prince Teano (*op. cit.*, vol. ii. p. 262) has exposed the improbabilities which attend this explanation, and he concludes that both traditions are equally untrustworthy, and doubts the authenticity of any part of the story of Ukeidir. It does, however, appear to me to be possible that the ruins of Dûmat el Ḥîrah which were standing in Yâḳût's day were no other than the abandoned palace of Ukheiḍir, though it is not necessary to accept either of Yâḳût's versions of the story of its foundation.

2. If the palace is to be ascribed to the period immediately succeeding the conquest, it would be a Mesopotamian representative of the group of pleasure palaces which were built upon the Syrian side of the desert by the Umayyad princes (Lammens: *La Badia et la Ḥîra, Mélanges de la faculté orientale,* Beyrout, vol. iv., p. 91). But whereas it was natural that the Umayyad khalifs should have constructed

hunting palaces in that part of the desert which lay on the direct road between their capital of Damascus and the spiritual capitals of their empire, Mecca and Medina, it is difficult to see why they should have selected a site so far from any of their habitual residences as Ukheiḍir. It is true that the Khalif 'Alî made Kûfah his capital for five years. He was assassinated there in A.D. 661. But during those years he was ceaselessly occupied in quelling rebellions, and I dismiss the possibility that he should have found leisure to build or to use the palace of Ukheiḍir.

3. I am not disposed to place Ukheiḍir as late as the Abbâsid period. The Abbâsid princes had lost the habit of the desert which was so strong a characteristic of their Umayyad predecessors. When they moved away from their capital of Baghdâd they built themselves cities like Raḳḳah and Sâmarrâ. Moreover, the architectural features of Ukheiḍir, both structural and decorative, present marked differences from those of the ruins at Raḳḳah and at Sâmarrâ, and on architectural as well as on historical grounds I am inclined to ascribe Ukheiḍir to an earlier age.

Whether that age be immediately before the Mohammadan conquest, or whether it fall shortly after the conquest, during the Umayyad period, I do not think we are as yet in a position to determine. It is to be borne in mind that the ruins of the palace bear witness to two different dates of building. The eastern annex and probably the edifice outside the enclosing wall to the north are an addition to the original plan and must be of a slightly later date.

CHAPTER V

KERBELÂ TO BAGHDÂD

March 30—April 12

To travel in the desert is in one respect curiously akin to travelling on the sea: it gives you no premonition of the changed environment to which the days of journeying are conducting you. When you set sail from a familiar shore you enter on a course from which the usual landmarks of daily existence have been swept away. What has become of the march of time? Dawn leads to noon, noon to sunset, sunset to the night; but night breaks into a dawn indistinguishable from the last, the same sky above, the same sea on every side, the same planks beneath your feet. Is it indeed another day? or is it yesterday lived over again? Then on a sudden you touch the land and find that that recurring day has carried you round half the globe. So it is in the desert. You rise and look out upon the same landscape that greeted you before—the contour of the hills may have altered ever so slightly, the hollow that holds your camp has deepened by a few yards since last week, the limitless sweep of the plain was not hidden a fortnight ago by that little mound; but here are the same people about you, speaking of the same things, here is the same path to be followed, yes, even the seasons are the same, and the dusty face of the desert is too old to flush at the advent of spring or to be wreathed in autumn garlands of gold and scarlet. Yet at the end of a long interval composed of periods recurrent and alike, you look round and see that the whole face of the universe has changed.

When we reached Kerbelâ we passed into a world of which the aspect and the associations were entirely new to me. I had set out from an Arab town in North Syria, and I emerged in a Persian city linked historically with the Holy

Places, with the first struggles and the only great schism of Islâm. At Kerbelâ was enacted the tragedy of the death of Ḥussein, son of 'Alî ibn abi Tâlib; the place has grown up round the mosque that holds his tomb, and to one half of those who profess the Mohammadan creed it is a goal no less sacred than Mecca. But it was not the golden dome of Ḥussein, though it covers the richest treasure of offerings possessed by any known shrine (unless the treasure in 'Alî's tomb of Nejef touch a yet higher value), nor yet the presence of the green-robed Persians, narrow of soul, austere and stern of countenance—it was not the wealth and fame of the Shî'ah sanctuary that made the strongest assault upon the imagination. It was the sense of having reached those regions which saw the founding of imperial Islâm, regions which remained for many centuries the seat of the paramount ruler, the Commander of the Faithful. Within the compass of a two-days' journey lay the battlefield of Ḳâdisîyah, where Khâlid ibn u'l Walîd overthrew at once and for ever the Sassanian power. Chosroes with his hosts, his satraps, his Arab allies—those princes of the house of Mundhîr whose capital was one of the first cradles of Arab culture—stepped back at his coming into the shadowy past; their cities and palaces faded and disappeared, Ḥîrah, Khawarnaḳ, Ctesiphon, and many another of which the very site is forgotten; all the pomp and valour of an earlier time fell together like an army of dreams at the first trumpet-blast of those armies of the Faith which hold the field until this hour. Then came the day of vigour; the adding of dominion to dominion; the building of great Mohammadan towns, Kûfah, Wâsiṭ, Baṣrah, and last of all Baghdâd, last and greatest. And then decline, and finally the transference of authority. This was the story that was unfolded before me as I stood upon the roof of a Persian house and gazed down into the gorgeously tiled courtyard of the mosque of Ḥussein, in which none but the Faithful may set foot. When I lifted my eyes and looked westward I saw the desert across which the soldiers of the Prophet had come to batter down the old civilizations; when I looked east I saw the road to Baghdâd, where their descendants had cultivated with no less renown, the arts of peace. The low sun shone upon the golden dome; the nesting storks held conversation from minaret to minaret, with much clapping of beaks and shaking out of unruffled wings; the Spirit of Islâm marched out of the wilderness and seized the fruitful earth.

There were other lesser things which aroused a more personal if not a keener interest. The oranges were good at Kerbelâ, as Fattûḥ had said. The shops were heaped with them and with pale sweet lemons: I fear I must have astonished my military escort, for I stopped at every corner to buy more and yet more, and ate them as I went along the streets, hoping to satisfy the inextinguishable thirst born of the desert. Side by side with the oranges lay mountains of pink roses, the flowers cut off short and piled together; every one in the town carried a handful of them and sniffed at them as he walked. After night had fallen I was invited to a bountiful Persian dinner, where we feasted on lamb stuffed with pistachios, and drank sherbet out of deep wooden spoons. And there I heard some talk of politics.

Under the best of circumstances, said one of my informants, constitutional government was not likely to be popular in the province of 'Irâḳ. Men of property were all reactionary at heart. They had got together their wealth by force and oppression; their title-deeds would not bear critical examination, and they resented the curiosity and the comments of the newly-fledged local press. Nor were the majority of the officials better inclined—how was it possible? To forbid corruption, unless the order were accompanied by a rise in salary corresponding to the perquisites of which they were deprived (and this was forbidden by the state of the imperial exchequer) meant for them starvation. A judge, for example, is appointed for two and a half years and his salary is £T15 a month, not enough to keep himself and his family in circumstances which would accord with his position. But over and above the expenses of living he must see to the provision of a sum sufficient to engage the sympathies of his superiors when his appointment shall have expired; otherwise he might abandon the hope of further employment. Most probably he would have to defray the heavy charges of a journey to Constantinople, to enable him to push his claim, not to speak of the fact that he might spend several unsalaried months in the capital before his request was granted. "And so it is that out of ten men, eleven take bribes, and, as far as we can see, nothing has come of the constitution but the black fez" (this because of the boycott on the red fez, made in Austria), "free speech and two towers, one at Kerbelâ and one at Nejef, to commemorate the age of liberty." Under the new régime Kerbelâ had received a mutesarrif whose story was a good example of the mistakes which men were apt to commit when first the old restraints were relaxed. He was of the Aḥrâr, the Liberals, and had begun his career as secretary to the Vâlî of Baghdâd. The people of Baghdâd raised a complaint against him, on the ground that in the fast month of Ramaḍân he had been seen to smoke a cigarette in the bazaar between sunrise and sunset, which showed clearly that he was an infidel, and he was dismissed from his post; but since he was one of the Aḥrâr and had friends in Constantinople, he was presently appointed to Kerbelâ. Now Kerbelâ, being a holy place inhabited mostly by Persian Shî'ahs, is one of the most fanatical cities in the Ottoman Empire, and a mutesarrif who brought with him so unfortunate a reputation could do nothing that was right. Some of his reforms were in themselves reasonable, but he was not the man to initiate them, nor was Kerbelâ the best field for experiments. The town, owing to blind extortion on the part of the government and to neglect of the irrigation system, is growing rapidly poorer and yields an ever diminishing revenue. This revenue is burdened by a number of pensions, and the mutesarrif, looking for a way of retrenchment, found it by depriving all pensioners of their means of livelihood. The pensioners were holy men, sayyids, whose duty it was to pray for the welfare of the Sultan. Some were old and some were deserving, some were neither, but all were holy, and the feelings that were aroused in Kerbelâ when they were left destitute baffle description.

"Yet," continued my host, "the Turks understand government. There was once in Baṣrah an excellent governor; his name was Ḥamdî Bey. When he came to Baṣrah it was the worst city in Turkey; every night there were murders, and no one dared to leave his house after dark lest when he returned he should find that he had been robbed of all he possessed."

"So it is now in Baṣrah," said I, for the town is a by-word in Mesopotamia.

"Yes, so it is now," he returned, "but it was different when Ḥamdî Bey was governor. For a year he sat quiet and collected information concerning all the villains in the place; but he did nothing. Now there was at that time a harmless madman in Baṣrah whom the people called Ḥajjî Beiḍâ, the White Pilgrim; and when they saw Ḥamdî Bey driving through the streets, they would point at him and laugh, saying: 'There goes Ḥajjî Beiḍâ.' But at the end of a year he assembled all the chief men and said: 'Hitherto you have called me Ḥajjî Beiḍâ; now you shall call me Ḥajjî Ḳara, the Black Pilgrim.' And then and there he cast most of them into prison and produced his evidence against them. And after a year's time the town was so peaceful that he ordered the citizens to leave their doors open at night; and as long as Ḥamdî Bey remained at Baṣrah no man troubled to lock his door. And at another time there was a Commandant in Baṣrah, and he too brought the place to order. For when he knew a prisoner to be guilty, yet failed to get the witnesses to speak against him, he would put the man to death in prison by means of a hot iron which he drove into his stomach through a tube. Then it was given out that the man had died of an illness, and every one rejoiced that there should be a rogue the less."

I made no comment, but my expression must have betrayed me, for my interlocutor added a justification of the commandant's methods. "In Persia," said he, "they bury them alive."

"My soldiers have told me," said I, not to be outdone, "that in Persia they cut off a thief's hand, and I think they regard it as the proper sentence, for they generally add: 'That is ḥukm, justice.'"

"It is the sherî'ah," he replied simply, "the holy law," and he recited the passage from the Ḳurân: "If a man or woman steal, cut off their hands in retribution for that which they have done; this is an exemplary punishment appointed by God, and God is mighty and wise."

I had intended to go straight from Kerbelâ to Babylon, but I was reckoning without full knowledge of the Hindîyeh swamp. The history of this swamp is both curious and instructive. A few miles above the village of Museiyib, north-east of Kerbelâ, the Euphrates divides into two channels. The eastern channel, the true bed of the river, runs past Babylon and Ḥilleh and discharges its waters into the great swamp which has existed in southern 'Iraḳ ever since the last days of the Sassanian kings. The western channel is known as the Nahr Hindîyeh; it waters Kûfah, now a miserable hamlet clustered about the great mosque in which the khalif 'Alî was assassinated, and flowing through the great swamp re-enters the Euphrates some way above the junction of the latter with the Tigris.[1] The dam on the Euphrates which regulated the flowing of its waters into the Hindîyeh canal has been allowed to fall into disrepair; every year a deeper and a stronger stream flows down the Hindîyeh, and matters have reached such a pass that during the season of low water the eastern bed is dry, the palm gardens of Ḥilleh are dying for lack of irrigation, and all the country along the river-bank below Ḥilleh has gone out of cultivation. The growth of the Hindîyeh has proved scarcely less disastrous.

[1] The history of Mesopotamian rivers is exceedingly complicated owing to the frequency with which they change their beds. Mr. Le Strange (*Lands of the Eastern Caliphate*, p. 70 *et seq.*) believes that the Nahr Hindîyeh, which is probably identical with the 'Alḳâmî of Ḳudâmah and Mas'ûdî, was considered in the tenth century to be the main stream of the Euphrates, though even at that time it was not so broad as the Ḥilleh branch. Writing in 1905 Mr. Le Strange speaks of the Ḥilleh branch as being undoubtedly the main stream in modern times, but in 1909 nearly all the water, as I shall describe, flowed down the Kûfah branch (the Hindîyeh canal) and the Ḥilleh branch lay dry all the winter. This, however, will, it is to be hoped, be rectified by the new irrigation schemes on which Sir William Willcocks is at present engaged.

The district to the west of the canal, in which Kerbelâ lies, is lower than the level of the stream, while the increasing torrents, bringing with them the silt of the spring floods, yearly raise the bed of the canal and add to the difficulty of keeping it within bounds. The Hindîyeh has become an ever-present danger to the town of Kerbelâ, and indeed in one year, when the stream was unusually high, the water flowed into the streets. It was the duty of the owners of the land, a duty prescribed by immemorial custom, to keep up the dykes, in order to save the cultivated country, and incidentally the town, from inundation. Needless to say they neglected to do so. A large part of the land—and here the story takes a very Oriental turn—had been bought up by a rich Mohammadan who proposed to do a good office by the holy city and to take the charge of the dykes upon himself. But as the canal silted up the charge became heavier, until at last the pious benefactor wearied of his task and refused to do another hand's turn in the matter. Thereupon the mutesarrif sent for him and ordered him to perform his lawful duty. But the landowner was an Indian and a British subject (at this point I realized that I had come once more into the net of our vast empire) and he refused to be bullied by a Turkish official. He pointed out that the floods were largely due to the negligence of the Arab tribes, who draw from the Hindîyeh ten times as much water as they need and let it go to waste upon the land, where it helps to form the redoubted swamp; and since, said he, the swamp was caused not by the will of God, but by the conduct of the Sultan's subjects, the government would do well to remedy the evil by applying to the dykes the forced labour which it has the right to exact from every man during four days in the year.[1] The mutesarrif replied that the Indian had not cultivated his land for four years and that it was therefore forfeit to the State;[2] the Indian countered him with the rejoinder that the land had been under pasture and had paid a regular tithe. So the matter stood in the

[1] It is known as the 'Amalîyeh Mukallifeh.

[2] This applies, I believe, only to lands leased from the State, arḍîyeh amîrîyeh.

spring of 1909; the town of Kerbelâ might at any time be flooded if the river rose, the Hindîyeh swamp was growing day by day, and the road to Babylon was impassable. No one seemed to regard these perils and inconveniences as otherwise than inevitable, and I with the rest bowed my head to the inscrutable decrees of God and took my way to Museiyib.

Museiyib, as I have said, lies on the Euphrates above the point where the Hindîyeh canal branches off from the river. For the last half of the day's journey we skirted the swamp. It was in reality much more than a swamp: it was a shallow lake extending over a vast area. It had invaded even the Museiyib road, which is the direct road from Kerbelâ to Baghdâd, and we, together with all other travellers, had to make a long détour through the desert. The other travellers were mainly Persian pilgrims, men, women and children riding on mules in panniers. It is the ardent wish of every pious Persian to make the pilgrimage to Kerbelâ once during his lifetime, and still more does he desire to make it once again after his death, that his body may lie in earth hallowed by the vicinity of Ḥussein's grave. Countless caravans of corpses journey yearly from Persia to Kerbelâ, and the living should bear in mind that the khâns of the towns are insalubrious, to say the least, owing to the fact that they are packed with dead bodies awaiting their final burial. The close connection between Kerbelâ and Persia has been during recent years of considerable political significance. The large Persian community, rich, influential and safely placed under the protection of the Turkish government, has more than once tendered advice to the struggling factions of its native country, and more than once the advice has been in the nature of a command. The European is not accustomed to think of the Ottoman Empire as a haven of refuge for the oppressed, but the Persian, comparing Turkish administration with his own, regards it as an unattainable standard of tranquillity and equity. Turkey must be judged by Asiatic, not by European, possibilities of achievement, and I tried to keep my thoughts fixed upon the pilgrims jogging sadly home to their intolerable anarchy; but it was difficult not to notice the bands of peasants who came wading through the shallow waters of the Hindîyeh floods, their fields submerged, their crops devastated, their houses reduced to mud-heaps and their possessions scattered over the swamp. Six hours from Kerbelâ we reached the Euphrates, a river much smaller than the one we had left at Hît, since a great part of its waters had been drawn off into irrigation canals. To my amazement it was provided with a practicable bridge of boats, by which we crossed, glorifying the works of man. It was the first, and I may add the only bridge over the Euphrates that I was privileged to see. We pitched camp on the further side just beyond the village of Museiyib.

On the following day we turned southwards to Babylon. For two hours we continued to do battle with the waters, not, however, with untamed floods, but with the almost equally obtrusive irrigation canals and runnels which the industrious fellâḥ conducts in all directions across his fields, regardless of road and path and of the time and temper of the wayfarer. At length we reached the high road from Baghdâd to Ḥilleh, beyond the belt of cultivation, and made the rest of the stage dry-footed. We crossed the Naṣrîyeh canal by a bridge near a ruined khân, and five hours from Museiyib we came to the village of Maḥawîl on a canal of the same name, also bridged. There I lunched under palm-trees—there are no other trees in these regions—and so rode on, catching up the caravan and crossing many another canal, now dry, now bringing water to villages far to the east of us. It was a very barren world, scarred with the traces of former cultivation, and all the more poverty-stricken and desolate because it had once been rich and peopled; flat, too, an interminable, featureless expanse from which the glory had departed. I was almost immersed in the rather jejune reflections which must assail every one who approaches Babylon, when, as good-luck would have it, I turned my eyes to the south and perceived, on the edge of the arid, sun-drenched plain, a mighty mound. There was no need to ask its name; as certainly as if temple and fortress wall still crowned its summit I knew it to be

Bâbil, the northern mound that retains on the lips of the Arabs the echo of its ancient title. I left the road, hoping to find a direct path across the plain to that great vestige of ancient splendours, but the deep cutting of a water-course, as dry and dead as Babylon itself, barred the way. My mare climbed to the top of the high bank that edged it and we stood gazing over the site of the city. A furtive jackal crept out along the bank, caught sight of Fattûḥ and fled back into the dry ditch.

"The son of retreat," said Fattûḥ in the speech of the people.

"Chaḳâl," said I, searching dimly for some familiar swell of sonorous phrases which the word seemed to bring with it. And suddenly they rolled out over the formless thought: "The wolves howl in their palaces and the jackals in the pleasant places."

For the past twelve years a little group of German excavators has lived and worked among the mounds of Babylon. To them I went, in full assurance of the hospitality which they extend to all comers. The traveller who enters their house, sheltered by palm-trees, on the banks of the Euphrates, will find it stored with the best fruits of civilization: studious activity, hard-won learning and that open-handed kindness which abolishes distinctions of race and country. As he watches the daily task of men who are recovering the long-buried history of the past, he will not know how to divide his admiration between the almost incredible labour entailed by their researches and the marvellous culture which their work has laid bare. "Only to the wise is wisdom given, and knowledge to them that have understanding."

Within the largest of the mounds, the Ḳaṣr, or castle, as the Arabs call it, lie the remains of Nebuchadnezzar's palace. Another eight or ten years' work will be needed to complete the ground plan of the whole structure, but enough has been done to show the nature of the house wherein the king rested. It is built of square tiles, stamped with his name and bound together with asphalt. The part which has been excavated consists of an immense irregular area enclosed by thick walls.

One of these (it forms the quay of a canal) is called by the workmen "the father of twenty-two," *i. e.* it is twenty-two metres across; another reaches the respectable width of seventeen metres, but usually the royal builder was content with five or six metres, or even less. Within the enclosure lies a bewildering complexity of small courts and passages with chambers leading out of them—the more bewildering because in many cases the bricks have disappeared, and the walls must be traced by means of the spaces left behind. For more than a thousand years after the fall of Babylon no man building in its neighbourhood was at the pains to construct brick-kilns, but when he needed material he sought it in Nebuchadnezzar's city. Greek, Persian and Arab used it as a quarry, and as you climb the stairs of the German house you will become aware of the characters that spell the king's name upon the steps beneath your feet. The small courts and chambers, which were no doubt occupied by retinues of officials and servants of the palace, formed a bulwark of defence for the king. His apartments lay behind a wide paved court. From the court a doorway leads into a large oblong chamber, in the back wall of which is a niche for the throne. This is believed to be the banqueting hall where Belshazzar made his feast, and on a fragment of wall facing the throne you may see, if you please, the fingers of a man's hand writing the fatal message. How this hall was roofed is an unsolved problem. No traces of vaulting have been found, yet the width from wall to wall is so great that it is doubtful whether it could have been covered by a roof of beams. If there were indeed a vault it would be the earliest example of such construction on so big a scale. Behind the banqueting hall are the private chambers, and behind all a narrow passage leading to an emergency exit, by means of which the king could escape to his boat on the Euphrates in the last extremity of danger.

Nebuchadnezzar's father, Nabopolassar, had built himself a smaller, but still very considerable, dwelling which occupied the western side of the mound. This Nebuchadnezzar destroyed; he filled up the walls and chambers with rubble and masonry and laid out an extension of his own palace above it. The plan both of the upper and of the lower palace has now been ascertained. Above the Babylonian walls are the remains of Greek and Parthian settlements, each of which has to be carefully planned before it can be swept away and the lower strata studied. I saw work being carried on in a mound which formed one of the most ancient parts of the city; the excavation pits had been sunk twelve or fifteen metres deep to dwelling-houses of the first Babylonian Empire. They passed through the periods of the Parthian and of the Greek, through the age of Nebuchadnezzar and that of the Assyrians, and each stratum was levelled and planned before the next could be revealed. Add to this that the most ancient walls were constructed of sun-dried brick, scarcely distinguishable from the closely-packed earth, and some idea can be obtained of the extreme difficulty of the work. The oldest Babylonian houses which have been uncovered rest themselves on rubbish-heaps and ruins, but deeper digging is impossible owing to the fact that water-level has been reached. The Euphrates channel has silted up several metres during the last six thousand years and the primæval dwellings are now below it. While we were standing at the bottom of a deep pit, a workman struck out with his pick a little heap of ornaments, a couple of copper bracelets and the beads of a necklace which had been worn by some Babylonian woman in the third millennium before Christ and were restored at last to the light of the sun.

The northern part of the palace mound is as yet almost untouched. Here can be seen a sculptured block which used to lie among the earth-heaps until a French engineer built a pedestal for it and set it up above the ruins (Fig. 104). It is carved in the shape of a colossal lion standing above the body of a man who lies with arms uplifted. The man's head is broken away and the whole group is only half finished, but the huge beast with the helpless human figure beneath his feet could not have been given an aspect more sinister. It is as though the workmen of the Great King had fashioned an image of Destiny, treading relentlessly over the generations

FIG. 104.—BABYLON, THE LION.

FIG. 105.—BABYLON, ISHTAR GATE.

FIG. 106.—BABYLON, ISHTAR GATE.

of mankind, before they too passed into its clutches. All along the east side of the palace stretches the Via Sacra, contracting at one point only its splendid width that it may pass through the gate that stands midway between the house of Nebuchadnezzar and the temple of the goddess Ishtar. The Ishtar gate—its name is attested by a cuneiform inscription—is the most magnificent fragment that remains of all Nebuchadnezzar's constructions. Four or five times did he fill up the Via Sacra and raise its level, and each time he built up the brick towers of the double gateway to correspond. The various levels of the pavements can now be seen on the sides of the excavation trench, while the towers, completely disclosed, rear their unbroken height in stupendous masses of solid masonry. They are decorated on every side with alternate rows of bulls and dragons cast in relief on the brick; the noble strength of the bulls, stepping out firmly with arched neck, contrasts with the slender ferocious grace of the dragons, and the two companies form a bodyguard worthy of the gate of kings and of gods (Figs. 105 and 106). Along the walls of the Via Sacra marched a procession of lions, fragments of which have been found and pieced together. They, too, were in relief, but covered with a fine enamel in which the colours were laid side by side without the intermission of cloissons. This art of enamelling is lost, and no modern workman has been able to imitate the lion frieze.

On the east side of the gate stands the little temple of Ishtar, raised on a high platform and commanding the city below. The temple is built of sun-baked brick, probably in accordance with hieratic tradition, which held to the ancient building material used in an age when the architects were unacquainted with the finer and more durable burnt brick. Small courts with side chambers lead into an inner holy of holies, where in a niche stood the symbol or effigy of the goddess. Behind the sanctuary there is a narrow blind passage where the priests could lurk behind the cult image and confound the common folk with mysterious sounds and hidden voices. The Via Sacra pursues from the gate its stately way, skirting along the edge of an immense open court that lay between the palace and the temple of the god Marduk, the patron divinity of Babylon. The mound in which the temple lies has not as yet been completely excavated, but a pit sunk in its centre has laid bare the walls of the entrance court. It will be no easy matter to continue the work here. The mound was thickly inhabited during the Greek and Parthian periods, and its upper levels consist chiefly of refuse-heaps. When the workmen cut down through them to reach the temple gate, the stench of the old rubbish-heaps, combined with the stifling heat of the pit, was so intolerable that their labours had to be interrupted for several days until a breeze arose and made it possible to continue them.

The excavations are carried on all through the summer heats, but the director, Professor Koldewey, was at the time of my visit paying a penalty for his tireless energy. He had been ill for some months owing to his exertions during the previous summer, and to my permanent loss I was unable to see him. I retain notwithstanding the most delightful memory of the days at Babylon, of the peace and the dignified simplicity of life in the house by the river, of the little garden in the courtyard where Badrî Bey, the delegate from the Constantinople museum, coaxed his roses into flower and his radishes into red and succulent root; of long and pleasant conversations with Mr. Buddensieg and Mr. Wetzel, wherein they poured out for me their knowledge of the forgotten things of the past; of quiet hours with books which they brought for me out of their library—and books were a luxury from which I had been cut off since I left Aleppo. When I rode out of an afternoon one of the zaptiehs of Babylon was detailed to accompany me. He knew the ruin-field well, having been the fortunate occupier of a post at the Expeditions-haus for several years. I would find him waiting in the palm-grove where my horses were stabled, alert, respectful and less ragged than his brothers in arms whose pay does not come to them through the hands of European excavators. One day I asked him to take me to the Greek theatre, wondering a little whether he would understand the request.

"Effendim," he said, "you mean the place of Alexander."

The great name fell strangely among the palm-trees, and from out of the horde of ghosts that people Babylon strode the Conqueror at the end of his course. So we rode to the place of Alexander, the theatre near the city wall, ruined almost beyond recognition, but preserving in the popular nomenclature the memory of the most brilliant figure in the history of the world.

And once the clouds gathered as we were riding through the palm-groves by the river. "Praise God!" said the zaptieh, "maybe we shall have rain." He shouted the good tidings to a peasant who drove the oxen of a water-wheel: "Oh brother, rain, please God!" But it was dust that was heralded by the darkness, and as we hastened to the great mound of Bâbil the wind bore down upon us and the parched earth rose and enveloped us. We left our horses standing with downcast heads under the lee of the mound and picked our way up the sides between the trial trenches of the excavators. In a few moments the dust-storm swept past, and we saw the wide expanse that was Babylon, embraced by gleaming reaches of river and the circuit of mound and ditch which marks the line of the city wall.

"Effendim," said the zaptieh, "yonder is Birs Nimrûd," and he pointed to the south-west, where, in the heart of the desert, rose the huge outline of a temple pyramid, a zigurrat. Legend has given it a notable place in the story of our first forefathers: it was believed to be no other than the impious tower that witnessed the confusion of speech.

I heard at Babylon some hint of the state of unrest, bordering on revolution, into which the province of 'Iraḳ had fallen. The German excavators had been sucked into the outer edges of the whirlpool. Their workpeople, drawn from different tribes (they had relinquished nomad life, but the tribal system still held good among them), had caught the infection of hatred and turned from the excavation pits to the settling of ancient scores—so effectually that many a score had been settled for ever, and the debtor came back to his place in the trench no more. Most of the survivors had been clapped into gaol by a justly incensed civil authority, and what with death and the serving out of sentences, Professor Koldewey and his colleagues had suffered from a scarcity of labour. This was nothing, as I was to learn at Baghdâd, to the confusion that reigned in other parts of 'Iraḳ, and it was fortunate that I had no intention of going south from Babylon; at that time it would have been impossible.

On the way to Baghdâd I was resolved to visit Ctesiphon, but we were obliged to follow, during the first day's journey, the Baghdâd road, re-traversing for some hours the line of our march from Museiyib. Ever since we had left Kebeisah the temperature had been exceedingly high, and from Babylon to Baghdâd we travelled through a heat wave very unusual at the beginning of April. The early morning was cool and pleasant, but by about ten o'clock the scorching sun became almost unbearable, even for people so well inured to heat as my servants and I. As long as we were moving, it was tempered by the breath of our progress, but if we stood still it burnt through our clothes like a flame. There was not a leaf or any green thing upon the plain, and the only diversion in a monotonous ride was caused by a peasant who caught us up with lamentations and laid hold of my stirrup.

"Effendim!" he cried, "you have soldiers with you; bid them do justice on the man who stole my cow."

"Where is the man?" said I in bewilderment.

"He is here," he answered, weeping more loudly than before, "but a quarter of an hour back upon the road. An Arab he is; and while I was driving my cow to Museiyib, he came out of the waste and took her from me, threatening me with his rifle."

"The effendi has nought to do with your cow," said one of the zaptiehs impatiently—and indeed the sun withered us as we stood. "Go tell the Ḳâḍî at Museiyib."

"How shall I get justice from the Ḳâḍî?" wailed the peasant. "I have no money."

The rejoinder struck me as correct, and I sent one of the zaptiehs back with the lawful owner of the cow, telling him to catch the thief if he were still upon the road and I would give a reward. The zaptieh re-joined us while we were lunching at the khân of Ḥasua, but he had not seen the cow, nor yet the thief, and perhaps it was unreasonable to expect that the latter should keep to the high road with stolen goods trotting before him. The khân at Ḥasua is large and built on the Persian plan for Persian pilgrims. We ate our lunch in the shadow of its gateway, and when we came out the sun struck us in the face like a sword. There was nothing to be done but to try and forget it; I summoned Fattûḥ and drew him into conversation.

"Oh Fattûḥ," said I, "is there any justice in the land of the Ottomans?"

"Effendim," replied Fattûḥ cautiously, "there is justice and there is injustice, as in other lands. Have I not told you of Rejef Pasha and the thief who stole from me £T28?"

"No," said I, settling myself expectantly in the saddle.

"It happened one year that I was in Baghdâd," Fattûḥ began, "for your Excellency knows that I drive the gentry back and forth between Aleppo and Baghdâd in my carriage, and so it is that I am often in Baghdâd."

"I know," said I. "Once you sent me some blue and red belts embroidered with gold that you had bought in the bazaars."

"It is true," said Fattûḥ. "One I gave to Zekîyeh, and the others I sent by the post for you and for their Excellencies your sisters. Please God they rejoiced to have them?" he inquired anxiously.

"They rejoiced exceedingly," I assured him for the fiftieth time; a present that has to be sent by the post is no small thing, and it would be matter for consternation if it did not please. "But what of Rejef Pasha?"

"Rejef Pasha was Mushîr of Baghdâd," Fattûḥ picked up his tale. "And God knows he was a just man. Now I had sold my carriage to one who needed it and gave me £T28 for it, which was a good price, for it was old. And as I was walking in the bazaars a thief stole the money from me, and when I put my hand into my pocket, lo, it was empty."

"Wah, wah!" commiserated the zaptieh.

"Eh yes," said Fattûḥ. "Twenty-eight Ottoman pounds.

Now I had heard men speak of Rejef Pasha that he was famed for justice, and I went to him where he sat in the serâyah and said: 'Effendim, I am a man of Aleppo, a stranger in Baghdâd; and a thief has stolen from me £T28. And there are many here who can speak for me.' Then Rejef Pasha sent into the bazaars and all the thieves he arrested."

"Did he know them all?" I asked.

"Without doubt," replied Fattûḥ. "He was Mushîr. And some he questioned and let them go, and others he caused to be beaten upon the soles of their feet with rods, and them too he released, until only three men remained, and then only one. And Rejef Pasha said: 'This is the thief.' Then they cast him upon the ground and beat him many times, and every time when they had beaten him till he could bear no more, he cried out: 'Cease the beating, and I will give back the money.' But when they ceased he said he had not so much as a mejîdeh. Then one of the soldiers caught him by the leg to throw him to the ground, and the man's garment tore in his hand, and out of it fell £T26 and rolled upon the floor. But two pounds he had eaten," explained Fattûḥ. "And Rejef Pasha cast him into prison. And when I was next in Baghdâd he was still in prison, and I visited him and lent him £T1, for he was very poor. And we ate together."

"Did you see him again?" said I, deeply interested in this simple history.

"Eh, wallah!" replied Fattûḥ. "I met him in Deir, and there I feasted him in the bazaar. And now he lives in Deir, and I go to his house whenever I pass through the town, for we are like brothers. But he has not returned me the pound I lent him while he was in prison," added Fattûḥ regretfully.

"Mâshallah!" said the zaptieh. "Rejef Pasha was a good man."

"But I will tell you another tale of Rejef Pasha, better than the last," pursued Fattûḥ, drawing, with the perfect art of the narrator, upon yet choicer stores of his memory—or was it of his imagination? "Effendim, I had a friend, and he hired from me one of my carriages that he might drive a certain daftardâr from Aleppo to Baghdâd. Now at Ramâdî the daftardâr spent two nights in the house of the son of his uncle, and when they reached Baghdâd the daftardâr searched in his box for the gold ornaments of his wife, and, look you, they were missing. And they cost £T60. Then the daftardâr said that the carriage driver had stolen them, and he caused him to be imprisoned for a period of three years. And soon after, I came to Baghdâd and inquired concerning my carriage; and a man in the bazaar told me that which had befallen, but I did not believe that my friend had stolen the gold ornaments of the daftardâr's wife. And the man in the bazaar said: 'You are his friend, and moreover you are a walad melîḥ, a good lad, and he has a wife and two little children in Aleppo. You will not let him starve in prison.' And when I heard him call me a walad melîḥ and thought upon the children in Aleppo, I went away and sold my two carriages for £T60, and set my friend free. And then," Fattûḥ continued his gratifying reminiscences, "I went to a scribe in the bazaar and gave him half a mejîdeh. And your Excellency knows that a scribe charges one piastre. And I said: 'Take this half mejîdeh and write a letter to Rejef Pasha that shall be worthy to be sent to the Sultan and explain to him the whole matter.' So the scribe wrote the letter, and I took it to the serâyah. Then Rejef Pasha called me before him, for he had not forgotten me, nor the £T28 that were stolen by the thief. And he said: 'My son, do not fear. I will get back your money if I have to pay from the treasury of our Lord the Sultan.' And he sent for the daftardâr and rebuked him for committing a man to prison without evidence, for he said that without doubt the gold ornaments had been stolen at Ramâdî. And the daftardâr paid me back £T60. Never was there a pasha like Rejef Pasha," concluded Fattûḥ. "He feared none but God. God give him peace—he died a year ago."

Late in the afternoon we came to Maḥmûdîyeh. The baggage got in half-an-hour afterwards, and found me established in the upper room of a khân which Jûsef had noted down as he passed through on his way to Kerbelâ as "the very place for our effendi." The room was cooler than a tent, and to sit in the shade and drink tea seemed to me to be the consummation of earthly happiness. My lodging opened on to a flat roof on which I dined, and realized that the more intolerably blasting the day, the more perfect was the soft and delicate night. The khânjî, when he heard that we were bound for Ctesiphon, declared that the Tigris was in flood and the road under water. We stood aghast, seeing a second enemy flow into the field just as we had circumvented the first, but a Kurdish zaptieh (his name was 'Abdu'l Ḳâdir) stepped up with a smart salute and bade us take courage, for he would lead us to Ctesiphon. He was as good as his word; there was, in fact, no water on the road. We reached the mounds of Seleucia in three hours, and in another half-hour camped by the Tigris under the ruined wall of the Greek city. The Tigris, where we came to it, was a mighty stream and a well-conducted. It flowed solemnly between its low banks, which it did not attempt to overstep, in spite of the fact that the snows were beginning to melt in the Kurdish hills and the river was in flood. A belt of cultivation ran like a narrow green ribbon beside it, intersected by a network of irrigation canals which were fed by a regiment of jirds along the bank. The whole area of Seleucia was covered with corn, but half-a-mile inland the relentless desert resumed its rule, for the crops that had been sown beyond the irrigation streams, in expectation of the usual sprinkling of winter rain, had never sprouted. Out of the cornfields rose the mounds of Seleucia, the capital of the Seleucid empire, which for two hundred years after the death of Alexander embraced Mesopotamia, North Syria and a varying part of Asia Minor. Of all cities in Turkey, Seleucia is perhaps the one which would yield most to the spade of the excavator. The Greek civilization of the Diadochi has given up few of its secrets in any of the regions where the generals of Alexander cut their empires out of the fruits of his victories, but in Mesopotamia we are completely ignorant of what the Greek conquest may have meant in the history of architecture and the lesser arts. We know only that at the end of the period of Greek rule the arts emerged profoundly modified, and thus modified governed the late antique and the early Christian world.

I had no sooner appointed a camping-ground than I embarked on the broad waters of the Tigris in a basket. The craft that navigate that river are known in Arabic as guffahs, but I have applied to them the correct English word (Fig. 110). They are round with an incurving lip, like any other basket, made of plaited withes and pitched without and within to keep them water-tight. Their size and the pitch alone differentiate them from their fellows in the European market, and I readily admit that when first you are invited to cross a deep and rapid stream in a guffah you feel a shadow of reluctance. But for all their unpromising appearance they are stout and trustworthy vessels, and when you have crossed once, you and your zaptieh and your mares all in the same guffah, and accustomed yourself to its peculiar mode of progression, you come to feel a justifiable confidence in it. The guffah cannot make headway against stream; it must be pulled up the river to a distance considerably above the point you design to touch on the opposite bank—the two guffahjîs push off, the basket spins upon its axis, and so spinning advances, on the principle of the moon's advance across space, or, for that matter, of the earth's; the guffahjîs paddle with a genteel nonchalance, first on one side and then on the other, and at the end of all you reach your goal.

My goal was Ctesiphon (Fig. 107). The huge fragment of the palace, which is all that remains of the Sassanian capital, successor and heir to Seleucia, lies about half-a-mile from the river on the edge of a reed-grown marsh. No more of it is standing than the central vaulted hall (and here half the vault has fallen) and the east wall of one of the wings (Fig. 108). The second wing has disappeared, and nothing is left of the rooms on either side of the hall [1] (Fig. 109). Even in this condition Ctesiphon is the most remarkable of all known

[1] The foundations were, however, traced by Dieulafoy, who has indicated them in his plan: *L'Art ancien de la Perse*, Vol. V. When he first visited Ctesiphon, the east wall of both wings and all the vault of the hall were perfect.

Sassanian buildings and one of the most imposing ruins in the world. The great curtain of wall, the face of the right wing, rises stark and gaunt out of the desert, bearing upon its surface a shallow decoration of niches and engaged columns which is the final word in the Asiatic treatment of wall spaces, the end of the long history of artistic endeavour which began with the Babylonians and was quickened into fresh vigour by the Greeks. Tradition has it that the whole wall was covered with precious metals. The gigantic vault, built over empty space without the use of centering beams, is one of the most stupendous creations of any age. It spans 25·80 metres: the barrel vaults of the basilica of Maxentius in the Roman Forum span 23·50 metres; the barrel vault that covered the aula of Domitian's palace on the Palatine spanned 30·40 metres, but it has fallen. The Roman vaults were built over centering beams, not over space on the Mesopotamian system, and the latter, what with the appeal which it makes to the imagination and the high ovoid curve which it involves, gives a result incomparably more impressive. In this hall Chosroes held his court. It must have lain open to the rising sun, or perhaps the entrance was sheltered by a curtain which hung from the top of the vault down to the floor. The Arab historian, Ṭabarî, gives an account of a carpet seventy cubits long and sixty cubits broad which formed part of the booty when the Mohammadans sacked the city. It was woven into the likeness of a garden; the ground was worked in gold and the paths in silver; the meadows were of emeralds and the streams of pearls; the trees, flowers and fruits of diamonds and other precious stones. Such a texture as this may have been drawn aside to reveal the Great King seated in state in his hall of audience, with the light of a thousand lamps, suspended from the roof, catching his jewelled tiara, his sword and girdle, illuminating the hangings on the walls and the robes and trappings of the army of courtiers who stood round the throne.

The pages of the historian who relates the Mohammadan conquest of Ctesiphon ring still with the triumph of that victory. The Sassanian capital comprised both the old Greek

FIG. 107.—CTESIPHON, FROM EAST.

FIG. 108.—CTESIPHON, FROM WEST.

FIG. 109.—CTESIPHON, REMAINS OF VAULT ON WEST SIDE OF SOUTH WING.

foundation on the west bank of the river and the later Persian town with its palaces on the east bank.[1] Sa'd ibn abi Waḳḳâṣ, the leader of the army of Islâm, had little to fear from the last of the Sassanian kings, Yazdegird, a boy of twenty-one, and having entered the western city (known to the Arabs as Bahurasîr) without striking a blow, he assembled his troops and, Ḳurân in hand, pointed to the fulfilment of prophecy: "Did ye not swear aforetime that ye would never pass away? Yet ye inhabited the dwellings of a people that had dealt unjustly by their own souls, and ye saw how we dealt with them. We made them a warning and an example to you."[2] "And when the Moslems entered Bahurasîr, and that was in the middle of the night, the White Palace flashed upon them. Then said Ḍirâr ibn u'l Khaṭṭâb: 'God is great! the White Palace of Chosroes! This is what God and his Prophet promised.'"[3]

But the fording of the Tigris was a serious matter, and some days passed before Sa'd announced to the army that he had resolved to make the venture. "And all of them cried: 'God has resolved on the right path for us and for thee; act thou.' And Sa'd urged the people to the ford and said: 'Who will lead, and guard for us the head of the ford that the people may follow him?' And 'Âṣim ibn 'Amr came forward and after him six hundred men. And he said: 'Who will go with me and guard the head of the passage

[1] It was founded by Anushirwân the Just after he had taken Antioch of Syria in 540. He transported the inhabitants of Antioch to the Tigris and settled them opposite Seleucia in a new city which is said to have been built on the plan of Antioch. Le Strange: *Lands of the Eastern Caliphate*, p. 33.

[2] *Sûrah*, XIV. vs. 46. The Arabs called the double town Medâin, the cities, but Ṭabarî uses the name for the eastern city and describes the western as Bahurasir. I have abridged Ṭabarî's account of the siege from the text of de Goeje's edition, Vol. V., Prima Series, under the years 15 and 16 A.H.

[3] The White Palace is not represented by the existing ruin on the east bank, which was known to the Arabs as Aywân Kisrâ, the hall of Chosroes. The White Palace was also on the left bank, but about a mile higher up. It had disappeared by the beginning of the tenth century. Le Strange, *op. cit.*, p. 34.

that the people may ford?' And there came forward sixty. And when the Persians saw what they did, they plunged into the Tigris against them and swam their horses towards them. And 'Âṣim they met in the forefront, for he had neared the head of the ford. Then said 'Âṣim: 'The spears! the spears! aim them at their eyes.' And they joined in contest and the Moslems aimed at their eyes and they turned back towards the bank. And the Moslems urged on their horses against them and caught them on the bank and killed the greater part of them; and he who escaped, escaped one eyed. And their horses trembled under them until they broke from the ford. And when Sa'd saw 'Âṣim at the head of the ford he said: 'Say: We call upon the Lord and in Him we put our trust and excellent is the Entrusted; there is no power nor strength but in God, the Exalted, the Almighty.' And when Sa'd entered Madâin and saw it deserted, he came to the hall of Chosroes and began to read: 'How many gardens and fountains have they left behind, cornfields and fair dwellings and delights which were theirs; thus we dispossessed them thereof and gave their possession for an inheritance unto another people.' And he repeated the opening prayer and made eight prostrations. And he chose the hall for a mosque; and in it were effigies in plaster of men and horses and they heeded them not but left them as they were, though the Mohammadans do not so. And we entered Madâin and came to domed chambers filled with baskets; and we thought them to be food, and lo, they were overflowing with gold and silver. And they were divided among the people. And we found much camphor and thought it to be salt, and kneaded it into the bread, until we perceived the bitterness of it in the bread. And Zuhrah ibn u'l Ḥawîyeh went out with the vanguard and pursued the fugitives till he reached the bridge of Nahrwân; and the fugitives crowded upon it and a mule fell into the water, and they struggled round it greedily. And Zuhrah said: 'Verily, I believe, billah, that the mule bears something precious.' And that which it bore was the regalia of Chosroes, his robes and his strings of pearls, his girdle and his armour covered with jewels, in which he was wont to sit, vaingloriously attired." . . .

In the grey dawn I returned to Ctesiphon. The moon was setting in the west and as we floated down the river the sun rose out of the east and struck the ruined hall of the palace.

"Allah, Allah!" murmured 'Abdu'l Ḳâdir, moved to wonder as he watched the vast walls, in their unmatched desolation, take on the glory of another day.

We rode up to Baghdâd along the edge of the Tigris, and as we went, Fattûḥ, who thought little of ruins except as a divertisement for the gentry, dilated upon the splendours that we were to witness. Especially was he anxious that I should not fail to see the famous cannon which stands near the arsenal, chained to the ground lest it should fly away. "For," said Fattûḥ, "the people of Baghdâd relate that in a certain year there was a great battle at a distance of many days' journey. Now the soldiers of Baghdâd were giving way before the enemy when one looked up and saw the cannon flying through the air to their help. And without the aid of hands it fired at the army of the foe and drove them back. Then they brought the cannon back with them and chained it by the arsenal, for they prized it mightily. So I have heard in Baghdâd."

"And what do you think of the story?" I asked.

"My lady," said Fattûḥ with a fine show of contempt, "the people of Baghdâd are very ignorant. They will believe anything. But we in Aleppo would laugh if we were told that a cannon had flown through the air."

Every few hundred yards we came upon the deep cutting of an irrigation canal and our road passed over it airily, borne on the most fragile of bridges. At first I could scarcely control my alarm as I saw rider and baggage animals suspended above the gulf, but the horses made light of it and no one can keep up a fear that is unshared by his comrades. We were fortunate in finding all the bridges intact, but our good luck deserted us in the middle of the day, and when we came to Garârah, where we hoped to cross the Tigris by a bridge of boats, we found that the bridge had been swept away and the keeper of the toll-house seemed surprised to learn that we had expected it to stand firm in time of flood. So we turned wearily round an immense bend of the Tigris and entered Baghdâd by the Ḥilleh road (Fig. 111). Here the pontoon bridge had been mercifully spared; it was crowded with folk, and as we pushed our way slowly across it I had time to offer up a short thanksgiving for the first stage of a journey successfully accomplished, new roads traversed, unvisited sites explored, another web of delightful experiences woven and laid by. At the end of the bridge we found ourselves in the bazaars and made our way to the British Residency. It is a pleasant thing to be English and to see the Sikh guard leap to the salute at the gateway of that palàce by the Tigris which is our much-envied Consulate General. My thanksgiving must certainly have broken into a hymn of praise when I found that the hospitable Resident and his wife were expecting my arrival and had prepared for me a room almost as spacious as the hall of Chosroes.

At Baghdâd I learnt that the rumours of a revolt which had reached Babylon fell far short of the truth. Two of the Tigris tribes were up in arms and had effectually blocked all communication with Baṣrah and the Persian Gulf. They were holding up five steamers at Amârah, together with a couple of gunboats, which had been sent down to clear the channel, and over two thousand soldiers. Among the passengers was Sir William Willcocks, who was at that time engaged on the irrigation survey, and the disturbance had therefore become a matter of grave concern to the Resident and to all others who had the interests of Turkey at heart. During the few days which I spent in Baghdâd, I saw many people and heard much talk concerning the state of affairs that prevailed in the delta, and I came to the conclusion that the government were garnering the ripe fruit both of their inaction and of their action. On the one hand, the Arab tribes had been allowed to reach an alarming excess of insubordination. For three years the boats of the Turkish and of the Lynch Company had been exposed to perpetual danger of attack, and in 1908 one of the steamers of the Lynch

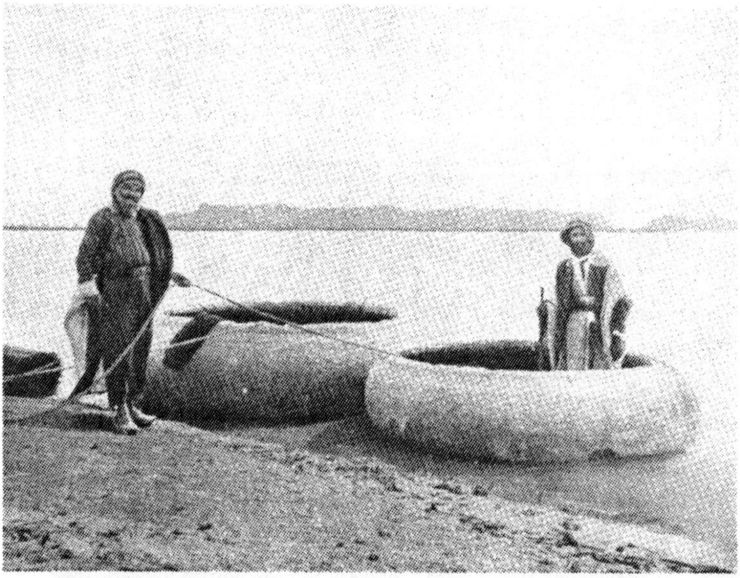
FIG. 110.—GUFFAHS OPPOSITE THE WALL OF SELEUCIA.

FIG. 111.—BAGHDÂD, THE LOWER BRIDGE.

FIG. 112.—BAGHDÂD, TOMB OF SITT ZOBEIDEH.

FIG. 113.—BAGHDÂD, INTERIOR OF SPIRE, SITT ZOBEIDEH

Company had been fired upon and several persons had been killed or wounded. Nevertheless no attempt has been made to bring the sheikhs to justice. In remoter districts, even where the land was under cultivation, the fiction of established government had been for all practical purposes abandoned. Where the tax-gatherers still ventured to put in an appearance they were bribed by the Arabs, and little money flowed through their hands into the imperial treasury, while not infrequently they did not dare to breathe the name of taxes. "The very shepherds are armed with rifles," said one, "and if I were to ask them to pay the aghnâm, the sheep tax, they would raise their guns to their shoulders, saying: 'Take the aghnâm.'" On the other hand, the authorities had sought to cover their weakness by setting one sheikh against another and thus fostering disorder. Individual officials had been guilty of methods of extortion almost unparalleled in the Ottoman empire, and a well-known sheikh had declared with some reason that to pay in the arrears which had been scored up against him would be little better than an act of madness, since the receipt given by one man would be pronounced invalid by the next and the whole sum would be demanded of him a second time. While I pondered over these tales, my interlocutor would generally add: "Wait till you see Môṣul. The vilayet of Môṣul is worse governed than the vilayet of Baghdâd."

The one ray of hope for the future sprang from the labours of the irrigation survey whose leader was lying imprisoned in midstream at Amârah. "He who holds the irrigation canals, holds the country," is a maxim which can be applied as well to Mesopotamia as it was to Egypt, and it was generally admitted that an irrigation system, justly administered, would be a better means of coercion than an army corps. The Arabs depend for their existence upon the river-side crops; the control of the water and the possibility of turning it off at any moment would prove an effective check on revolt. Moreover the man who has something to lose is never on the side of anarchy; prosperity is the best incentive to orderliness, and prosperity might in time be brought back to districts which had been for many ages the richest in the world. The native of 'Irâḳ, gazing upon the empty desert which now meets his eye, is accustomed to allude proudly to the days when "a cock could hop from house to house all the way from Baṣrah to Baghdâd," and the saying illustrates the fundamental truth that the present poverty-stricken condition of the land is due not to the niggardliness of nature, but to the destructive folly of man. The forerunner of effective reform must always be honest administration, and how was that to be attained where corruption was as natural as the drawing in of the breath? Even to this, perhaps the most critical of all the questions that beset the new government, there seemed to me to exist the germs of an answer in the growth and free expression of popular opinion. In Baghdâd the public mind was on the alert and the public tongue was no longer to be silenced. One day when I went down into the bazaars I heard on every lip the rumour that a noted Arab from one of the rebellious tribes had arrived in the town, his hands filled with gold which he was prepared to transfer to those of a certain high military authority. The next day the tale was in the local papers, the official was mentioned by name, and if it were indeed true that the Arab had been sent on the mission with which he was credited, his distinguished patron would have found it hard to accept the money intended for him and impossible to carry out his part in the proposed bargain. But the press, though it was as yet inefficient enough, was the best asset of the new order. Not even the most optimistic could assert that constitutional government had taken deep root in Baghdâd. The local committee was a negligible quantity, and men of all creeds were persuaded that the revolution was still to come and that it would come with bloodshed. But it must be added that when the news of the counter-revolution in Constantinople reached Baghdâd, not a finger was lifted nor a voice heard to support anything that would approach to a return to the old régime, and the military authorities of Baghdâd were among those who telegraphed to the Committee with offers of assistance when the fate of the latter hung in the balance.

Here as elsewhere the chief bar to progress was the political fatalism of the people themselves. But amid the universal scepticism there was one section of the community which showed a desire to profit by the advantages which had been promised. The Jews form a very important part of the population, rich, intelligent, cultivated and active. One example of their attitude towards the new order will be enough to show their quality. It had been given out that all the subjects of the Sultan would ultimately be called upon to perform military service; the law (which has since been passed) had not yet assumed a definite shape and many were of the opinion that it would be found impossible to frame it. Not so the Jews of Baghdâd. As soon as the idea of universal service had been conceived, a hundred young men of the Jewish community applied for leave to enter the military school so that they might lose no time in qualifying to serve as officers. The permission was granted, and I trust that they may now be well on the road to promotion. The Christians showed no similar desire to take up the duties of the soldier. On the contrary, all those who were in arrears with the payment of their exemption money hastened to make good the sum due, that they might show that they had fulfilled their obligations under the old system and claim acquittal from those imposed by the new.

I heard these tales by snatches as I explored Baghdâd and tried to reconstitute the city which had been for five centuries the capital of the Abbâsid khalifs, a period during which it had witnessed a magnificence as profuse and destruction as reckless as any others on the pages of history. Of the original Mohammadan foundation, Manṣûr's Round City, built in A.D. 762 on the right bank of the Tigris, no vestige remains.[1] The site of the great quarters which sprung up to north and south of the Round City are marked only by the tomb of

[1] Bricks stamped with Nebuchadnezzar's name have been found along the quays, and there was a flourishing Persian Baghdâd on the west bank of the Tigris towards the end of the Sassanian period. The chief authority for the history of Baghdâd is Mr. Le Strange's admirable book, *Baghdâd during the Abbâsid Caliphate,* which has made it possible to understand the very complicated topography of the town.

Sheikh Ma'rûf and the celebrated Shi'ah sanctuary of Kâẓimein. The west bank is at present occupied by a small modern quarter, about and below the pontoon bridge which we crossed when we arrived. As early as Manṣûr's time a palace had been built on the east side of the river and the eastern city gradually eclipsed the western in importance. But it did not occupy the site of modern Baghdâd; it lay to the north of the present town and the sole relic of it is the shrine of Abu Ḥanîfah in the village of Mu'aẓẓam, which is now situated some distance to the north of Baghdâd. Finally the existing town grew up round the palaces of the later khalifs, and its walls and gates are the same as those which were seen and described by Ibn Jubeir in the twelfth century. It no longer fills the circuit of those walls; between them and the modern houses there are large empty spaces which were once occupied by streets and gardens. I drove out one windy morning to the village of Mu'aẓẓam and gazed respectfully from a house-top at the tiled dome which covers the tomb of the Imâm Abu Ḥanîfah. He was the founder of the earliest of the four orthodox sects of the Sunnis and he aided Manṣûr in the building of Baghdâd. Even in Ibn Jubeir's time the city had retreated from the shrine and he describes it as lying far outside the walls, as it does to-day. We then crossed the Tigris by an upper bridge of boats and visited the Kâẓimein. Here too a village has sprung up round the sanctuary which shelters the remains of the seventh and ninth Shî'ah Imâms.[1] The place is now purely a Shî'ah shrine, though its original sanctity was due to the fact that somewhere in this region stood the tomb of Ibn Ḥanbal, the founder of the last of the four orthodox Sunni sects. His tomb still existed when Ibn Baṭûṭaḥ visited Baghdâd in 1327, but it fell subsequently into ruin and has now disappeared. No infidel is permitted to enter a Shî'ah mosque, and it is well not to linger with too

[1] It is perhaps unnecessary to explain that the Shî'ahs regard 'Alî ibn abî Tâlib, who lies buried at Nejef, as the only lawful khalif. He and his eleven immediate heirs are known as the Twelve Imâms, the twelfth being Muḥammad III al Mahdî, who is credited with having been concealed in a cave at Sâmarrâ whence he will emerge at the end of days and re-establish the true faith.

great a show of interest at the gates, so as to avoid the ignominy, which you are helpless to avert, of being hustled out of the way by a fanatical crowd. I went therefore to a neighbouring building, the tomb of Sir Iḳbâl ed Dauleh, brother to the king of Oudh, and begged the wakîl to allow me to look upon the Kâẓimein from his roof. The wakîl, the guardian of Sir Iḳbâl's tomb, was a charming and cheerful mullah, dressed in long robes and a white turban. He turned a friendly eye upon me, partly out of the innate sociability of his character, and partly in view of the fact that I was a fellow subject of his departed master. Not only did he grant my request, but he presented me with a bunch of pomegranate flowers and entertained me with coffee and sherbet.

"Why," said he, "do you travel so far?"

I replied that I had a great curiosity to see the world and all that lay therein.

"You are right," he answered. "Man has but a short while to live, and to see everything is a natural desire. But few have time to accomplish it—what would you? we are but human." And he drew his robe round him and sipped contentedly at the sherbet, repeating as he did so his elegy on the race: "Insân! we are human."

With that he turned his attention to the things of this brief world and gave me his opinion of a high official of the empire. "He is mad," he declared, "majnûn."

"He is a man of books rather than of deeds," said I, for I knew the official in question and held him in respect.

"That is what I call majnûn," replied the mullah sharply.

When I had finished the sherbet I took my leave and went to the tomb of Sheikh Ma'rûf, who was a contemporary of Hârûn er Rashîd and by origin a Christian, but having professed Islâm he became noted as the ascetic of the age and the imâm of his time. He was one of the four saints who by their intercessions protected Baghdâd, however inadequately, from the approach of evil. The existing tomb, though it has frequently been repaired, probably covers the very site of the earliest shrine. It is surrounded by a large cemetery in which stands a building known as the tomb of the Sitt Zobeideh, the wife of Hârûn er Rashîd (Fig. 112). The attribution does not appear earlier than 1718 and is undoubtedly erroneous. The Princess Zobeideh was buried in the Kâẓimein, her tomb has long been destroyed and its exact site forgotten.[1] A very cursory inspection of the architecture is enough to prove that the building near the tomb of Ma'rûf cannot date from the ninth century.[2] It has been in great part reconstructed and contains nothing of architectural interest except the form of its cone-like roof, narrowing upwards by a series of superimposed alveolate niches or squinches (Fig. 113). I have never seen any roof of this kind which could be dated as early as the ninth century.

In the city on the east bank, the modern Baghdâd, by far the most interesting relic of the age of the khalifs is the line of the enclosing wall with its gates. The wall itself is largely destroyed, but its position is marked by a mound and a deep ditch; of the gates the two on the eastern side are the best preserved. One of these, the Bâb eṭ Ṭilism, is dated by a fine inscription of the Khalif Nâṣir in the year A.H. 618 (A.D. 1221) (Fig. 114). It is a splendid octagonal tower, but the door has been walled up ever since the Sultan Murâd IV, the Turkish conqueror of Baghdâd, rode through it in triumph in the year 1638. Round the top of this closed gateway runs a remarkable decoration consisting of a pair of dragons with the wreathed bodies of serpents (Fig. 115). They confront one another with open jaws above the summit of the pointed arch and between them sits cross-legged a small figure with a hand outstretched into each gaping mouth. The serpent motive is not unknown in the decoration of Islâm; it appears, as has been said, upon the gateway of the citadel of Aleppo, where the inscription in dated in the year 1209. I have seen it upon

[1] The whole argument is given by Le Strange, *Baghdâd,* p. 160 *et seq.*, and pp. 351–2.

[2] From its relation to similar buildings (for instance at Ḥadîthah on the Euphrates and at Dûr on the Tigris) in places which probably flourished until the time of the Mongol invasion, *i.e.* towards the end of the thirteenth century, I should, however, place the tomb of Sitt Zobeideh earlier than 1200.

FIG. 114.—BAGHDÂD, BÂB EṬ ṬILISM.

FIG. 115.—BAGHDÂD, DETAIL OF ORNAMENT, BÂB EṬ ṬILISM.

FIG. 116.—BAGHDÂD, MINARET IN SÛḲ EL GHAZL.

many a lintel of the churches in and near Môṣul, which are generally to be dated in the thirteenth century and owe their decorative motives entirely to the arts of Islâm. There the snakes are sometimes combined with the cross-legged figure, precisely as at Baghdâd, and frequently the figure appears seated between a pair of rampant lions. I am inclined to regard the whole snake-and-figure or lion-and-figure scheme as Inner Asiatic, possibly it is due to Chinese influence. The seated figure, as has been noticed by de Beylié,[1] bears a curious resemblance to the Buddha type, and at Môṣul the affinities with early Buddhist motives are even more strongly accentuated in the art of the thirteenth century. The second of the eastern gates, the Bâb el Wusṭânî, consists also of a domed octagonal chamber outside the wall, connected with the city by a low bridge, with walls on either hand, that leads across the moat. The dome, set on eight niches, is a fine piece of construction.

Within the town the traces of the Baghdâd that existed before the Mongol invasion are woefully scanty. There is a beautiful minaret in the Sûḳ el Ghazl (Fig. 116) which is dated by an inscription of the Khalif Mustanṣir in the year 1236,[2] and at the end of the lower pontoon bridge stand considerable remains of the Mustanṣirîyeh College, completed by the Khalif Mustanṣir in the year 1233 and now used as a custom house. A splendid inscription of Mustanṣir runs along the wall facing the river to the north of the bridge. Behind the wall there are parts of a court with ruined chambers round it, and to the south of the bridge I was conducted through another series of chambers which look as if they had belonged to a bath. The mastery of structural problems shown by the architects of Islâm in the thirteenth century is nothing short

[1] See de Beylié: *Prome et Samara*, p. 34.

[2] Mr. Le Strange gives good reasons for believing that Mustanṣir did not found the mosque to which this minaret belongs, but that it is no other than the Jâmi' el Ḳaṣr, built by the Khalif el Muktafî (A.D. 902) as a Friday Mosque adjoining the palace of his father Mu'taḍid. The palace was known as the Ḳaṣr et Tâj, the Palace of the Crown: *Baghdâd*, p. 269.

of amazing. Every trace of decoration has disappeared from the walls of these buildings, yet the admirable quality of the brick masonry and the feats performed in the vaulting make the half-ruined halls as beautiful as a palace. The octagonal rooms are covered by very shallow brick domes set over the angle on squinch arches of patterned brick.[1] Square chambers are invariably roofed with four-sided domes, and over long rectangular halls the four-sided dome again appears, the two extremities being parted by a span of absolutely flat brick roof which depends for its solidity upon the excellence of the mortar.[2] Not far from the custom house is a twelfth-century khân, Khân Orthma,[3] and in the Khâṣakî Jâmi' there is a very beautiful miḥrâb cut out of a single block of stone.[4] Beyond these there was but one other place which I desired to see. I had read[5] that there existed in the arsenal some fragments of one of the palaces of the khalifs, beautifully decorated with stucco, and accordingly I set out in all innocence to visit them. The arsenal lies at the extreme north end of the bazaar, not far from the northern gate, and to reach it I passed by the khân where my servants and horses had found a lodging. Fattûḥ and Jûsef were standing at the entrance and they gave me a cordial greeting.

"Please God," said Fattûḥ, "your Excellency has seen the cannon which is chained to the ground?"

I confessed that I did not know where it was to be found.

"But it is here in the Maidân, close at hand," exclaimed Fattûḥ, and hurried out to conduct me to the spot. There it

[1] These are exactly copied in the domes over the carrefours in the bazaars, which are certainly much later in date.

[2] I have been able to give an illustration of this system from Khân Khernîna; the chambers at Baghdâd were so dark that photography was almost impossible.

[3] Some admirable photographs of it are given by De Beylié, *op. cit.*, p. 33 *et seq.*

[4] A good photograph has been given by Viollet: *Le Palais de Al-Moutasim, Mémoires présentés à l'Acad. des Inscrip. et Belles-Lettres*, Vol. XII. Part II. Viollet believes it to have come from a church. See too Herzfeld: "Die Genesis der islamischen Kunst," in *Der Islâm*, Vol. I. Part I.

[5] De Beylié, *op. cit.*, p. 30. He gives several illustrations.

was, sure enough, a rusty piece of artillery and an ancient, chained to the ground under a big tree. Fattûḥ gazed upon it with an interest that was not unmixed with contempt.

"In Aleppo," said he, "we do not chain our cannon."

At the arsenal I was received by a polite officer to whom I explained my errand. He asked me whether I had brought with me a letter from the English Resident, and I replied that I had not, but that I could easily obtain one.

"Good," said he. "If you will return to-morrow with the letter you shall see all that you will."

On the following day I returned, letter in hand. I gave it to a sentry and desired him to convey it to the Commandant, to whom it was addressed. After a due interval an officer descended the stairs below which I was sitting; he regretted, said he, that I could not be shown the palace of the khalifs, it must be for another day. Upon this the hasty European blood, which no amount of sojourning in the East can bring to subjection, rose in revolt, and brushing aside (I blush to relate it) the officer and the sentry, I sprang up the stairs, drew back a heavy leather curtain and burst unannounced into a room filled with distinguished military men. They were, I suppose, the Mesopotamian equivalent for an army council, and if I am not mistaken they were composing themselves to slumber—the hour was the somnolent hour of noon and the day was hot. But my advent galvanized them into wakefulness. They listened with the greatest courtesy to my tale, and when I had finished, one who sat behind a green baize table pronounced judgment.

"The letter," said he, "is addressed to the Commandant and may be opened by none but he."

"Effendim," said I, "could it not be given to the Commandant?"

"Effendim," he replied, "the Commandant Pasha is in his house, asleep, but if you wish I will send the letter."

I thanked him and begged him to do so, saying that I would go with it.

The Commandant's house was a stone's throw from the arsenal. I was greeted by a smiling major-domo who said that the Commandant should be informed of my arrival, and meantime would I please to look at the lions upon the roof. I agreed to this suggestion—as who would not?—and together we climbed up to the housetop, where a pair of Mesopotamian lions, thin, poor beasts, and ill-conditioned, were confined in an exiguous cage. And they too were spending the midday hour in the approved fashion. After we had succeeded in rousing them, I was conducted into the Commandant's reception-room, where the Commandant in full uniform awaited me. We exchanged salutations and sat down.

"Effendim," said the Commandant, "I trust you were satisfied with the lions."

I expressed complete satisfaction, mingled with astonishment at finding them upon his roof.

"They are now rare," said the Commandant. "I had them captured in the swamps near Amârah while they were yet young."

"Effendim," said I, "I have seen them pictured upon the ancient stones of the Assyrians."

"Indeed!" he replied. "They were no doubt more plentiful in the days of the Assyrians." At this point coffee was handed to us, and I ventured to put forward my request.

"Effendim," I said, "I would now gaze upon the rooms of the khalifs in the arsenal, if your Excellency permit."

The Commandant took a moment for reflection and then gave me his answer. It was in three parts. He said, firstly, that those rooms were much ruined and not worth seeing, secondly, that they were full of military stores, and thirdly, that they did not exist. I recognized at once that I had lost the game, and having thanked the Commandant for his kindness, I bade him farewell. So it came about that I never set eyes on what remains of the palace of the khalifs, but I did not realize till afterwards that the clue to the whole situation had been the military stores, the most jealously guarded of all the treasures of the Turkish empire. And upon reflection my sympathies are with the Commandant, the lions and the military council.

Besides the great shrines at the Kâẓimein and Mu'aẓẓam,

there is a much-frequented place of pilgrimage which lies within the area of the modern city. It is the mosque and tomb of 'Abdu'l Ḳâdir, the founder of the Ḳâdirîyeh sect of dervishes, a widespread order which has many votaries in India. 'Abdu'l Ḳâdir died in Baghdâd in 1253; his tomb was erected a few years before the Mongol invasion, and is therefore one of the last of the buildings that fell within the days of the Abbâsid Khalifate. Connected with the mosque is a large tekîyeh, a house for the lodging of pilgrims, richly endowed and visited by the pious from all parts of the world. The ordering of this establishment, the distribution of its funds and the cares of its maintenance rest upon the descendants of 'Abdu'l Ḳâdir. The head of the family, who is known by the name of the Naḳîb, a title of honour applied to the chief of a tribe, is an important person in Baghdâd, lord of great possessions and still greater sanctity—important, too, to us, since his tekîyeh is the resort of many subjects of our empire. As I was strolling through the streets I happened to pass by the gateway of his house opposite to the tekîyeh. The Residency ḳawwâs, who was my guide (and very efficient he proved himself), stopped short and said, "Does not your Excellency wish to visit the Naḳîb?" Before I could answer he had addressed himself to the gatekeeper and informed him that a beg who was staying with the Resident stood at the door, and in another moment I was ushered into the garden and into the presence of its master. The Naḳîb was taking the air under his orange-trees. He received me with cordiality and appeared to regard the introduction of the ḳawwâs as a sufficient basis for acquaintance. After compliments had passed between us, he gathered his cloak round him, mounted the stairs and led me into a cool upper chamber furnished with a divan. "Bismillah!" said he as we sat down upon the cushions, "in the name of God." Conversation came easily to the Naḳîb, and the two hours which I spent with him passed lightly away. Hearing that I was interested in antiquities he gave me a short sketch of the history of the world, beginning with the days of Hammurabi and ending with our own times, during the course of which he proved that all human culture had originated in Asia. He then turned to a review of the English rule in Egypt, and I pricked up my ears, for it is not often that a high dignitary of Islâm will give his impartial opinion on such subjects. He had nothing but good to say of our administration, and he deplored the unpopularity into which it had fallen. According to him this unpopularity dated from the Denshâwî incident. He detailed the events that had taken place at Denshâwî in the version under which they have become known to Asia, a version irreconcilable with the facts, though it was repeated by the Naḳîb in all good faith and with implicit confidence. He said that the whole Mohammadan world had been outraged by the story and had learnt from it to distrust the character of the English. "When you conquered India you won it by love and gentleness" (oh shade of Clive and Warren Hastings!), "thus showing how excellent was your civilization; but when we heard that at Denshâwî you had shot down women and children, we knew that you had fallen from your lofty place." I did not attempt to answer these charges; it would have been useless, for the Naḳîb would not have believed me—and had not some of my country-people brought similar accusations against their own officers?—but I would point here a simple moral. It is that Islâm is like a great sounding board stretched across Asia. Every voice goes up to it and reverberates back; every judgment pronounced in anger, every misrepresentation, comes down from it magnified a thousandfold. At the end of the interview the Naḳîb sent one of his servants with me to show me the tekîyeh. It is a very remarkable sight. Thousands of pilgrims can be lodged in the two-storeyed rooms which surround the broad courts, and men of every nationality were washing at the fountain and strolling under the arcades. Such foundations as these are the meeting places of Islâm; here news is circulated from lip to lip, here opinions are formed, here the Mohammadan faith realizes its unity.

The day before I left Baghdâd was Easter Sunday, Yaum el Âzirah as it is popularly called, the Day of the Silk

Mantles, on account of the gorgeous garments worn by the Christian women. They walked through the streets dressed in cloaks of every soft and brilliant hue, woven in exquisitely contrasting colours. The Greek Catholic church, where I went to Mass, looked like a garden of tulips, but one of the priests, an Austrian by nationality, whom I met as I came away, deplored the scene and said that his congregation thought of nothing but clothes and adornments. The Catholic community is increasing, so he told me; when he came to Baghdâd eleven years ago it numbered but 4,000, and now he reckoned it at 10,000. He proposed that I should see the school, which was close at hand, and accompanied me thither to introduce me to one of his colleagues, a French father. It was an exalted moment at the school; the black-eyed children were sitting in rows upon the floor and eating their Sunday breakfast. Usually this breakfast consists of the simplest fare, but on the Day of the Silk Mantles there are bowls of steaming hot crushed grain and succulent chunks of meat, a feast to satisfy the children of kings.

With this I returned to the roses and green lawns of the Residency garden, to dream of brightly-robed women and far-travelled pilgrims, of the clash and contest of creeds, and of truth, which lies somewhere concealed behind them all.

CHAPTER VI

BAGHDÂD TO MÔṢUL

April 12—April 28

WE left Baghdâd on the wings of a strong south wind. My kind host mounted and rode with me for the first half-hour, and we parted in a dust-storm at the upper bridge. When he was gone, I joined my servants, who welcomed me with solicitous inquiries as to how I had passed my time in the city of Baghdâd. I replied that I had passed every moment enjoyably, and that I trusted that they had been equally well pleased. Fattûḥ hastened to satisfy me on this head. His friends had vied with one another in providing entertainments, and he and the muleteers had been plunged into a vortex of luncheon and dinner parties.

"And last night," concluded Fattûḥ, "we supped at the Kâẓimein."

"You had far to go," said I. "How did you get back in the darkness?"

"Effendim," began Fattûḥ—but I cannot remember his exact words, for they were at once absorbed into the recollection of a more famous utterance; the upshot of his explanation was, that the rule laid down by Mr. Jorrocks is observed in Baghdâd, with one exception. Where you dines you sleeps, but you do not have breakfast; you rise at 4 a.m. and hurry home, since it would be an infringement of the social law to appear to expect that your host should provide the morning meal.

We were riding by a narrow path along the top of the ṣidd, the steep embankment of the Tigris, and as we went, the wind grew more and more violent and the difficulty of preserving a foothold on that knife-edge of a road greater and greater. The loaded pack animals were ever struggling away from an imminent brink, towards which the following wind buffeted them, first on one side and then on the other, according to the windings of the path. During the course of the day one of the horses, unwarily presenting a full flank to the blast, was swept off its feet and rolled into a cornfield, but by good luck this accident occurred after we had descended from the ṣidd on to level ground. The dust was so intolerable that we welcomed the heavy raindrops which presently came driving down upon the storm; but they could not pacify the unruly earth, and dust and rain together formed an atmospheric mud ocean, churned by the wind into whirlpools and breakers. Never have I ridden through such a hurricane. Six hours from the bridge we reached the khân of Musheidah [1] where we had intended to pitch camp. No tent ropes would have held for half-an-hour in that wind, if it had been possible to unfurl the tents, which it was not, and we rode into the khân to seek a lodging. But the khân provided only for the needs of pack animals and contained not a single room for their masters. Fattûḥ looked gloomily down the long vaults of the stables into which the rain was beginning to penetrate, and still more gloomily he returned to the gate and eyed the maddened universe. There was one small edifice besides the khân; the khânjî, being interrogated, informed us that it was the barracks, whereupon Fattûḥ strode resolutely out into the rain and beat upon the door. We waited some time for an answer; the howling blast, which could not keep the soldiers awake, prevented us from rousing them. At length one stumbled to the door and led us into a muddy courtyard, unpromising in appearance. The barracks (perhaps it should only be dignified with the name of guardhouse) consisted of a small stable with two rooms above it. Without any hesitation, Fattûḥ took possession of one of these last, piled into a corner the hay with which it was half filled, swept it out, and garnished it with my camp furniture. Meantime the soldiers busied themselves with coffee making, and I, being warm and dry and well fed, mocked at the storm that battered against

[1] Kiepert calls it Khân eṭ Ṭarniyeh.

the mud walls, and spent the evening with the books which had served as guides down the Euphrates.

It was not to those red-bound volumes which we are accustomed to associate with travel that I turned, but to the best of all guide-books to Mesopotamia, the Anabasis and Ammianus Marcellinus. In a moment I was back in the ranks of the Ten Thousand and of the Roman Legions, but what a change had come over them since we parted from them at 'Ânah! Cyrus had fallen in the disastrous confusion of Cunaxa, which, but for his fatal wound, might have crowned his campaign with victory. Julian, misled by omens, had turned away from Ctesiphon, where Sapor awaited him in terror; he had thrown his army across the Tigris and had met with his end on the further side, venerating the everlasting God that he should die with honour fairly earned in the midst of a career of glory. And by a "blind decision of fortune," as Ammianus Marcellinus relates, the timid Jovian had been elected to his place. The Roman army continued its retreat along the east bank, and I did not fall into the line of its march until I crossed the Tigris, but Xenophon and the Ten Thousand passed close to Musheidah and came down to the river at Sitace, where they found a bridge of boats. There they crossed and marched four days up the river to Opis.[1]

[1] Sitace cannot be placed with certainty. Ritter (Vol. X. p. 21) conjectures that the bridge must have lain about four hours above Baghdâd. After the battle of Cunaxa, a field of which the site is not determined, the Greeks pursued the Persians to a village on a mound where they passed the night. Here they learnt that Cyrus was dead. Next day they joined Ariæus and marched in one day to some unnamed Babylonian villages. They then marched through fertile country for a space of time not specified, probably a day, to well-supplied villages, where they stayed twenty-three days. In three days from these villages they reached the Median Wall, under the guidance of Tissaphernes, who must have led them by a tortuous course across Mesopotamia, and in two days more they came to Sitace, which was a populous city lying on an island formed by the Tigris and a canal. Sitace is perhaps Pliny's Sittace (Bk. VI. ch. xxxi.), though his confused statement would seem to place it on the left bank of the Tigris. Ptolemy mentions a place called Scaphe, which Müller is inclined to connect with the Sablis of the Tab. Peut., but it appears to have been some distance to the east of the Tigris (*Ptolemy*, ed. Müller, p. 1006). The placing of Sitace depends upon the position of Opis, which is not satisfactorily determined.

The topography of this country is difficult to grasp. The Tigris changed its course during the Middle Ages and now runs considerably to the east of its former channel. Besides the old bed of the river, there is also the cutting of a great canal, the Dujeil of the era of the khalifs, which has long been devoid of water except in its upper reaches.[1] Each of these dry channels is set thickly with the ruins of towns and villages belonging to Mohammadan as well as to earlier times. The northern reaches of the Dujeil still bring water from the Tigris, and here villages and cultivation continue to exist; but the canal is much smaller than it was originally, and it no longer rejoins the Tigris at the lower end of its course.

The soldiers of Musheidah, though they were unexceptionable as hosts, were inefficient as guides. When I announced that I wished to ride by the old Tigris bed they exclaimed in horror that it was unsafe to leave the high road. At this Fattûḥ laughed outright, and remarking that we had travelled over many a worse desert, laid hands upon a peasant who happened to be listening to the discussion, and engaged him to accompany me for the day. The peasant (his name was Ḳâsim) was an Arab of the Benî 'Amr, and he was full of the recent history of the land. All this district had been granted by the Sultan Murâd to the Ma'amreh, the Benî 'Amr, to have and to hold in perpetuity, "and we possess his 'Irâdeh signed by his hand," said Ḳâsim. But about twenty years ago, 'Abdu'l Ḥamîd, seeing it to be valuable property, ousted the Arabs, sold half the land to a man of Baghdâd and turned the other half into Senîyeh (royal estates).[2] The Benî 'Amr were thus left destitute, "and by God who created the heavens and the earth," declared Ḳâsim, "I have nothing

[1] There was an earlier Dujeil which started from the Euphrates a little below Hît, crossed Mesopotamia and joined the Tigris above Baghdâd, but by the tenth century its eastern end had silted up. The later Dujeil was a loop canal from the Tigris; it left the river opposite Ḳâdisîyah and rejoined it at 'Ukbarâ. These complicated questions may easily be understood by referring to the first map in Mr. Le Strange's *Baghdâd*.

[2] The term is the equivalent of the northern Chiflik. The latter is a Turkish word signifying merely farm, but it designates especially a farm belonging to the Sultan.

but the mercy of God." When the constitution was granted and it was made known that the Senîyeh would be handed over to the State, the men of the Benî 'Amr, like many others who had suffered in a like manner, began to speculate as to whether their rights would meet with acknowledgment, but how the matter has been settled I do not know. We rode from Musheidah to a number of ruined sites lying somewhat to the west of the present Tigris channel, and I could see, still further to the west, the line of mounds which mark the lower course of the Dujeil, now waterless; Ḳâsim gave me their names as Sagr, Tâṣir, Bisheh and Baghût. In an hour and a half we came to a series of big mounds called Mdawwî, which lie upon the banks of the old Tigris bed. In time of flood the river overflows the land as far west as Mdawwî. From here we crossed a plain, all of which must have been inhabited, for it was scattered with mounds and covered with fragments of Mohammadan coloured pottery, blue and green, yellow and purple, and in three-quarters of an hour we reached Tell Bshairah, where there were quantities of potsherds and bits of burnt brick. The land round it is watered in flood time by canals from the Tigris, and at that time sown with summer crops. The mounds of 'Ukbarâ [1] lie an hour further to the north. A little to the west of these mounds is a small ruin known as Kahf 'Alî consisting of two chambers of baked brick, one of which had been covered by a dome set on squinch arches. I suppose that it was a shrine or tomb of the late Abbâsid period. Thence we rode up the dry

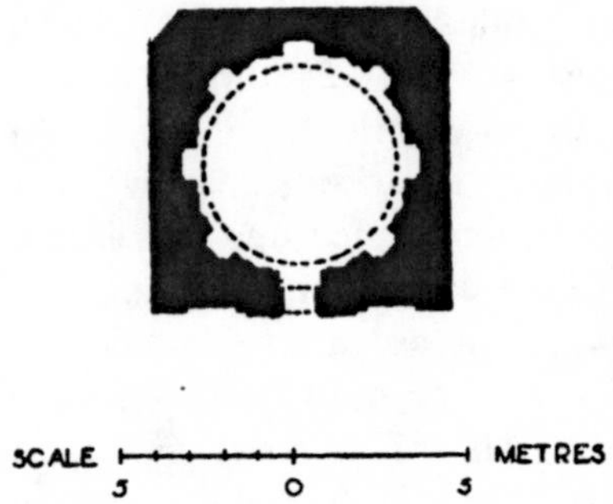

FIG. 117.—WÂNEH, IMÂM MUḤAMMAD 'ALÎ.

[1] 'Ukbarâ was a well-known place in the days of the Khalifate. Muḳaddasî (ed. de Goeje, p. 122.) It lay on the east bank of the Tigris, *i.e.* on the east bank of the old channel. Le Strange, *Lands of the Eastern Caliphate*, p. 50.

FIG. 118.—WÂNEH, IMÂM MUḤAMMAD 'ALÎ.

FIG. 119.—ḲÂDISÎYAH FROM SOUTH-EAST.

FIG. 120.—SÂMARRÂ, RUINED MOSQUE FROM SOUTH.

FIG. 121.—SÂMARRÂ, FROM MALWÎYEH.

FIG. 122.—SÂMARRÂ, RUINED MOSQUE, INTERIOR OF SOUTH WALL.

bed of the old Tigris to the tomb of the Imâm Muḥammad 'Alî lying among mounds that mark the site of the village of Wâneh (Fig. 117). The tomb is built of fine burnt bricks measuring 20 × 20 × 6 c., pale in colour, nearing to yellow, like the bricks I had previously seen scattered over the mounds. It is a square-domed building, but the dome rests on an interior octagon and is set at each of the eight angles on a shallow pointed squinch arch (Fig. 118). Pointed arched niches occupy seven of the sides; in the eighth is the door. There is a system of niching on the facade which has been considerably destroyed by the addition of a rude porch of sun-dried brick. The mazâr is a typical example of the small Mohammadan memorial shrine, and from the excellence of its workmanship and the character of the brick I should place it within the Abbâsid age.[1] From Wâneh we rode in an hour to Sumeikhah, where we found our tents pitched in a charming palm garden. Sumeikhah is a modern village lying on the Dujeil at a point where a little water still flows down the canal from the Tigris, enough to satisfy the inhabitants and keep their palm gardens in a flourishing condition. Like all Senîyeh villages it has a prosperous appearance. The peasants are well to do, having been exempted under the old régime from the greater part of the ordinary taxes and from military service. With the memory of the previous night of storm freshly in our minds we felt that we had reached an agreeable haven. The temperature had fallen by an average of ten degrees after the rain; the palm garden was a delicious

[1] Kiepert marks Wâneh to the south of 'Ukbarâ, whereas I should place it a little to the north. We rode to Sumeikhah in about an hour from the Imâm Muhammad 'Alî, which would have been impossible from Kiepert's Wâneh, or for that matter from his 'Ukbarâ. I am relying, however, for the names upon the not too certain testimony of Ḳâsim. Both 'Ukbarâ and Wâneh are mentioned by Muḳaddasî, but he gives no indication of their relative position. He provides us with no more information about Wâneh than its name (ed. de Goeje, pp. 54 and 115), which he spells Aiwanâ. The customary mediæval spelling is Awânâ, and other authorities place the town on the west bank of the old Tigris bed, while 'Ukbarâ lay opposite to it on the east bank (Streck: *Die alte Landschaft Babylonien*, p. 227). This would correspond fairly well with my itinerary. I rode from 'Ukbarâ in a north-westerly direction and reached Wâneh in forty-five minutes.

camping-ground, which we shared in all amity with a family of storks who had built their nest on the angle of the enclosing wall. And we knew as little as they of the counter-revolution which had overwhelmed Constantinople that very day.

Next morning I left my caravan to follow the straight road and turned again to the east. In an hour we reached Tell Hir, where there had been a considerable town on the old Tigris; thirty-five minutes further there was a similar mound, Tell Ghazab, and in thirty-five minutes more we came to Tell Manjûr. From Tell Manjûr to Tell edh Dhahab, three-quarters of an hour to the north, a large area, stretching down to the Tigris, is completely covered with mounds and strewn with pottery. The pottery is not coloured or glazed, but ornamented with roughly scratched patterns and narrow raised bands, a Mohammadan ware with which I was to become very familiar at Sâmarrâ. The whole site must therefore have been inhabited in the Mohammadan period, but in all probability it was occupied by a city of earlier fame. On the east bank of the Tigris, above the point where it is joined by the river 'Aḍêm, and therefore exactly opposite the mounds which I saw on the west bank, Ross discovered a great stretch of ruins and believed them to be the ruins of Opis.[1] The Tigris, when it changed its course, must have cut through the area of Opis, so that one half of its mounds now lie to the east of the river and one half to the west. Opis is mentioned by Xenophon [2] and by Herodotus.[3] It was the most important city of Babylonia after Babylon. Alexander's ships touched there on their voyage up the Tigris, and Strabo observes that the river was navigable up to that point.[4] But in Strabo's time it was no more than a village, and Pliny does not mention it, unless his Apamea is a later name for Opis.[5]

[1] *Journal of the Geog. Soc.*, Vol. XI. p. 124.

[2] *Anabasis*, Bk. II. ch. iv. 25.

[3] Bk. I. 189.

[4] Bk. XVI. ch. i. 9.

[5] Bk. VI. ch. xxxi. Though I believe that the ruins on the east bank seen by Ross and the extensive ruin field on what is now the west bank of the Tigris must represent Opis, the locating of the city is complicated by the fact that Xenophon took four days to reach Opis from Sitace.

The mounds and pottery continued uninterruptedly almost up to the Mazâr of Sayyid Muḥammad, which we reached in an hour from Tell edh Dhahab. The mazâr is a mosque with a fine great dome decorated with coloured tiles; and near the mosque is a large khân. I do not know whether there was an older shrine here; the present mosque is dated by an inscription: A.H. 1310, *i.e.* A.D. 1893. An hour from the mazâr we came to Balad, a large village on the Dujeil. It existed in the thirteenth century for it is mentioned by Yâḳût, but it can scarcely have been more flourishing then than it is now, with its walled gardens filled with fruit-trees, its well-laid roads and well-bridged irrigation canals. There was no need to ask who was landlord here, so clearly did the place bear the stamp of the Senîyeh estates, nor is it necessary to point out that if the irrigation system were restored to its old perfection, the country from Baghdâd to Balad might again be as thickly populated as it was in the Abbâsid age.[1]

We rode down to the Tigris ferry in two and a half hours, and the way was beguiled by the conversation of an Arab of the Mujamma', who happened to be going in our direction. He gave us the news of the desert, telling us of Kurdish raids on the east bank of the river (commonly called the Khawîjeh) and of jealousies between the 'Anazeh and the Shammar on the west bank, the Jezîreh. We breathed a familiar air, even though the Kurds were a new element in

---

Now if Sitace is anywhere near Baghdâd it is strange that the Greeks should have marched four days and got no further than a town situated immediately to the north of the 'Aḍêm. The Physcus, which Xenophon crossed by a bridge of boats before coming to Opis, may be the 'Aḍêm, but some have supposed it to be the great Ḳâṭûl-Nahrawân, a loop canal on the east bank of the Tigris. I do not know, however, that there is any record of a canal here before the Sassanian period (Le Strange: *Lands of the Eastern Caliphate*, p. 57). Chesney tried to solve the difficulty of Xenophon's march by placing Opis higher up the river at Ḳadsîyeh, but that would leave the great ruin field lower down unidentified, and would, besides, leave too long a time for the march from Opis to the Great Zâb, which occupied the Greeks eleven days. For the site of the Babylonian Opis, see King: *Sumer and Akkad*, p. 11.

[1] It is probably one of the districts which were ruined by the Mongol invasion.

desert politics. The Arab did not hold these episodes to be of great account, in spite of the fact that the Kurds had completely blocked the post-road from Baghdâd to Kerkûk; "Ghazû mazû!" he said, using an expressive Turkish locution, "raids maids."[1] We found the caravan in the act of crossing at the ferry. I sat down upon the bank to wait for the return of the ferry-boat and fell into talk with the owner of a pair of performing monkeys.

"Where are you going?" I asked, after I had fed the monkeys.

"Ila'l wilâyah," he replied vaguely, "to the capital," and I gathered that he was making his way to Môṣul. But he thought better of it when he got to the other side of the river, and for that night he interrupted his journey that he might enjoy our company. He was wise, since he and the monkeys were invited to share our supper, but I fear it was not the man who moved me to hospitality. As we crossed the Tigris the ferrymen composed and sang a piece at my intent. It was of a purely utilitarian character and ran thus—

Jenâh es Serkâr: Ḥôsh, ḥôsh!
Fi khidmat: Ḥôsh, ḥôsh!
Bakhshîsh: Ḥôsh, ḥôsh!

Her Excellency the Governor: draw together!
In her service: draw together:
A gratuity: draw together!

There were many more verses, but the gist of all was the same. From our camp by the water's edge we could see the famous spiral minaret of Sâmarrâ, the Malwîyeh, and watch the keleks going down from Diyârbekr to Baghdâd. Now a kelek is a raft made of logs or brushwood laid over inflated skins, and it carries all the merchandise of the Tigris.

We were lying within the dry cutting of a canal dug by Hârûn er Rashîd, and now called the Nahr el Ḳâim. It is connected with the Tigris by several cross-cuttings, over one

[1] *i.e.* "raids and so forth"; the second word is merely a repetition of the first with the initial letter *r* changed to *m*. This convenient form is very common in Turkish.

of which we passed a quarter of an hour from the camping-ground, and found upon the further side the ruins of Ḳâdisîyah[1] (Fig. 119). They are nothing but a crumbling wall of sun-dried brick enclosing an octagonal area, but whether this space was ever covered with buildings it is difficult to determine[2]; I noticed, however, that the surface of the ground was piled into low mounds such as are left by the decay of sun-dried bricks. The octagon is far from regular. I paced the eight sides of the enclosing walls and found them to vary considerably from interior angle to interior angle, the smallest side being 565 paces, the largest 725 paces. Each angle is provided with an exterior round bastion, and at intervals of from twenty-eight to twenty-nine paces smaller round bastions project from the face of the wall. Six of the sides are broken by three gates apiece, one by four gates and one by two. The double-gated wall is the northern side of the octagon, and in the middle part of its length, between the two gates, there is a series of ten small vaulted chambers (3.55 m. wide by 3.65 m. deep) set against the interior face of the wall. The barrel vault of some of these chambers is still fairly well preserved. It is built of sun-dried brick laid in slices against the head wall on the Mesopotamian system, by which centering was avoided. Round the interior of the octagon, at a distance of thirteen paces from the wall, runs a shallow ditch, ten metres wide, having on its inner side a low mound which occupies a space about seventeen metres wide. The mound is no doubt the remains of a wall. Opposite each of the

[1] This Ḳâdisîyah must not be confounded with the battlefield near Ḥirah where Khâlid ibn u'l Walîd overthrew the Sassanians.

[2] Sarre thinks it was empty, and holds that the town was never finished or inhabited. He would therefore place here Ḳâṭûl, the site first fixed upon for his capital by the Khalif Mu'taṣim when he left Baghdâd. Finding Sâmarrâ to be better placed, he abandoned Ḳâṭûl before the work there was completed: *Ya'ḳûbî*, ed. de Goeje, p. 256. Sarre: *Reise in Mesop. Zeitsch. der Gesell. fur Erdkunde zu Berlin*, 1909, No. 7, p. 437. Schwartz, however, suggests that Ḳâṭûl may have lain to the north of Sâmarrâ: *Die Abbâsiden-Residenz Sâmarrâ*, p. 5. Ross thought that Ḳâdisîyah was Sassanian, but I am persuaded that he was in error. (A Journey from Baghdâd to Opis, *Journal of the Geog. Soc.*, Vol. XI. p. 127.) Jones gives a plan: *Memoirs*, p. 8.

doorways in the outer wall, a causeway has been laid across the ditch. A wall and ditch upon the inner side of a strong fortification such as the enclosing wall of Ḳâdisîyah are singular features. They can scarcely have been intended for defence, indeed I am not certain that they extend round the whole enclosure. The ditch may have been a canal bringing water to the palace or fortress.

We rode out of one of the western gates of Ḳâdisîyah and in a little over an hour reached the enigmatic tower of Ḳâim. It stands in the angle formed by the Tigris and the channel of the Nahr el Ḳâim, which has silted up so that no water runs down it from the river. The tower is a truncated cone composed of pebbles and concrete; there is no chamber inside it and no means of climbing to the top of it. It looks as if it had received some sort of facing, and in that case the existing cone is only the core of the tower, but whether it was intended merely to mark the opening of the canal, or whether it is, as Ross supposed, a relic of remoter antiquity, it would be impossible to determine, though I incline to the view that it is ancient. Having crossed the Nahr el Ḳâim, we found ourselves almost immediately among vestiges of the immense city of Sâmarrâ, of which the bazaars and palaces stretched uninterruptedly along the east bank of the Tigris for a distance of twenty-one miles. This city, which was during the brief time of its magnificence the capital of the Abbâsid empire, sprang into existence at the bidding of the Khalif Mu'taṣim and was inhabited by seven of his successors, who added market to market, palace to palace and pleasure-ground to pleasure-ground. After a period of forty years (836–876 A.D.) the Khalif Mu'tamid removed the seat of his government back to Baghdâd; with his departure the walls of Sâmarrâ crumbled back into the desert from which they had arisen, and like the rose-scented clay of Sa'dî's apologue when the fragrance had vanished, became once more the dust they had been. A glory so dazzling, so abrupt a decline, can scarcely be paralleled on any other page of history. Encompassed by a league-long expanse where the surface of the waste is tumbled into confused masses of mounds or marked off by the vast rectangular enclosures of palace and garden, stands the modern town of Sâmarrâ, no better than a walled village, except that above its mean roofs hang the incomparable domes of the Shî'ah sanctuary, one a-glitter with gold, the other jewelled with precious tiles. And behind the town the huge Malwîyeh, the spiral tower of Mutawakkil's mosque, lifts its head high over the wilderness.[1]

Mu'taṣim's choice of Sâmarrâ as the site of his new capital when Baghdâd had become distasteful to him was, according to the Arab historians, determined by the purest hazard. Ya'ḳûbî, writing at the close of the ninth century when Sâmarrâ had recently been abandoned, relates that Mu'taṣim fixed first upon Ḳâṭûl, a point lower down the river, but that the site did not prove satisfactory.[2] And upon a certain day he rode out to the chase; "and he continued upon his way until he came to a place called Surra man raa" (who sees it rejoices), "which is a desert of the Tîrhân district; there were no buildings in it, and no inhabitants, except a Christian monastery. And he stopped at the monastery and spoke with those who were in it, and said: 'What is the name of this place?' And one of the monks said: 'We find in our ancient books that this place is called Surra man raa, and that it was a city of Shem son of Noah.'" Mu'taṣim accepted the good omen, together with other prophetic matter

[1] The Malwîyeh can scarcely be any other than the minaret described by Balâdhurî among Mutawakkil's buildings: *Futûḥ ul Buldân*, p. 306, Cairo edition of 1901. The ruins of Sâmarrâ have not yet received the detailed study which they deserve, but Professor Sarre and Dr. Herzfeld are about to begin an exhaustive examination of the site. Sketch plans have been published by De Beylié (*Prome et Samarra*), and at about the same time Herzfeld brought out a small monograph entitled Sâmarrâ. I had this monograph with me, and finding the plans to be incorrect and the drawings inexact (for example, the ornament drawn in fig. 5 gives little idea of the original), I measured and photographed all the ruins over again. Meantime Viollet has published a short account of his journey in Mesopotamia, in which he has given plans of the ruins of Sâmarrâ: *Le Palais de Al Moutasim, etc. Mémoires of the Acad. des Inscrip. et Belles-Lettres*, Vol. XII. Part II. His attempt to reconstruct the ground plan of the palace of which the Beit el Khalîfah forms part, is of great interest.

[2] Ed. de Goeje, p. 256.

related by the monks, and chose the place for his capital. The etymology was, however, as fortuitous as was the khalif's selection; the name Sâmarrâ has in reality nothing to do with the Arabic phrase. A town had existed on the Tigris bank long before Arabic was spoken there; it was called in Aramaean Sâmarrâ, and Ammianus Marcellinus alludes to it as Sumere.[1]

Half-way between Ḳâim and the modern Sâmarrâ we came to the first of the palace enclosures, a large oblong space surrounded by a ruined wall of sun-dried bricks set with round bastions. The remains of a gateway decorated with niches led into another enclosure similar to the first, and both stretched down to the river-bank. From this point the surface of the ground is seamed with ruin mounds, and just before we reached Sâmarrâ (about an hour from Ḳâim) we passed another clearly-marked enclosure by the river. My camp had gone on while I was examining Ḳadsîyeh, and Fattûḥ had pitched the tents on the brink of the high bank that overhangs the Tigris. When I saw it I rejoiced, like Mu'tasim, for the position could not have been bettered; and moreover the modern town of Sâmarrâ stands somewhat back from the river, so that we did not molest its Shî'ah inhabitants, neither did they disturb us.

There is only one way of appreciating the extent of the Abbâsid city, and that way lies up the spiral path of the Malwîyeh tower (Fig. 121). It is seldom that the desert offers so wide an expanse to the eye, since nowhere else is the gazer mounted upon a lofty steeple in its very midst. Below the minaret lies the enclosure of the great mosque, a massive brick wall with round bastions; but the colonnades that protected the worshippers from sun and rain have all vanished and are indicated only by even trenches, marking the place from which the columns or piers have been removed. In the central court, surrounded by the colonnades, lies the shadowy outline of a fountain, and beyond the walls a long low mound shows that the precincts must have been bounded by an outer enclosure.[2]

[1] *Lands of the Eastern Califate*, p. 53. Am. Mar., Bk. XXV. ch. vi. 4.
[2] This is marked in Viollet's plan.

South of the mosque, in open hummocky ground, the little town of Sâmarrâ with its glittering domes is set down like a child's toy upon the waste—a toy half broken and thrown away. All round it the uneasy desert has rolled in over the city of the khalifs, covering but not obliterating the streets and courts, of which the walls are dimly apparent, as though they struggled through a veil of silted sand. To the north are the shattered walls and bastions of a great rectangular enclosure, Madaḳḳ eṭ Ṭabl the Arabs call it (the Place of the Beating of Drums), and about it the parallel streets of the city are drawn upon the surface of the earth, ruled out by the pencil of a giant artist. Still further north the three halls of the palace of the khalifs stand amid an immense area of shapeless mounds, and far away a second spiral tower, the minaret of Abu Dulâf, lifts its head out of the plain. The waters of the Tigris bring no colour to the vast landscape; the dead and silent world is like a battlefield, wherein men fought out the secular contest with the wilderness, and lost, and left it empty of all but ruins.

I came down from the tower and set to work upon the mosque.

To measure a wall would not seem to be a complicated business, yet I do not care to remember how many hours I spent upon the mosque. Its great size is no advantage when seen over the edge of a metre tape, and the action of the wind upon its masonry has been fatal to accuracy. The face of the brick is destroyed higher than a man can reach by the constant scrub and wear of the heavier sorts of desert dust, which makes the exact noting of angles exceedingly difficult. The buildings on the west bank of the river, among which I spent the two succeeding days, were even more disfigured, and the palace of the khalifs, except for its three vaulted halls, a crowning confusion of mounds and rock-cut subterranean chambers. It was not until I had made acquaintance with all these that I found time to visit the modern town. I had been spending a few final hours in the great mosque and was beginning to wonder whether a metre tape and a camera are advantageous additions to the equipment of travel, a doubt which was shared by the zaptieh and Jûsef, whose duty it was to stretch the one and carry the other over weary acres of crumbling ruin. When at last we turned our horses' heads to the little town lying out upon the plain, we felt that there was a great deal to be said for prejudices which forbid the measuring and photographing of mosques that cover the bones of saints. The town walls have recently been rebuilt, for the acquisition of merit, by a pious Persian; he neglected, however, to turn his attention to that which they enclose, and the first few hundred yards of sacred Sâmarrâ is a vacant desolation, the home of dust and dirt. Having crossed this area we plunged into mean and narrow streets. All the windows facing outwards had been blocked up, and within or without there was no living soul to be seen as we rode down the silent ways. But when we drew near the mosque we became aware that Sâmarrâ was not quite uninhabited. Grave Persians and ragged Arabs sat at the tea-shops before the gateway; they gave me the salute as I passed, and I was careful not to gaze too curiously through the arch where the big chain hangs across the entrance of the shrine. Inside, under a dome of priceless tiles, are the tombs of the tenth and eleventh Shî'ah Imâms, while the smaller dome of gold covers the cleft into which vanished the Mahdî, who will appear again when the time is ripe. Therefore when you see black ensigns, black ensigns coming out of the east, then go forth and join them; for the Imâm of God will be with those standards, and he will fill the world with equity and justice.

We left Sâmarrâ early in the morning and rode through almost continuous ruin-heaps to Shnâs, which we reached in an hour and forty minutes. It is nothing but a great enclosure, the walls and towers built of sun-dried brick, and consequently much ruined. The towers are placed astride the wall instead of upon one side of it only.[1] A few minutes further north lies an oblong enclosure nearly a third of a mile across, with a walled triangle to the north of it, in

[1] Herzfeld, *Samarra*, p. 61, places the old quarter of Karkh at Shnâs and Dûr 'Arabâyâ at Eskî Baghdâd. Karkh is the Charcha of Ammianus Marcellinus.

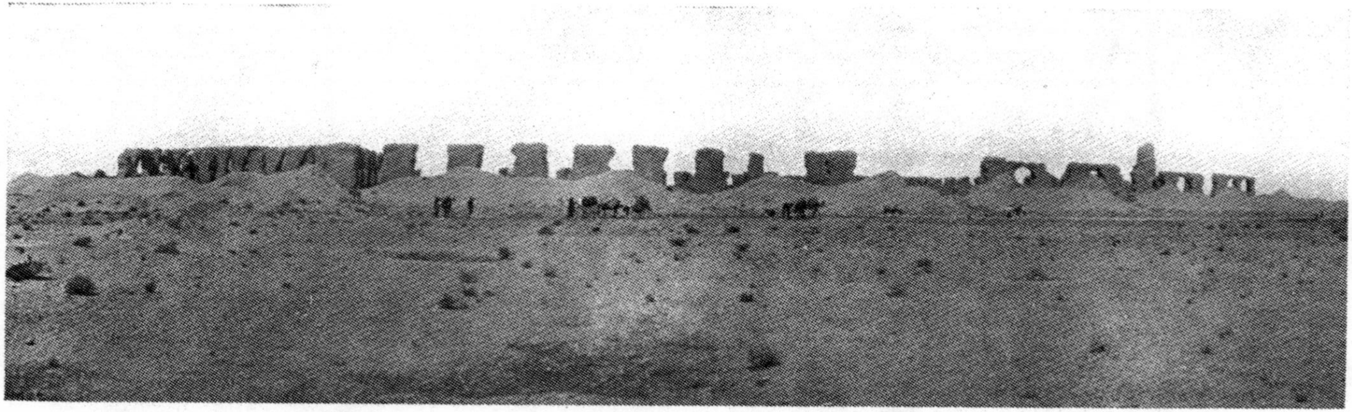

FIG. 123.—ABU DULÂF, FROM EAST.

FIG. 124.—ABU DULÂF, INTERIOR, LOOKING NORTH.

FIG. 125.—NAHRAWÂN CANAL.

FIG. 126.—IMÂM DÛR.

which is a small square enclosure near the river, with foundations of burnt brick. Still further north are some ruin-heaps which are said to represent the tomb of a holy man. This group of ruins is known as Eskî Baghdâd, but the name is applied loosely to the whole area round Abu Dulâf. We crossed a dry watercourse and rode on over mounds for another hour and a half, when we came to the mosque of Abu Dulâf (Fig. 123). Now Abu Dulâf is brother and complement to the mosque at Sâmarrâ, for whereas at Sâmarrâ the arcades have fallen and the outer wall stands, at Abu Dulâf the arcades stand and the outer wall is ruined. I looked in vain for traces of a water-basin in the centre of the court, but being no true antiquarian, I was well consoled for its absence by finding a tall borage plant where the fountain should have been. It lifted its blue flowers gaily out of the dust, and every time I crossed the court I made a circuit that I might look into its clear eye. It was the first flower that we had seen upon the face of the desert for many weeks, and it heralded the end of the region wherein the drought had wrought such havoc. Late in the afternoon I got down to my camp by the Tigris. Fattûḥ had sought a lodging for the night inside the enclosing walls of a palace, and whatever prince it was who housed us, he gave us a lavish hospitality as regards sunset and rising stars and gleaming curves of river.

Half-an-hour's ride brought us on the following morning to the northern limit of Sâmarrâ. In the angle between the Tigris and the Nahrawân canal lie the remains of Mutawakkil's tragic palace, built in a year, inhabited for nine months, destroyed and deserted, together with all the quarter round it, when Muhammad el Muntaṣir caused the khalif his father to be murdered within its walls. Immediately beyond it we crossed the dry channel of the Nahrawân, which was cut by the Sassanian kings in order to bring water to the fertile regions below Sâmarrâ (Fig. 125). At the point where our path crossed it are the brick foundations of a bridge, below a large artificial mound.[1] The dry bed of the canal, hewn for

[1] Mutawakkil began a new canal from the Tigris to the Nahrawân,

scores of miles, straight as a Roman road, through the solid rock, is as impressive as the most magnificent of ruins; for the king who could bid rivers to flow and crops to spring in the barren wilderness was indeed lord of the earth.

As we reached the village of Dûr, an hour further to the north, we met a number of the inhabitants coming out along the road, and all were armed with rifles. We stopped and asked them whither they were bound, and they in turn inquired of us whether we had seen anything of a caravan of merchandise from Sâmarrâ. It was due to arrive at Dûr that morning and they felt some anxiety as to its safety, since the desert was much disturbed. There are no soldiers posted on the left bank of the Tigris, and every man must protect his own property. But we, having come only from Abu Dulâf, could not reassure them. On the outskirts of Dûr the plain is once more tossed into ruin-mounds, probably of the Mohammadan period. The village stands upon an old site; Dûr is mentioned by Ammianus Marcellinus in his account of Jovian's retreat. It is remarkable only for the shrine of the Imâm Dûr (Fig. 126), Muḥammad ibn Mûsa ibn Ja'far ibn 'Alî ibn Ḥussein—his genealogy goes back to a respectable Shî'ah ancestry, and I read it on an inscription cut upon a marble slab by the door. Moreover, while we waited for the mullah to appear with the key, one of the villagers busied himself with scraping away the whitewash which covered the lower part of the inscription, and we deciphered the date, 871 of the Hijrah, which is 1466 A.D.[1] While we were thus engaged the

the latter having silted up by the ninth century, but the labour of cutting through the hard conglomerate was found to be too great and the work was abandoned. I do not know whether the canal I crossed was of his making, but I fancy it was the Nahrawân itself, perhaps cleared and deepened by him. Ross (*op. cit.*, p. 129) speaks of bridge foundations formed of large "artificial stones" (concrete?) "joined together by iron clamps and melted lead." I saw nothing but brick, but Ross's bridge may well be, as he conjectured, earlier than the Mohammadan period. since it probably spanned the Sassanian canal. I thought the artificial mound to be pre-Mohammadan.

[1] There is some doubt about this inscription. Professor Sarre copied it without noticing the date, which was covered with whitewash; he gave it to Professor van Berchem, who decided that the shape of the

mullah joined us, a rubicund old man in a spotless turban. The reluctance which he displayed on being invited to unlock the door was terminated by the zaptieh, who took him aside and explained that I was employed by the government as a surveyor; upon which the mullah, with perhaps a silent reflection on the laxity of the age in the matter of official appointments, threw open the door and bade me enter (Fig. 127). The shrine is a high square tower of fine brickwork, laid at the top so as to form patterns, and, on the north side, inscriptions. Above this tower rises a conical roof constructed, like the roof of the Sitt Zobeideh at Baghdâd, by means of a series of alveolate niches or squinches. In the interior this pointed dome is covered with plasterwork of a character totally different from the stucco decorations of Raḳḳah and Sâmarrâ, to which it stands in the same relation as baroque to cinque cento work. It cannot belong to the same period as the brick walls of the chamber, for it blocks the windows, and my impression is that the whole roof is considerably later than the lower part of the shrine. The mullah, in full assurance of my distinguished position, and sustained by lively hopes of a sufficient reward, looked on with benignant interest while Jûsef and I measured the shrine; but his hopes were to prove as ill-founded as his assurance, for when I opened my purse, prior to departure, it contained nothing but three piastres. I had emptied it the night before on behalf of an obliging person who had accompanied us to Abu Dulâf, and had forgotten to replenish it. To crown all, the money-bags were

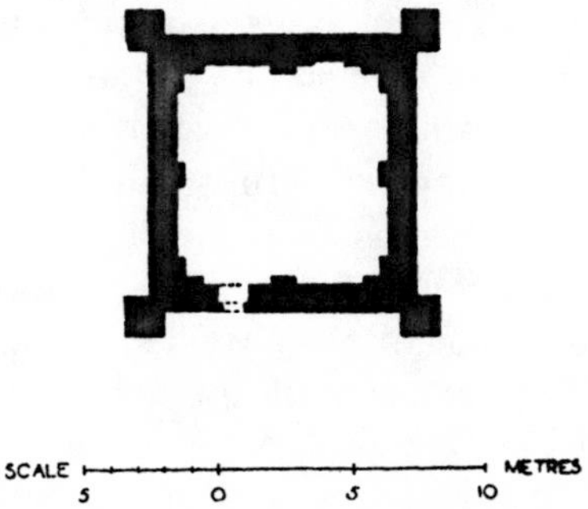

FIG. 127.—IMÂM DÛR.

---

letters pointed indubitably to the ninth century. Professor van Berchem's authority in such matters is not to be questioned, but the date must be accounted for. Perhaps it was a later addition, put in when the shrine was repaired.

with the caravan, and the caravan was a full two hours ahead on the road to Tekrît. I do not know who was the more disconcerted by this unlucky accident, but the mullah bore it with the greater dignity. After I had confounded myself in explanation and apology, he nodded his head, folded his hands into his sleeves and dismissed me smilingly.

"Naṣîb!" he said, "a misfortune. Go in peace."

The subsequent events of the day must have been intended as a judgment upon me. By the time we came down to the river bank opposite Tekrît, three hours from Imâm Dûr, a strong wind had arisen, and we found the caravan standing dejectedly at the water's edge while Fattûḥ called upon God to hasten the movements of the ferrymen. His prayers were far from efficacious (moreover, he had forgotten to put up a supplication for a water-tight boat), and the crossing was longer and more tiresome than any we had experienced (Fig. 128). It was near sunset before we got into camp on the high ground behind Tekrît, and the last of the muleteers did not come in with the riding horses until after dark.

No sooner were the tents pitched than a messenger waited upon me to ask whether I would receive Ḥmeidî Beg ibn Farḥân. I returned an answer couched in respectfully cordial terms, since no one who has travelled in the desert is ignorant of the name of Farḥân, who was the Sheikh of Sheikhs of all the northern Shammar. Since the death of Ibrahîm Pasha, the Shammar and the 'Anazeh share, without amity, the lordship of Mesopotamia, as they did before the Kurd rose into power. The road from Tekrît to Môṣul is in Shammar territory, so far as it can be said to be in the territory of any one. Not a caravan passes up and down but it pays tribute to Mejwal ibn Farḥân, a beshlik (three piastres) on every mule, and half a beshlik for a donkey, unless the travellers happen to be escorted by a zaptieh as I was. Muleteers cannot afford zaptiehs, and when they see two spearmen of the tribe upon the road, they pay and lodge no complaint in deaf ears. Sheikh Mejwal, who is the strongest of Farḥân's fourteen sons, levies a tax from all the Jebbûr, the tribe that camps along the river, and I was told that whereas the Jebbûr

FIG. 128.—TEKRÎT FERRY.

FIG. 129.—COFFEE-MAKING, SHEIKH 'ASKAR.

FIG. 130.—TEKRÎT, THE ARBAÎN.

FIG. 131.—KHÂN KHERNÎNA, MIḤRÂB.

had once been breeders of horses, now they breed none, finding it an unprofitable labour with the Shammar sheikhs alert to seize every likely mare. Ḥmeidî is said to be the mildest of Farḥân's brood. He is a handsome man of middle age, with deepset eyes and a gentle, rather indolent expression. He had come to Tekrît on some business connected with sheep stealing, and hearing of my arrival he hastened to bid me welcome to these deserts and to make me free of the Shammar tents. I asked him news of his cousins in Nejd, where the Shammar princes of the Benî Rashîd hold with much bloodshed a hazardous authority, and when he had spoken of these matters he gave me a piece of news which he thought, and rightly, might be of no less interest. It was rumoured that the Sultan had dismissed the deputies, but how or why no one knew, though the counter-revolution was now more than a week old.

Tekrît is the birthplace of Saladin. It is seen to the best advantage from the other side of the Tigris, where the bold bluffs and steeply falling banks to which its houses cling are imposing to the eye. The distant promise is not fulfilled; the modern town is devoid of interest and little remains of the mediæval town but ruin-heaps, the line of a wall and part of the lower gateway of the citadel. Tekrît was the seat of a bishopric; Ibn Ḥauḳal, writing in the tenth century, states that most of the inhabitants were Christians, and Rich speaks of the remains of ten churches.[1] Beyond the ruins of the old town, which extend far to the west of modern Tekrît, there lies the Moslem shrine of the Arba'în, the Forty, much dilapidated, though two small chambers covered with domes are still intact. These chambers, and the ruined precincts adjoining them, are decorated with stucco of the same character, and I should say of the same date, as the ornaments of Imâm Dûr (Fig. 130).

We set out from Tekrît with a large and unusually nondescript company, or perhaps it would be truer to say that they

[1] *A Residence in Koordistan,* Vol. II. p. 147. The book was published in 1836.

set out with us, a European and a couple of zaptiehs being valuable assets on the Môṣul road. Half-a-dozen Kurds from above Mardîn and as many Nestorians from the mountains south of Lake Vân marched with my pack-animals, and presently we fell in with the Father of Monkeys, as Fattûḥ called him, who had not made much haste on his way to the capital. There was also a young sayyid, white-turbaned and somewhat forbidding of aspect; with him too I made friends after I had conquered the distaste born of his over-godly looks. "I love thieves and pigs," murmured one of the muleteers, "Yezîd and Druze, but I do not love sayyids or mullahs." This particular descendant of the Prophet addressed me systematically as Queen, and I experienced a not unnatural gratification at being raised to royal rank, though whether it is higher than that of consul I cannot be sure. With the Nestorians I was immediately on terms of intimacy. They were sturdy, bearded mountaineers of a type which it is impossible not to appreciate, even at first sight, and they marched cheerfully through dust and heat with no possessions but a water-flask and a crust of bread. Their pointed felt caps and close-fitting cotton trousers formed a costume which was new to me, and as they walked beside my mare I asked them who they were and whence they came.

"We are the people of Mâr Shim'ûn," said one, naming the hereditary patriarch of their faith. "Effendim, we have no friends but the English—Islâm, Armenians, all are our foes."

A struggling sect is the ancient community of Mâr Shim'ûn, harassed by the Kurds in their mountain fastnesses, but if they may be judged by their brave and independent looks, they do not turn the other cheek to the striker.

We rode for three hours through monotonous country, a barren and stony wilderness raised high above the river. When we dropped down to the water's edge we found the land to be partly cultivated by the men of Tekrît, but the Tigris is eating away the right bank and in places field and

FIG. 132.—KHÂN KHERNÎNA, DETAIL OF FLAT VAULT.

FIG. 133.—KHÂN KHERNÎNA, VAULT, SHOWING TUBE.

FIG. 134.—KHÂN KHERNÎNA, SETTING OF DOME.

FIG. 135.—TELL NIMRÛD.

path have been destroyed by the depredations of the stream.[1] We camped that night six and a half hours from Tekrît, near a ḳishlâ which has recently been built at the expense of a very beautiful khân. The ḳishlâ represents a spasmodic attempt on the part of the government to control the tribes; it holds from forty to fifty foot soldiers, who, since they are unmounted, cannot pursue or punish the marauding Arabs. The walls of Khân Khernîna, a magnificent Mohammadan building of the finest period, have therefore been laid low to no purpose, and the soldiers lead a miserable and useless existence in the ḳishlâ, which has been erected out of its bricks. The khân is now so much ruined that I did not attempt to plan it. It is a rectangular enclosure with round bastions in the walls, and fine gateways covered with pointed arches. Along the south side stretches a vaulted corridor, interrupted towards the middle of its length by a chamber which has served as a mosque. This chamber contains a miḥrâb decorated with exquisite arabesques in stucco; of the inscription which was placed beneath the pointed arch only a few letters remain (Fig. 131). The barrel vaults of the corridor, corbelled slightly forward from the wall and built without centering, are splendid examples of Mesopotamian brick construction. The roof of a small chamber at the south-east angle, and the four-sided dome of the mosque, show the singular arrangement which I had noticed at Baghdâd of a flat piece of masonry laid over the summit of the vault (Fig. 132). A square chamber near the mosque had been covered with a dome, and in one corner a squinch arch, decorated with a tiny ornamental arcade, is still standing (Fig. 134). On the flanks of the barrel vaults I observed the same system of tubes which exists at Ukheiḍir (Fig. 133). The masonry and the plan of the building are closely akin to thirteenth-century work in Baghdâd, and to that period I should assign it.[2]

[1] Ḳal'at Abu Rayâsh, which is marked in Kiepert's map, has almost disappeared, the high ground on which it stands having fallen away and carried the walls and towers with it.

[2] Khân Khernîna is not mentioned by Ibn Jubeir nor by Ibn

There is another guard-house thirty minutes further up the Tigris, Sheramîyeh is its name. Here we stopped on the following morning to water our horses, for our road now led us far from the river. A low line of rocky hills, the Jebel Ḥamrîn, borders the west bank for several hours' journey. It runs crosswise over the desert and the river cuts through it by the Fetḥah gorge. The hills drop sheer into the stream, leaving no space for a path, and caravans are obliged to skirt the western slopes, where there is little water and no settled population, though we saw a few encampments of the Deleim far out in the desert. The cups and hollows of the plain were filled with a scanty growth of grass. We rejoiced over the unwonted sight as if each blade were a separate benediction, and Fattûḥ began to calculate the sums we might save on provender when the horses could be pastured every evening on fresh herbage.

"God is great," said the zaptieh, "but it has been a year of ruin for poor men. We have not known where to look for food for our horses, and more than that, I have received no pay for six months."

"Please God the new government will give you your pay," said I.

"Please God," he answered. "But when it comes the ḍâbiṭs" (officers) "eat it. Effendim, once I travelled with a ḍâbiṭ who received £T18 a month, wallah! And my pay was 100 piastres a month. Yet whenever he drank coffee he left me to defray the expense. Where is eighteen pounds and where a hundred piastres!"

"God exists," said the sayyid. "Oh Queen, He exists."

"Wallah, He exists," said the zaptieh hopefully.

We camped that night six hours from Sheramîyeh in a sheltered place among the hills beside a spring of which the waters were bitter with sulphur and not unmixed with pitch; our companions drank of it, but my servants and I quaffed

---

Baṭûṭah, who both travelled by this side of the Tigris from Tekrît to Môṣul, the one at the end of the twelfth century, and the other in the middle of the fourteenth century.

royally from the flasks which Jûsef had filled at the Tigris. While the tents were being pitched I walked to the top of the hills, and on the banks of watercourses that had but recently run dry I found flowers, blue larkspurs and purple gentians and a wide selection of the thistle family. A bowl of larkspurs was set upon my dinner-table, and Jûsef was very loath to throw them away when we struck camp, so rare and delicate a possession did they seem to us. But I assured him that the German professors at Ḳal'at Shergât would have flowers fairer than these. A more wonderful sight was in store for us on the next day's march. We had travelled barely two hours when we splashed into a pool of rain-water, and then into another; there was grass round them, green, abundant grass: "More than we have seen all the way from Aleppo!" exclaimed Jûsef. The region of the drought was over, and when our path led us to the top of the Jebel Ḥamrîn, here sunk to a low hog's back, I was scarcely surprised to see the slopes down to the Tigris red with poppies. But even the poppies could not withhold the eye from the great mound of Ḳal'at Shergât by the river's edge, the mound of Asshur, crowned with the crumbling mass of a huge zigurrat, the temple pyramid of the tutelary god of the Assyrians. With the general aspect of the first capital of Assyria I was already familiar, thanks to the excellent photographs published by the German Orient-Gesellschaft, but I was not prepared for so magnificent a prospect. The Tigris in high flood washed the foot of the temple mound; far away to the north ran the snow-clad barrier of mountains whence its waters flow—a barrier which Nature planted in vain against the valour of the Assyrian armies; and across the river the fertile plain stretched away in long undulations to where Arbela lies behind low hills. Bountiful gods had showered their gifts upon the land.

We rode down into the ruin-field and found one of Dr. Andrae's colleagues at work in the trial trenches. He directed us to the house set round with flowers, as I had predicted, wherein the excavators are lodged. There Dr. Andrae and Mr. Jordan made me so warmly welcome that I felt like one returning after absence into a circle of life-long friends. They had grave news to give me, news which was all the more disquieting because it was as yet nothing but a rumour. Constitutional government had foundered suddenly, and it might be for ever. The members of the Committee had fled from Constantinople, the Liberals were fugitive upon their heels, and once more 'Abdu'l Ḥamîd had set his foot upon the neck of Turkey. So we interpreted the report that had reached Asshur, but since there was no means of allaying or of confirming our anxieties we turned our minds to more profitable fields, and went out to see the ruins.

A site better favoured than Kal'at Shergât for excavations such as those undertaken by Dr. Andrae and his colleagues could scarcely have been selected. It has not given them the storied slabs and huge stone guardians of the gates of kings with which Layard enriched the British Museum; they have disappeared during the many periods of reconstruction which the town has witnessed; but those very reconstructions add to the historic interest of the excavations. Asshur was in existence in the oldest Assyrian period, and down to the latest days of the empire it was an honoured shrine of the gods; there are traces of Persian occupation; in Parthian times the city was re-built, walls and gates were set up anew, and the whole area within the ancient fortifications was re-inhabited. Valuable as are the contributions which Dr. Andrae has been able to make to the history of Assyria, the fact that he is bringing into the region of critical study a culture so shadowy as that of the Parthians has remained to us, in spite of its four hundred years of domination, adds greatly to the magnitude of his achievement. His researches in this direction have been pursued not only at Asshur, but at the Parthian city of Hatra, a long day's journey to the west of the Tigris, where the famous palace is at last receiving the attention it merits.

The temple of the god Asshur, of which the zigurrat is the most notable feature of Ḳal'at Shergât, goes back to the earliest Assyrian times, but the greater part of it is occupied by a Turkish guard-house, and has not yet been excavated (Fig. 136).

FIG. 136.—ḲAL'ÂT SHERGÂT, THE ZIGURRAT AND RUINS OF NORTH WALL.

FIG. 138.—SÂMARRÂ, INTERIOR OF SOUTH GATE, RUINED MOSQUE.

FIG. 140.—SÂMARRÂ, RUINED MOSQUE, SMALL DOOR IN WEST WALL.

The court between temple and zigurrat lies open; in a later age the Parthians adorned it with a splendid colonnade, and it is here that Dr. Andrae has succeeded in piecing together large fragments of Parthian architectural decoration which throw a new light both upon the arts of Parthia and upon the succeeding era of the Sassanians. Fortunately there exist upon the mound other temples of the Assyrian period which he has been better able to study. Chief of these is the double shrine of the gods Anu and Adaḍ, lords of heaven and of the thunderstorm, the excavation of which cost him many months of difficult work. The temple was finished by Tiglathpileser at the end of the twelfth century before Christ, but in the course of some three hundred years it fell into complete decay; Shalmaneser II, he who received the homage of Jehu, as is recorded on the Black Obelisk in the British Museum, filled in the ruins of the earlier shrine and set a new edifice upon them, preserving almost exactly the plan of the old. No Assyrian temple has hitherto been studied accurately, save one of Sargon's at Khorsabâd, later by more than a century than the second temple of Anu and Adad; it was therefore necessary to get an exact record of both the periods at Asshur, and in order to leave Shalmaneser's work undisturbed, Dr. Andrae was compelled to trace that of Tiglathpileser by means of a system of underground tunnels. "I have never," he observed, as he surveyed his handiwork, "done anything so mad." But the results have more than justified the labour. The scheme of the Assyrian temple has now been established by examples ranging over a period of four hundred years, and it is conclusively proved that it differed in a remarkable degree from the Babylonian temple plan, and was related to the plan adopted by Solomon. In Babylonia the chambers are all laid broadways in respect of the entrance; that is to say, the door is placed in the centre of one of the long sides, so that he who enters has only a narrow area in front of him, and must look to right and left if he would appreciate the size of the hall. At Jerusalem and in Assyria the main sanctuary ran lengthways, an immense artistic advance, inasmuch as the broadways-lying hall was at best a clumsy contrivance which could never have given the sense of space and dignity conveyed by the other. To the genius of what builders are we to attribute this masterly comprehension of spatial effect? The question cannot as yet be answered, but Dr. Andrae is inclined to seek outside Syria and Mesopotamia for the prototypes of Asshur and Jerusalem. In the palaces, be it noted, the lengthways hall was never adopted, but palace architecture is not well illustrated at Asshur, those buildings having been the first to suffer at the hands of the spoiler.

The walls to the north of the temples are perhaps the most impressive part of the excavations. The mound on which the city is built reaches here its greatest elevation, and the gigantic masses of the fortifications rear themselves up from its very base. Time after time the kings of Assyria renewed these bulwarks, setting them forward further and further against the river, which once washed their foundations—its bed runs now a little more to the east, where the stream still flows under the eastern quays of Asshur. The upper parts of the walls are of unburnt brick, but the lower, as Xenophon observed at Nimrûd, are cased in massive stone. The stone-work was not in reality as durable as the brick, for the Assyrians had no binding mortar, and the stones, being set together with mud, could not resist a pressure from behind, such as that which was offered by the mound itself. A mortar of asphalt is sometimes used in sun-dried brick, but binding mortar seems to have been a discovery of the age of Nebuchadnezzar, since it is first found in constructions of his time at Babylon. The fortifications sweep round southwards to the Gurgurri Gate, well known in inscriptions, and identified by epigraphic evidence. Between the gate and the temple and palace area, a great part of the ground is covered with a network of streets and houses belonging to a late Assyrian period. The larger houses consist of an outer court with rooms for servants and dependents, roughly floored with big cobblestones and traversed by a pathway of smaller cobbles whereon the masters could cross to the inner paved court round which their chambers lay. Every house, however small, is provided with a bath-room. The whole complex has the appearance of another Pompeii, though it is more ancient than the Italian Pompeii by six or seven hundred years. Down in the plain, outside the city walls, stood a magnificent building which has been christened by the excavators the Festhaus. It is a fine open court, surrounded on two sides by a colonnade, while on the side opposite to the gate there is a raised platform of solid masonry. The court must have had the aspect of a formal garden, for at regular intervals there are holes in the hard conglomerate of the floor which the excavators conjecture to have been filled with earth and planted with shrubs. In this colonnaded garden was celebrated the spring sacrifice, the annual festival in honour of the fruitful earth. The plan of the building is not Assyrian —the column itself is a non-Mesopotamian feature—but whence it was derived it would be impossible as yet to say.

Throughout the area of the city a series of deep trial trenches have been dug, cutting through the Parthian period, through the late Assyrian, and down to the earliest times. These trenches afford materials for the most fascinating studies. One of the earliest cities that stood upon the mound of Asshur is, curiously enough, the easiest to trace. The houses are in an unusually perfect state; their walls, preserved not infrequently to a height of several feet, enclose little cobbled courtyards with narrow cobbled streets between. These worn and ancient ways, emerging from under the steep sides of the trench and disappearing again into the earth at its furthest limit, give the observer a sense as of visualized history, as though the millenniums had dropped away that separate him from the busy life of the antique world. It is probable that the city to which they belong was destroyed by some overwhelming catastrophe, laid desolate, perhaps by an onslaught of the Mitanni kings of northern Mesopotamia or of the Babylonians from the south, and so left in age-long ruin until a later generation completed the filling up of court and street which had been begun by time, levelled the whole and built their dwellings upon foundations of the past. The Assyrians were content to leave their story inscribed on clay cylinder or on stone; they did not, like the Egyptians, rear for their dead enduring monuments, but each man in turn was thrust into a clay sarcophagus or sepulchral jar lying immediately below the floor of his own dwelling—we counted as many as fifteen burials in one of the smaller houses—or placed, with a slightly greater regard for the comfort of the living, in an adjoining subterranean chamber vaulted with brick.

As Dr. Andrae led me about the city, drawing forth its long story with infinite skill from wall and trench and cuneiform inscription, the lavish cruel past rushed in upon us. The myriad soldiers of the Great King, transported from the reliefs in the British Museum, marched through the gates of Asshur; the captives, roped and bound, crowded the streets; defeated princes bowed themselves before the victor and subject races piled up their tribute in his courts. We saw the monarch go out to the chase, and heard the roaring of the lion, half paralyzed by the dart in its spine, which animates the stone with its wild anguish. Human victims cried out under nameless tortures; the tide of battle raged against the walls, and, red with carnage, rose into the palaces. Splendour and misery, triumph and despair, lifted their head out of the dust.

One hot night I sat with my hosts upon the roof of their house. The Tigris, in unprecedented flood, swirled against the mound, a waste of angry waters. Above us rose the zigurrat of the god Asshur. It had witnessed for four thousand years the melting of the Kurdish snows, flood-time and the harvest that follows; gigantic, ugly, intolerably mysterious, it dominated us, children of an hour.

"What did they watch from its summit?" I asked, stung into a sharp consciousness of the unknown by a scene almost as old as recorded life.

"They watched the moon," said Dr. Andrae, "as we do. Who knows? they watched for the god."

I have left few places so unwillingly as I left Ḳal'at Shergât.

We rode northwards for eight hours and camped at Tell Gayârah, near to which there are some small pitch springs.

The land of Assyria grew ever more fertile as we journeyed up into it, and that night the horses were picketed knee-deep in grass, to the boundless satisfaction of the muleteers. I was anxious on the following day to visit Nimrûd, the Assyrian city mentioned in Genesis as Calah, but in order to do so it was necessary to find a ferry across the Tigris, which was a doubtful undertaking. Even if it were found, the flood might make ferry-boats unprofitable vessels, therefore I detached Fattûḥ from the caravan and bade him ride with the zaptieh and me, Fattûḥ being master of a thousand wiles with which to baffle difficulty, and possessor foreby of a remarkably strong right arm. We rode in two hours to Mangûb, where there are a few ruined huts. On the opposite bank of the Tigris a number of mounds mark the site of ancient villages. The grass grew thick by the river, and on the higher ground it had also sprouted abundantly, though it was now withered. Presently we spied upon the path in front of us an effendi on horseback, who carried a big umbrella to protect himself from the sun. His state was further enhanced by the presence of a few zaptiehs.

"He is coming to Gayârah," said my soldier. "They have sent him from Môṣul to judge a dispute about the crops. Four men were murdered last week at Gayârah, and ten are lying fatally wounded."

This was news to me. I had been peacefully unconscious of the dead and dying as I watched my horses knee-deep in the grass. The effendi, when he came up to us, addressed me as follows:

"Bonjour, Madame. Comment aimez vous le désert?"

"Mais beaucoup," said I, somewhat astonished to hear the French tongue spoken in it. And then I added quickly: "What tidings have you from Constantinople?"

The effendi drew his brows together.

"We hear that troops from Salonica have entered the town and captured two barracks."

"Did they take them without difficulty?" I asked.

"We do not know," he returned.

"Please God!" said I.

"Adieu," he replied hurriedly, and rode upon his way. In those days of uncertainty it was not wise to be drawn into a definite expression of opinion.

Our road took us up a ridge, and when we came to its crest I drew bridle, for the history of Asia was spread out before my eyes. Below us the Great Zâb flowed into the Tigris; here Tissaphernes murdered the Greek generals, here Xenophon took over the command, and having crossed the Zâb at a higher point, turned and drove back the archers of Mithridates. To the north the mound of Nimrûd, where the Greeks saw the ruins of Calah, stood out among the corn-fields; eastward lay the plain of Arbela, where Alexander overthrew Darius. The whole world shone like a jewel, green corn, blue waters, and the gleaming snows that bound Mesopotamia to the north; but to my ears the smiling landscape cried out a warning: the people of the West can conquer but they can never hold Asia, no, not when they go out under the banners of Alexander himself.

We rode up the bank of the Tigris, and when we came opposite to Tell Nimrûd there, by good fortune, was a ferry-boat, plying across the river with the men and flocks of the Jebbûr. The cause of their migration to the left bank was hopping about our feet—locusts, newly issued from the rocky ground and swarming over every blade of grass and corn.

"In two days there will be no pasture, and our flocks will die," explained an aged shepherd. "Let the consul cross!" he shouted, as the ferry-boat drew up beside the bank and half the tribe clambered into it.

We ejected two calves, a mare and a few goats and installed ourselves in their place. The ferry-boat was as tightly packed as the ark and the passengers nearly as varied; they all talked, whinnied, baa-ed and bleated at once as we pushed out into the swift stream. I climbed on to the back of my mare, which seemed the cleanest and the roomiest spot, and we busied ourselves in catching locusts and throwing them into the water, for, alas! they had embarked with us by the hundred.

The mound of Nimrûd, when I saw it, lay in a waving sea

of corn. The holes and pits of Layard's diggings were filled to the brim with grass and flowers, and the zigurrat of the war god Ninib reared its bare head out of a field of poppies. But except for the flowers, Nimrûd, whence we obtained many of the treasures of our museum in London, is a pitiful sight for English eyes. Its neglected state stands in sharp contrast with the pious care which the German excavators are expending upon the ruins of Asshur. Carved and inscribed blocks have been left exposed to the malicious attacks of Arab boys,[1] who hold it a meritorious act to deface an idol, and to the even slenderer mercy of the winter rains and frosts. In one place a stone statue projects head and shoulders out of the ground, the face of the king or god which it represents being already terribly battered (Fig. 135). The number of Assyrian statues known to us is exceedingly small —not more than seven or eight have been brought to light —yet this splendid example is allowed to fall into decay for want of a handful of earth wherewith to cover it. The city of Calah is associated with some of Layard's most memorable triumphs; for the sake of our own honour it would be well that we should take steps to preserve the works of art that remain in it, and that, if we cannot find money to transport them to the museum at Constantinople, we should at least employ a few men to re-bury them until more enthusiastic archæologists turn their attention to Nimrûd.

Sheikh 'Askar of the Jebbûr, who had accompanied me from his tents by the river, listened sympathetically while I lamented over the statue, and volunteered to bury it under the earth as soon as his men should have brought over their flocks from the west bank. I applauded the suggestion and encouraged it with bakhshîsh, but unless I am much mistaken, the sheikh's resolve has not yet reached the point of execution. We sat in his tent while we waited for the ferry-boat, and with eager hospitality he set before us coffee, bread, and a mess of apricots—it was the last Arab coffee fire that was to be lighted in our honour (Fig. 129). So we ferried

[1] Not, I believe, by Layard, who was always careful to cover what he did not remove.

back, climbed a bluff alive with locusts, and cantered through sweet-smelling crops to the sulphur springs of Ḥammâm 'Alî. A few minutes beyond the village our tents were pitched in deep luxuriant grass.

We struck camp next morning with an agreeable sense of excitement. Môṣul was only four hours away, and the advantages of city life—consulates, rest from travel, news of the outer world—shone very brightly before us. The rising sun, the dewy cornfields, the flowering grass, lent their enchantment to our breakfast, and gaily we stepped out upon the road. Before us lay a little ridge that separated us from Môṣul; we had journeyed towards it for half-an-hour when there fell upon our ears a sound that made our hearts stand still. It was the boom of cannon.

Said Fattûḥ: "What is that?" But none of us could answer.

We went on through the smiling sunny landscape and the green corn, where the peasants stood by the irrigation trenches, their work suspended, their faces turned towards that ominous sound, and presently we met an old man. He too listened.

"Why are they firing cannon in Môṣul?" I asked.

"God knows!" he answered, and wrung his hands together. "Perhaps it is news from Stambûl. One man says one thing and one another, and God knows what is true."

A little further a ragged pair came down the road toward us.

"When did you set out from Môṣul?" said Fattûḥ.

"At the first dawn," they answered, and fear was in their eyes.

"What was happening there?" asked Fattûḥ.

"Nothing," they replied. "When we set out, wallah! there was nothing."

We left them standing in the road with anxious faces turned towards the town. And still the cannon boomed over the hill.

"Môṣul is an evil city," said Fattûḥ to the zaptieh.

"It is evil," he answered. "Blood flows there like the water of the Tigris."

After a few minutes two Arabs galloped up behind us on their mares, and one carried a great lance.

"Whither going?" cried Fattûḥ.

"To Môṣul," they shouted.

"What is your business?" he called out.

"We heard the cannon," they replied, and galloped up the hill. The zaptieh went with them.

"He will be little use if Môṣul is up," observed Fattûḥ.

At this moment the cannon ceased, and we saw a party of four or five soldiers riding over the brow. The Arabs and my zaptieh stopped to speak to them, and then turned back with them, coming slowly towards us down the ridge.

"These know," said Fattûḥ.

They stopped when they reached us, and the moment was big with Fate.

"Peace be upon you," they said.

"And upon you peace," I returned. "What is the news?"

And one answered: "Reshâd is Sultan."

"God prolong his existence!" said I.

Upon this we parted, and they went down the hill, and we in silence to the top of the ridge. The silver Tigris and the green plain lay before us, and in the midst the city of Môṣul, which had published the accession of another lord.

"Praise God!" said I, looking down upon that fair land.

"To Him the praise!" echoed Fattûḥ.

And then the zaptieh gave voice to his thought.

"All the days of 'Abdu'l Ḥamîd," he said, "we never drew our pay."

THE RUINS OF SÂMARRÂ[1]

THE ruined mosque at Sâmarrâ has an interior measurement of 240 x 157·60 m., the greater length being from

[1] Dr. Herzfeld has been so good as to send me the chapter of his forthcoming work (written in conjunction with Professor Sarre), in which he gives a further account of Sâmarrâ. When it reached me my description of the ruins was already printed, and I can do no more than acknowledge, with gratitude, his kindness.

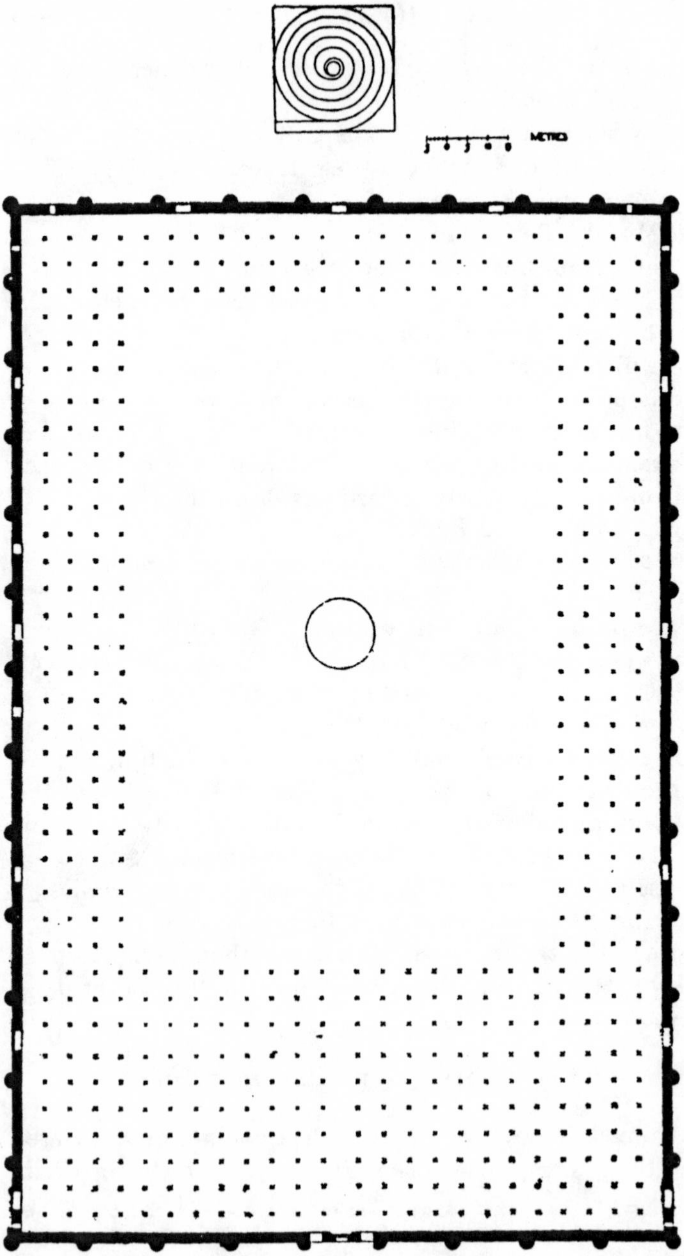

FIG. 137.—SÂMARRÂ, MOSQUE.

FIG. 141.—SÂMARRÂ, RUINED MOSQUE, SOUTH-WEST ANGLE TOWER.

FIG. 142.—SÂMARRÂ, RUINED MOSQUE, WINDOW IN SOUTH WALL.

FIG. 143.—SÂMARRÂ, RUINED MOSQUE, BIG DOOR IN NORTH WALL.

FIG. 144.—SÂMARRÂ, EL 'ASHIḲ, WEST END OF NORTH FAÇADE.

north to south (Fig. 135). The four angle towers are larger in diameter than those which are set along the walls. The intermediate bastions are perfectly regular in size and shape except the two on either side of the southern gate, from which a segment is cut off by the door openings, and the bastion immediately to the west of the same gate which has a small addition to the western part of its curve, an addition which I do not believe to be later in date though the brickwork is of a slightly different character. The southern gate is a triple opening in the middle of the wall where it would be natural to look for the miḥrâb (Fig. 138). There are remains of mouldings round the inner face of the central opening (Fig. 139). The upper part of the south wall is pierced by twenty-four windows, two of them being placed over the smaller openings of the central gateway (Fig. 122). These windows, together with the trenches in the interior of the mosque which mark the line of the columns, determine the number of the colonnades; there must have been twenty-four, each one ending against the wall between the windows. The central aisle which terminated at the main gate and was wider than the rest, was not provided with a window. The space between the colonnades was undoubtedly roofed with beams; the holes into which the large cross-beams were fitted can still be seen on the inner side of the south wall. The windows, placed with regard to the aisles, bear no relation to the position of the round bastions on the exterior of the wall. They break into them at haphazard, frequently impinging upon their sides, while in one instance a window is cut straight through a tower (Fig. 120). On the inner face the windows are covered by a cusped arch (Fig. 142). The east and west walls are broken by

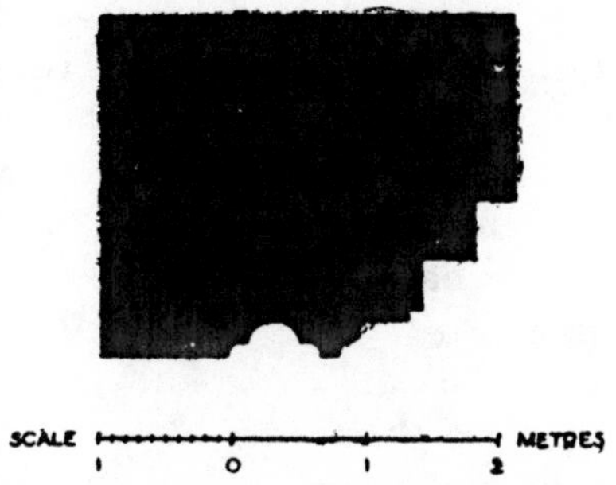

FIG. 139.—SÂMARRÂ, MOSQUE. DETAIL OF PIER, SOUTH DOOR.

numerous doors. Beginning from the southern end there is first a small entrance, 1·25 m. wide, close to the angle bastion (Fig. 141). A wall about a metre in length projects from the main wall to the south of the door opening and has been connected with the top of the main wall by a section of vaulting. Immediately beyond this postern there is a large gateway 4·55 m. wide, and then another which is still larger, being 4·75 m. wide. The next door is 3·85 m.; the fifth, which is only 2·62 m., is found in the west wall alone. Then follows another of the larger doors, about 4 metres wide, beyond which there is, in the west wall only, a door 2·62 m. wide; then on both sides a large door 4·05 m. wide and a small door 1·50 m. wide. The north wall is broken by five gates, the two at the outer ends averaging 1·50 m. and the other three 4 metres in width. All the smaller doors exhibit an exceedingly curious piece of construction (Fig. 140). The brickwork of the wall runs uninterruptedly over the door opening without the intermission of arch or lintel. It is as if the door had been cut out of the wall with a knife, and the bricks above it, so far as they keep their place, do so only by reason of the excellence of the mortar. The wall above the larger doors has in every case fallen away, but there is evidence of the former existence of some kind of lintel or arch strengthened by wooden beams, the round holes for the beams being visible in the existing masonry (Fig. 143). I incline to the theory of a lintel; the faced wall above the holes leaves no room for an arch. Above this lintel there would seem to have been a row of small arched windows two or three in number (*cf.* the two side openings of the south gate where there is a single window above the arch). Along the top of the east, west, and north walls runs a brickwork decoration consisting of a series of recessed squares, each of which contains the recessed segment of a sphere. The walls are seamed from top to bottom with narrow runnels, which were no doubt connected with the drainage system of the roof. There is no unanimity of opinion among those who have planned the mosque concerning the number of the colonnades in the

interior. As I have already said, it seems to me evident that
there were twenty-four rows of columns or piers, from east to
west, at the northern and southern ends of the mosque. I
made out the colonnades to be ten deep upon the south side
and three deep upon the north, while upon the east and west
sides I counted four rows of columns.[1] The supports of the
arcades must have been either columns or small piers.
From the absence of any structural remains, such as might
have been expected if the supports had taken the form of
brick piers, I incline, with Herzfeld, to the view that the roof
must have been carried on columns. Their total disappearance may possibly be accounted for by the fact that they were
of wood,[2] though Muḳaddasî, writing at the end of the tenth
century, relates that the mosque of Sâmarrâ was built upon
marble columns and his evidence cannot be wholly dismissed.
In the centre of the open court was placed, in all probability,
the famous stone basin called the Kâs i Fir'aun (Pharaoh's
Cup), which is described by Mustaufî.[3] The minaret, with its
singular spiral path, stands to the north of the mosque. The
summit, though somewhat ruined, still retains a decoration of
niches. There can be little doubt that the mosque is that which
was erected by Mutawakkil (A.D. 847–861) to replace Mu'tamid's Friday mosque, but Yâḳût asserts that the minaret is
a relic of Mu'tamid's foundation. Yâḳût, however, wrote in
1225 when Sâmarrâ had long been in ruins.

Next in importance to the mosque is the castle or palace
on the opposite bank of the Tigris, known as the 'Ashiḳ
(Fig. 145).[4] The first time I visited it we crossed in a guffah
from a point a little below the town where there is usually a
bridge of boats. The bridge had been swept away by the floods
and the guffah landing was very bad. It was a full hour's

---

[1] Viollet puts them ten deep to the south, four deep to the north and
five deep to east and west.

[2] In Manṣûr's mosque at Baghdâd, the roof was borne by wooden
columns. See Le Strange, *Baghdâd*, p. 34.

[3] *Lands of the Eastern Califate*, p. 56.

[4] Its original name is doubtful. In the twelfth century it was called
the Ma'shûk, for Ibn Jubeir alludes to it under that name in the
twelfth century, and so does Ibn Baṭûṭah in the fourteenth century.

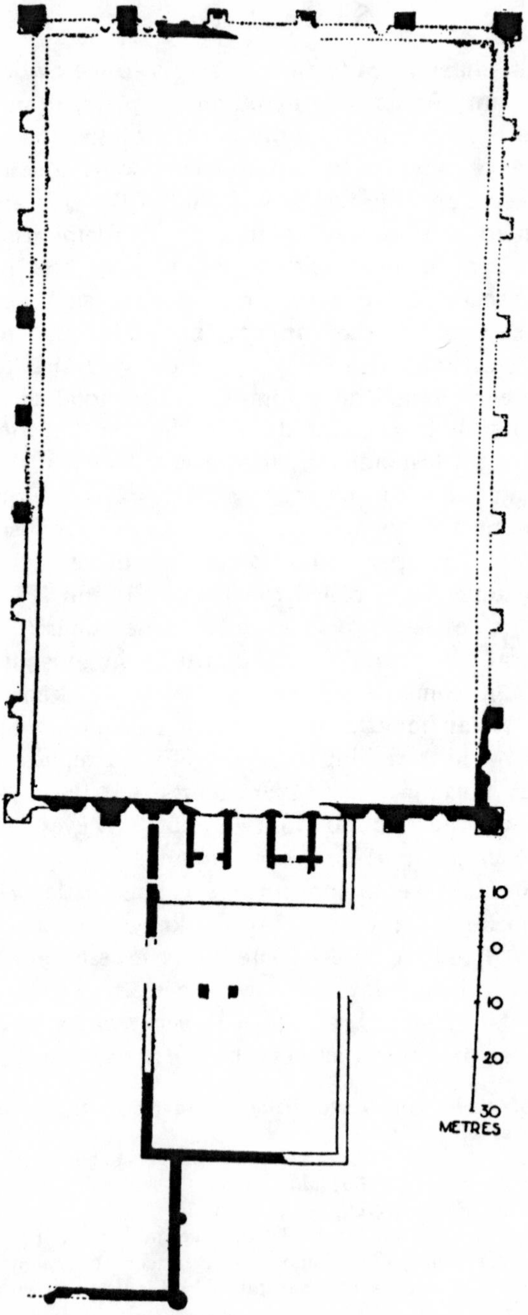

FIG. 145.—EL 'ASHIK.

ride up the river to El 'Ashiḳ, but I was rewarded for my trouble by finding indubitable traces of a masonry bridge in the low ground almost exactly opposite a curious little building called Ṣlebîyeh. My attention was called to the bridge by seeing men digging out the brick piers and arches for building material. The peasants told me that when the river is low, piers can be seen in the bed of the stream and that the bridge ran in the direction of the Beit el Khalîfah. I give this information for what it is worth. Ya'ḳûbî mentions a bridge of boats (ed. de Goeje, p. 263): it is not impossible that pontoons may have been thrown across the deepest and swiftest part of the river and connected with the high ground on the west bank, which is at some distance from the stream, by a series of masonry arches of which I saw the remains. The piers and arches would therefore have stood on ground which was under water in time of high flood. This is exactly the arrangement of the modern bridge at Môṣul. The castle of the 'Ashiḳ consists of a great enclosure, 123 metres from north to south and 85 metres from east to west, surrounded by a wall with round bastions which are set upon a rectangular base (Fig. 146). All the buildings that may have stood within the wall have vanished, but adjoining the north wall there are remains of a gatehouse consisting of five parallel chambers opening on to a corridor or platform. The chambers and the corridor are built upon a substructure of vaults. Under the corridor the vaults run from east to west, except in the central part where the vault running from north to south is a continuation of the vault under the central chamber. Under the five chambers all the vaults run from north to south.[1] The vaults are built of flat tiles laid in slices against the head-wall without centering. They have the usual small set forward from the wall, but in one case, perhaps in more than one, there is a slight divergence from the customary arrangement. From the spring of the vault the tiles are laid horizontally for the first sixteen or seventeen courses, projecting forward so as to form a shallow curve;

[1] Viollet has given a section of them, pl. xviii.

above these horizontal courses the tiles are laid upright and in slices; they form an ovoid curve more abrupt than the curve of the lower part of the vault. The fourth of the upper chambers, reckoning from east to west, is the best preserved. It shows the remains of a doorway, 1·85 m. wide, covered on the same principle as the small doors of the mosques, *i.e.* without lintel or arch. A moat or trench runs all round the castle and passes to the north of the gatehouse. A bridge, of which small trace remains, connected the gatehouse with a rectangular outpost. To the north and east of this outpost there are fragments of a wall and towers which encompassed a rectangular area.[1] The most interesting feature in the ruins is the niche decoration between the bastions of the north wall (Fig. 148). The niches have

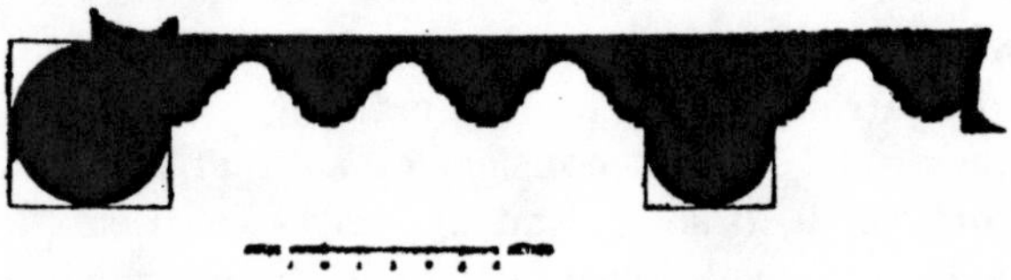

FIG. 148.—EL 'ASHIḲ, DETAIL OF NICHING ON NORTH FAÇADE.

been in part filled up—no doubt they were found to be too dangerous a weakness to the wall—but their scheme is clearly apparent (Fig. 144). Each niche consisted of a high cusped arch above a rectangular recessed panel which enclosed in turn a smaller arched niche. High up on the wall, near the western angle tower, there are traces of an upper order of niches. There is some indication that the niches were continued in the first north bay of the west wall, but the remainder of this wall, together with the whole of the east wall, is completely ruined. The disadvantage of these deep niches is evident in the south wall where the niche has been broken through at its weakest point and has now the appearance of a door. In the two central towers on this side there seemed to have been small flat-roofed chambers (Fig. 147). The building materials used in the castle are burnt and sun-dried brick. The foundations of the

[1] Viollet's plan, pl. xvii, is here more complete than mine.

FIG. 146.—SÂMARRÂ, EL 'ASHIḲ FROM NORTH.

FIG. 147.—SÂMARRÂ, EL 'ASHIḲ FROM SOUTH.

FIG. 150.—SÂMARRÂ, ṢLEBÎYEH.

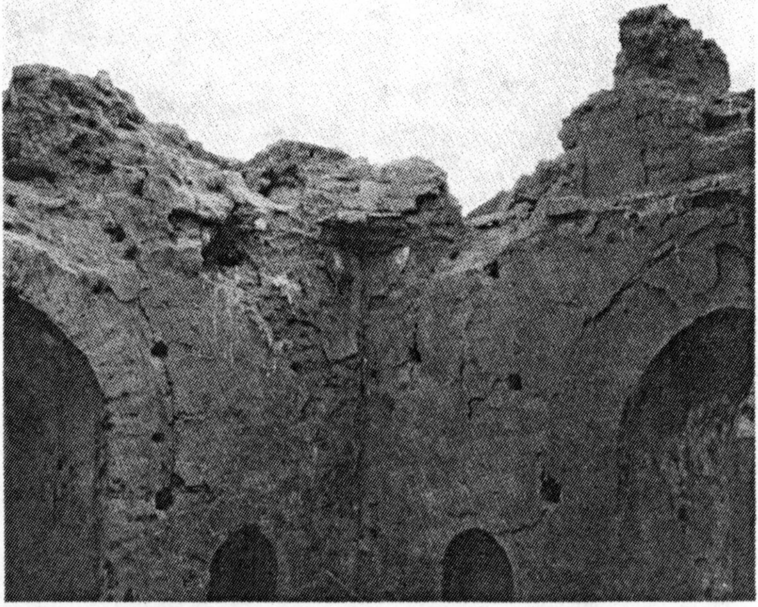

FIG. 151.—SÂMARRÂ, ṢLEBÎYEH, SETTING OF DOME.

walls and towers, the vaulted substructures, the niched face of the north wall and its towers, together with what remains of the south wall and towers are of burnt brick, but all the rest of the structure, including the partition walls of the gate-house, are of sun-dried brick, and the same material is used to fill up the niches in the north wall.

I rode northwards from the 'Ashiḳ for exactly an hour to the ruins of Ḥuweiṣilât where there are traces of a wall set with towers. One tower alone stood to any height; it appeared to mark the north-west corner of a rectangular enclosure, in the centre of which was a mound covered with fragments of tiles, but the east side of the enclosing wall was so completely destroyed that I could not make out the line of it. One important point is to be noted: the wall and towers were not built of brick, but of pebbles set in concrete, exactly similar to the masonry of the Ḳâim tower, and I think it possible that both Ḳâim and Ḥuweiṣilât may belong to an age prior to the Abbâsid period. It must, however, be added that the gateway of the castle at Tekrît, which is undoubtedly Mohammadan, is built of the same materials. South of the 'Ashiḳ is the ruin known as Ḳubbet es Ṣlebîyeh (Fig. 149). It consists of a small square central chamber, octagonal upon the exterior, encompassed by an octagonal corridor (Fig. 150). The central chamber had been covered by a dome which was set on a simple bracket over the angles of the substructure (Fig. 151); the corridor had been barrel vaulted. Fragments of the transverse arches that helped to carry the vault are still in place. Ṣlebîyeh was built of sun-dried brick covered with plaster.

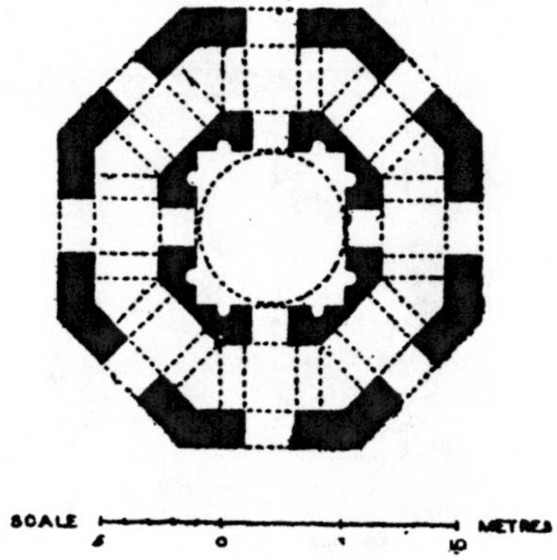

FIG. 149.—ṢLEBÎYEH.

When I went to the 'Ashiḳ for the second time I sent a

guffah up the river to above Lekweir and dropped down-stream to the ruins of the castle, whence we floated down to the camp. On this most pleasant expedition I took occasion to examine Lekweir. It lies about an hour's ride above Sâmarrâ, and unlike all the other ruins, it is in the low ground by the water's edge. Its complete destruction is perhaps due to its having been at the mercy of the flooded river. Great blocks of fallen brickwork lie upon the bank and in the stream, while a massive brick wall forms a sort of quay. A large building must have adjoined this quay, for the ground is tossed into mounds for a considerable distance and the mounds are strewn with broken brick and with fragments of thin marble slabs, pink, green and greyish-white in colour.

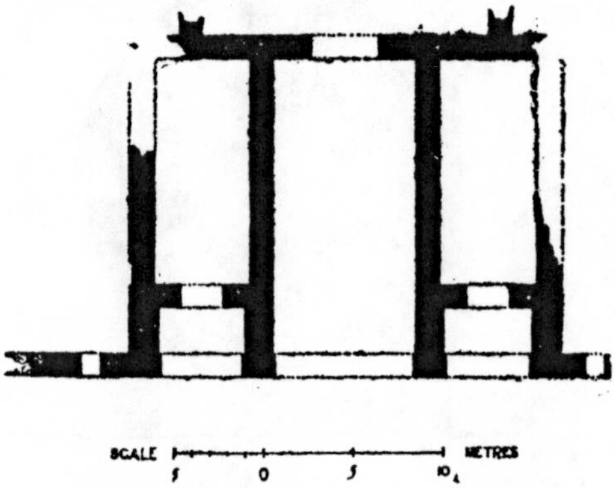

FIG. 152.—SÂMARRÂ, BEIT EL KHALÎFAH.

The only other edifice which has escaped complete destruction is the Beit el Khalîfah (the House of the Khalif) (Fig. 152).[1] It is a triple-vaulted hall standing above the Tigris (Fig. 153.)[2] The central hall was no doubt the audience chamber of the palace; it corresponds to the great hall at Ctesiphon. The two wings are divided into a small ante-chamber, covered with a semi-dome set on squinches (Fig. 154), and a larger room roofed with a barrel vault. The vaults are all slightly pointed and all are built on the Meso-

[1] I give a plan of the three vaulted halls, but Viollet has made a sketch plan of the ground behind which furnishes indications of the whole scheme of the palace. The Beit el Khalîfah is perhaps the Dâr el 'Ammeh, the first palace built by Mu'taṣim upon the site of the monastery: Herzfeld, *Sâmarrâ*, p. 63.

[2] Ross distinguished in 1834 a substructure of "arches" (*op. cit.*, p. 129) by which he must mean vaults like those at the 'Ashiḳ.

FIG. 153.—SÂMARRÂ, BEIT EL KHALÎFAH.

FIG. 154.—SÂMARRÂ, BEIT EL KHALÎFAH, DETAIL OF VAULT OF SIDE CHAMBER.

FIG. 156.—SÂMARRÂ, BEIT EL KHALÎFAH, STUCCO DECORATION.

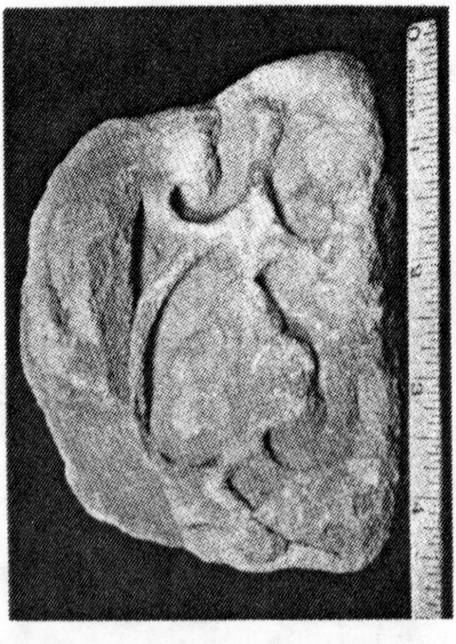

FIG. 157.—SÂMARRÂ, BEIT EL KHALÎFAH, FRAGMENT OF RINCEAUX WORKED IN MARBLE.

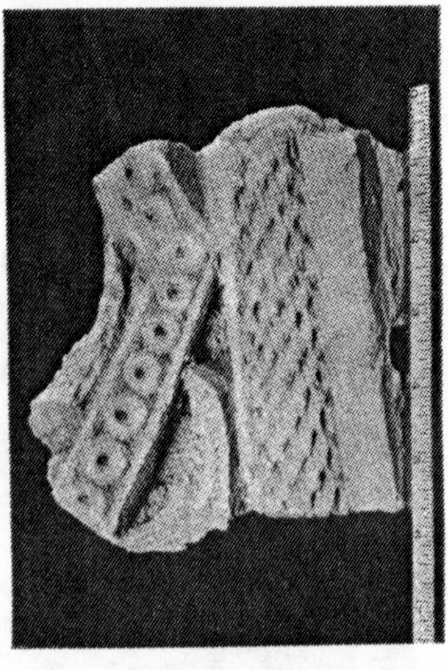

FIG. 158.—SÂMARRÂ, BEIT EL KHALÎFAH, STUCCO DECORATION.

potamian system, without centering and with a small corbelling forward from the wall. Under this outset there are a series of square holes as if for beams, though it is scarcely conceivable that beams can have been laid across the halls at this point. Round wooden poles were certainly used in the body of the walls; the wood has perished leaving the round hole which it occupied. The windows (or doors?) of the chambers on either side of the triple hall were covered without lintel or arch in the manner already described. The decoration of the palace must have been mainly of stucco, worked in relief or frescoed. Lying upon the ground were small fragments of plaster bearing a frescoed pattern of a simple kind, a row of circles outlined in red and yellow; a small piece of moulded stucco is still attached to the inside of the arch over the opening of the central chamber (Fig. 155) and I picked up other pieces (Fig. 158). While I was at work a peasant came to me and inquired whether I would like to see a picture which he had just unearthed. I went with him to a trench close at hand, where he had been digging for bricks, and found a beautiful piece of plaster work adhering to a wall (Fig. 156). It was doomed to instant destruction that the bricks behind it might be removed. I inquired whether such decorations were frequently discovered, and promised a reward for any piece that was brought to me, with the result that before I left I had been provided with four other examples. Three showed variants of a continuous pattern (Figs. 159 and 160), while the third was worked with a fret motive (Fig. 161). To the east of the triple hall there are some underground chambers hollowed out of the rock. They have been explained in various manners and fully described by Viollet. Here as elsewhere in Sâmarrâ the rock begins immediately below the surface of the ground. It is a conglomerate of pebbles in a bed of lime, exceedingly hard to work and covered with so thin a layer of earth that

FIG. 155.—BEIT EL KHALÎFAH, FRAGMENT OF STUCCO DECORATION ON ARCH.

no cultivation is possible. The cornfields and vineyards of the Abbâsid Sâmarrâ lay on the opposite bank of the Tigris in the low alluvial soil beneath the ridge on which stand Ḥuweiṣilât, the 'Ashiḳ and Ṣlebîyeh. Near the underground chambers of the Beit el Khalîfah there are considerable mounds, and in some places fragments of building which appertained to the palace. The walls are of sun-dried brick

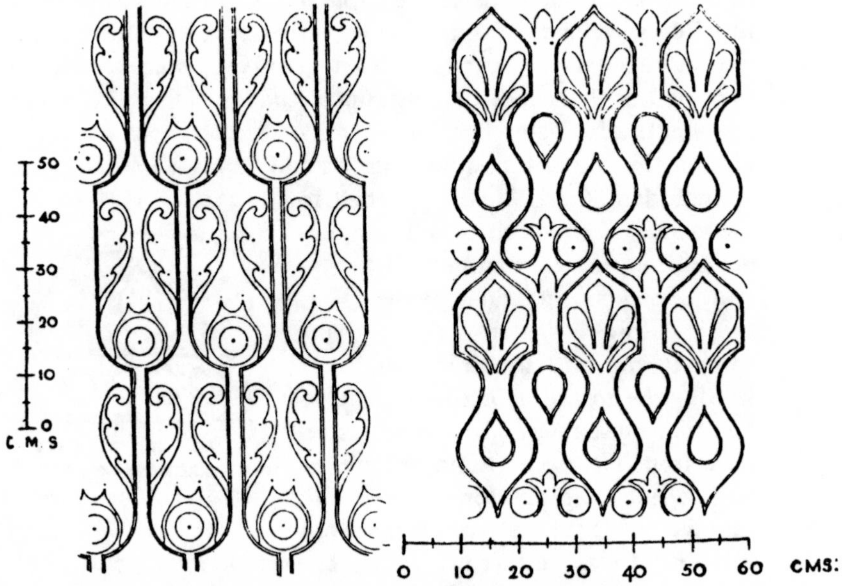

FIG. 159.—STUCCO DECORATIONS, SÂMARRÂ.

and the rooms have been covered with domes and semi-domes resting on squinch arches.

Almost due east of the Beit el Khalîfah there rises out of the middle of the plain a large artificial mound, Tell 'Alîj.[1] It is surrounded by a moat, and beyond the moat there are traces of a circular wall. A little to the east of north a raised causeway leads down from the top of the tell, crosses the moat by what must once have been a bridge and runs straight as an arrow over the space between moat and wall

[1] An account of it, together with a sketch plan, was given by Ross, *op. cit.*, p. 130.

FIG. 160.—SÂMARRÂ, STUCCO DECORATION.

FIG. 161.—SÂMARRÂ, STUCCO DECORATION.

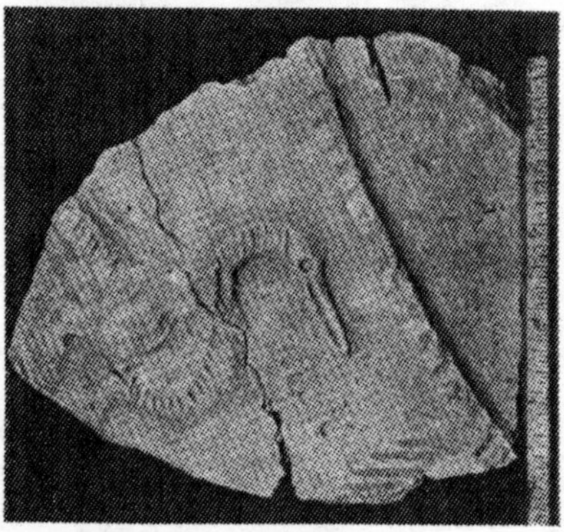

FIG. 162.—SÂMARRÂ, FRAGMENT OF POTTERY.

FIG. 163.—SÂMARRÂ, FRAGMENT OF POTTERY.

FIG. 165.—ABU DULÂF, ARCADE.

FIG. 166.—ABU DULÂF, NICHED PIER OF NORTHERN ARCADE.

(Ross made it 110 paces) and across the plain for about half-a-mile. It ends at a low mound where Ross found remains of brickwork. On either side of the point where the causeway reaches the outer edge of the ditch, a low mound, fanning out from the causeway, stretches from ditch to rampart. These mounds are the remains of walls that protected the causeway. Local tradition says that the moat was fed with water by a canal from the Tigris; Ross adds that the ḳanât, or cut as he calls it, brought water from a channel (he uses the word tunnel, by which he probably means ḳanât, underground conduit) which ran from the Jebel Ḥamrîn to Sâmarrâ. What this singular fortified mound can be I do not know, but I should be surprised if it did not belong to a period earlier than the days of the Abbâsids.

All the area of the city is strewn with Mohammadan potsherds, but the pottery is markedly different in character from that of Raḳḳah. Coloured ware, though it is not entirely absent, is rare; by far the greater number of pieces are unglazed and ornamented only with incised patterns which are frequently divided into zones by raised notched bands. I saw, too, a few fragments of a better class of pottery with beautiful patterns or inscriptions in relief, worked with the utmost care. When the peasants discovered that the patterned clay excited my interest they brought basket loads of broken pots to my tents and I drew and photographed innumerable examples, two of which I here reproduce (Figs. 162 and 163).

In the mosque of Abu Dulâf (Fig. 164)[1] the arcades are carried on massive brick piers and the effect of the long, half-ruined aisles is very imposing (Fig. 165). The area embraced by the outer wall of sun-dried brick is slightly smaller than at Sâmarrâ (213·20 × 136·50 m.) and the arcades are more widely spaced, but the type of plan is the same, even to the spiral minaret to the north. Although the enclosing wall is no better than a crumbling mound, it is possible to make out the

[1] Viollet has given a plan of Abu Dulâf. Herzfeld did not publish it in his *Sâmarrâ*, for he had not at that time visited it, but he has since published a plan: *Zeitschr. für Gesch. der Erkunde zu Berlin*, 1909, No. 7, pl. viii. My plan differs considerably from his, but only a re-examination of the mosque can prove which of us is right.

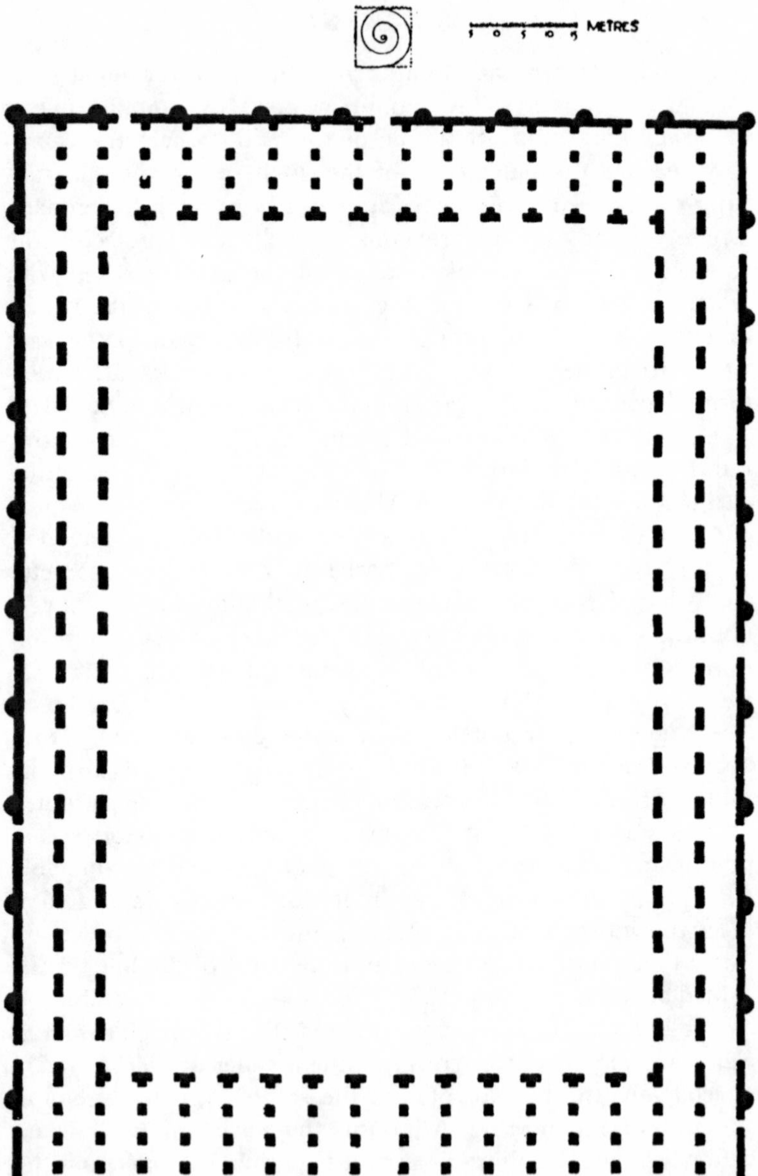

FIG. 164.—ABU DULÂF.

gateways, inasmuch as the jambs, which were built of burnt brick, stand more or less intact. The arcades and their returns against the wall are also of burnt brick, and so are the remains of the three bastions which are all that can be seen in the south wall. In the centre of this wall there is another fragment of burnt brick which might be the curve of a miḥrâb but is more probably a door leading into a small building or vestibule,[1] of which the shapeless mounds can be distinguished immediately to the south of the wall. There is a space of 10·40 m. between the outer wall and the southernmost row of piers, and the ruins give no indication of its having been roofed over. But if this transept were open to the sky it is unlikely that the miḥrâb should have been placed in it, and I should therefore place a door in the centre of the south wall as at Sâmarrâ. The space between the arcades at the northern and southern ends of the mosque averages 6·20 m., but the alley which conducts to the central door at either end measures 7·33 m. in width. Similarly the alley conducting to the central doors leading into the court from east and west is 4·90 m. wide, whereas the average width of the intercolumniation of the east and west arcades is 4·15 m. The plan exhibits everywhere noticeable irregularities; the arcades vary in width, sometimes by as much as ten centimetres. The small piers in the ḥaram average 2·10 × 1·73 m., the greater length being from north to south. The piers of the arcades to east and west of the ṣaḥn average 4·03 × 1·57 m.; the small piers of the northern arcades 2·18 × 1·52 m. All the piers bordering the central court are adorned upon the face which is turned towards the court with a brick niche covered with a cusped arch and placed high up on the pier (Fig. 166). There is also a decoration of small niches upon the north side of the base of the minaret; the other sides are too much ruined to have retained the trace of it. The north wall of the mosque

[1] This vestibule is present opposite the south gate of the Sâmarrâ mosque. Herzfeld has made an attempt to reconstruct the vestibule of Abu Dulâf. Viollet has given a bare indication of it, and this is all that exists. Viollet has also marked the line of an outer wall, which, as at Sâmarrâ, enclosed the precincts of the mosque.

is the best preserved, and shows in places the same drainage runnels that were described at Sâmarrâ.

The ruins of which I have here given a brief account are of the first importance for the elucidation of the early history of the arts of Islâm. They can all be dated within a period of forty years falling in the middle of the ninth century, and are therefore among the earliest existing examples of Mohammadan architecture. They bear witness to the Mesopotamian influences under which it arose. The spiral towers of Sâmarrâ and Abu Dulâf [1] are an adaptation of the temple pyramids of Assyria and Babylonia which had a spiral path leading to the summit; the technique of arch and vault was invented by the ancient East and transmitted through Sassanian builders to the Arab invaders; the decoration is Persian or Mesopotamian and almost untouched by the genius of the West.[2] In the palaces and mosques of Sâmarrâ, we can see the conquerors themselves conquered by a culture which had been developing during thousands of years on Mesopotamian soil, a culture which had received indeed new elements into its composition, which had learnt from the Greek and from the Persian, but had maintained in spite of all modifications its distinctive character. Side by side with Sâmarrâ stand the ruins at Raḳḳah, where the mosque repaired by Nûr ed Dîn probably preserves a plan which can be dated even earlier than the two mosques on the Tigris; and finally the scheme and decoration of the Mesopotamian mosque is reproduced with certain variations in the latter half of the ninth century by Ibn Ṭûlûn, and the last descendant of the Babylonian zigurrat is the minaret of his mosque at Cairo.[3]

[1] Abu Dulâf was probably built by Mutawakkil when he erected a whole new quarter three farsakhs north of Shnâs: Ya'ḳûbî, ed. de Goeje, p. 266.

[2] The spiral tower occurs also in Sassanian architecture, witness the Atesh Gah of Jur, Dieulafoy: *L'Art ancien de la Perse*, Vol. IV. p. 79.

[3] Thiersch has indicated the true relation of Ibn Ṭûlûn's minaret both to the zigurrat of Mesopotamia and to the pharos of Alexandria. His objections to Herzfeld's theory that the Cairo minaret is purely Hellenistic in origin are conclusive. Thiersch: *Pharos*, p. 112.

CHAPTER VII

MÔṢUL TO ZÂKHÔ

April 28—*May* 10

THE city of Môṣul has a turbulent record which has lost nothing of its quality during the past few years. It lies upon the frontier of the Arab and the Kurdish populations, and the meeting between those two is seldom accompanied by cordiality or good-will on either side. Upon the unhappy province of Môṣul hatred and the lust of slaughter weigh like inherited evils, transmitted (who can say?) through all the varying generations of conquerors since first the savage might of the Assyrian empire set its stamp upon the land. The town is distracted by the ambitions of powerful Arab families who ruled, until less than a century ago, each over his estate in undisputed sovereignty. These lordlings have witnessed, with an antagonism which they are scarcely at the pains to hide, the hand of the Turk tightening slowly over the district; nowhere will the Arab national movement, if it reaches the blossoming point, find a more congenial soil, and nowhere will it be watered by fuller streams of lawless vanity. Cruel and bloody as Ottoman rule has shown itself upon these remote frontiers, it is better than the untrammelled mastery of Arab beg or Kurdish âghâ, and if the half-exterminated Christian sects, the persecuted Yezîdîs, the wretched fellaḥîn of every creed, who sow in terror crops which they may never reap, are to win protection and prosperity, it is to the Turk that they must look. He, and he only, can control the warring races of his empire, and when he has learnt to use his power impartially and with rectitude, peace will follow. But it is yet far from Môṣul, and seldom has it seemed further than in the beginning of the year 1909.

Except inasmuch as a greater distance from Constantinople and Salonica meant a thinner trickle of western ideas, I do not believe that there existed in Môṣul a more definite opposition to the new order than in other places, though there, as elsewhere in Asiatic Turkey, the forces of reaction were numerous and strong. But Môṣul has always been against the government, whatever form it should happen to assume; the begs have always played with the authorities as you play with a fish on the hook, and the fact that they were now constitutional authorities gave an even better zest to the sport and barbed the hook yet more sharply. The affairs of the Committee had been ill managed. The local committee, which had formed on the proclamation of the constitution, had received with open arms the delegates who were sent from Salonica to instruct it in its duties—indeed the whole town had gone out to meet them, with the Vâlî and other notables at its head. But the delegates had been unfortunately chosen. Both were ignorant and tactless; one was a native of Kerkûk, the bitter rival of Môṣul, and he had, besides, anything but an unclouded personal reputation. The local committee lost rather than gained by their coming, and when they left, they rode unescorted across the bridge, and no one took notice of their departure. With them vanished the slender hopes of improvement which the proclamation of liberty, fraternity and equality had excited, and the begs were left with a clear field. To their ears the words had sounded like a knell. Universal liberty is not a gift prized by tyrants, and equality stinks in the nostrils of men who are accustomed to see their Christian fellow citizens cower into the nearest doorway when they ride through the streets. They had no difficulty in causing their dissatisfaction to be felt. The organization of discord is carried to a high pitch of perfection in Môṣul. The town is full of bravos who live by outrage, and live well. Whenever the unruly magnates wish to create a disturbance, they pass a word and a gratuity to these ruffians; the riot takes place, and who is to be blamed for it? The begs were all in their villages and could have had no hand in the matter; it was Abu'l

FIG. 167.—MÔṢUL.

FIG. 169.—MÔṢUL, MÂR JIRJIS.

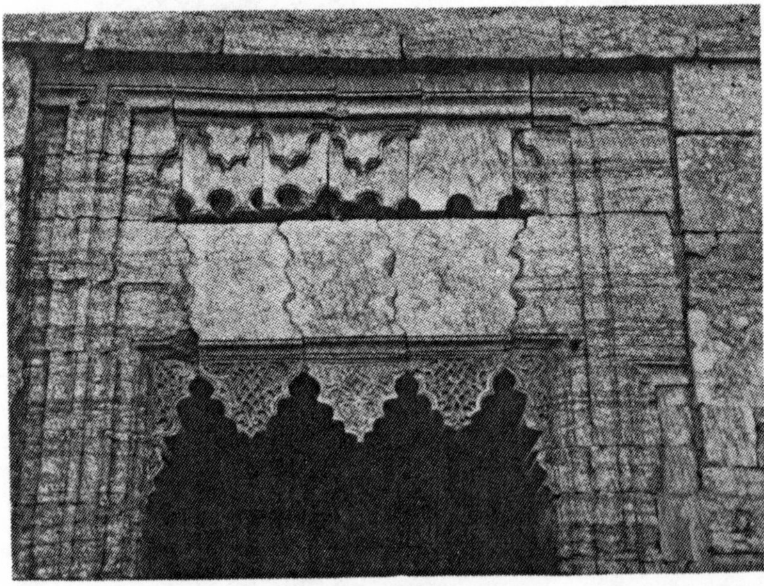

FIG. 170.—MÔṢUL, MÂR TÛMÂ.

Ḳâsim, the noted bandit, it was Ibn this or Ibn that. As for the opportunity, it is never far to seek, and upon this occasion it occurred on the last day of the feast of Bairam, January 1, 1909. The people were out in the streets, dressed in their best, as is proper to a festival, when a man of the Kurdish mule corps from Kerkûk insulted (so it is said) a Moslem woman of Môṣul. In an instant arms were out, the Arab soldiery attacked the Kerkûkî sowwârs, a fight ensued that lasted many hours, and in the confusion several Mohammadan women, holiday-makers, who had not had time to seek refuge in their houses, were killed and wounded, a most unusual disaster. Meantime, the Vâlî sat trembling in the serai and lifted not a finger to restore order. Late at night the Kerkûkîs retired to their own barracks, surrendered at discretion to the government, and gave up their arms. This episode might be dismissed as a natural ebullition of racial animosities, but the events of the following day can scarcely be explained except on the assumption that they were instigated by the begs. In the morning a rabble assembled before the serai and cried out for vengeance on the Kerkûkî sowwârs, who were awaiting judgment at the hands of the government. The Vâlî hesitated, and the ringleaders called upon the crowd to arm. The people executed this order with the alacrity of the forewarned, shops and private houses barred their doors and the town was thrown into a state of civil war.

There lived at that time in Môṣul a certain Kurdish holy man, a native of Suleimânîyeh on the Persian frontier. Some years earlier Sheikh Sayyid had fallen foul of the Turkish authorities—his own influence having swelled into too great a force—and had received a summons, which was regarded as implying the blackest misfortune, to present himself in Constantinople. It happened, when he arrived in the capital, that a favourite son of the Sultan was lying sick, and since the sheikh had a great reputation for sanctity, his punishment was delayed while he put up an intercession on behalf of the child. It was effectual: the boy recovered, and the sheikh returned in honour to his native place, with a chaplet of priceless pearls about his neck and a celebrity immensely enhanced. He was old and had long been harmless, but his sons traded upon his position and presently made Suleimânîyeh too hot to hold them. The whole family was under the direct protection of 'Abdu'l Ḥamîd; it was considered advisable to remove them to a spot where they would be equally directly under the eye of his deputy, the Vâlî, and they were brought to Môṣul. They came in like princes on a triumphal progress. The streets were choked with the mules that carried their possessions, and a house opposite the serai was assigned to them as a lodging.

No sooner had the rioters reassembled with arms on January 2, than they were directed to the house of the Kurdish family. Sheikh Sayyid was a man of eighty-five, but he had the courage of his race. When he heard the mob storming at his doors, he took the Ḳurân in his hand and clothed in years and sanctity stepped out into the street, intending to take refuge in the serai. Its door was opposite his own, and the Vâlî from a window watched the scene. The rabble gave way before the venerable figure clasping the holy book, but before he could reach the serai, it closed in upon him, he was cut down and hacked to pieces. His house was then sacked and seventeen of his descendants were murdered. If the leaders of the reactionary party had wished to embarrass the government and to show up its weakness, they were more than commonly successful. During the six weeks that elapsed before the arrival of troops from Diyârbekr and elsewhere, Môṣul was in a state of complete anarchy. Christians were openly insulted in the streets, the civil and military authorities were helpless, and no less helpless was the local committee of Union and Progress. When the troops came some degree of order was restored, but the reactionary movement was not arrested. The formation of the League of Mohammad, which was designed as a counterblast to the Committee of Union and Progress, went on apace. It appealed to Moslems of the old school, who had a genuine dread of the effects of the new spirit upon the observance of the laws of Islâm; it appealed to the ignorant, to whom the conception of the equality of Christian and Moslem is incomprehensible, and it was eagerly welcomed by all who were opposed to constitutional government on grounds more or less personal to themselves. One great magnate went through the bazaars collecting the signatures of adherents to the Muḥammadîyeh, and for a time the situation was exceedingly critical. It was however significant that the Naḳîb of Môṣul, the leading doctor of Islâm, steadily refused to sign the papers or to have anything to do with the League. Meanwhile a new and capable Vâlî had been appointed to the province, but he had gone straight to Kerkûk, where matters were in a still more parlous state, and lawlessness walked abroad unchecked in the streets of Môṣul. At length the Vâlî realized the dangers that threatened the province through its capital, and being a man of action he travelled post haste to Môṣul, and set about the restoration of order. He arrested and imprisoned a number of persons and administered severe rebukes to the leading Moslems, together with assurances that the government would protect the rights of the Christians. These warnings were repeated in strong language the day after the accession of Muḥammad Reshâd when the first rumours of a massacre of Armenians at Adana reached the bazaars.

The fall of 'Abdu'l Ḥamîd set an immediate term to the agitation. In all likelihood the counter revolution of April 13 had caused no surprise to the organizers of the League of Mohammad, but the swift action of the Salonica committee had not been foreseen. The story ran that after the flight of the deputies from Constantinople the Vâlî had received a telegram bidding him obey no orders from the capital of the empire—I cannot vouch for the truth of the tale, but it is not in itself improbable. The Vâlî was backed by an unwontedly large body of troops (those who had been sent in to quell the disturbances which had arisen out of the murder of Sheikh Sayyid), and all over Turkey the troops stood loyal to the constitution. The city waited with a growing apprehension as day by day telegrams arrived reporting the advance of the Salonica army on Constantinople, nor was it unknown that a message from Baghdâd, offering instant help to the constitutional party, had passed through Môṣul. Then on a sudden came word that 'Abdu'l Ḥamîd had been deposed, and, except to the country folk and to me upon the high road, it had been half expected. So it was that when I came to Môṣul I found the town, which is one of the worst conducted in the Ottoman empire, submissive and quiet. In the week during which I remained there we had no further intelligence save the vague rumour of an outbreak at Adana; even the assurance that Muḥammad V was sultan in his brother's place we accepted from Turkish official sources, neither had we any means of ascertaining whether he had been recognized by the Powers of Europe. Turkish official sources are apt to be tainted, and few regions can be further removed than Eastern Turkey from the pure fountain of the truth; nevertheless the British Embassy in Constantinople did not see fit to acquaint its vice-consuls in Asiatic Turkey with the accession of a new sovereign. I leave this observation without comment. But if we in Môṣul were uncertain as to the turn events had taken in Europe, we had valuable opportunities of gauging local conditions. In Môṣul not a voice was raised against the second triumph of the new order. With the entire lack of initiative which characterizes the Asiatic provinces, men resigned themselves to a decree of Fate which was substantially backed by the army. Whether this second victory was to prove more decisive and more permanent than the first was open to question; the doubt kept people to their houses and affected the attitude of some of the most powerful of the begs, who, being lords of great possessions which they desired to enjoy in peace, would have given a whole-hearted support to the new Sultan, but held back lest his government should not prove strong enough to defend them against their ill-conditioned brethren. In vain the Vâlî filled the prisons to overflowing with noted malefactors; if he brought them to trial he knew that no one would dare to advance evidence against them, and in the meantime the gaols were growing more dangerously crowded every day. There was undoubtedly some personal feeling for

'Abdu'l Ḥamîd, but it was rare. I made the acquaintance of a citizen of Môṣul, a splendid type of the old school, for whom it was impossible not to feel sympathy, even though I know him to have been one of the instigators of the murder of Sheikh Sayyid: this man watched from a room in the serai the proclamation of Muḥammad V, and when he saw the soldiery tear down and trample under foot edicts which were signed with 'Abdu'l Ḥamîd's name, he, being alone but for one other, who was my informant, threw himself upon the ground and wept. "The dogs!" he cried. "Yesterday they would have been proud if their name had been mentioned in the same breath with his." To me he was more guarded; moreover he had had time to recover his balance. But he predicted wreck and ruin, bloodshed, revolution and all other evils for his country.

"Is there no remedy?" said I.

"If the source is pure the whole stream is pure," he answered enigmatically.

"Was the source pure?" I asked.

He hesitated a moment, and then replied: "No, by God and the Prophet! A king should go about among his subjects, see them and hear them. He should not sit imprisoned in his house, listening to the talk of spies."

I know another, poles asunder from the first, one of the richest men in the town and one of the most evil: a slave by birth, he might not sit in the presence of his former master, although the master, great gentleman as he was, could scarcely outmatch the wealth of the liberated slave. Him I asked whether there was any strength behind the Arab movement.

"The Khalîfah should be of the tribe of the Ḳureish," he answered significantly.

"Who would be Khalîfah if he were chosen from out of the Ḳureish?" I asked.

"The Sherîf of Mecca is of that blood," he answered. "The Arabs would govern themselves."

He left me to reflect upon his words, for I was well aware that if he chose to support them with force, all the rogues with whom the city abounds were at his command, and all the plots and counterplots of the vilayet were familiar to him.

I sat long in the guest chamber of a third acquaintance, the head of the greatest family in Môṣul. So stainless is his lineage that his sisters must remain unwed, since Môṣul cannot provide a husband equal to them in birth. His forebears were Christians who migrated from Diyârbekr two hundred years ago. The legend runs that his Christian ancestor, soon after he had come to Môṣul, went out in the morning to be shaved, but when he reached the barber's shop it was filled with low-born Moslems and the barber kept him waiting until the heads of the Faithful had been trimmed. "Shall a man of my house wait for such as these?" he cried, and forthwith abjured the creed of slaves. His descendant was one of those who would gladly have seen the new order triumph and give peace to the land. He called down vengeance upon the head of Aḥmed 'Izzet Pasha, one of the worst of the late Sultan's sycophants, and upon that of his brother, Muṣṭafâ, sometime Vâlî of Môṣul. "If he had stayed two years more he would have ruined the town," said he. But his hatred of 'Izzet Pasha had not blinded him to the dictates of honour. It happened that by those methods of persuasion of which 'Izzet was master, he had induced my friend to present him with a valuable piece of land. Two months later 'Izzet fell and fled in terror of death from Constantinople, but the beg would not revoke a gift which the disgraced favourite was powerless to exact from him. *Noblesse oblige.*

I had also the advantage of conversing with several bishops. Now there are so many bishops in these parts that it is impossible to retain more than a composite impression of them. They correspond in number to the Christian sects, which are as the sands of the sea-shore, but as I was about to journey through districts inhabited by their congregations, I made an attempt to grasp at least the names by which their creeds are distinguished from one another. As for more fundamental distinctions, they depend upon the wording of a metaphysical proposition which I will not offer to define, lest I should fall, like most of my predecessors, into grievous heresy. The most interesting, historically, of these several denominations are the people of Mâr Shim'ûn, some of whom I had met upon the road. They are currently known as Nestorians, though, as Layard has observed, this title is misapplied. The followers of Mâr Shim'ûn are the representatives of the ancient Chaldæan Church, and their race is probably as near to the pure Assyrian stock as can be expected in regions so often conquered, devastated and repeopled. Their church existed before the birth of Nestorius, and was not dependent upon him for its tenets;[1] its doctrines are those of primitive Christianity untouched by the influence of Rome, and its creed, with unimportant verbal differences, is that of Nicæa. After the Council of Ephesus, in 431, the members of the Chaldæan Church separated themselves from those who acknowledged the authority of the Pope. Politically they were already a separate community, for they lived, not under the Byzantine, but under the Sassanian empire. Their missionaries carried Christianity all over Asia, from Mesopotamia to the Pacific. Their patriarch, whose title was, and still is, Catholicos of the Eastern Church, was seated first at Ctesiphon; when Baghdâd became the capital of the khalifate, the patriarchate was removed thither, and upon the fall of the Arab khalifs it was transferred to Môṣul. During the sixteenth century a schism took place which led to the existence of two patriarchs, one living at the monastery of Rabbân Hormuzd near Alkôsh, and one at Kochannes in the mountains south of Vân. The first, with his adherents, submitted, two centuries ago, to the Pope; they are known as the Chaldæans,

[1] I believe it is generally admitted by the learned in these matters that Nestorius was not guilty of the heresies for which he was condemned in 431, at the second œcumenical council held at Ephesus. I remember to have heard a distinguished English Catholic, who was also an acute historian, express his definite opinion that Nestorius was in the right, for all his expulsion beyond the pale of western Christianity. An excellent account of the rise of the Eastern Churches is contained in Wigram's recently published book, *The Assyrian Church.*

and they are said to bear the yoke of Rome very unwillingly. The second is now the only patriarch of the old independent church, which has been dubbed Nestorian. The office may be termed hereditary; it passes from uncle to nephew in a single family, for the patriarch is not permitted to marry; the holder of it is always known as Mâr Shim'ûn, the Lord Simeon. It is generally believed that if the new government were to succeed in establishing order, so that the protection of a foreign Power should cease to be of vital importance, the Chaldæan converts would return in a body to their former allegiance to the Catholicos of the East.

A similar division exists among the Jacobites, the Syrian monophysites, who were condemned in 451 by the fourth œcumenical council, held at Chalcedon. A part of this community has submitted to Rome and is known as the Syrian Church, while those who have retained their independence have retained also their old title of Jacobites. To this pious confusion Protestant missionaries, English and American, have contributed their share. There are Syrian Protestants and Nestorian Protestants—if the terms be admissible—though whether the varying shades of belief held by the instructors are reflected in the instructed, I do not know, and I refrained from an inquiry which might have resulted in the revelation of Presbyterian Nestorians, Church of England Jacobites, or even Methodist Chaldæans.

None but the theologian would essay a valuation of the relative orthodoxy of converted and unconverted, but the archæologist must hold no uncertain opinion as to their merits. The unification, so far as it has gone, of the two ancient Churches with Rome is an unmitigated misfortune. The Chaldæans and the Syrians, instigated perhaps by their pastors, have been so eager to obliterate the memory of their former heterodoxy that they have effaced with an unsparing hand all, or nearly all, Syriac inscriptions older than the date of their regeneration, and in Môṣul it is rare to find any written stone earlier than the end of the seventeenth century. This is the more provoking as several of the churches are of great architectural interest, and it is much to be regretted that the epigraphic record of their history should not have been preserved. So far as I could judge, the oldest parts of the oldest churches may probably be dated in the twelfth or thirteenth centuries. All have been considerably remodelled; some were entirely rebuilt after the siege of Môṣul by Nâḍir Shah in 1743 and others have been rebuilt in recent years.[1] Moreover there are several which would seem to have been first founded as late as the eighteenth century. But whatever may be their date, they all exhibit the same simple plan, a plan which I believe to be essentially Mesopotamian and more ancient by many centuries than the existing churches. It is that of the barn church, the church with two aisles and a nave, covered by parallel barrel vaults so equal in height as not to admit of a clerestorey.[2] The nave and aisles are invariably cut off from the sanctuary by a wall—it is too substantial to be called an iconostasis—broken by three large doors. This complete separation is not typical of primitive ecclesiastical architecture; it results, as a rule, from a development of the ritual; but it appears to be here a part of the original plan. The sanctuary is almost invariably divided into three parts, corresponding to the nave and aisles, and, as a rule, the central altar is covered by a dome set upon squinch arches. The church of Mâr Ahudânî will serve as a typical example (Fig 168); it is now in the hands of the Chaldæans. A flight of steps leads down to it from the street, and the fact that it lies so far below the modern level is one of the indications of its antiquity. The stair opens into a small atrium with a cloister to east and west. The church is to the south of the atrium and there is no means of approach to it from any other side. The present atrium is comparatively modern and the church shows many signs of reconstruction and repair. The doorway from the nave to the sanctuary is richly decorated with Arabic inscriptions, with

[1] I am relying upon local tradition, upon comparison with churches in the country districts, and upon the character of the ornament compared with Moslem ornament in Môṣul which can be dated with tolerable accuracy.

[2] The barn church is more fully defined in *The Thousand and One Churches*, published by Sir W. Ramsay and myself, p. 309.

mouldings and entrelac, Mohammadan in character, and I should say not far removed from the early thirteenth century in date. There are also motives which are repeated with variations upon all the churches of a like epoch, grotesque lions and the cross-legged figure which has been described upon one of the gates of Baghdâd. The building was so dark that my photographs were not successful, but an outer doorway of Mâr Girjis gives an adequate idea of the

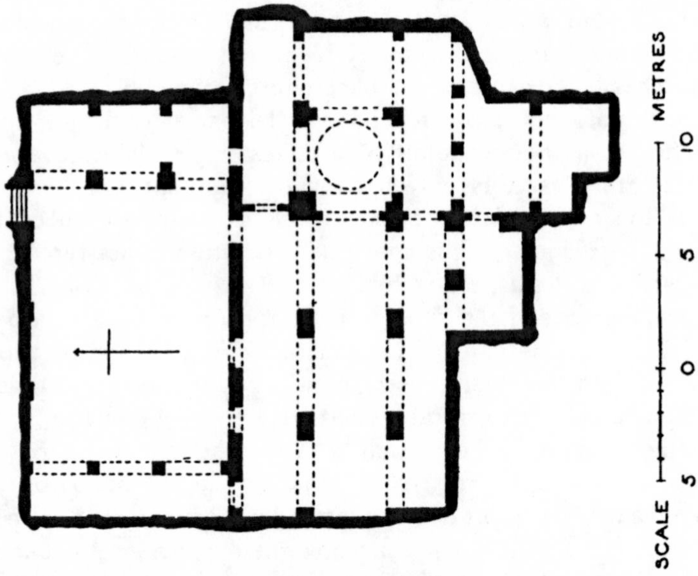

FIG. 168.—MÂR AHUDÂNÎ.

scheme of decoration (Fig. 169). The straight arch, which serves here as lintel, is a universal characteristic; so, too, are the ornaments pendant from the voussoirs. The doorways in the cloister that lies to the west of Mâr Tûmâ, the episcopal church of the Syrians, exhibit beautiful variants of the same theme (Fig. 170).[1] In this church the door leading from the nave to the sanctuary is framed by an entrelac enclosing in its windings the figures of Christ and the Twelve Apostles.

[1] There is a description of Mâr Tûmâ in Rich: *Residence in Koordistan*, Vol. II. p. 118.

FIG. 171.—MÔṢUL, MÂR TÛMÂ.

FIG. 172.—MÔṢUL, MÂR SHIM'UN.

FIG. 173.—MÔṢUL, PLASTER WORK IN ḲAL'AT LÛLÛ.

FIG. 174.—MÔṢUL, TOMB OF THE IMÂM YAḤYÂ.

Three extra aisles have recently been added to the original building, and I understood the church to be shared between the Syrians and the Chaldæans. If the Christian architects continued to make use of a primitive Oriental plan, it is even more certain that they continued to be dependent upon Eastern artists for their decorative schemes, and were in no way linked with the West. Their decoration is the same as that which is to be found in contemporary Mohammadan buildings. For instance, a lintel which now lies in the atrium of Mâr Shim'ûn, a church which has been almost entirely rebuilt, is carved with an entrelac unmistakably Mohammadan (Fig. 172). Over one of the doors of Mâr Tûmâ there is a band of ornament which may perhaps have been taken from a Mohammadan building, though it is more probable that it formed part of the original Christian work (Fig. 171).[1] The style of this deeply undercut relief is so marked that it imprints itself upon the memory. I saw other examples of it in the beautiful tomb of the Imâm Yaḥyâ which, according to an inscription, was built by the Sultan Lûlû (Fig. 174).[2] A mosque for the Friday prayers existed in the time of Ibn Baṭûṭah close to the Tigris, and this is in all probability the building which is praised by Mustaufî, who says that "the stone sculptured ornament is so intricate that it might stand for wood carving."[3] This particular kind of stone relief, which is to be found both in Moslem and in Christian buildings, does in fact closely resemble wood carving, and the Christian examples cannot be of a different date from the Moslem. The first recorded mosque in Môṣul was built by Marwân II, the last of the Omayyad khalifs (744–750), not far from the Tigris, according to Ibn Ḥauḳal; so far as I know, no trace of it has survived. Nûr ed Dîn, the Atabeg

[1] All the doors in the atrium of Mâr Tûmâ look as if they had been patched together out of older materials, but I suspect that these materials came from the church itself and that the patching is due to repair.

[2] Badr ed Dîn Lûlû, 1233–1259, according to Lane Poole: *Mohammadan Dynasties*, p. 163; Ritter, following Desguignes, makes him regent from 1213–1222, and an independent sovereign from 1222–1259.

[3] Le Strange: *Lands of the Eastern Caliphate*, p. 89.

(1146-1172), built a second Friday mosque in the bazaar, and this must be the great mosque with the leaning minaret which stands in the centre of the town, but how much of the original work remains I could not determine, for Mohammadan feeling was running high when I was in Môṣul, and at such times it is wiser not to ask for admittance into mosques.[1] Finally a third Friday mosque was erected near the Tigris (represented, as I conjecture, by the tomb of the Imâm Yaḥyâ), and to Lûlû's day belongs also the ziyârah of 'Abdullah ibn Ḥassan in the heart of the town. The entrelac round the door of this ziyârah is very similar to the decoration of the sanctuary door in Mâr Tûmâ, except that the figures are absent. In the interior there is a band of deeply-cut stone relief of the wood-work type. The fluted cone-like roof with which the ziyârah is covered is found in all the Moslem tombs of Môṣul. There is another fragment of Lûlû's handiwork which, ruined though it be, is of great architectural importance, the Ḳal'at Lûlû on the Tigris bank, not far from the tomb of the Imâm Yaḥyâ.[2] Only the eastern end of two vaulted halls is standing, but in one of these remains of stucco ornament still cling to the walls (Fig. 173). The ornament consists of a band of inscription and a band of tiny arcades, each arch containing the representation of a nude human figure, depicted from head to waist.[3] Below this band there has been another design of larger arches covered with rinceaux which are adorned with flowers and birds. The town walls are comparatively modern, but the Sinjâr Gate, on the west side, is worthy of note. It resembles the gates of Aleppo, and like them it bears a blazonry of lions.

One other memory of the days at Môṣul stands very freshly in my mind. There exists in the town a small and indigent Jewish community—neither too small nor too poverty-stricken

[1] Oppenheim, *Vom Mittelmeere zum persischen Golf*, Vol. II. p. 176, gives a short description of it.

[2] De Beylié has given a good photograph of the general view: *Prome et Samarra*, p. 49.

[3] This decoration is curiously akin to some of the Buddhist Græco-Bactrian work.

to have attracted the watchful care of the Alliance Juive.[1] Under their auspices, M. Maurice Sidi, a courageous and highly cultivated Tunisian, has opened a school for the children, and by precept and example he imparts the elements of civilization, letters and cleanliness, to young and old. The English vice-consul, who had witnessed his efforts with great sympathy and admiration, invited him to bring a deputation of his co-religionists to the consulate while I was there, and a dignified body of bearded and white-robed elders filed one morning into the courtyard. We returned their visit at the school, where we were received by a smiling crowd, dressed in their best, who pressed bunches of flowers upon us. The class-rooms were filled with children proudly conscious that their achievements in the French, Arabic and Hebrew tongues had called down honour upon their race. The scholars in the Hebrew class, who were of very tender years, were engaged in learning lists of Hebrew words with their Arabic equivalents, Hebrew being an almost forgotten language among the Jews of Môṣul. M. Sidi drew forward a tiny urchin who stood unembarrassed before us, and gazed at him expectantly with solemn black eyes.

"What do you know?" said the master.

The black-eyed morsel answered without a shadow of hesitation: "I know Elohim." And while I was wondering how much of the eternal secret had been revealed to that small brain, he began to recite the first list in the lesson-book, which opened with the name of God: "Elohim, Allah"—I do not remember how it went on, neither did he remember, without M. Sidi's prompting. Elohim was what he knew.

Over against Môṣul lies Nineveh. The pontoon bridge that spans the Tigris had been swept away by the floods; the masonry arches on the further side stood out into the river, but where the causeway dips down to meet the bridge of boats it met nothing but the swiftly-flowing stream. We crossed therefore by a ferry, and so rode up to the mound of Kûyûnjik, where Xenophon saw the ruins of Nineveh and

[1] In the middle ages it was more numerous. Benjamin of Tudela found a colony of 7,000 Jews at Môṣul: Ritter, Vol. X. p. 254.

thought them to be a city of the Medes. His description of the immense area they covered scarcely seemed incredible as we stood upon the mound. The line of the walls ran out far to the north, far, too, to the south, embracing the neighbouring mound of Nebî Yûnus, which is the site of one of Jonah's many tombs. The corn grew deep on Ḳûyûnjik, and the blue bee-eaters flew in and out of Layard's excavation pits; across the fertile plain rose the towers of Môṣul; the broad Tigris ran between, which Saladin sought to turn from its bed when he laid siege to Nûr ed Dîn. His imperious folly is as forgotten as the splendours of Sennacherib—

> "And such plenty and perfection, see, of grass
> Never was!
> Such a carpet as this summer time o'erspreads
> And embeds
> Every vestige of the city . . ."

Had the poet been dreaming of Nineveh when he wrote *Love Among the Ruins?*

> "Shut them in
> With their triumphs and their glories and the rest . . ."

We rode from Nineveh through blazing heat for four hours across a plain where the peasants were harvesting the barley while the locusts harvested the green wheat, which was not ripe enough to save. The sun beat so fiercely upon us that I sought refuge in the house of the village sheikh at 'Amrḳân, and ate in his guest-chamber a lunch which was made more palatable by the sour curds which he set before us. An hour and a half further we came to Mâr Behnâm, and found the tents pitched upon the slopes of a mound above a deep round pool. On the one side of our camp lay the monastery of Mâr Behnâm, on the other the shrine that covers his grave.[1]

[1] An account of Mâr Behnâm has been published by Pognon: *Inscriptions de la Mésopotamie*, p. 132. He believes that the existing church is due to a reconstruction that took place in the twelfth century, but its original form seems to him to be the same as that of Mâr Gabriel of Kartmîn in the Ṭûr 'Abdîn, a church which I should date not later than the sixth century. The history of Mâr Behnâm would therefore offer an exact analogy to that of the churches of Môṣul, according to my theory;

The monastery has the appearance of a small fort. Its outer walls have been many times ruined and repaired, and the interior buildings, all except the beautiful church, are modern. The doorways leading from the porch into the church and from the nave and aisles into the sanctuaries are covered with lacework patterns, interspersed with small figures of angels, lions and snakes, together with Arabic and Syriac inscriptions. In the porch, between the two doors, there is a small niche worked with arabesques, the very counterpart of a Moslem miḥrâb. There are square chambers leading out of the aisles, roofed with pointed domes which are elaborately worked with stucco ornaments. Upon the east wall and on one of the piers of the nave are two stucco plaques, one representing St. George on horseback, the other a full-length figure of a saint. On both there are traces of colour.[1] I paid my respects to the saint's tomb in company with a number of pilgrims from Môṣul who were spending the night in the monastery. At dusk the villagers assembled under the mound, which marks the spot as some small suburb of Nineveh, and watered their flocks at the pool; I watched them from my tent door and thought that the scene must have changed but little in the past three thousand years.[2]

---

it is a mediæval building following the lines of a very early structure. Pognon gives a good illustration of the altar niche in the tomb (Pl. VIII), which is dated the year of the Seleucid era corresponding to 1306 A.D. The superstructure he takes to have been a baptistery.

[1] They must be dated before 1550, according to Pognon's reasoning. He speaks of them with great contempt, and they are not very remarkable works of art, though they seemed to me to be of considerable interest. The Moslems call the monastery Deir el Khiḍr, Khiḍr being the Mohammadan counterpart of St. George. The village close at hand is known as El Khiḍr.

[2] The following notes on the decorations of the church are perhaps worth recording. S.W. door in porch: on lintel, a pair of birds on either side of a cross; over lintel, two snakes, tail to tail, with open jaws turned to what looks like a piled-up cup; in the corners, lions with tails ending in the head of a snake; band of entrelac and round it a band of Syriac inscriptions surrounding the door. N.W. door in porch: on lintel, an angel on either side of a cross; over lintel, small crosses with a boss between, two circles with a star in each; at either corner the figure of a saint; entrelac and inscriptions. Door from nave into

We rode next day in two and a half hours to Ḳaraḳôsh, where there are no less than seven churches. Three of them stand outside the village, each surrounded by its fortress wall, which usually encloses one or two small living-rooms besides the church. They reminded me forcibly of the walled Coptic monasteries of Egypt, but the monastic buildings were smaller. Between them stretched fields of barley wherein the villagers, standing in line, were pulling up the crops to the strains of the bagpipes. The churches were oriented almost at haphazard, and provided with the smallest doors, and windows to correspond. The interiors were so dark that I abandoned all hope of photographing the ornaments upon the inner doors,[1] though I made a rapid sketch of the lintel

FIG. 175.—ḲARAḲÔSH, DECORATION ON LINTEL OF MÂR SHIM'ÛN.

over the sanctuary door of Mâr Shim'ûn (Fig. 175). Above it was a slab bearing a floral Persian pattern incised upon the stone. Inside the town several of the churches had recently been repaired, or were in process of reparation. A young priest, Kas Yûsef, showed me the work, and gloried in the replacing of old and ruined churches by new and brand-new

---

apse; on lintel, a lion's head forming a central boss, on either side St. George and the Dragon. Door into S.E. chapel: on lintel a cross; round door, small niches formed by an interlacing rope (*cf.* the sanctuary door of Mâr Tûmâ at Môṣul), the niches alternately filled with a saint and a decorated cross; above the door two of the niches are filled with representations of: (1) the baptism in Jordan; (2) the entry into Jerusalem, with an ass and palms in the background. The spandrils between the upper niches are filled in with dragons' heads with open jaws.

[1] Pognon found inscriptions of the thirteenth, fifteenth, and sixteenth centuries at Ḳaraḳôsh (*op. cit.*, p. 129), but the inscriptions inside the churches have not, so far as I know, been recorded.

edifices. New lamps for old, but it was the old lamp that could summon the genius, and I realized the sound moral of the fairy story as I watched the refurbishing of ancient walls at Ḳaraḳôsh; but I did not impart my impression to the Syrian priest, whose ardour it would have been unkind to damp. The Syrians have annexed most of the larger churches, so said the worthy Jacobite father who brought me the key of Mâr Shim'ûn, and he told his tale not without a touch of bitterness. Yet it would have been folly to blink the fact that he was no match for Kas Yûsef, who was young and eager, and had been trained in a French school at Môṣul. Twenty minutes beyond Ḳaraḳôsh we came to the ruined church of Mâr Yuhanna Deleimoyya (St. John the Deleimî), which no one has troubled to repair, though it had beautiful carved lintels and domes adorned with plasterwork. Thence we rode for an hour through cornlands to Bârtallâ, and saw Bâ'ashikâ at the foot of the hills. They were real hills which lay before us, not the bare desert ridges which were all the heights we had seen since we crossed over Lebanon on the way to Aleppo. Here were the buttresses of mightier ranges than Lebanon, the alps of Kurdistân which end the land of the two rivers. As we climbed upwards, the corn grew greener, the grass deeper, the flowers more brilliant along the edge of trickling streams. But my companions paid no heed to these marvels. Jûsef's thoughts were busy with the great cities he had seen since he set forth on his travels, and especially with Môṣul, last and therefore fairest in his memory. He rehearsed its advantages to the Môṣul zaptieh, and 'Abdullah was well pleased to listen to such talk.

"Not even in Aleppo," said Jûsef magnanimously, "do you find better bread."

"However many places there may be in the world," pronounced 'Abdullah, "there is none where the bread is so good."

"It is sweet," assented Jûsef.

"And if you take tobacco from Môṣul to Baghdâd," 'Abdullah pursued, "it rots there. The air of Baghdâd is not like the air of Môṣul."

"Wallah, no!" said Jûsef the much-travelled, weighing city against city in the finest judicial manner.

We rode through exquisite meadows, and in about five hours and a half from Ḳaraḳôsh crossed a mountain stream that rippled between banks rosy with oleander—Solomon in all his glory was not arrayed in robes so softly flushed. Beyond it my camp was pitched upon a swelling slope below the steep rocks of Jebel Maḳlûb, wherein, placed high among the hills, stood the monastery of Mâr Mattai, a grey wall hanging over a precipice. I left my horse at the camp, and taking 'Abdullah with me, set out on a half-hour's climb up a narrow gorge, full of the western sun, which was golden now, and clement. Every crevice between the stones was gay with a small starry campanula, gentian-blue, mountain-blue, the full clear colour of an upland flower; and thrusting their strong roots under the rocks, the terebinths hung glossy foliage over the path—I found myself, as I looked once more upon the divine curves of leafy twig and bough, heaping contempt upon the recollection of that leggy vegetable, the palm. A ragged boy opened the monastery gate and conducted us by a long stair to a terrace from which the bishop had watched our progress up the gorge. He bade me go quickly, while the sun still shone, to see the church and the tombs of Mâr Mattai and of Bar Hebræus, but the church had been rebuilt, the inscriptions on the tombs were already known, and my desire turned towards the bishop, and the coffee which he was preparing for us, and the room on the terrace where the cushioned windows opened on to the Assyrian plain. The bishop was old and very garrulous; the monastery, high set above the world, was beyond the reach of mundane intelligence, the only monk had gone down to Môṣul, and in the Jebel Maḳlûb men were still uncertain under which lord they served. Was it indeed true, asked the bishop, that Muḥammad Reshâd was Sultan of Turkey? and he rejoiced greatly when we confirmed the rumour. But his thoughts wandered back to older histories, and hearing that we had come from Mâr Behnâm, he began to instruct us in matters pertaining to that shrine.

"My daughter, listen," said he, and I lay back upon the cushions and watched the light redden and fade over the plains of Assyria, while the sweet mountain silence fell more closely in the gorge, and the bishop's rambling tale filled the idle hour like some voice out of the past. 'Abdullah sat cross-legged upon a pile of carpets at the end of the room, rolling cigarettes and nodding his head in approval as the venerable weaver of romance unfolded his chronicle. "Senherib, king of Assyria, king of kings," he began, "to him a son was born whose name was Behnâm. And it happened upon a day that the Amîr Behnâm was hunting, and he lost his gazelle and night came upon him while he pursued her. And being weary with the chase he fell asleep beside a fountain. Then in his sleep an angel appeared unto him and bade him hearken to one whom he should meet next day upon the road. And when he had journeyed but a little way he met Mâr Mattai. And Mâr Mattai stopped him and said: 'Oh prince, why do you worship idols that have eyes that see not, ears that hear not, lips that speak not, instead of worshipping the living God, who made heaven and earth, al ins w'al jins w'al jami?'—mankind and different kinds and all kinds. And Behnâm answered: 'Give me a sign.' Then said Mâr Mattai: 'What sign shall I give you?' And he said: 'Heal my sister who is sick.' And they went on their way towards Nineveh, and as they went, Behnâm was full of fear, for he dared not take the saint into his father's city. But when they reached Bârtallâ, Mâr Mattai was weary and could walk no further. And he said: 'If I make water to gush out of the rock, will you believe?' And Behnâm answered: 'I will believe.' And the water gushed forth. Then Behnâm returned to Nineveh, and he refused to worship idols that have eyes that cannot see and ears that cannot hear and lips that cannot speak."

"It is true," said 'Abdullah.

"Neither would he worship the sun," pursued the bishop, "nor the moon, nor the stars, nor anything but the living God, who created heaven and earth, mankind and different kinds and all kinds."

"It is written in the book," said 'Abdullah.

"My son," said the bishop, "it is written." And Christian and Moslem met on the common ground of scripture. "Then Senherib put him and his sister to death. But the king was old and sick unto death, and he repented of what he had done, for he had no heir to inherit the kingdom. Therefore he sent for Mâr Mattai and entreated him to bring his son to life. And Mâr Mattai answered: 'Oh king, I will raise him from the dead if you will build me a monastery in the Jebel Maḳlûb.' And Senherib built the house wherein we sit," concluded the bishop.

"And who built Mâr Behnâm?" said I, anxious to prolong the recital.

"My daughter," he replied, "the house of Mâr Behnâm was built by Isḥâk the merchant. For Isḥâk was journeying to Baghdâd, and upon the road he fell ill, and Mâr Behnâm appeared to him and healed him. Verily the Assyrians were idolators, but they came to know the true God. So the world changes." The bishop broke off abruptly at this confusing point in the narrative, for even he felt that it would be an anachronism to assert that the Assyrian empire was Christian. But the historical sequence of events was nothing to 'Abdullah.

"God is great," he assented. "The world changes." And he rolled another cigarette.[1]

We ran down the path in the dusk and found my dinner-table spread under the moon. Round the camp-fire sat al ins w'al jins w'al jami' and watched the boiling of Ḥâjj 'Amr's rice-pot.

However many countries there may be in the world there are none so rich in faiths as the mountain frontiers of eastern Turkey. Beliefs which have been driven out with obloquy by a new-found truth, the half-apprehended mysticism of the

[1] The bishop had not perhaps retained a clear memory of his facts—if facts they can be called; but Rich seems to have found the history of Mâr Mattai and Mâr Behnâm scarcely less involved than I did: *Residence in Koordistan*, Vol. II. p. 75. See, too, Pognon, *op. cit.*, p. 132, note 1.

East, echoes of Western metaphysics and philosophy, illusive memories of paganism—all have been swept together into these hills, where creeds that were outlined in the childhood of the world are formulated still in terms as old as themselves. Islâm, with the lash of its simple, clear-cut doctrine, has herded them into remote places. Cowering there under centuries of persecution they have hidden their sacred things from the eyes of the spoiler, in silence they endure the reproach which dogs the most innocent practices of a secret cult, and each sect awaits, through ages of misery, the reward and the redeemer which its peculiar revelation has promised. These outcast communities make a potent appeal to the imagination and to the sympathy. I have no desire to pry into that which they choose to conceal, neither have they any wish to take me into their special confidence; but their hospitality is unfailing, and whenever I find myself among them I find myself among friends.

We were now entering the country which is the headquarters of the Yezîdîs, who, from their desire to conciliate or to propitiate the Spirit of Evil, are known to Moslem and Christian as Devil Worshippers. By Moslem and by Christian they have been placed beyond the bounds of human kindness, and while the Mohammadan has been unremitting in his efforts to bring them, by methods familiar to dominant creeds, to a sense of their short-comings, the Christian has regarded the wholesale butchery which has overtaken them from time to time as a punishment justified by their tenets. I had journeyed before among Yezîdî villages, in the mountains of north Syria, and had been struck by the clean and well-ordered look of the houses, and by the open-handed friendliness of the people, as well as by their courage and industry. The Mesopotamian Yezîdîs I knew only through the descriptions contained in Layard's enchanting books, but I carried a letter to 'Alî Beg, the head of the sect, and proposed to visit him in his village of Bâ'adrî and to see, if he would permit, the most sacred of all Yezîdî shrines, Sheikh 'Adi. 'Abdullah, when he learnt my intention, expressed his entire approval of 'Alî Beg as a man, but he would hear nothing of his religious convictions because they were not founded upon a book.

"Effendim," he said, "Moslems and Jews and Christians have a book; it is only the infidels which have none, and the Yezîdîs are infidels. They worship the Sheitân."

"You must not speak of him while we are at Bâ'adrî," said I, for the Yezîdîs never take the name of the Devil upon their lips and to mention him in their presence is a shameful insult.

"God forbid!" replied 'Abdullah.

We rode over flowery foot-hills that were bright with hollyhock and gladiolus, borage and mullein, and in an hour and a half from our camping-ground we reached the village of Jezarân.

"These are Shabbak," observed 'Abdullah.

"What are Shabbak?" I asked.

"They are not true Moslems," he replied. "God knows what they believe. They resemble the Shî'ahs. Effendim, they came with the armies of the 'Ajam, and after the 'Ajam departed, they remained." The 'Ajam are the Persians, or, roughly speaking, any barbarians.[1]

We went down into a lovely valley where the storks waded wing-deep through grass and buttercups—Chem Resh is its Kurdish name, Wâdî Aswad in Arabic, and both mean the Black Valley. Everywhere I was now given a Kurdish as well as an Arabic name for the villages, and the mother-tongue of the inhabitants was Kurdish, though, as a rule, they

[1] I fancy that 'Abdullah's explanation was not far from the truth. Layard, who is the best of all authorities on this country, makes the following remarks about the Shabbak: "Though strange and mysterious rites are as usual attributed to them" (*i.e.* as is usual with regard to a secret creed), "I suspect they are simply the descendants of Kurds who emigrated at some distant period from the Persian slopes of the mountains, and who still profess Sheeite doctrines. They may, however, be tainted with Ali-Illahism, which consists mainly in the belief that there have been successive incarnations of the Deity, the principal having been in the person of Ali, the celebrated son-in-law of the prophet Mohammad. The name usually given, Ali-Illahi, means 'believers that Ali is God.' Various abominable rites have been attributed to them, as to the Yezidis, Ansyris, and all sects whose doctrines are not known to the surrounding Mussulman and Christian population." *Nineveh and Babylon*, p. 216.

spoke Arabic also. Three hours from the camp we crossed a stream in the Wâdî 'Ain Sifneh, and half-an-hour beyond it we rode through the first Yezîdî village, Mukbil. The Yezîdîs, being of Kurdish race, do not differ in appearance from the rest of the population, except in one particular of their attire: they abhor the colour blue and eschew it in their dress, but red they regard as a beneficent hue, and their women are mostly clothed in dark-red cotton garments. The valley in which Mukbil lies is of uncommon fertility. Rice is cultivated here, and cotton; the emerald green of the grass indicated the presence of swampy ground, and the heavy air was full of the perfume of growing things. I lunched under a fig-tree near a Yezîdî hamlet; the village elders brought me curds and bread unasked, and refused to take payment. Having climbed a green ridge, we dropped into the valley of Baviân, crossed a deep river and rode up its bank till we came, four hours from Mukbil, to the famous rocks which are carved with Assyrian reliefs and inscriptions. Under them we pitched out tents, and a more exquisite camping-ground you might go far to seek. Fattûḥ knew the place. He had been here with one of whom he spoke as Meesterr Keen. This legendary personage appears frequently in Fattûḥ's reminiscences, and I suspect him to be no other than Mr. King, of the British Museum. "He gazed long upon the men and animals," observed Fattûḥ, with indulgent recollection, "and many times he photographed them. And then, wallah! he climbed up the rocks, and all the writing he took down in his book. Not many of the gentry are like Meesterr Keen, and your Excellency need not trouble to copy the writing once more."

I troubled not at all, but looked in amazement at the great figures of gods mounted on lions, and kings standing in adoration which Shalmaneser II had carved upon the cliff (Fig. 176). Behind some of the groups rock-cut chambers have been hollowed out in a later age, their doorways breaking through the figures of the reliefs, and the stream eddies round the feet of winged beasts and bearded men, walking in procession, cut upon huge boulders which have been dislodged from the face of the hill.[1] When I had seen these wonders I wandered up the valley to a point where the cliff bends round and holds the river in the curve of its arm. Here lay a deep still pool, the banks of which were starred with daisies and poppies and the rocks with campanulas and orchids. The water, dyed to a ruddy brown by recent rains, was like a disk of polished bronze in a setting of green and white and scarlet enamel. I sat for a little and listened to the birds singing about their nests in the cliffs, and the river breaking over the stones below the pool, and then I swam in the warm brown water and went upon my way rejoicing.

A fortunate chance sent other travellers to visit the reliefs that day, Dominican fathers from the monastery of Mâr Ya'ḳûb, two days' journey to the west of Baviân. They gave me much valuable information before they rode away on their mules, and I only hope that they enjoyed my tea half as much as I enjoyed their conversation. They were bound for Sheikh 'Adî, and hearing that I also was on my way thither, they told me of the underground chambers of the shrine, now seldom shown to strangers, and of the spring that runs through them from basin to basin; of the Yezîdî adoration of fountains, and of the baptismal rites which they practise, ceremonies which they borrowed from another Mesopotamian sect, the Mandæans, who are called the Christians of St. John. So sacred is the element of water that a Yezîdî will not enter a Moslem bath, nor will he eat of fish, which is born of water. They spoke too of the religions of dualism, of which the Yezîdî faith is one, though it is probably derived, through Manichæanism, from an ancient Babylonian source, rather than directly from Zoroaster, since it preserves the reverence for the sun which sprang from Mani's identification of light with the Principle of Good; and out of their wide experience of local customs they drew parallels

[1] A full description of the reliefs is contained in Layard's *Nineveh and Babylon*, p. 207. Mr. King is so kind as to inform me that the smaller panels at Baviân were carved in the reign of Sennacherib, between the dates 689 B.C. and 681 B.C. The larger sculptures are to be assigned to Shalmaneser II (860–825 B.C.).

FIG. 176.—ASSYRIAN RELIEFS AT BAVIÂN.

FIG. 177.—'ALÎ BEG.

FIG. 178.—THE KHÂTÛN AT THE DOOR OF SHEIKH 'ADÎ.

from the Christian sects, whose observances reflect those of primitive cults, and told me of Christians who, like the Yezîdîs, turn to the sun to pray. Then they left me with the birds and the river and the Assyrian gods, to reflect upon the unchanging persistence of human beliefs.

It is a five-hours' ride from Baviân to Bâ'adrî, and during the course of it I began to learn something of the terrible lawlessness which turns the beautiful Kurdish mountains into a hell upon earth. We passed upon our way a small Kurdish settlement, of which the houses burrowed into the hill-side like the lairs of wild animals. It is the winter quarters of one Hassan Jângîr, a robber chief of the Kochars, the nomad Kurds. Two days before it had been raided by the government, in retribution for innumerable outrages, and such of the population as yet lived had fled into the hills. The feudal lord of Hassan Jângîr is Sheikh Hajjî, who was at that time, to the satisfaction of the whole country-side, imprisoned in Môsul, but his liegeman had joined forces with another redoubted malefactor, Sheikh Nûrî, and it was rumoured that the pair with their followers had been encamped the previous night on the heights above Baviân. It was not without reason, as I now perceived, that the Vâlî of Môsul had insisted on providing me with four zaptiehs instead of the customary two.

The village of Bâ'adrî clings to the green slopes of the foot-hills, and 'Alî Beg's whitewashed house stands over it like a miniature fortress. The beg, who is the descendant of the other 'Alî to whom Layard stood godfather (with some misgivings as to what might be the duties of the sponsor of a devil-worshipping baby), received me in his divan with the utmost cordiality. He is a man of middle age with a commanding figure and a long beard, light brown in colour, that curls almost to his waist. He was dressed from head to foot in white, and as we sat together in the divan, I thought that I had seldom drunk coffee in more remarkable company. I told him that I knew his people in the Jebel Sim'ûn and that they had spoken of him as the ruler of all.

"The ruler of us all," he replied gravely, "is God."

In the courtyard were a pair of peacocks, in honour, no doubt, of the Angel Peacock, who rules the age of 10,000 years in which we live, and is the symbol of him who must not be named. His bronze effigy is carried by the Ḳawwâls, the higher priesthood of the Yezîdîs, when they journey among the scattered communities of the sect, and to whatever dangers they may be exposed, it is said that the image has never been allowed to fall into the hands of infidels.[1] The Yezîdî women are neither secluded nor veiled, and when 'Alî Beg took me to see his wife we found her in the midst of her household, male and female, giving orders for my entertainment. She was a handsome woman dressed in a robe of purple cotton, with a black velvet cap placed over the muslin veil which was wrapped about her head and under her chin, but did not conceal her face. On her wrists she wore heavy gold bracelets set with turquoises. She talked nothing but Kurdish, so that my greetings and my gratitude were conveyed to her through the beg's secretary, a Chaldæan from Alkôsh. Few Yezîdîs can either read or write, such knowledge being forbidden to them, and I doubt whether the beg himself had any acquaintance with letters. In the women's quarters I knitted an instant friendship with 'Alî Beg's small son, Sa'îd Beg, and though we had no common language in which to express our feelings, our intimacy advanced silently by leaps and bounds while he sat upon the largest of my camp-chairs and watched me eat the sumptuous meal with which his father had provided me. When I had finished there was enough and to spare of rice and mutton, bread and semolina pudding and sour curds to satisfy all my servants and soldiers. Meantime the beg had made preparations for my visit to Sheikh 'Adî, whither two Yezîdî horsemen and all my four zaptiehs were ordered to accompany me, lest we should meet with Kurdish robbers in the hills. 'Alî Beg with a dignified retinue of elders, one of whom was a ḳawwâl who had that day returned from

[1] It has been described and drawn by Layard: *Nineveh and Babylon*, p. 48.

FIG. 179.—SHEIKH 'ADÎ.

FIG. 180.—ZÂKHÔ.

FIG. 181.—BRIDGE OVER THE KHÂBÛR.

the Jebel Sinjâr, watched our departure (Fig. 177). Their fine grave heads and flowing beards gave them a singular resemblance to the kings and gods upon the rocks of Baviân, and perhaps the likeness was not merely fanciful, for the higher dignitaries of the Yezîdîs intermarry with none save those of their own rank, and who knows what ancient blood may flow from generation to generation through their veins?[1] We rode into the folds of the hills by a path so stony that we were forced at times to dismount and lead our horses. Bushes of flowering hawthorn grew among the rocks, oak-trees, in newly opened leaf, were scattered over the steep slopes, and the grass was full of poppies and the last of the scarlet ranunculus. The Yezîdîs hold the ranunculus in high esteem, its bright-red colour being of good omen in their eyes, and I regard it with no less favour, though perhaps for more superficial reasons. After a climb of close upon two hours, we reached the summit of the hill and the path dipped down, through sturdier oak woods, into a secluded valley, out of the heart of which rose the fluted spires of Sheikh 'Adî, a sanctuary and a tiny village embosomed in planes and mulberries and ancient fig-trees (Fig. 179). We sat down by the edge of a clear fountain while one of my Yezîdî guides went forward to announce our arrival to the khâtûn, the sister of 'Alî Beg. She came to meet me in the outer court of the shrine, a tall and slender woman wrapped in white robes, with a black cap upon her head and a heavy linen veil thrown over it and drawn tightly under her chin. She took me by the hand, and bidding me welcome in the few words of Arabic which she had at her command, led me past the booths where the hucksters spread out their wares during the days of the great yearly festival—they stood empty now under the mulberry branches. We passed through a doorway into a small paved court, still and peaceful and half-shaded by mulberries. The further side was bounded by the wall of the shrine, which opens into the court by a single

[1] In the photograph 'Alî Beg is seated and the ḳawwâl stands to the right of him. The figure on the left is the Christian secretary, and the close-shaven man behind the beg is Fattûḥ.

door. Upon the wall near the door a snake is carved in relief upon the stones and painted black (Fig. 178). With a singular magnetic attraction it catches and holds the eye, and the little court owes to its presence much of the indefinable sense of mystery which hangs over it as surely as hang the spreading branches of the mulberry-trees. I took off my shoes and followed the khâtûn as she stepped softly over the grass-grown pavement. At the door she paused, touched with her lips the stone, and murmured a Kurdish prayer in which I heard the frequent repetition of Sheikh 'Adî's name. In her white robes and heavy veil she looked like some strange priestess: the sibyl of the Delphic shrine might have stood so, robed in white, and kissed the marble gateway of the sun-god's house. A cool darkness and the murmur of water greeted us as we entered. We found ourselves in a large oblong chamber lying, as near as I can guess, from east to west, and divided into two vaulted aisles, of about the same width, by a row of seven piers. From under the wall on our left hand flowed a streamlet of clear water that ran into a square tank, and out of it down the length of the southern aisle. In the north aisle there was a tomb covered over with coloured cloths: "Holy man's grave," whispered the khâtûn as we passed it. But we had not yet reached the sanctuary which holds Sheikh 'Adî's bones. The eastern end of the north wall is broken by a door which leads into a dark chamber containing a second tomb. This chamber is covered by the smaller of the two spires. To the west of it is a second square room, bigger than the first, and here Sheikh 'Adî's tomb stands under the larger spire. It was totally dark: the wick floating in a saucer of oil carried by the khâtûn did little to illuminate it, and I lighted a coil of magnesium wire, to the delight of my guide, who interrupted her prayers to Sheikh 'Adî to utter ejaculations of pleasure each time that the white flash leapt up into the dome. For my part I would as soon study by the flame of a will-o'-the-wisp as by the uncertain brilliance of magnesium wire, coupled as it is with the assurance that the burning tendril will ultimately expend itself upon my skirt, and I got no more profit from the display than the gratification of the khâtûn and the knowledge that the high cone was set over the angles of the chamber on squinch arches—a construction which I could have predicted while it was still wrapped in darkness. Beyond the tomb chamber, and parallel with the north aisle, lies a long vaulted room, pitch-dark like the other, and filled with oil jars. "For Sheikh 'Adî," said the khâtûn, and kissed the well-oiled door as we entered.[1] Still further west we came to a vaulted gallery, running along the north side of the court; it, too, was dark except where the light shone through a few cracks in the wall. We went back through the two domed rooms, and when we reached the smaller tomb-chamber the khâtûn turned to me, saying, "Come." Up to this point we had been accompanied by the zaptiehs and by the Yezîdîs from Bâ'adrî; to these she pointed the way into the aisled hall, and taking my hand she led me to a low door in the eastern wall of the tomb-chamber. She bent her slender figure and passed through it, holding up her lamp to light my path. I followed her down half-a-dozen steps into a small chamber, dimly illumined by faint rays that struggled through chinks in the masonry of the south wall. The north wall was, so far as I could see, cut out of the solid rock; from under it gushed a spring which is said to take its source in the well Zemzem at Mecca. As in the upper building, the water flowed into a small square basin and through a hole in the wall at the eastern end of the room, but it flowed at its own pleasure, or perhaps the well Zemzem had been overfilled by the rains and the stream was greater than is usual, for it covered the floor to the depth of several centimetres. I stood doubtfully upon the lowest step and then decided that the wisest course would be to pull off my stockings—bare feet take no harm from a watery floor, though feet accustomed to be shod will tread unsteadily upon the sharp pebbles with which the spring has plentifully bestrewn the pavement. The khâtûn

[1] Layard mentions that the oil for the lamps is provided out of the funds of the shrine: *Nineveh and its Remains*, Vol. I. p. 291.

was much distressed to see me reduced to this plight: "Bîchâreh!" she said, "poor one." We splashed across the chamber and into a low passage which turned at right angles and conducted us into a second room. The stream came with us and was caught in yet another basin. In the dim twilight my companion turned quickly towards me and laid her hand upon my arm.

"Are you not afraid?" she whispered.

I looked up into the white and gentle face, wrapped round with the whiter veil, on which the burning wick cast a ghostly light, and because of my deep ignorance I was much perplexed.

"No," I answered.

"I am afraid," said she. And then I understood that if I had known how holy was the ground whereon we trod, not even the sharp pebbles would have prevailed over my mind against its awe-inspiring shades.

The stream gushed out under the east wall, the khâtûn opened a small door beside its mouth, and we passed out, blinking, into a sunny courtyard, half filled with piles of firewood, which I believe to be the wood used in the annual sacrifice of the white bull to Sheikh Shems, who is the sun.[1] We returned round the south of the building, past the house which is occupied by the khâtûn and by 'Alî Beg when he comes to the festival, and rejoined the zaptiehs in the inner court. There we sat long under the trees, eating freshly-baked bread and drinking bowls of milk with which the khâtûn provided us. It was with difficulty that I persuaded her not to kill a lamb and add it to the meal, which she considered far too modest for our merits or for her reputation as a hostess.

Little is known of the saint whose tomb is the central shrine of the Yezîdî faith. He is variously reported to have sprung either from the regions near Aleppo, or from the Haurân, and he died in the year A.D. 1162. He was one

[1] Layard pointed out the connection between the white bull offered annually to the Yezîdî solar saint and a similar sacrifice in the Assyrian ritual: *Nineveh and its Remains*, Vol. I. p. 290.

of a number of illuminators of whom the Sûfî mystic, Manṣûr el Ḥallâj, was another—he who suffered martyrdom for asserting the permeation of all created things by the Deity with the phrase: "I am God."[1] The Angel Jesus is a third —not the phantom Jesus whose death is recorded in the New Testament, but the spirit whose place that other had usurped;[2] and many of the Jewish prophets are revered in the same manner. There is a tradition that the building which is now Sheikh 'Adî's tomb was once a Christian church, but though I looked sharply for evidences that might confirm this report, I could not be sure that they existed. It is certain that there were earlier edifices upon the present site, and the building has been so often destroyed and restored that its original form must have been almost obliterated.[3] Round the doorway there are re-used stones covered with the net-like patterns which are to be found in the churches at Ḳaraḳôsh. An Arabic inscription, built into the same wall, bears the date 1115, but this date undoubtedly refers to the Mohammadan era, and the inscription is therefore barely two centuries old. Below it a second representation of a serpent is carved upon the wall, not painted like the one near the doorway, and lying parallel with the ground instead of standing upright. What the black snake signifies I do not know, neither did I ask for an explanation which would not have been accorded. Layard says that the Yezîdîs repeatedly assured him that it was without significance, and I should have been given no other answer.[4] 'Abdullah, who knew as little as I, volunteered the

[1] This doctrine is, however, older than the Sûfîs; it was held by the Mandæans and is a part of the Asiatic heritage of religious ideas out of which the Yezîdî creed has been formed. The transmigration of souls, another Mandæan tenet, is also professed by the Yezîdîs.

[2] This, too, is an article of the Mandæan faith.

[3] The late Lord Percy, who visited Sheikh 'Adî in 1897, found nothing but the outer shell and the roof intact. It had been wrecked by a Turkish general who had made a resolute attempt to convert or exterminate (the two expressions are practically synonymous) the Yezîdîs: *Notes from a Diary*, p. 184.

[4] *Nineveh and Babylon*, p. 83.

information that a Yezîdî will never kill a black snake, but when I asked whether there were many such reptiles in the hills, he replied that so far as he knew there were none, and his testimony as to the practices of the Yezîdîs when confronted with them did not seem to me to be of much value. Before I left Bâ'adrî I received an invitation to be present at the summer festival. Of the ceremonies performed at this time Layard has left two wonderful descriptions,[1] and if ever I find myself at Môṣul in the height of the summer, I shall not forget 'Alî Beg's proffer of hospitality.

It was near sunset when we reached Bâ'adrî. After night had fallen Sa'îd Beg came to fetch me to his mother's quarters. We held converse through the Christian secretary, and our talk was mostly of the child who sat beside me smoking one cigarette after another.

"In my country children may not smoke," said I. "Oh Sa'îd Beg, little children like you should be asleep at this hour."

The khâtûn smiled at him tenderly. "We can deny him nothing," said she.

And the secretary added: "The 'araḳ they give him is worse for him than the cigarettes." Sobriety is not, I fear, to be numbered among the Yezîdî virtues.

I left next morning at an early hour, and the secretary saw to the comfort of my departure and received my thanks for the kindness which had been shown to us, but neither he nor any other of 'Alî Beg's people would accept a reward. As I was about to mount, he said that the beg would ask a favour of me.

"Upon my head and eyes," said I.

"Will you leave with us some of your fire ribbon. He would light the tomb with it at the next festival." I broke off half the roll, and by this time the fame of magnesium wire must have spread to the Jebel Sinjâr, or even to the Jebel Sim'ûn, and in the skirts of many a pious person a hole has doubtless been burnt.

[1] *Nineveh and its Remains,* Vol. I. p. 280, and *Nineveh and Babylon,* p. 81.

Having breakfasted with Devil Worshippers, I lunched with the prior of Rabbân Hormuzd. The monastery, which is a very ancient and famous Nestorian house, once the seat of a patriarch, now belongs to the Chaldæans, that is, to the Catholic Nestorians. It lies high up in the hills above Alḳôsh, a village four hours to the west of Bâ'adrî. When we reached Alkôsh I sent my caravan forward, and with Jûsef and 'Abdullah climbed for half-an-hour up a narrow rocky valley by a winding path which led us to a postern in the wall. In the flourishing Nestorian days innumerable hordes of monks lodged in caves among the rocks; many of these caves are still extant (though many have crumbled away with the crumbling of the stone) but few are tenanted. Rich, who has left an interesting account of Rabbân Hormuzd,[1] was of opinion that the amphitheatre of cliffs, honeycombed with caves, was an ancient Persian burial-place converted into a Christian monastery. Traditions differ as to the history of the tutelary saint; some say that he was martyred in the persecution of Yazdegird, king of Persia, and some in that of the emperor Diocletian. The date of the foundation of the monastery is generally given as falling within the fourth century, though the prior, Kas Elyâs, told me that it was founded in the seventh century. Exceedingly little of the original monastery remains, and Rich relates that at the time of his visit it had recently undergone a comprehensive restoration. The present buildings (and no doubt the ancient buildings were much the same) climb in tier above tier up the precipitous hill-side. The house of Kas Elyâs stands highest of all, and there I sat in the window-seat and gossiped with the jolly prior. We brought him news of the accession of Muhammad V, on the hearing of which he bubbled over with satisfaction, and declared that Salonica was the saviour of the empire and that all his allegiance was given to the Young Turks, and all his hopes depended upon them. Even in the last six months order had been foreshadowed in the Kurdish hills, and with Muhammad V upon the throne

[1] *Residence in Koordistan*, Vol. II. p. 91.

and Sheikh Hajjî in prison, who could predict how far it might not be carried? It was encouraging to listen to views so optimistic, even though I knew that the prophecies of Kas Elyâs must be slow of fulfilment. I began to forget the weariness caused by the heavy steaming heat of the plain, and half-an-hour in the prior's lofty house, together with a lunch of omelettes and honey and sour curds, completed the cure. Thus restored, I followed him into the church. The main part of it, according to him, is about four hundred years old, but a chapel (which is obviously later in date) was, said he, erected about a hundred years ago. For English eyes it has an interest out of all proportion to its age, for upon the doorway are carved the names of James and Mary Rich, with the date 1820, and of Henry Layard, with the date 1846. An age of splendid achievement in travel was that which saw Rich and Layard, Chesney and Ainsworth and Rawlinson; for much of our knowledge of the remoter parts of Asia we depend still upon the bountiful information with which their learning and their courage supplied us. To the south of the church a passage is hollowed out of the cliff. It leads into a tiny rock-cut chamber, to the ceiling of which two iron rings are fastened. "From these," observed the prior, "Rabbân Hormuzd suspended himself when he fell into meditation, and here it is the custom for pilgrims to make their offerings." The hint, I need hardly say, was effectual. The baptistery lies south-west of the church; it is built of masonry and covered by a dome on squinches. To it, and to the vaulted chamber adjoining it, I should give an earlier date than to the rest of the edifice.

Much cheered in mind and body, and laden with roses from the monastery garden, we rode down into the insufferable heat of the low ground. Shortly after leaving Alḳôsh our path turned into the hills to the right, climbed by a charming valley with a rushing stream in its depth, crossed a low pass and led us out into the broad green plain which lies between the Jebel Alkôsh and the Jebel Dehûk. Flowering grasses brushed our stirrups as we rode, but, in spite of its fertility, the plain is almost uncultivated. The few villages, Moslem and Christian, are harried by the robber bands of Sheikh Nûrî, and whenever the miserable peasants have gathered together such modest wealth as their resources permit, the nomad Kurds fall upon them with rifle and with firebrand. Thus it is that long tracts of land are unpeopled and the hamlets that exist are more than half in ruin. One we passed that had been looted and left a smouldering heap of ashes two years earlier, but the newly aroused hopes of firmer government had induced the peasants to return to it, and the houses were springing up again. The deep grass through which we journeyed, both on this day and on the next, is looked upon as a sore peril, since it tempts the Kurds down into the lowland pastures. To avoid this annual reign of terror, the peasants are wont to set it on fire as soon as it ripens, leaving but a small patch round each village. For a week the plain is wrapped in flame and smoke, and the stifling heat of the burning rises up to the hill-top monastery of Mâr Ya'ḳûb, where the Catholic priests are witnesses to the appalling destruction of what might have been a rich harvest, and to the bitter oppression which turns the bounty of nature into a recurring threat. Jûsef, whose imagination is not tc be roused except by considerations of a soundly practical character, cast his eye over the fields and observed thoughtfully: "The muleteers of Baghdâd must starve this year to buy fodder for their cattle, yet here is enough to feed all the Jezîreh." Heaven send peace to this fair country.

We camped near the small village of Grê Pahn (Arabic: Tell' Arîḍ = the Broad Mound), where we found our tents pitched. It had taken us three and a half hours to reach it from Alḳôsh, but the caravan time had been somewhat longer. Upon the following day we had a hard march; the caravan was ten hours upon the way and I, with 'Abdullah and Jûsef, considerably more, for we began the day with an excursion from the road to the Assyrian reliefs above Malthai. We turned to the right, up the valley that leads to Dehûk, and leaving our horses at the foot of the hill under the care of Jûsef, 'Abdullah and I climbed up and sought for the sculptures. It was rough going and we had been insufficiently directed, so that for long we sought in vain. At last in despair I sent 'Abdullah back to fetch a guide and sat down to wait for him under a rock. Clumps of flowering saxifrage covered the stones; campanula pyramidalis lifted its tall spires out of the crevices, the wide green valley lay below, its sparsely scattered villages each clustering about an ancient mound, and beyond it rose the mountain chains of Kurdistân. The air was full of the fragrance and the freshness of the hills and alive with the sound of their waters. To all the high places of the world I have given allegiance—all exercise a like authority and confer like privileges, and in these distant solitudes I claimed and was accorded an old-established right of mountain citizenship.

'Abdullah's mission came abruptly to a successful termination. We had climbed high above the reliefs, and his keen eye espied them as he made his way down. They are four in number, and on each precisely the same scene is depicted. A king stands in adoration before a procession of seven gods, six of whom are mounted upon the backs of beasts, while one is seated upon a throne borne by a lion. Another, or perhaps the same, king follows the company of gods on foot. A tomb or cell has been broken through one of the reliefs, as at Baviân. In subject and in style the reliefs in both places are closely alike, and though there are no inscriptions at Malthai, the learned have concluded that the work there must be of the same epoch as that at Baviân, and have dated it in the reign of Shalmaneser II (860–825 B.C.).[1] They have yet to solve the difficult problems connected with the interchange of religions and artistic conceptions between the Assyrians and the Hittites, whose sculptures show, at a far earlier date, the same strange motive of a divinity standing upon the back of a wild animal.

For the rest of the day we journeyed along the foot of the hills by the Môsul high road. In the middle of the afternoon 'Abdullah observed conversationally:

[1] Layard: *Nineveh and its Remains*, Vol. I. p. 230. See, too, Perrot and Chipiez: *Histoire de l'Art*, Vol. II. p. 642.

"That is the house of a bandit," and he nodded his head towards a small white fort under the hills. The bandit was at that period imprisoned at Môsul, but his empty dwelling served 'Abdullah as a peg whereon to hang a denunciation of the Kurds, root and branch.

"As God is almighty," said he, "they fear not God nor the Sultan. They take the load and the camel with it. Allah al wakîl! they fire at the soldiers of the government; they seize the load and the mule."

"Where do they buy arms?" I asked.

"From Ibn Sabbâh of Kuweit," he replied. "They travel down the Tigris to the Gulf in keleks, and there they buy a rifle for three Ottoman pounds, and sell it here for ten pounds—with a rich merchandise, wallah! they return from the Gulf of Persia. And how can we prevail against them when 'Abdu'l Hamîd showed them favour? Sheikh Hajjî was a shepherd in the hills—a shepherd with a shepherd's staff guarding the sheep—till 'Abdu'l Hamîd made him a beg. Praise God he is now in the Môsul prison—may God curse him!"

"God strengthen the new government," said I.

"Please God," he answered.

After five hours' quick riding from Malthai the post-road turned to the right, over the hills. We did not follow it, but rode straight on for another forty minutes to our camp at the Kurdish village of Koleh. I had heard of a fortress which lay upon the western slopes of the Jebel el Abyad, half-an-hour beyond Koleh, and thither I went next morning. It proved to be the ruins of a fortified town of which nothing but the outer wall was standing. The spurs of the Kurdish mountains are covered with fortress ruins, outlying strongholds of the highland races against the inhabitants of the plains, or else defences serving to protect the fruitful lowlands from the inroads of the tribes. They date, so far as I can judge, from every period, from the Assyrian to the Ottoman, but the majority are undoubtedly Kurdish, robber fastnesses of the marauding chiefs who have spread terror over the countryside for many a century. In this last category I should not, however, place Za'ferân. The wall is built of fine masonry; it is about 1·70 metres thick, the outer and the inner faces being of dressed stones, the core of rubble and mortar. It runs up to the top of a rocky bluff which has been divided from the area of the town by a cross wall. The rock forms a natural citadel, but I could see no signs of masonry, other than the wall, upon its summit—indeed the ground falls so sharply that there is little room for building. From this elevated position the town wall can be seen stretching out in an irregular, elongated semicircle, and the plain slopes down from it towards the Tigris, which lies two or three miles to the south. In the centre of the town there is a large mass of ruin near which are some rock-hewn sarcophagi. Two clearly marked streets cross the enclosed area at right angles to one another, the one passing by the central ruin and running down to a gate in the south wall, the other running from east to west and probably from gate to gate—the eastern gate is visible, but the western part of the wall is so much ruined that the position of its gateway is not to be determined. The lintel and door jambs of the south gate are standing, the width of the opening is only two metres, and the lintel here and in the east gate (where it has fallen to the ground) is unadorned and uninscribed. The character of the masonry and the existence (as is proved by the lines of street and ruin heap) of a town carefully planned upon an ordered system, point to a date prior to the Mohammadan conquest, and I am inclined to seek for a Byzantine origin for Za'ferân. Perhaps it may be a relic of the triumphant, though brief, re-occupation by Heraclius of the provinces ceded to the Persians by Jovian.

I followed my caravan back to the Môṣul highway and so across the hills to Zâkhô. We climbed up the pass by as good a road as any in Turkey, but while we were rejoicing over its excellence, it broke off short and left us to find our way down the opposite side of the pass as best we might along a bridle-path strewn with boulders. So we came down into the valley of the Khâbûr and saw before us the snowy wall of the Kurdish Alps (Fig. 180). At the gate of the pass stands Zâkhô, "old and isolated," as Ainsworth says, and it would be difficult to better the phrase.[1] The more ancient part of the village is built upon an island in the Khâbûr. The right arm of the river is spanned by a masonry bridge, the left arm washes round the castle, a fortress which must have had a long and checkered history, though I can find no record of it.[2] The masonry is of many different periods. The finest and probably the oldest part is an octagonal tower which juts out into the stream on the south-east side. The outer walls are all fairly well preserved and make an imposing appearance, but the interior is terribly ruinous. In the upper part of the building there is a large hall with windows opening on to the river. The engaged columns which support the interior pointed arches of these windows are covered with a delicate tracery of carving very like Seljuk work of the thirteenth and fourteenth centuries. This part of the castle cannot be dated later than the fourteenth century, but the foundations and the octagonal tower must be considerably older. Last of all the Turkish garrison has supplemented the ancient work with wretched structures of rubble and mortar, and these, too, have fallen into ruin and have been given over to the storks, who nest contentedly among them. In Zâkhô lies buried the first missionary to Kurdistân, the Dominican Soldini, who died here in 1779. The quarter that

[1] *Travels in the Track*, p. 144.

[2] Zâkhô must be the place known to the Arab geographers as Ḥasanîyeh (I see that Hartmann comes to the same conclusion: *Bohtân, Mitt. der Vorderas. Gesell.*, 1896, II. p. 39), but their information is, as usual, exceedingly meagre and the castle is mentioned by none. Muḳaddasî, in the tenth century, says that it is a day's journey from Ma'lathâyâ (Malthai) to Ḥasanîyeh (ed. de Goeje, p. 149), and notes the bridge over the Khâbûr above the town (p. 139). Yâḳût, in the thirteenth century, observes that it is two days from Môṣul on the road to Jezîret ibn 'Umar. Ainsworth conjectures it to be the spot described by Xenophon as "a kind of palace with several villages round it," which was reached by the Greeks in five days' march from Mespila-Nineveh, but it must be admitted that Xenophon's description is not exactly suited to Zâkhô. Ritter thinks that a memory of the people called by Strabo Saccopodes may be retained in the name Zâkhô (Vol. IX. p. 705). With regard to the name Ḥasanîyeh it is perhaps preserved in Ḥasanah, a small village on the opposite side of the Khâbûr valley.

stands upon the right bank of the Khâbûr is mainly Christian and contains, I believe, two small churches of no very great age, but my curiosity was quenched before I reached them, by a violent thunderstorm which drove me back to my tents. It swept down the valley from Amadîyeh, and rolling away, left the mountains so magically beautiful that I could give no further thought to any architecture but that of their white pinnacles and spires.

CHAPTER VIII

ZÂKHÔ TO DIYÂRBEKR

May 10—*June* 4

THE Babylonians, and after them the Nestorians and the Moslems, held that the Ark of Noah, when the waters subsided, grounded not upon the mountain of Ararat, but upon Jûdî Dâgh. To that school of thought I also belong, for I have made the pilgrimage and seen what I have seen. The snows that gleamed upon us from under the skirts of the thunderstorm when we camped at Zâkhô were the springtime wreaths of Jebel Jûdî, and resisting all other claims, we turned our faces towards them on the following day. Selîm, the muleteer, gloried in this decision. He was a native of the hills above Killiz, and like all mountain people his spirits rose with the rising ground. Above Zâkhô the Khâbûr is spanned by a masonry bridge of four arches (Fig. 181), but when we came to Durnakh, we found the Ḥeizil Sû innocent of bridge or ferry-boat. The river, which is the principal affluent of the Khâbûr, ran deep and swift by reason of the melting snows. In midstream its waters touched the top of my riding-boots and buffeted my mare, so that I thought she would certainly fall; indeed she would have fallen but for two of the inhabitants of Durnakh who, with garments rolled round their waists, held bravely up her chin. Another pair was attached to each of the baggage animals, the muleteers joined in the sport, and we reached the further side without loss. Four hours and a half from Zâkhô we passed by Tell Kobbîn, an ancient mound with a village of the same name a little further to the north,[1] and in two hours more we

[1] Ainsworth thinks that it may mark the site of the village at which the Greeks camped on the second day from Zâkhô: *Travels in the Track*, p. 146. Xenophon mentions neither the Khâbûr nor the Ḥeizil.

entered the foothills and lunched in an oak grove near the village of Gerik. Our path led us over rising meadows to Geurmuk and Dadar, and so into the mouth of a gorge where Ḥasanah nestles under rocky peaks. The clouds gathered over the mountains and thunder came booming through the gorge as we pitched our tents by the edge of the stream, nine hours from Zâkhô. Ḥasanah is a Christian village inhabited partly by Nestorians and partly by the converts of American missionaries. The pastor of the Protestant Nestorians, if I may so call him (when I asked him what was his persuasion, he replied that he was Prôt), came at once to offer his respects, coupled with a bunch of pink roses from his garden, and I, being much attracted by his sturdy figure and simple open countenance, asked him to guide me next day through the hills. Over and above his personal charms, Kas Mattai had the advantage of a knowledge of Arabic. He spoke besides Kurdish and Syriac, but his native tongue was Fellâḥî (the Peasant Language), which is no other than Assyrian. His brother Shim'ûn, who accompanied us on all our expeditions (he climbed the rocks like a cat or a Grindelwalder), had nothing but Fellâḥî and Kurdish and a cheerful face, but with one or the other, or all three, he made his way deep into my affections before we parted. We walked up the narrow valley, where flowers and flowering shrubs nodded over the path in an almost incredible luxuriance, and climbed the steep wooded hill-side to a point where the rock had been smoothed to receive the image of an Assyrian king, though none had been carved upon it. Above it rose a precipitous crag clothed on one side with hanging woods through which zigzagged a very ancient path, lost at times among fallen rocks and trees, while at times its embankment of stones was still clearly to be traced. On the summit of the crag were vestiges of a small fortress. The walls were indicated by heaps of unsquared stones, many of which had fallen down the hill, where they lay thickly strewn; the evidence afforded by them, and by the carefully constructed path, made it certain that we were standing upon the site of some watch-tower that had guarded the Ḥasanah gorge. On the opposite side rises a second crag whereon, said

FIG. 182.—ḤASANAH, ASSYRIAN RELIEF.

FIG. 183.—SHAKH, ASSYRIAN RELIEF.

FIG. 184.—NOAH'S ARK.

Kas Mattai, are ruins of the same description. That the valley was held by the Assyrians there can be no doubt, for it is signed with their name. Below and to the west of the crag to which we had climbed there is another smoothed niche in the rock (Fig. 182), and here the work has been completed and the niche is carved with the figure of an Assyrian king, wearing a long fringed robe and carrying a sceptre.[1] At a later age, the mountains had been occupied by Christians. Kas Mattai showed me at the foot of the crag a few vaulted chambers which he declared to be the ruins of a Nestorian monastery, and walking westward for an hour or more along the wooded ridges, we came to a second and larger monastic ruin, with a garden of fruit-trees about it, and groves of tall blue irises which had escaped from the cemetery of the monks and wandered over the hill-side.

In the high oak woods I forgot for a few hours the stifling heat which had weighed upon us ever since we had left Môṣul. Each morning we had promised one another a cooler air as we neared the mountains; each evening the thermometer placed in the shade of my tent registered from 88° to 93° Fahrenheit. The heavy air was like an enveloping garment which it was impossible to cast off, and as I walked through the woods I was overmastered by a desire for the snow patches that lay upon the peaks—for one day of sharp mountain air and of freedom from the lowland plague of flies. Sefînet Nebî Nûh, the ship of the Prophet Noah, was there to serve as an excuse.

Accordingly we set out from camp at four o'clock on the following morning. Kas Mattai and Shim'ûn in their felt sandals, raishîkî, a proper footgear for the mountaineer, Selîm, whom Providence had marked out for the expedition, 'Abdu'l Mejîd, a zaptieh from Zâkhô, who had been ordained as pointedly to walk upon flat ground, and the donkey. "As for that donkey," said Fattûḥ, "if he stays two days in the camp eating grass, Selîm will not be able to remain upon his back." He was Selîm's mount, and Selîm, who knew his mind better than any other among us, was persuaded that he

[1] Mr. King, who has visited Jûdî Dâgh, tells me that all the reliefs are of Sennacherib and were carved in the year 699 B.C.

would enjoy the trip. The donkey therefore carried the lunch. We climbed for two hours and a half through oak woods and along the upper slopes of the hills under a precipitous crest. But this was not what I had come out to see, and as soon as I perceived a couloir in the rocks, I made straight for it and in a few moments stepped out upon an alp. There lay the snow wreaths; globularia nudicaulis carpeted the ground with blue, yellow ranunculus gilded the damp hollows, and pale-blue squills pushed up their heads between the stones and shivered in the keen wind. Selîm had followed me up the couloir.

"The hills are good," said he, gathering up a handful of snow, "but I do not think that the donkey will come up here, nor yet 'Abdu'l Mejîd."

We returned reluctantly to the path and walked on for another half-hour till Kas Mattai announced that the Ark of Noah was immediately above us. Among asphodel and forget-me-nots we left the zaptieh and the donkey; Selîm shouldered the lunch-bags, and we climbed the steep slopes for another half-hour. And so we came to Noah's Ark, which had run aground in a bed of scarlet tulips (Fig. 184).

There was once a famous Nestorian monastery, the Cloister of the Ark, upon the summit of Mount Jûdî, but it was destroyed by lightning in the year of Christ 766.[1] Upon its ruins, said Kas Mattai, the Moslems had erected a shrine, and this too has fallen; but Christian, Moslem and Jew still visit the mount upon a certain day in the summer and offer their oblations to the Prophet Noah. That which they actually see is a number of roofless chambers upon the extreme summit of the hill. They are roughly built of unsquared stones, piled together without mortar, and from wall to wall are laid tree-trunks and boughs, so disposed that they may support a roofing of cloths, which is thrown over them at the time of the annual festival. To the east of these buildings there is an open court enclosed by a low stone wall. The walls both of the chambers and of the court are all, as I should judge,

[1] Ritter, Vol. XI. p. 154.

constructions of a recent date, and they are certainly Mohammadan, since one of the chambers contains a miḥrâb niche to the south, and in the enclosing wall of the court there is a similar rough niche. Further to the west lie the ruins of a detached chamber built of very large stones, and perhaps of an earlier date. Beneath the upper rocks upon which these edifices stand, there is a tank fed by the winter snows which had not entirely disappeared from the mountain-top. Still further down, upon a small plateau, are scattered fragments of a different architecture, carefully built walls, stone door-posts, and lintels showing above the level of the soil. Here, I make little doubt, was the site of the Nestorian monastery.

The prospect from the ziyârah was as wild, as rugged and as splendid as the heart could desire, and desolate beyond measure. The ridge of Jûdî Dâgh sinks down to the north on to a rolling upland which for many miles offers ideal dwelling-places for a hardy mountain folk. There were but four villages to be seen upon it. The largest of these was Shandokh, the home of a family of Kurdish âghâs whose predatory habits account for the scantiness of the population. To the east of it lay Heshtân, which is in Arabic Thamânîn (the Eighty), so called because the eighty persons who were saved from the Deluge founded there the first village of the regenerated world when they descended from Jebel Jûdî.[1] Further to the north an endless welter of mountains stretched between us and Lake Vân. They rose, towards the east, into snowy ranges, and very far to the south-east we could see the highest snow-peaks of Tiyârî, where the Nestorians, grouped under a tribal system, defend their faith with their lives against the Kurdish tribes—a hereditary warfare, marked with prodigies of valour on the part of the Christians, and with such success as the matchlock may attain over the Martini rifle.

[1] So said Kas Mattai, but the Arab geographers would seem to place it to the south of Jûdî Dâgh, not to the north. For example, Muḳaddasî says that Thamânîn, the village of the eighty who were saved from the flood, stands on the river Ghazil (the Ḥeizil Sû), a day's march from Ḥasanîyeh (Zâkhô), ed. de Goeje, pp. 139 and 149. Sachau, however, speaks of Bêtmanîn as being behind Jûdî Dâgh, *i.e.* he bears out my information : *Reise*, p. 376.

Because the light air breathed sharply off the snows, and because the vista of mountains was a feast to the eye, we lay for several hours in the sanctuary of the Prophet Noah. There can be no manner of doubt that I ought to have completed the pilgrimage by visiting his grave, but it lay far down upon the southern slopes of Jûdî Dâgh, and I was making holiday upon the hill-tops; therefore when we turned homewards, we bade Shim'ûn conduct the donkey and 'Abdu'l Mejîd to Ḥasanah and ourselves kept to the crest of the ridge. Half-an-hour from the summit we met some Kurdish shepherds near a small heap of ruins, concerning which they related the following history: Once upon a time there was a holy man who took a vow of pilgrimage to the ship of Noah, and for a month he journeyed over hill and vale until he reached the spot on which we stood. And there he met the Evil One, who asked him whence he came and whither he was going. The holy man explained that he was bent on a pilgrimage to the ship of Noah. "You have still," said the Devil, "a month's journey before you." Thereat the pilgrim, being old and weary, lost heart, and since he could not return with his vow unfulfilled, he built himself a hut and ended his days within sight of the goal, if his eyes had not been too worn to see. The presence of the shepherds upon Mount Jûdî was not to be attributed to any pious purpose. They had come up from the villages below to escape from the sheep tax which was about to be levied for the second time within a twelvemonth, once for last year's arrears, and once for this year's dues. Their lawless flocks skipped among the boulders and the snow-wreaths as light-heartedly as the wild goat, which no government can assess, but the owners lived in anxiety, and when, half-an-hour further, we encountered a second company, they took us for soldiers and greeted us with rifle shots. Kas Mattai grasped the situation and shouted a justification of our existence, which was not received without hesitation. I was standing, when the shots began, in the middle of a *névé*, and thinking that I must offer a fine mark, I stepped off the snow and sat down upon a grey rock to await developments. But as soon as we had made it clear that we were simple people with no official position, we were allowed to pass. "It was well," observed Kas Mattai, as we clambered down the crags, "that 'Abdu'l Mejîd was not with us. They would have killed him."

At the foot of the rocks we sat down to rest beside a bubbling spring.

"Have you suffered at the hand of the government?" I asked my guide.

"We suffer from the Kurds," he replied, "and there is no one to protect us but God. Effendim, the âghâwât from Shandokh come over the pass and claim hospitality from us. We are poor men—in all Ḥasanah there is not one who is ignorant of hunger; how shall we feed the âghâwât, and their mares, and the followers they bring with them? And how shall we refuse when they are armed with rifles?"

"Have you no arms?" said I.

"We have no money to buy rifles," he answered; "and if we bought them, the Kurds would take them from us. And when we have killed our last sheep that we may entertain them, they seize upon all we possess before they leave us."

"Oh Merciful!" ejaculated Selîm.

"Sir," said Kas Mattai, "last year they took my bed, and that which was too worthless to carry away they broke and threw upon the fire. But if we resisted they would burn the village."

We ran down through the oak woods and got into camp at four in the afternoon.

"God prolong your existence!" cried Fattûḥ. "Have you seen the ship of the Prophet Noah?"

"Oh Fattûḥ," I replied, "prepare the tea. I have seen the ship of the Prophet Noah." So it is that I sŭbscribe in this matter to the wisdom of the Kurân: "And immediately the water abated and the decree was fulfilled and the Ark rested upon the mountain of Jûdî."

Next morning the camp was sent straight to Jezîreh, which it reached after a six-hours' march, but I, with Shim'ûn as guide, followed the line of the hills. We rode for two hours through the oak woods, and then crossed a gorge wherein lies the Moslem village of Evler. The incomparable beauty of these valleys passes belief. Evler was buried in a profusion of pomegranate and walnut, fig, almond and mulberry trees; the vines were wreathed from tree to tree, the ground beneath was deep in corn, and the banks of the stream aglow with oleander. An hour further we reached the Nestorian village of Shakh, where a ruined castle protects the entrance of the gorge. The walls climb up the hillside towards a citadel placed upon a high peak; above the village two deep valleys run up into the mountains, and each has been walled across, so that Shakh was guarded from attack on every side. I should judge these fortifications to be Kurdish, but there are traces of an older civilization on the rocks above them (Fig. 183). Of the four Assyrian reliefs that are reported to exist, I saw only three, the fourth being cut upon the face of the cliff and unapproachable except with ropes. Each of the three niches which I was shown (after an hour's climb in the hottest part of the day) contained a single figure, like that of Ḥasanah; each had been covered with cuneiform inscriptions, but in two cases both the figure and the inscriptions had all but weathered away. We left Shakh at midday, stopped for half-an-hour to lunch by the stream, and reached Jezîret ibn 'Umar at four o'clock. The camp was pitched upon a high bank overhanging the Tigris, but the bridge of boats which should have connected us with the town was broken, and I crossed by a ferry on the following day.

Jezîret ibn 'Umar is built upon an island formed by the Tigris and a small loop canal. It is called after a certain Hassan ibn 'Umar of the tribe of Taghlib, who lived in the ninth century.[1] Upon the river's edge stands a much-ruined

[1] It has been identified with the Bezabde of Ammianus Marcellinus, the Saphe of Ptolemy (ed. Müller, p. 1005), and the Sapha of the Peutinger Tables. Ammianus Marcellinus is generally supposed to have confused Bezabde-Jezîreh with Phœnice-Finik, saying that the two names are applied to the same place. In his account of the capture of Bezabde by Sapor II, in A.D. 360, his description applies better to Finik than to Jezîreh (Bk. XX. ch. vii. 1. See, however, Hartmann: *Bohtân*, Part II. p. 98). He relates further that Constantius attempted in vain to re-

FIG. 185.—JEZÎRET IBN 'UMAR, GATE OF FORTRESS.

FIG. 186.—JEZÎRET IBN 'UMAR, BRIDGE.

FIG. 187.—JEZÎRET IBN 'UMAR, FOUNTAIN OF MOSQUE.

FIG. 188.—JEZÎRET IBN 'UMAR, RELIEFS ON BRIDGE.

castle of which the masonry is mostly of alternate bands of black basalt and white limestone. Over one of the doors are carved a couple of rudely executed lions (Fig. 185). The town walls still exist in part and belong to the same date as the castle; so too does the fragment of a masonry bridge which spanned the Tigris about half-an-hour's ride below the town (Fig. 186). On our way to it we forded the moat which was at that time quite shallow. One of the bridge piers is decorated with a key pattern of black and white stone, and with some curious reliefs representing the signs of the zodiac, of which the work is similar in character to that of the lions upon the castle gate (Fig. 188). Each relief bears an inscription in Arabic naming the zodiacal sign which it depicts.[1] As we came back through the town we stopped at the principal mosque, which has a pair of fine bronze doors, with bronze knockers worked in a design of intertwined dragons. A small dome, set upon columns that may have been taken from an earlier building, covers the fountain in the courtyard (Fig. 187).[2] Jezîret ibn 'Umar has a bad reputation for the fever which is bred in its marshy moat; moreover it was stifling hot. I hurried through a cursory sight-seeing and ferried back to the opposite bank, where I found the baggage animals loaded and ready to start. Having followed the Tigris bank for half-an-hour, I left the caravan to pursue its way to Finik and turned up the valley of the Risür Chai. In less than two hours from Jezîreh we came to a ruined Kurdish fort, standing on either side of the stream and blocking effectually the passage of the gorge;

---

capture Bezabde (Bk. XX. ch. xi.), but in this passage he must mean Jezîreh. I can find little in the history of Jezîreh except the mention of sieges: by Tîmûr for example (Ritter, Vol. IX. p. 709), and by the emirs of Bohtân (Rich: *op. cit.*, Vol. I. p. 106). When Moltke visited it in 1838 it was a heap of ruins (*Briefe aus der Turkei*, Berlin, 1893, p. 251), and it was not much more when I saw it.

[1] Sachau notices these reliefs. In his opinion the inscriptions are of no great age: *Reise*, p. 379.

[2] Ibn Baṭûṭah, in the fourteenth century, mentions an old mosque in the market place, which is probably the same as the one I saw, though it has undergone many alterations and reparations since his day.

and carved upon the rocks of the left bank there is a more ancient guardian of the pass, a warrior armed, and mounted upon a bounding horse (Fig. 189). His companion, who went on foot, has fallen into the stream, and I know no other record of him than Layard's woodcut.[1] The figure of the horseman is much defaced by time. The winter rains have worn thin his armour, the spring floods have undermined the rock on which he stands, but shadowy though his image may be, it marks the triumph of a European civilization, and its prototypes are to be sought not among the bearded divinities and winged monsters of Assyria, but in the work of Western sculptors. The Parthian, who was the bitter enemy of the Roman empire, carved it upon the rocks of Ḳaṣr Ghellî, and bore witness with his own hand to the overmastery of Roman culture.

We cut across the hills back to the Tigris, and rode by a memorably inadequate path—equally memorable for the profusion of oleanders through which it ran—up the bank to Finik. The high ground on either side of the valley falls sharply to the water, and the river bursts here through the last barrier of mountain which divides it from the Mesopotamian plain. Finik has been from all time the key of the ravine. Before we reached the side-gorge in which the village lies, we passed a great enclosure of ruined walls and towers, and below it, among the ricefields that occupy a cape jutting into the stream, there are remains of similar fortifications. Beyond the gorge of Finik we rode under a crag which is crowned by the most commanding of the many castles, and less imposing fortress ruins are clustered about its foot. We made our way through groves of pomegranate down to the camp, pitched in clover pastures by the river. A ferry-boat was drawn up upon the bank, and with its help we designed to convey ourselves next morning to the further side, but the boat was ancient and the stream swift, and I suspected that the passage would be a long business. Therefore I left Fattûḥ to cope with the ferrymen and went up, while he did

[1] *Nineveh and Babylon*, p. 55.

FIG. 189.—PARTHIAN RELIEF, ḲAṢR GHELLÎ.

FIG. 190.—PARTHIAN RELIEF, FINIK.

FIG. 191.—THE HILLS OF FINIK.

so, to the village. A tumbling stream and masses of oleander fill the gorge; the greater part of the inhabitants of Finik are lodged in caves, preserving, no doubt, the customs of their remotest ancestors whose rock-cut dwellings they have inherited.[1] We climbed up to the castle by a winding path and entered it on the side furthest from the Tigris, the face of the hill turned towards the river being a precipitous rock. The castle wall is partly of masonry and partly of the natural rock, and the gate is tunnelled through the cliff and flanked by small rock-cut chambers. Within the enclosure there are a number of underground chambers, and on the highest peak the rooms are rock-hewn and vaulted with masonry. How old the rock cutting may be I cannot tell; the masonry is not very ancient, some of it may be modern, while none could safely be dated earlier than the Middle Ages. But the position overhanging the Tigris is superb, and it is difficult to think that the Phœnice which Sapor overthrew stood on any other crag. The rolling plateau of the Ṭûr 'Abdîn stretched away to the south-west, and since I observed that the ferrying of my caravan was taking as long a time as I had anticipated, I sat down and made a comfortable survey of the country we were about to traverse. We returned to the village by the way we had come (there is no other) and climbed the rocks on the opposite side of the valley, where Layard found a much-effaced Parthian relief. It depicts the figures of a man and a woman, clad in short tunics which hang in heavy folds over loosely-fitting trousers (Fig. 190). Above the man's head are traces of an inscription which even in Layard's day was indecipherable. Our guide hurried back to the village while I was examining the tablet, and when we came down we found him spreading a meal of omelets and bread and bowls of irân (a most delectable drink made of sour curds

[1] The caves are carefully excavated and I should say that they are ancient. Layard (*Nineveh and Babylon*, p. 54) speaks of them as tombs and some may have been intended as burial-places, but I do not doubt that many were from all time used by the living. The troglodyte habits of the dwellers in these mountains are still strongly marked. Above Bâ'adrî I saw an underground village; at Ḥiṣn Keif, higher up the Tigris, the people live in rock-hewn chambers.

beaten up in water) under the shade of some mulberry-trees —a welcome sight to those who have breakfasted early and climbed over many rocks. A less pleasing surprise awaited us when we reached the Tigris; not half the horses had crossed, and the ferry-boat was engaged in intricate and lengthy manœuvres on the opposite side. There was nothing to be done but to wait for its return, and I lay down among the clover under a hawthorn-bush.

It was here that we were to bid a final farewell to the Greeks who had accompanied us from the outset of the journey (Fig. 191). "When they had arrived at a spot where the Tigris was quite impassable from its depth and width, and where there was no passage along its banks, as the Carduchian mountains hung steep over the stream, it appeared to the generals that they must march over those mountains, for they had heard from the prisoners that if they could cross the Carduchian heights they would be able to ford the sources of the Tigris in Armenia."[1] They turned north, therefore, and fought their way through the land of the Carduchi, which are the Kurds, until they reached the sea, while we, having a ferry-boat at our disposal and a smaller force to handle, passed over the Tigris into the Ṭûr 'Abdîn. So at length we parted, and Cheirosophus in advance with the light-armed troops scaled the hills of Finik and led slowly forward, leaving Xenophon to bring up the rear with the heavy-armed men. Their shields and corselets glittered upon the steep, they climbed, and reached the summit of the ridge, and disappeared. . . .

"Effendim!" Fattûḥ broke into my meditations. "Effendim, the boat is ready."

"Oh Fattûḥ," said I, "the Greeks are gone."

Fattûḥ looked vaguely disturbed.

"The Greeks of old days, who marched with us down the Euphrates," I explained.

The history of the Ten Thousand is not included in the Aleppine curriculum, and since Fattûh can neither read nor

[1] *Anabasis*, Bk. IV. ch. i.

write, he is debarred from supplementing the acquirements of his brief school-days, but he searched his memory for fragments of my meaningless talk.

"Those?" he said. "God be with them!"

We had more reason to invoke the protection of the Almighty on our own behalf. The ferry-boat was packed with our baggage animals, standing head to tail; the current was very swift. We shot down it, heading aslant, until we neared the further shore; the ferrymen thrust their long poles sharply into the water, and the boat heeled round until the gunwale touched the level of the stream Thereat the horses tumbled over like ninepins, one upon the other, and I, sitting high in the stern, was saved by the timely clutch of a zaptieh from plunging headlong into the stream. "Allah, Allah!" cried the ferrymen, and we ran aground upon the bank.

The Ṭûr 'Abdîn, which we now entered, is a lofty plateau that stretches from Finik on the east to Mardîn and Diyârbekr on the west, and south to Nisîbîn. The Tigris embraces it to north and east; on the south side the heights of the plateau fall abruptly into the Mesopotamian deserts which, interrupted only by the long hog's back of the Jebel Sinjâr, extend to the Persian Gulf. The Mount of the Servants of God—such is the meaning of its beautiful name—was known to the ancients as Masius Mons and Izala Mons, Mount Izala occupying the eastern end of the plateau.[1] This country lay upon the confines of the Roman and the Persian empires, and in the confused accounts of the campaigns of Constantius, Justinian and Heraclius the frontier fortresses of Izala and Masius play a conspicuous part. While war raged round Amida, Marde, Dara and Nisibis, the secluded valleys of the Ṭûr 'Abdîn were falling peacefully into the hands of the Servants of God. The Mount was a stronghold of the Christian faith; monastery after monastery rose among the oak woods, the rolling uplands were cleared and planted with

[1] Ammianus Marcellinus, when he speaks of Izala, evidently intends the name to cover the whole Ṭûr 'Abdîn: Bk. XVIII. ch. vi. 11, and Bk. XIX. ch. ix. 4.

vineyards, and the ancient communities of the Eastern Church multiplied and grew rich in their almost inaccessible retreat.[1] Very little has been published concerning the architectural remains of the district, but I had happened to see in Môṣul some photographs which had awakened my curiosity, and the Dominican fathers whom I met at Baviân had raised it still higher.[2]

The morning was half spent before we landed on the west bank of the Tigris. Our path climbed up on to the plateau and led us over downs sweet scented with clover and very thinly populated: during the five hours' journey from the Tigris to Azakh we saw only three villages.[3] Azakh, where we camped, is inhabited mainly by Jacobites, some of whom have modified their creed under the influence of American missionaries. The Protestant pastor paid me a visit and brought disquieting news. While we were still at Môṣul we had heard rumours of a massacre of the Christians which had taken place at Adana. The Ṭûr 'Abdîn was full of these reports. It was impossible to make out whether the events which were related to us were past or present, how serious the massacre had been or whether it were now at an end, and it was not until I reached Cæsarea that I learnt the truth with regard to the double outbreak in Cilicia. For a month we were greeted wherever we went with details of fresh calamities that were in part the reverberation of those of which we had already heard, and everywhere these histories were accompanied by the assurance that a deliberate attempt had been

[1] The Jacobites and the Syrians (*i.e.* Jacobites who have submitted to Rome) have now ousted the Nestorians, who must have been the first to occupy the Ṭûr 'Abdîn. When this change took place I do not know, but the Nestorians were in possession of the monastery of Mâr Augen as late as 1505: Pognon, *op. cit.*, p. 109.

[2] Pognon's account of the churches, and his publication of the inscriptions, is the best work on the subject (*Inscriptions de la Mésopotamie*); Parry (*Six Months in a Syrian Monastery*) gives a short description of the churches and some sketch plans.

[3] Tigris ferry 9.25; Handak (Christian) 9.45; Thelailah (Moslem) 10.40; Kôdakh—marked in Kiepert—we saw at 12.15, a little to the south of our route.

made from without to stir up massacres in the districts through which we passed. No direct proof of this statement was offered; I never met the man who had set eyes on the reported telegram, nor any one who could tell me what signature it bore. But in the East, conviction does not wait upon evidence. I learnt to realize the evil power of rumour, and experience taught me how hard it is to keep the mind steadily fixed upon the proposition that two unsupported statements (or the same often repeated) will not make a certainty. The atmosphere of panic which surrounded us is the true precursor of disaster, and I found good reason to respect the statecraft of the Turkish officials whose firmness saved the population from the consequences of their own loudly expressed suspicions. I bear testimony to the fact that all that I saw or heard of the agitation which attended the events of April 1909 led me to the conviction that the local authorities had set their face against bloodshed, and by so doing had averted it.

Next morning we rode for six hours to Bâ Sebrîna, over wide uplands almost entirely uncultivated and covered with small oak-trees. The country was so like the swelling, thinly wooded hills that lead out of the Belḳâ towards the Syrian Desert that at times I could have sworn that we were riding from Gilead into Moab.[1] The characteristic feature of the Ṭûr 'Abdîn is the absence of streams; even when we crossed a deep valley, as we did twice during the course of the morning, there was no running water in it. The water supply of the villages is derived from pools which are fed by the winter rains and snows. In the second valley we found the ruined monastery of Mâr Shim'ûn, placed among thickets and deep herbage, but, to my disappointment, it was of little architec-

[1] Our itinerary was as follows: 5.30 Azakh; 6.30 a ruined site (marked in Kiepert); 7.5 Salakûn (Kiepert: Salekon Kharabe), a small Moslem village; 8 Middo (marked in Kiepert), a Christian village on the further side of a deep gorge (here we got into the oak woods); 9 Irmez, about a mile to the south of our road; 9.25 Arba', a Christian village also about a mile south; 9.45–10.45 Deir Mâr Shim'ûn, a ruined monastery; 11.30 Deir Bar Sauma, the first monastery of Bâ Sebrîna.

tural interest. The village of Bâ Sebrîna is wholly Christian. It has been an important place, and though it has now fallen to the estate of a small hamlet, it contains innumerable monasteries. Several of these are beyond the limits of the town. They lie, each in its own enclosing wall, like small forts upon the hills, and each is garrisoned by a single monk. The monastic buildings are exiguous, and I doubt whether they can have been intended for more than one or two persons; perhaps they should be regarded as clerical rather than as monastic foundations,[1] and the living-rooms were intended for the lodging of those who served the shrine. The first monastery which we reached upon the outskirts of Bâ Sebrîna was of this character. Its high and rather tapering rectangular tower, and strong walls, gave it from afar a striking appearance, but the vaulted chapel and the rooms set round a tiny court were rudely built of undressed stones, almost totally dark, and devoid of decorative features. I looked at several of the monastic houses within the village, and always with the same results: they had no pretension to architectural interest and were without ornament or inscriptions by which to determine their date. But at the monastery of Mâr Dodo I found a clue to the history of Bâ Sebrîna. The church, which is the largest in the place, stands upon the north side of a walled court round which are placed insignificant living-rooms, store-rooms and stables. The church consists of a closed narthex running along the south side of a vaulted aisleless nave, with a single apse to the east. On the east side of the court, south of the church, there is an exedra covered by a semi-dome and provided with a stone reading-desk on which to set the holy books. All the masonry is rude and unskilful, and the carved capitals and moulded arch of the exedra bear no sign of great antiquity, while the engaged capitals in the church are merely blocked out. Now this scheme of a single-chambered church, with a narthex to the south and an external exedra, filled me with amazement, for it was unlike any that I had seen, but I was

[1] Monasteria clericorum. See *The Thousand and One Churches*, p. 461.

subsequently to learn that it is one of the oldest ecclesiastical plans of the Ṭûr 'Abdîn, and its combination at Bâ Sebrîna with rough masonry and late decorative details is explained by a Syriac inscription above the porch which states that the church was built in the year 1510 of the Seleucid era, *i. e.* A.D. 1200. Whether this be the date of the first foundation or of a fundamental reconstruction upon an older site I cannot be certain, though from the absence of all trace of early work I incline to the former alternative, and I conclude that the old architectural scheme of the Ṭûr 'Abdîn was adhered to closely at a later date, when a second period of building activity saw the foundation of the churches and monasteries of Bâ Sebrîna. But since I did not then know that these edifices were exact copies of more ancient work, their recent date was a rude shock, and I began to wonder whether the Mount would prove to be as fruitful a field as I had hoped. Bâ Sebrîna, at any rate, had been drawn blank, and we rode down for three-quarters of an hour through vineyards to the village of Sâreh. As soon as we had settled upon a camping-ground—no easy matter on account of the interminable vineyards—I walked down to the village to examine the church. The âghâ of Sâreh belongs to one of the leading Kurdish families of these parts. I found him in an open space near the church, entertaining friends who had ridden over from a neighbouring village. They too were âghâs of a noble house, and they were tricked out in all the finery which their birth warranted. Their short jackets were covered with embroidery, silver-mounted daggers were stuck into their girdles, and upon their heads they wore immense erections of white felt, wrapped round with a silken handkerchief of which the ends stuck out like wings over their foreheads. They pressed me to accept several tame partridges which they kept to lure the wild birds, and while we waited for the priest to bring the key of the church, they exhibited the very curious stela (Fig. 192) which stands upside down in the courtyard.[1] Meantime the village priest had arrived, and I

[1] Pognon : *op. cit.*, p. 108. The stela has not, as Pognon feared, been destroyed. The script is in an unknown alphabet, which Pognon believes

followed him unsuspiciously into the church. But I had not stood for more than a minute inside the building than I happened to look down on to the floor and perceived it to be black with fleas. I made a hasty exit, tore off my stockings and plunged them into a tank of water, which offered the safest remedy in this emergency.

"There are," said the priest apologetically, "a great many, but they are all swept out on Sunday morning. On Sunday there are none."

I confess to a deep scepticism on this head.

The incompleteness of the maps and the absence of trustworthy information led us far astray upon the following day. I had heard of a very ancient monastery that lay upon the outer edge of the Ṭûr 'Abdîn: upon the way thither I proposed to visit the castle of Ḥâtim Ṭâi. Accordingly I spread out Kiepert, and drawing a bee-line across the blank paper, told Fattûḥ to take the camp to Useh Dereh (Kiepert calls it Useden), and provided him with a zaptieh and a guide. Another villager accompanied Jûsef and me and the second zaptieh, and undertook to guide us via the castle to Useh Dereh. We set forth from Sâreh at 5.30 and rode through uninhabited oak woods till 8.10, when we reached a ruined village from which we could see the castle of Ḥâtim Ṭâi standing up boldly on the opposite side of a deep valley. There was no road by which to reach it—not so much as a bridle path. We struggled down through the woods, dragging our horses over rocks and fallen trees, and by the special mercy of Providence reached at 9.15, and without accident, the foot of the castle hill. A path led round it to the Yezîdî village of Gelîyeh, and thither I sent Jûsef and the zaptieh with the horses, while the man of Sâreh climbed the hill with me. Ḥâtim Ṭâi was a renowned sheikh of the Arab tribe of the Ṭâi, but the castle which is called after him has a far longer history. The summit of the hill is enclosed in a

---

to be the prototype of Pehlevî. He gives excellent photographs of the two inscriptions; my photograph shows the relief on the third side. The fourth side is much weather-worn.

FIG. 192.—STELA AT SÂREH.

FIG. 193.—ḲAL'AT ḤÂTIM ṬÂI, CHAPEL.

FIG. 194.—MÂR AUGEN.

double line of fortification following the contours of the slopes. The lower ring is provided with towers at the angles of the wall, and with round bastions of very slight projection. Within the inner enclosure stands the citadel, now completely ruined and bearing evidences of frequent reconstruction. The oldest parts are unmistakably of Byzantine masonry, and contain a chapel of which the apse is well preserved (Fig. 193). The castle must have been rebuilt during the Mohammadan period, and then again rebuilt, for in one of the walls of the citadel there is a fragment of an Arabic inscription, which is not in its original position, neither is the inscription complete.[1] The Yezîdîs declare that the castle was one of their strongholds until it passed into the hands of the Ṭâi, and this might account for a reconstruction of the citadel at a late period. The only other inscription which I could find is also Arabic. It is apparently a name, with no date or further qualification, cut upon the main gate of the outer wall.[2] In the space between the two walls there are a number of small rock-hewn cisterns, some of which were probably intended to hold corn and other provisions. The main water supply was drawn from a large cistern in the citadel. So far as I could judge, the ruins, therefore, exhibit Yezîdî or Arab work (or both) upon Byzantine foundations, and I think it exceedingly likely that the castle of Ḥâtim Ṭâi is that Rhabdium which, according to Procopius, was fortified by Justinian. It lay, says he, on a steep rock upon the frontiers of the Roman and the Persian empires, two days from Dara. Below it was the Ager Romanorum, which has been identified with the plain between Môṣul and the Ṭûr 'Abdîn. Since there was no water near it (there is none, as I have said, in the Ṭûr 'Abdîn), Justinian was obliged to cut a number of cisterns.[3] The whole of this description exactly fits the castle of Ḥâtim Ṭâi, and the presence of Byzantine masonry among the ruins is strongly in favour of the identification. The position of the

[1] I sent the photograph to Professor van Berchem. The inscription is merely a date: 630 (=A.D. 1232–3), or possibly 639.

[2] The name itself is unintelligible.

[3] *The Buildings of Justinian* (Palestine Pilgrims' Text Society), p. 51.

fortress is exceedingly fine. The hills drop down sharply from its very walls into the Mesopotamian plain, where the long line of the Jebel Sinjâr, a mountain occupied almost exclusively by the Yezîdîs, alone breaks the desolate expanse.

A cruel disillusion awaited us when we reached the valley. The Yezîdîs, who were feasting Jûsef and the zaptieh on bread and bowls of milk, declared that there was no getting to Useh Dereh except by taking the path down into the plain and climbing up into the hills again by a pass at Ḳal'at ej Jedîd. Even the direction from which we had come was blocked to us, for we refused to contemplate a return through the woods down which we had pushed our way with so much difficulty. The Yezîdîs, who had heard from Jûsef that we had recently visited 'Alî Beg, begged us to stay the night in their caves (the village of Gelîyeh is all underground), and offered to kill a sheep for us, and when I was obliged to decline this eagerly proffered hospitality, one of their number accompanied us for some distance to show us the way. Riding through oak woods where the bees had hived in every hollow trunk we came to a small and dilapidated Yezîdî shrine, where my guide paused to kiss the largest of the trees. "It belongs to the ziyârah," he said in answer to my question. "We do not collect the honey out of any of these trees; all the wood here belongs to the ziyârah." We left Gelîyeh at 10.30 and in two hours found ourselves in the familiar Mesopotamian landscape, an interminable flat strewn with big mounds, each with its village near it. The climate, too, was familiar, and we rode wearily through a burning heat to which we had not thought to return. At 11.30 we passed near Kalka; at 12.30 we came to Kinik, where we spent half-an-hour trying to re-shoe one of our horses. But the farrier was dead, so we were informed, and though we had the shoe with us the whole village could not produce a single nail. When once the Yezîdî was gone none of our party had any special knowledge of the way, but Kiepert (upon whom be praise!) served us well, and with his help we hit off the valley which led up to Ḳal'at ej Jedîd, and at five o'clock we found ourselves, tired and hungry, under its towers. It soared above us, no less splendidly placed than Ḳal'at Ḥâtim Tâi, and guarded this second pass just as Ḥâtim Ṭâi had guarded the other. If we had been certain that we should reach our camp before nightfall I should have climbed up to it, but in the mountains no one can make a sure calculation of distances, and we dared not stay. I know nothing, therefore, of Ḳal'at ej Jedîd but its magnificent outer aspect, and it remains in my memory as a vision of wall and tower and precipitous rock rising into the ruddy sunset light above a shadowy gorge, a citadel as bold and menacing as any that I have seen.[1] We led our horses up the rugged gorge, and at 6.40 regained the plateau of the Ṭûr 'Abdîn. A little village, Bâ Dibbeh, stood at the head of the pass, and before us stretched a rolling, thickly wooded country. We stopped at the village pool to inquire our way, and were given the general direction of Useh Dereh, coupled with a vague assurance that it was not far. The paths were too stony for riding, and to walk was a relief after so many hours of the saddle; I left my companions to bring on the horses and turned into the darkening oak woods. For close upon an hour I followed the course of a shallow winding valley; the trees, standing close about the path, obscured all view; a brooding silence, unbroken by man or beast, hung over the forest, the dark deepened into cool, sweet-smelling night, and still the narrow rocky path wound on between wooded banks. And just as I was wondering whether it had any end, the trees fell back round an open patch of corn and vine, and the lights of my camp shone out upon the further side.

If we had travelled far in the body upon that day, we travelled further in the spirit upon the next. There lies upon the lip of the hills, overlooking the wide desolation of Meso-

[1] I would suggest that Ḳal'at ej Jedîd may occupy the site of the Sisaurana of Procopius, which was destroyed by Belisarius. Sisaurana, however, lay three miles from Rhabdium, and even as the crow flies the distance between Ḳ. Hâtim Tâi and Ḳ. ej Jedîd must be greater. But the important position of K. ej Jedîd on one of the few passes up from the plain suggests that the spot must have been fortified in ancient times. Sisaurana is no doubt the Sisara of Ammianus Marcellinus: see Ritter, Vol. XI. p. 150 and pp. 400–401.

potamia, a monastery which is said to be the mother house of all the Ṭûr 'Abdîn. Into these solitudes, according to the tradition of the mountain, wandered at the beginning of the fourth century a pupil of St. Antony, whose name was St. Eugenius. He had learnt from his master the rule of solitude and had overcome with him the devils that people the Egyptian sands; among the rocks of Mount Izala he laid down his pilgrim's staff, gathered disciples about him and founded the monastery that still bears his name. It was at first no more than a group of cells hollowed out of the cliff, but as its fame increased, the monks built themselves a church upon a narrow shelf between precipice and precipice, and helped out the natural defences of the mountain by a strong wall of masonry. The cave cells increased in number until the rocks were honeycombed on every side, and disciples of the first founder led forth companies of monks to raise fresh monasteries over the Ṭûr 'Abdîn.[1] The Jacobite priest of Useh Dereh, when he heard that we proposed to visit Mâr Augen, offered to accompany us, saying that he wished to pay his respects to the bishop who lived there (this was a figure of speech, for the bishop is not to be seen of any man), and he guided us for an hour through the woods to the southern edge of the hills.[2] The path to the monastery was a rock-cut staircase, but we succeeded in dragging the horses down it and left them by the gate (Fig. 194). Under the crag stands the church with its tiny cloister and walled court, and it did not take long to discover that, in spite of many rebuildings, the tradition as to its age could not be far wrong. A church must have stood here in the sixth century, if not in the fifth;

[1] Though tradition links these foundations with Egypt, it is quite possible that they may have had a yet closer connection with Syria, where in the fourth century monasticism and the solitary life had already taken a strong hold. Duchesne: *Histoire de l'Eglise*, Vol. II. p. 516.

[2] Kiepert marks a "Gr. Cœnobium von Izala," which is, I imagine, intended for Mâr Augen, but its position relatively to Ḳ. ej Jedîd and Useh Dereh, as marked in the map, cannot be correct. Mâr Yuhannâ, which lies to the east of Mâr Augen, approaches more nearly to Kiepert's site. I have published a short account of these and other monasteries and churches of the Ṭûr 'Abdîn in *Amida* (Strzygowski and Van Berchem).

some of the old capitals have been re-used at a later time, and the ancient plan is preserved in church and cloister. Ten monks are lodged in the rock-cut cells of their remote forerunners—I met with one of them in the cloister and he carried intelligence of my arrival to the prior, who came in haste to do the honours of his church. He was a man of some thirty years of age, with melancholy eyes. We sat together in the shadow of the cloister, while he explained to me the rule under which he and his brethren lived, and as he spoke I felt the centuries drop away and disclose the ascetic life of the early Christian world. They spend their days in meditation; their diet is bread and oil and lentils; no meat, and neither milk nor eggs may pass their lips; they may see no woman—

"But may you see me?" I asked.

"We have made an exception for you," explained the prior. "Travellers come here so seldom. But some of the monks have shut themselves into their cells until you go."

The cell of St. Eugenius stands apart from the others, hollowed out of the cliff to the west of the church. The prior had spent a lonely winter there, seeing no one but the brother who brought him his daily meal of bread and lentils. As we stood in the narrow cave, which was more like a tomb than a dwelling-place, I looked into the young face, marked with the lines drawn by solitude and hunger.

"Where is your home?" I asked.

"In Mardîn," he answered. "My father and my mother live there yet."

"Will you see them again?" said I.

"Perhaps not," he replied, but there was no regret in his voice.

"And all your days you will live here?"

He looked out calmly over rock and plain. "Please God," he said. "It seems to be a good place for prayer."

It is the habit of the monks to let no traveller depart without food, a habit well known to the neighbouring Kurds who claim more hospitality than the monastery can well afford. While I worked at the church, the prior betook himself to the cave kitchen and prepared an ample meal of eggs and bread, raisins and sour curds for me and for my men. When we had eaten I asked whether it would not be seemly to thank the bishop for the entertainment which had been offered to us.

"You cannot see him," said the prior. "He has left the world."

"The kas from Useh Dereh came to-day to visit him," I objected.

"He came to gaze upon his cell," answered the prior, and with that he led me out of the church and pointed to a cave some fifty feet above us in the cliff. Three-quarters of the opening had been filled with masonry, and I could see that it was approached by a stair of which the lower part was cut out behind a gallery and the upper on the face of the rock. An active novice might have thought twice before attempting the path to the bishop's cell.

"Is he old?" said I.

"He is the father of eighty years," replied the prior, "and it is now a year since he took a vow of silence and renounced the world. Once a day, at sunset, he lets down a basket on a rope and we place therein a small portion of bread."

"And when he dies?" I asked.

"When he is sick to death he will send down a written word telling us to come up on the next day and fetch his body. Then we shall see his face again."

"And you will take his place?" said I.

"If God wills," he answered.

We walked across the hills for half-an-hour to Mâr Yuhannâ, a monastery founded by a disciple of St. Eugenius. It is neither so finely placed nor so interesting architecturally as Mâr Augen, though the rough walls of church and monastic building, which cling to the rocky slopes, are not without a certain wild beauty. The bishop who rules over the house of Mâr Yuhannâ is less exclusive than the prelate at Mâr Augen, for he shares a tower with his four monks, but he was still too exclusive to receive my visit. The aged prior was all for serving us with a meal, but I could not undertake to dispose of another omelet, nor did I realize that my refusal would be regarded as a shocking breach of the social code. The prior was so deeply hurt that he would not bid us farewell, and we left under the cloud of his displeasure. We climbed back to the summit of the hills and rode home to Useh Dereh, and if any one should wonder why a recluse from Egypt should have sought so distant a dwelling-place as Mount Izala, I can give a sufficient answer. It was because he found Iris Susiana growing among the rocks. The great grey flowers lift their heads in every open space between the oak-trees, gleaming silver in the strong sun, and so perfect are they in form, so exquisite in texture, that I stood amazed at the sight of them, as one who gazes on a celestial vision.

It is just an hour's ride from Useh Dereh to Mâr Melko,[1] which stands fortress-like upon the top of a hill. The bishop (for there was a bishop here also—the number of prelates in the Tûr 'Abdîn is scarcely to be reckoned) was singularly unlike his colleagues of the other monasteries. He carried sociability to so high a point that I doubted whether I should be allowed to proceed that day upon my journey, but with the regrettable incident at Mâr Yuhannâ fresh in my memory, I put force upon my appetite and ate the second breakfast upon which his hospitality insisted, while the zaptieh and Jûsef, who were not in the habit of counting breakfasts, did fuller justice to the remains of it. The monastery is a rambling building with a chapel upon an upper floor and a crypt containing the tombs of priors. The tomb of the patron saint is in the church itself. Over it hangs a rude picture of Mâr Melko with the devil beside him : upon inquiry the bishop explained that the saint had been renowned for his power of casting out devils, and he pointed to a collar and chain attached to the wall and observed that men who were afflicted with fits or madness came here to be cured, and all

[1] Kiepert places Mâr Melko too far from Useh Dereh. My itinerary was as follows : Useh Dereh to Mâr Melko, 1 hr. ; Mâr Melko to Kharabah 'Aleh, 30 min. ; Kharabah 'Aleh to Kernaz, 2 hrs. 15 min. ; Kernaz to Deir el 'Amr, 1 hr. 15 min. All these places are marked in the map.

went away sound, no matter what their creed.[1] The buildings bore evidences of frequent reconstruction, and parts of the church were still in the state of ruin in which a recent Kurdish raid had left them. It is almost impossible to date architecture of this kind, for the new work and the old have much the same character, but the plan of the church is the ancient monastic scheme, as I learnt at Mâr Gabriel and at Salâh, and in all probability Mâr Melko is to be counted among the oldest foundations of the Tûr 'Abdîn. Like Mâr Gabriel it is some distance removed from the nearest village, and depends for its security upon its own strong walls. After we had passed through Kharabah 'Aleh, which contains the ruins of a church, we wandered among the rolling, wooded hills, and had gone needlessly far to the north before we caught sight of the monastery of Mâr Gabriel standing upon an eminence, with my tents pitched beside it. The inevitable bishop was away and I could not regret his absence, since it implied a relaxation of the social duties which I should otherwise have been obliged to fulfil, and permitted me to give my whole attention to the building.

The house of St. Gabriel of Kartmîn was, during the Middle Ages, the most famous and the richest of Jacobite establishments. It is said to have been founded in the reign of Arcadius (395-408) and rebuilt under Anastasius (491-518), and I see no reason to doubt that the great church of Mâr Gabriel is, as it now stands, a work of the early sixth century. There are two other churches within the existing monastic precincts, one dedicated to the Virgin, the other to the Forty Martyrs, but neither of these is as old as that which is dedicated to the tutelary saint (Fig. 197). A large area of ruins beyond the walls gives some indication of the former magnificence of the monastery which gained, as early as the days of Justinian, a reputation for holiness second only

[1] Niebuhr heard that Mâr Melko was famed for the curing of epilepsy: *Reisebericht*, Vol. II. p. 388. Not having penetrated into the Ṭûr 'Abdîn, he thought that the report that there were seventy monasteries in the hills must be an exaggeration, but I expect that it was not far from the truth.

FIG. 195.—THE BISHOP OF MÂR MELKO.

FIG. 196.—KHÂKH, THE NUN.

FIG. 197.—NARTHEX OF MÂR GABRIEL.

FIG. 200.—KHÂKH, CHURCH OF THE VIRGIN.

to Jerusalem. It bore at that period the name of St. Stephen; St. Gabriel was bishop of the monastery during the reign of Heraclius. When the Arab invaders drove out the forces of the Byzantine empire, he obtained from the Khalif 'Umar ibn u'l Khaṭṭâb rights of jurisdiction over all Christians in the Ṭûr 'Abdîn, for which reason the monastery is sometimes called after him, Deir Mâr Gabriel, and sometimes after the khalif, Deir 'Umar. It was despoiled by Tîmûr towards the close of the fourteenth century, and many a harrying it must have endured from the Kurds before it sank into its present state of poverty and decay. One monk and a single nun, well stricken in years, were its sole occupants at the time of my visit. The church of Mâr Gabriel is built upon a plan which I conjecture to be monastic as distinguished from parochial. The two types, which are quite unlike each other, are also unlike all churches known to me outside the Ṭûr 'Abdîn. The parish church (Fig. 198), which has no domestic buildings attached to it, or nothing but a few chambers for the lodging of clerks, follows invariably the plan that I have described at Bâ Sebrina; at Mâr Gabriel, and in the other monastic churches (Fig. 199), the atrium and narthex lie to the west, the vaulted nave is placed with its greater length running from north to south, and three doors in the east wall communicate with a triple sanctuary. From what prototypes did the Christian architects of the Ṭûr 'Abdîn derive the singular feature of the nave lying with its greater length at right angles to the main axis of the building? I

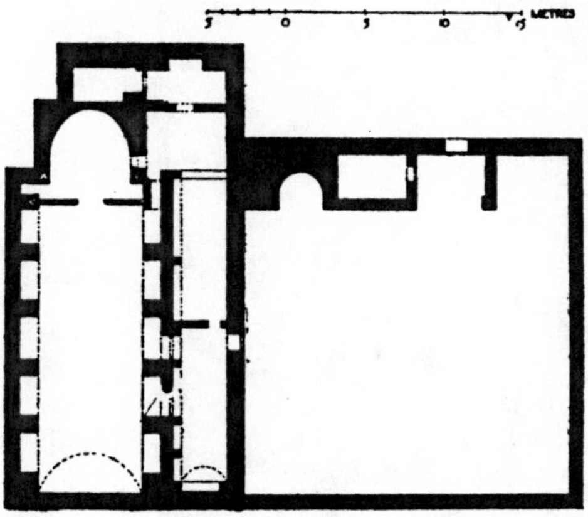

FIG. 198.—KEFR ZEH, MÂR 'AZÎZÎYEH; PARISH CHURCH.

can only suggest that they may have preserved the ancient scheme of the Babylonian temple and palace hall, which was retained by the Assyrians in their palaces, but not in their temples; and if this be so, the monastic churches of the Ṭûr 'Abdîn are the last representatives of the oldest Oriental architecture. The walls and vault of the nave of Mâr Gabriel are devoid of ornament, but the vault of the central sanctuary is adorned with mosaics. The accumulated soot of centuries of candle-smoke has not entirely obscured the glory of its golden ground, of the great jewelled cross laid over the centre of the vault, and the twisted vine scrolls with which it is encircled. It is said that similar mosaics once covered the whole church and were destroyed by the soldiers of Tîmûr.

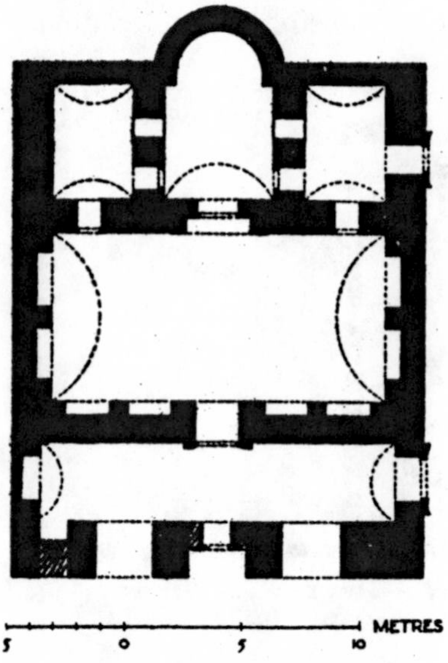

FIG. 199.—SALÂH MÂR YA'KÛB; MONASTIC TYPE.

We rode next morning into Midyâd,[1] and camped beside the ruined church of Mâr Philoxenos which, since it has not been recently repaired, is of greater interest than any other in the town.[2] The task of planning it was a labour of hatred. The population of Midyâd, men, women and

[1] Deir 'Umar, 5.30; Mezîzakh, 8.15; Midyâd, 9.15.

[2] I visited inside the town Mâr Shim'ûn, which is in process of being rebuilt, and Mâr Barsauma, which has been completely rebuilt. Outside the town is the monastery of Mâr Ibrahîm and Mâr Hôbel. It has recently been repaired, but much of the masonry is ancient. The two churches, dedicated to the two patron saints, belong to the monastic type of Mâr Gabriel; the mouldings round the doors, and the cyma cornice are old. There is also a small chapel, dedicated to the Virgin; it is square in plan and covered by a dome on squinches, but it appeared to me to be of later date. I was shown in this monastery a

children, stationed themselves upon the ruined walls, and for them it was no doubt the most entertaining afternoon which they had spent for many a long week, but for me, and for the patient bearers of the measuring tape, the hours were charged with exasperation. The Ḳâimmaḳâm, when he appeared upon this agitated scene (Midyâd is the seat of government in the Ṭûr 'Abdîn), succeeded in clearing the ruins for a few moments, but as soon as he had turned his back, the hordes reassembled with a greater zest than before.

My Christian servants returned in the evening from the bazaar gravely disquieted by the gossip which was current there. It was rumoured that the wave of massacre had spread to Aleppo and they trembled for the fate of their wives and families. The news which was causing us so much anxiety was in fact nearly a month old, but we did not learn until we reached Diyârbekr that Aleppo had escaped with a week of panic.

The next day was devoted to three churches which I visited and planned on the way to Khâkh, Mâr Yâ'ḳûb at Ṣalâḥ, Mâr Kyriakos at Arnâs and Mâr 'Azîzîyeh at Kefr Zeh. I doubt whether there exists anywhere a group of buildings

---

very remarkable silken vestment. The ground is of green satin covered with a repeated pattern in gold, silver and coloured silks, representing a woman in a red robe seated in a howdah upon the back of a camel. A man naked to the waist is seated upon the ground with his head bowed upon his hands. A variety of animals and floral motives are scattered round the principal figures. The subject is no doubt taken from the story of Leila and Majnûn. The date of this brocade is probably somewhere between 1560 and 1660. A fragment showing a like pattern is in the possession of Dr. Sarre. The monastery possesses besides a small bronze thurible, of which I succeeded in procuring a counterpart. A similar thurible exists in the British Museum (No. 540 in the catalogue of Early Christian and Byzantine Antiquities); it is said to have come from Mâr Musa el Habashi, between Damascus and Palmyra. The Kaiser Friedrich Museum has obtained several in Cairo and Trebizond (Wulff: *Altchristliche Bildwerke*, Teil I, nos. 967–970). These are ascribed to the sixth and seventh centuries. Mr. Dalton, to whom I owe this information, gives me references to two others, one in the Bargello collection at Florence (No. 241 in the catalogue of the Carraud Collection, published in 1898) and one published in the *Echos d'Orient*, VII., 1904, p. 148.

more precious to the archæologist than these three churches and the little domed shrine of the Virgin which stands almost perfect among the ruins of Khâkh (Fig. 201). It is close upon a miracle that in this forgotten region, long subjected to the tyranny of the Kurds, such masterpieces of architecture should have escaped destruction; the explanation is probably to be found in the rugged mountain frontiers of the Ṭûr 'Abdîn. Even though it lay upon the edge of country which was for over a hundred years the battle-ground of the Persian and the Byzantine, war seems to have penetrated but little into its heart. The Christian communities, from their rock-cut cells in the crags of Mount Izala, must have listened to the rumours of advance and flight and siege; they could almost witness the encounter of armies in the plain below. But "the lofty mountain, precipitous and almost inaccessible," as Procopius describes it, was a sure refuge, and Procopius himself can scarcely have been acquainted with the wooded uplands and fertile valleys where already in his time stood the churches and monasteries of Ṣalâḥ and Arnâs, Kefr Zeh and Khâkh. The Arab conquerors left the Christians undisturbed; they bowed the head and suffered under the fierce blast of Tîmûr's invasion and under the secular persecution of the Kurds; but decimated and stripped of their wealth, they held firmly to the bare walls of their religious houses, and the meagre, ragged choirs still chant their litanies under vaults which have withstood the assault of fourteen centuries. Into this country I came, entirely ignorant of its architectural wealth, because it was entirely unrecorded. None of the inscriptions collected by Pognon go back earlier than the ninth century; the plans which had

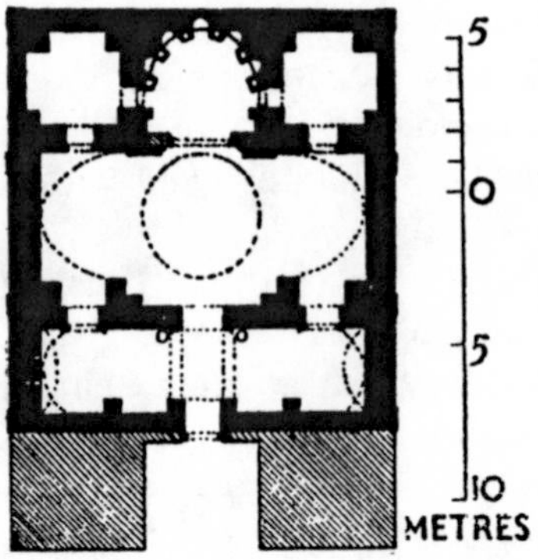

FIG. 201.—KHÂKH, CHURCH OF THE VIRGIN.

FIG. 202.—KHÂKH, CHURCH OF THE VIRGIN, CAPITALS.

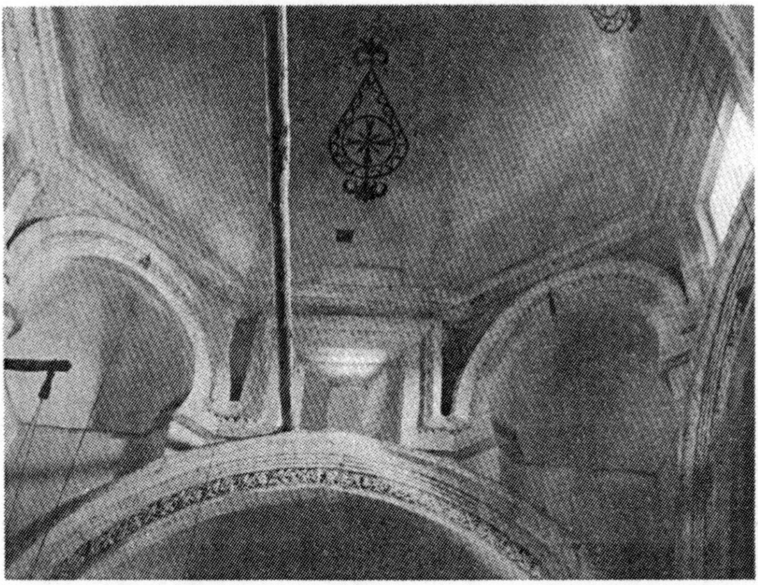

FIG. 203.—KHÂKH, CHURCH OF THE VIRGIN, DOME ON SQUINCH ARCHES.

FIG. 204.—THE CHELABÎ.

FIG. 205.—FORDING THE TIGRIS BELOW DIYÂRBEKR.

been published were lamentably insufficient and were unaccompanied by any photographs. When I entered Mâr Yâ'ḳûb at Ṣalâḥ and saw upon its walls mouldings and carved string courses which bore the sign manual of the Græco-Asiatic civilization I scarcely dared to trust to the conclusions to which they pointed. But church after church confirmed and strengthened them. The chancel arches, covered with an exquisite lacework of ornament, the delicate grace of the acanthus capitals, hung with garlands and enriched with woven entrelac (Fig. 200), the repetition of ancient plans and the mastery of constructive problems which revealed an old architectural tradition, all these assure to the churches of the Ṭûr 'Abdîn the recognition of their honourable place in the history of the arts.

It was evening when we rode over the last of the wooded hills and saw the village of Khâkh lying upon a green knoll in the midst of a fertile plain. The rays of the setting sun touched the dome of the church of the Virgin, the tower of Mâr Sobo and the terraced houses; they flashed upon the pool below the village, by the edge of which my camp was pitched, and were mercifully unrevealing of poverty and ruin. It seemed to me that I had ended the most wonderful day since that which had brought me to Ukheiḍir by dropping into a village of the fifth century, complete and prosperous in every part. The searching light of morning disclosed a different picture. The houses were mere hovels, and except for the church of the Virgin, not one of the ancient buildings but had fallen into the extremity of decay. That church is, however, the jewel of the Ṭûr 'Abdîn (Figs. 200, 202, 203). It has suffered scarcely any change since the builders completed it, and it points a way to the solution of many a problem of Byzantine architecture. Its plan suggests a memorial rather than a monastic type; the domestic buildings near it are small and modern and I saw no trace of an ancient monastic house. A nun and the village priest occupied the rooms that now stand to the north of the courtyard. The nun was young and personable, and she found the religious life very much to her taste. Her sacred calling gave her the right to come and go as she pleased, to mix in male society and even to put forth her opinion in male councils. Moreover it provided her with an excuse for claiming audience of me on the evening of my arrival.

"I have come to see my sister," I heard her announce. "Does she speak Arabic?" And before Fattûḥ could answer, she had presented herself at the tent door. The object of her visit was to ask me for a revolver.

"What do you want with a revolver?" I said.

"We are afraid," she replied. "We are all afraid of massacre."

The little community of Jacobites snatch their daily bread from field and vineyard which lie at the mercy of marauding Kurds, whose practices were not, unfortunately, to remain for us a matter of hearsay. The second night at Khâkh was marked by the only misadventure that has befallen me in Turkey. We had intended to leave the village early on the following morning and everything was prepared for our departure; even my saddle-bags, duly packed with note-books and camera, were lying ready in my tent. In the middle of the night I was awakened by a rustling noise, and starting up I saw the figure of a man crouched in the door-way. We had grown careless with months of safe journeying in dangerous places, and neither Fattûḥ nor I had taken the trouble to set a guard over the camp. The thieves had found us an easy prey; before the servants and zaptiehs were roused, they had made off into the night and we were left to reckon up our loss. What money I had with me had been taken out of my tent, the servants had been robbed of all their spare clothing, and various other small objects were missing, but the real disaster was the disappearance of the saddle-bags which contained my note-books. We stood helpless, gazing into the darkness into which had vanished the results of four months' work. A rifle shot fired by Selîm had awakened the priest, who came hurrying down to inquire into our case. Deeply distressed was he, poor man, to hear of our misfortune, for we were the guests of the village, and he feared that ill might fall upon him and his flock for suffering us to come to harm. I listened to a great deal of divergent advice, and finally decided to send for the Chelabî, who is the feudal chief of the Kurdish tribes in the Ṭûr 'Abdîn. Accordingly at the first dawn Fattûḥ and a zaptieh were dispatched across the hills to bear him the news. A certain village lay under suspicion, a little robbers' nest situated in the depths of a wild and rocky valley a few miles to the east. The people of Khâkh were well used to the depredations of the men of Zâ'khurân, and during the course of the day we were provided with more positive evidence against them. It chanced that the thieves had carried off a parcel of my gloves, and these they shed along the path as they ran. Gloves lying upon the rocky ways of the Ṭûr 'Abdîn are exceptional objects, and the path by which they were found was that which led to Zâ'khurân. Evening brought the Chelabî, pacing sedately upon his mare with twenty men behind him, all dressed in white garments and armed with rifles (Fig. 204). I went out to welcome them and brought their leader to my tents, where he listened to my tale over a cup of coffee and gave me many assurances of redress. This done, he repaired with great dignity to the roof of the priest's house, converted for the time into a court of justice, and received, until late into the night, deputations from the neighbouring villages. Next day the judgment seat was removed to Zâ'khurân, and Fattûḥ went with it as witness to the crime and representative of the plaintiff; at dusk he returned and reported that the Chelabî had arrested four men, selected, so far as could be ascertained, by empirical methods from among the inhabitants of the district, but that no clue had been found to the missing note-books. It was now time to invoke a higher power, and I entrusted a zaptieh with a letter to the Ḳâimmaḳâm of Midyâd and with a telegram which was to be sent from Midyâd to the Vâlî at Diyârbekr. The Ḳâimmaḳâm entered into the business like a man. On the following evening ten zaptiehs arrived from Midyâd, and next morning fifty foot soldiers marched into our camp. The nature of evidence is not clearly grasped in the East, and by the third day after the robbery there was no person in the country-side, except, I believe, myself, against whom a charge of complicity had not been raised, but there continued to be no further proof than that which we had had from the beginning, and it pointed to Zâ'khurân. To Zâ'khurân, therefore, the miniature army took its way, leaving me divided between regret for the disturbance which my own carelessness had brought about, and gratitude for the good-will displayed on every side. So difficult, however, had it become to protect the innocent, that but for the note-books I should have left the guilty in peace. My servants were plunged in grief; their honour was gone—indeed whose honour was left intact?—and in sackcloth and ashes we passed the day. And then . . . in the grey dawn we were wakened by a voice shouting from the hills: "Your goods are here! your goods are here!" Every man in the camp leapt up and ran in the direction of the sound, and there, lying upon a rock among the oak scrub, was all that we had lost. Nothing had been injured, nothing was missing, except some money, which was subsequently refunded to me by the Ottoman government, at the instance of the British Vice-Consul in Diyârbekr—and it may well be questioned whether any other government would have recognized a like liability. The villagers of Khâkh assembled round the tents and shed tears of thankfulness over the recovered objects, and I mounted in haste and rode off to Zâ'khurân to set a term to the pursuit of criminals. The cause of the restitution was there apparent. The village was deserted; men, women and children had fled into the hills taking with them all that they possessed, and it was reported by a picket that the Chelabî and the soldiers were engaged in capturing the flocks of the community. I sent a messenger after them and rode myself to Midyâd to ask for a universal amnesty. Revenge is not so sweet as it is said to be, nor is it so easy when wrong is afoot to determine who is the more wronged.

Two days and a half of journeying brought us to Diyârbekr. The way was without interest, except for that which was supplied by the dragoman of the British Consulate, who had

FIG. 206.—DIYÂRBEKR, MARDÎN GATE.

FIG. 207.—DIYÂRBEKR, YENI KAPU.

FIG. 208.—DIYÂRBEKR, CHEMIN DE RONDE, NORTH WALL.

FIG. 209.—DIYÂRBEKR, COURT OF ULU JÂMI'.

come to Midyâd to help me out of difficulties. A cheerful travelling companion he proved, and a well-informed. We camped on the second evening under the mound of Karkh, not far from the Tigris, and shortened our way next day by fording the river, which was now a shallow stream, and cutting across a wide bend (Fig. 205). This route had the advantage of giving us a first view of Diyârbekr under its finest aspect. It stands upon the high crest of the Tigris bank, a great fenced city built of basalt—"black are the dogs and black the walls and black the hearts of black Amid," says the proverb. Since the days when Ammianus Marcellinus took part in the desperate resistance to Sapor, and watched from the towers of Amida the Persian hosts "collected for the conflagration of the Roman world," the din of battle has never been far from Diyârbekr. The town passed to and fro between the Byzantine and the Sassanian. Constantius fortified it and lost it to Sapor; Anastasius recaptured it and lost it to Kobâd and won it back; Justinian rebuilt the fortifications, but it fell with Mesopotamia to the Moslem invaders. The Kurdish Marwânds made it their capital, and after them the Turkmân Ortuḳids; Tîmûr burst through the famous walls and put the inhabitants to the sword, and finally the Turk conquered it in A.D. 1515 and holds it still. But there is no peace for the lawless capital of Kurdistân. Warring faiths struggle together as fiercely as rival empires, and the conflict is embittered by race hatreds. The heavy air, lying stagnant between the high walls, is charged with memories of the massacres of 1895, and when I was in Diyârbekr the news from Cilicia had rekindled animosity and fear. Moslem and Christian were equally persuaded that the other was watching for an opportunity to spring at his throat. Tales of fresh outbreaks in different parts of the empire were constantly circulated in the bazaars, and the men who listened went home and fingered at their rifles. If there had been any sign of further disturbance at Constantinople, Diyârbekr would have run with blood.

With the population in this temper it would have been futile to inquire into the prospects of constitutional government. I spent a day among ancient churches;[1] and a day upon the walls, which are as fine an example of mediæval fortification as any that exists. They hang, upon the south and south-east sides, high over the Tigris—it was from this direction that Sapor's troops effected an entry through a hollow passage that led down to the water's edge. On the south-west they crown a slope set thick with gardens of mulberry and vine, and towards the north the wall bends round to join the curve of the river. Four great gateways break this circuit. The Mardîn Gate commands the terraced gardens, and the road that passes through it runs down to an ancient bridge over the Tigris (Fig. 206). To the north-west and north the Aleppo or Mountain Gate and the Kharpût Gate open on to a fertile plain, and the Yeni Kapu, the New Gate, stands above the precipitous southern bank (Fig. 207).[2] The lie of the ground makes it certain that the oldest fortifications of the city must have occupied much the same position as those which still surround it, and though the latter are proved by numerous inscriptions to be Mohammadan work of different periods, I should judge them to be built mainly upon ancient foundations. The north wall with its round towers is perfectly preserved; even the domed chambers inside the towers, together with the stairs that gave access to the *chemin de ronde*, are intact. All the arches and domes in the interior of the towers are of brick. Between the Kharpût and the Aleppo Gates a small aqueduct brings water to the town, the few springs within the walls being unpleasantly brackish. The citadel commands the north-east angle above the river; most of the space surrounded by its enclosing wall is occupied by modern buildings and by a mound whereon stood the castle of the first Mohammadan princes. The domed arsenal is said to have been a Christian

[1] I have published photographs and plans of the Jacobite church of the Virgin and the Greek Orthodox church of Mâr Cosmo in *Amida:* Van Berchem and Strzygowski.

[2] The Yeni Kapu differs in plan from the other three. It has square bastions, whereas they are protected on either side by massive round towers. The round towers extend all along the northern parts of the wall; on the other sides the towers are rectangular.

church, but remembering my unsuccessful attempts to visit the arsenal at Baghdâd, I did not ask permission to enter it.[1] From a postern gate in the north wall a road leads down to the river, passing under a cliff out of which gushes a sulphurous spring. As I watched the soldiers of the garrison washing their clothes in its waters, I tried to reconcile it with "the rich spring, drinkable, indeed, but often tainted with hot vapours," which Ammianus Marcellinus describes as rising under the citadel, and to see the men of the 5th Parthian Legion in the ragged groups standing about it.[2] From the citadel we walked to the Mardîn Gate along the *chemin de ronde*, a fine course, lifted high above the close air of the city and swept by the breezes that come down from Taurus (Fig. 208). Between the Aleppo Gate and the Mardîn Gate stand two huge round towers, larger than any others and later in date.[3] Near the Mardîn Gate the *chemin de ronde* is for some distance vaulted over and lighted only by small loop-hole windows on the inner side. To the south of the Mardîn Gate the wall runs out abruptly, and the salient angle thus formed holds a great hall of which the vault is borne on columns. The two main streets lie from gate to gate, intersecting each other at right angles, and since this is in accordance with an ancient scheme of city planning, the line of the streets may be as old as the first foundation of the town. Not far from the point of intersection stands the Ulu Jami' with its famous courtyard, enclosed to east and west by a two-storeyed portico, which has been conjectured to be either the remains of a church built by Heraclius or a Byzantine palace (Fig. 209). The buildings need a more exhaustive

[1] A sketch plan, made by De Beylié, is published in *Amida*.

[2] His phrase "under the citadel but in the very heart of Amida" is difficult to understand. It does not seem to imply a spring outside the walls, yet there is no place "under the citadel" and within the walls.

[3] One is known by inscriptions to have been erected by the Ortoḳid Sultan Malek Shah in the year A.D. 1208–1209, and the other must belong to the same period. The inscriptions have been published by Van Berchem, see Lehmann-Haupt: *Materialen zur älteren Geschichte Armeniens und Mesopotamiens*, p. 140. They are more fully published in *Amida*, but that work has not appeared in time for me to make any accurate reference to it.

study than the fanaticism of the Mohammadan population will at present admit, and the correct plan of mosque and court has yet to be made. The older part of the work is closely related to the ancient architecture of the Ṭûr 'Abdîn.

Even this hasty survey of Diyârbekr was sufficient to convince me that the treasures which it contains are still unexplored. Of its many mosques only the Ulu Jami' has been so much as photographed, though the square minarets scattered over the town are probably an indication of an early date. Once or twice as I walked in the bazaars I looked through gateways into the courts of splendid khâns, where the walls were decorated with contrasted patterns in limestone and basalt, and stripes of black and white masonry are used in many of the houses and mosques. The final history of Amida must wait upon a much more careful investigation of the town than any which has yet been undertaken.

CHAPTER IX

DIYÂRBEKR TO KONIA

June 4—July 1

THE frontier between the Arabic and the Turkish-speaking peoples is not sharply defined. Through the southern parts of the Kurdish hills it is common to find men acquainted with one or both languages in addition to their native Kurdish; among the Christians of the Ṭûr 'Abdîn a knowledge of Syriac is not rare; in Diyârbekr, where there is a considerable Arab population, Arabic, Turkish and Kurdish are spoken about equally, but north of Diyârbekr Arabic ceases to be heard, and as we journeyed along the road from Kharpût to Malaṭiyah, Kurdish died out also. Fattûḥ, in addition to many other qualifications for travel, speaks Turkish fluently, though in a manner peculiar to himself; the muleteers who were with me had some knowledge of the language, and I have enough to wish that I had more of that singularly beautiful and flexible tongue. Thus equipped we set out to make our way across Taurus and Anti-Taurus on to the Anatolian plateau.

As far as Malaṭiyah we followed the high road which led us at first across a fertile plain celebrated for its gardens ever since the days of Ammianus Marcellinus. Outside the village of Tarmûr [1] we spent the night somewhat uneasily by reason of certain wedding festivities which were there in

[1] Our itinerary was as follows: Diyârbekr, 7; Shilbeh, 8; Uch Keui, 9.5; Dereh Gechid Chai, a deep valley once noted for brigands, 10.45; Tolek, a village on the opposite side of this valley, 11. Here followed 35 minutes' halt during which the caravan caught us up and passed us, but we came up with it again before we reached Ḳara Khân Chai, a small river, at 1 o'clock. We got to Tarmûr at 2.45. I give these hours since Kiepert's map is frequently mistaken as to relative distances.

progress. Not only did the merry-makers keep up their rejoicings until close upon dawn, but the inhabitants of a neighbouring village judged the occasion to be propitious for mule-lifting, and were driven off with rifle shots. Peace was restored by daybreak, and the marriage procession conveying the bride to her husband's house set off to the strains of fife and drum. We passed it upon the road, a motley crowd, mounted and afoot. The bride was enveloped in a silken cloak of vivid magenta, which will not, I fear, be needed again for many a long day, if her opportunities for the wearing of finery may be measured by the aspect of her future home, for a more poverty-stricken collection of hovels than the bridegroom's village it would be difficult to picture. We left her in her brief glory to take up her daily task of preventing her husband's roof from falling about her ears, and rode on to the hill of Arghana, a bold spur of the Taurus mountains, with a village perched among its crags. I sent the baggage animals along the carriage road and climbed with a zaptieh to the village, and thence by a steep path to the Armenian monastery of the Virgin, which stands on the summit of the rocks.[1] We were rewarded by a magnificent view and by a pleasant talk with the prior who informed me, as I drank his excellent coffee, that the monastery was founded in the first century of the Christian era, a tradition which calls for weightier confirmation than any which he advanced. Be that as it may, the existing house must have been largely rebuilt in the Middle Ages, perhaps towards the fourteenth century—I hazard this date on the evidence supplied by the decoration of the church which had the character of Mohammadan work of about that period. We led our horses down the north side of the hill, by a stony

[1] The day's march was Tarmûr, 6; Kayden Keui, 6.30; Shawa Keui, 6.50 (both these villages lay about three-quarters of an hour to the right of the road); Tulkhum, a mile to the left of the road by a big mound, 7.10; we climbed a low ridge and dropped into a little plain in which we crossed a stream at 8.15; Kadi Keui to the right, 8.30; road up to Arghana, 9; monastery, 10.10–10.55; crossed the Ma'den Chai by Kalender Koprüsi at 1; Khân above Arghana Ma'den, 3; the caravan had arrived a few minutes before us.

FIG. 210.—ARGHANA MA'DEN.

FIG. 211.—GÖLJIK.

FIG. 212.—KHARPÛT, THE CASTLE.

FIG. 213.—IZ OGLU FERRY.

path that ran between bramble hedges enclosing fruit gardens, rejoined the carriage road and crossed the Ma'den Chai, which is the local name for the main arm of the Tigris, by a bridge near Kalender Khân. We had now fairly entered into the mountains, and our road took us over high bare ridges and down again to the Ma'den Chai at the village of Arghana Ma'den, the mines of Arghana. On a shelf of the opposite hill-side the smoke drifted perpetually from the smelting furnaces of the richest copper mines in Turkey (Fig. 210). The metal, smelted on the site, is cast into disks, two of which go to a camel load, and sent across the hills to Diyârbekr and Cæsarea, Sivâs and Tokat. The valley of the Ma'dan Chai, where the village lies, is so narrow that it offers no camping-ground; we lodged, therefore, in a charming khân above the village by the water's edge—but for the fact that it was innocent of furniture I could have fancied myself in an English country inn by the side of a rushing trout stream. The rain fell heavily in the night, and we rode for the greater part of the next day through an alternate drizzle and downpour, and were unable to determine which we enjoyed the most. The river cuts here through a deep rocky gorge, and the road climbs up by the side of the stream. The mists, clinging to the precipitous slopes, added to the sombre grandeur of a pass which opened at its upper end on to an exquisite little fertile plain, set like a jewel among the hills. Through its cornfields the infant Tigris, a rippling brook, wandered from willow clump to willow clump; we parted from it two hours from its source, and set our faces towards the hills which divide it from its mightier brother, the Euphrates. At their foot lies the Little Lake, Göljik, encircled by peaks, of which the northern slopes were white with snow patches (Fig. 211). It is slightly brackish, and its waters have no outlet. We turned aside from the carriage road and took a bridle path along the northern side of the lake, and up the hills beyond it. Before we reached the crest of the slopes we struck the road again and by it crossed the water parting, and saw below us the rich and smiling plain of Kharpût bounded by mountains, through which wound the silver streak of the

Euphrates. We camped that night at the foot of the pass in the Armenian village of Keghvank, our tents being advantageously placed in a grove of mulberry-trees, loaded with ripe fruit.[1] Kharpût, or rather the lower town, Mezreh,[2] which is the seat of government of the vilayet of Ma'mûret el 'Azîz, lies three hours from Keghvank. The plain between is exceedingly fertile; it is scattered over with villages about half of which are inhabited by Armenians, who suffered cruelly in the massacres of 1895. At Kezerik, half-an-hour to the south-east of Mezreh, two finely-cut inscriptions, commemorating the expedition of Domitius Corbulo in A.D. 65, are built into the walls of a ruined church. They are well known, but I, coming from far beyond the limits of the Roman empire, turned aside with pious enthusiasm and read the high-sounding titles of Nero, as one who glories in their achievements of his own people: Nero Claudius Cæsar Augustus Germanicus Imperator Pontifex Maximus, the words rang out with greater splendour from those remote stones than from any lying within the walls of Rome.

Kharpût is set upon the summit of the hills beyond Mezreh. The castle, standing upon the highest crag, guards a shallow ravine wherein is stretched the greater part of the town, but the houses climb up on to the rocky headlands overhanging the plain and, from below, the mountain seems to be crowned with a series of fortresses (Fig. 212). The streets are so narrow that a cart can hardly pass along the cobbled ways; very silent and peaceful they seemed, the shops heaped with cherries, the cool breezes stirring the vine tendrils that wreathed together overhead. The castle, for all its frowning walls and bastions, is nothing but a heap of ruins within. I looked in vain for the dungeons in which Sukmân, the son of the Turkman officer Ortuḳ, founder of the Ortuḳid dynasties,

[1] The day's march was as follows: Khân of Arghana Ma'den, 6.20; Khân of Pünoz, at upper end of gorge, 9.40 (the village of Pünoz lies up a rocky valley to the right); Ḳâsim Khân, at further side of plain, 10.55–11.30—there is no village here; Göljik, 11.55; Shabyan, a small village near the water parting, 1.40; Keghvank, 4.

[2] Mezreh is perhaps Ptolemy's Mazara (ed. Müller, p. 945), and it bears the same name in the Peutinger Tables.

imprisoned Baldwin of Edessa and Jocelyn of Courtney in the early years of the twelfth century. The Crusaders, gathering together their forces, seized the fortress in 1123 and held it until Balak, Ortuḳ's grandson, recaptured it and threw the garrison over the battlemented rock into the plain below.[1] On an inner wall, not far from the gate, there are traces of an Arabic inscription, together with two stones carved in relief, the one bearing a lion and the other a ram, memorials, I make no doubt, of the Ortuḳid rule. The walls are of many periods of building. The masonry of one of the eastern towers is laid in alternate stripes of red and white stone. The eastern side of the hill drops steeply into a deep valley filled with houses which are terraced one above the other. Here there is a Jacobite church of ancient origin, its plan repeating the old scheme of the parochial church of the Ṭûr 'Abdîn. The priest assured me that it dated from the first century, and in proof of his assertion showed me a couple of curious oil paintings, a Crucifixion and a Virgin and Child, Byzantine in type, so far as I could make out through the dust of ages.[2]

My tents were pitched on the plain near Mezreh. There in the evening I received the Vâlî, a cheerful Cretan, and the Mu'âvin Vâlî,[3] and after they had departed, several other visitors. Their conversation left me groping my way through the intricate labyrinths of the Oriental mind, and even more bewildered than usual. Kharpût and Mezreh and the villages of the plain had felt yet more sharply than Diyârbekr and the Ṭûr 'Abdîn the wave of panic that had emanated from Cilicia. Three days after the first outbreak at Adana, the Kurdish peasants had trooped into the Chris-

[1] The garrison consisted of 65 men and 80 beautiful ladies, a proportion of the sexes which may have contributed to Balak's victory.

[2] Kharpût has been identified with Carcathicerta, which was the royal city of Sophene, according to Strabo.

[3] Since the outbreak of 1895 a Christian governor has been appointed in all vilayets which contain a large proportion of Armenians. The Mu'âvin Vâlîs are nominally co-rulers with their Moslem colleagues, but report, I know not with how much justice, credits them with little influence and less initiative.

tian villages and announced their intention to kill, while in Mezreh the Vâlî was besieged by demands that he should give the signal for massacre. To his credit be it recorded that he held out against these appeals, though the abject terror of the Armenians did much to increase the danger of the situation. When the news of 'Abdu'l Ḥamîd's deposition reached the vilayet, the agitation went out like a candle in the wind; the Kurds returned peaceably to their houses, and the fears of the Christians were allayed. This was strange enough, but that which followed was stranger still. The district had suffered during the spring from lack of rain and the drought became at length so serious that the whole harvest was threatened. The leading mullah of Mezreh called upon the people to assemble in a neighbouring village, where there was a much-respected Mohammadan shrine, that they might raise a common supplication for rain. The population answered his call to a man; Christian and Moslem, who but five weeks before had with difficulty been restrained from leaping at each other's throats, stood side by side and listened to the sermon which the mullah delivered to them. All, said he, were brothers, all were children of one God, all alike were in danger of perishing from the drought, and it behoved all to pray together for the beneficent rain which would save them from famine. His eloquence reduced the assembled audience to tears, and for three days their united orisons rose to heaven. And then the miracle came to pass. The rain fell abundantly, that same rain over which we had rejoiced in the Tigris gorge, without knowing that we owed it to the prayers of the Moslems and Christians of Kharpût, nor yet how many fevers it was assuaging, more fatal than the sun-fever in our veins; for it was admitted that this most fortunate coincidence would do more to bring about amity than the fall of many sultans.

I sat long into the night and gazed upon the shattered crags of Kharpût and the hollow plain, clothed in abundance of fruits, and sheltered by its ring of noble hills. What is it that leads to massacre? whence does that sudden frenzy spring, whither vanish? Like a tornado it bursts over the peaceful earth, blots out the daily life of town and village, destroys, uproots and slays—and passes. My thoughts were still busy with these unanswerable problems when we rode upon our way next morning. One of my muleteers was a Moslem, a ḥajjî, a Mecca pilgrim. I had known him for many years and he had served me well during months of hard travel. When the road was long he had not wearied; when the sun was hot he had not complained; when the wind blew cold he drew more closely about him the duffle coat which I had given him in Aleppo, and every evening after the tents were pitched and the horses picketed, I had seen him building up the fire under the big rice-pot and stirring the savoury mess on which my camp was to sup. To-day as I looked into his simple honest face, I wondered what unexpected ferocity lay behind its familiar wrinkles.

"Ḥâjj 'Amr," I said, "in the day of slaughter, would you kill me?"

"My lady, no," he replied, "not you. I have eaten your bread."

"Would you kill Fattûḥ and Selîm and Jûsef?" I asked.

"No, no," said he, "not them. We are brothers."

"But other Christians you would slay?"

"Eh wallah!" he answered; "in the day of slaughter."

I ceased my questionings and rode on, but the subject was to come up again. It happened in this manner.

We had journeyed over the plain to Khân Keui and climbed on to a low spur of the hills. Having crossed it, we rode down a long valley with high hills on either hand.[1] It chanced that Fattûḥ and I and a zaptieh were on ahead, and as we went we fell into talk. Now Fattûḥ is a Catholic Armenian, and in the old days we have experienced many a difficulty over his teskereh, owing to the ominous word

[1] Mezreh, 6.5; Khân Keui, 9.25; Tell Maḥmûd, left of road, 9.45; Chaghullah, left of road, 9.55; Sapolar (left), 10.5; Harnik (right), 10.20; Melekjân (about a mile to the right), 10.35; Cholak Ushagî, where there is a khân, 11–11.45. Here we crossed a ridge into a valley which runs down to the Euphrates. Tutli Keui (left), 2.5; over another ridge and down to Kömür Khân at 3.35; Iz Oglu, 5.45.

Armenian which is inscribed upon it. At the end of the last journey he had vowed that he would change his faith, which does not sit very heavy upon him—Fattûḥ being a philosopher touching the finer distinctions of creed—and I now asked him whether he had carried out this determination.

"Effendim," he replied, "two years ago, when I returned to Aleppo, I told the bishop that I would become Brotestant or Latîn (Protestant or Roman Catholic). And he argued with me and said he would send a priest to pray with me. But I said No, for I and my family are Brotestant."

"And are you a Protestant?" said I.

"God knows," replied Fattûḥ. "On my teskereh I am still written down a Catholic Armenian, but that I cannot be, for I refused to let the priest come into my house to pray. Therefore I belong to no religion but the religion of God."

"We all belong to that religion," said I.

"True, wallah," said the zaptieh.

Presently there came up the road towards us a train of loaded camels.

"These are men of Ḳaisarîyeh," said Fattûḥ. "I know them by their dress." And as the first string of camels drew near, he shouted to the man sitting half-asleep upon the leading animal: "Are you from the port, the port of Beilân?"

"Evvet, evvet," he answered drowsily, and his body rocked with the long rocking of the camel's stride as they plodded past.

"Nasl Kirk Khân?" cried Fattûḥ. "How does Kirk Khân?"

Kirk Khân is a Christian village at the foot of the Beilân Pass, between Aleppo and Alexandretta.

The next cameleer had come up with his string and he answered the question.

"The giaour are all killed," he answered, taking Fattûḥ for a Moslem.

"And how are the houses, the houses of the giaour?" Fattûḥ called out. The leader of the next string answered—

"They are all burnt."

"Praise God," said Fattûḥ, and the zaptieh laughed.

When the camel-train had passed I said:

"Why did you call the people of Kirk Khân infidels?"

"Because the camel-driver called them so," Fattûḥ replied.

"And why did you praise God?"

"Effendim, they praised God when they saw Kirk Khân in ashes, and they rejoiced to tell the tale—what else should I say?" He rode on silently for a few minutes, and then he added: "All the men of Kirk Khân were my friends. Every time I drove my carriage from Aleppo to Alexandretta, I stopped to eat with them, and they, when they were in Aleppo, came to my house. Now they are dead—God have mercy on them."

His sorrowful acceptance of an outrage which the Western mind, accustomed to regard the protecting of human life as the first obligation of society, refused to contemplate, revealed to me the magnitude of the gulf which I had been attempting to bridge, and as I followed the channel of Fattûḥ's thought, I saw Fate, in the likeness of a camel-train, moving, slow and heavy-footed, towards the inevitable goal.

Our road climbed over a bluff and dropped again into a ravine at the lower end of which stands Kömür Khân, an old, red-roofed caravanserai, stately in decay. Near to it flows the Murad Su, which is the Euphrates, and though we were now far from its Mesopotamian reaches, it was already a great river whose waters had received the tribute of many snows. Below Kömür Khân it enters a narrow gorge where the hills fall sheer into the water, and above the khân, carved upon a slab of rock, a Vannic inscription bears witness to the high antiquity of the road.[1] The ferry is a couple of hours further up stream, but we reached it late in the afternoon and were too weary to cross that night. We pitched our tents on the bank—it was our last Euphrates camp—opposite the village and great mound of Iz Oglu.

The next day's ride took us over hill and dale to Malaṭiyah.[2]

[1] It is probably the ancient caravan road from Cæsarea and Ephesus to Babylon.

[2] Iz Oglu (on the west bank of the Murad Su), 8; Masnik, 10.15; a big chiflik of which I do not know the name, 12–12.30; we climbed a long hill, reaching the summit at 2.15, and got to Malaṭiyah at 2.45.

The road was planted with mulberry-trees that dropped their ripe fruit at our feet; the swelling slopes were deep in corn, and water-loving poplars stood in the meadows at the valley bottoms—I do not think that we broke the record of travel upon this stage: there were too many temptations urging us to loiter. Modern Malaṭiyah occupies the site of Azbuzu, a village which was once the summer quarters of the parent city. In 1838, during the war between Turkey and Egypt, Azbuzu became the head-quarters of the Turkish general, Ḥâfiẓ Pasha. Old Malaṭiyah, which is situated about two hours to the north-west, was at that time in great part destroyed for the enlarging of Azbuzu, and has since lain deserted and almost uninhabited. Moltke, who joined the Turkish army in 1838 and remained with it for a year, describes the wonderful luxuriance of the gardens of Azbuzu in his enchanting volume of letters, the most delightful book that has ever been written about Turkey, with the sole exception of *Eothen*. The gardens are no less exquisite now than they were in his time, and as we rode down the hill-side the houses were scarcely to be seen through their screen of fruit-trees. Even upon a nearer view the walnuts and mulberries are far more striking than the buildings of Malaṭiyah, which are constructed, as Moltke says, out of exactly the same material as that with which the swallows make their nests. We camped in the midst of poppy-fields by one of the many streams for which Malaṭiyah is famous, and I spent the afternoon exploring the town, but could find nothing of interest in it, except some Hittite reliefs which had been brought from Arslân Tepeh.[1] I had already determined to visit old Malaṭiyah, and the sight of these stones sent me round by the mound from which they had come. We rode for half-an-hour through gardens to Ordasu, itself buried in gardens, and thence to a ruined monastery, a quarter of an hour up the hill-side. A small chapel has been patched together in the north aisle of the original church. Slabs carved with Latin crosses, or

[1] They had been published, but not very satisfactorily. I gave my photographs to Mr. Hogarth, who published them in the *Annals of Archæology and Anthropology*, Vol. II. No. 4.

FIG. 214.—MALAṬIYAH ESKISHEHR.

FIG. 215.—VALLEY OF THE TOKHMA SU.

FIG. 216.—TOMB AT OZAN.

with the Greek cross encircled by a victor's wreath, lay about among the ruins or were built into the walls, and upon the piers of the old nave the capitals were roughly carved with acanthus. None of this work seemed to me to be earlier than the eighth or ninth centuries, but I saw in the grass-grown court finely-moulded column bases which were of earlier date. They may have been brought from the city of Melitene, which was the forerunner of old Malaṭiyah.[1] An hour's ride from the monastery stands the big mound of Arslân Tepeh surrounded by gardens and poppy-fields. Without the evidence of the reliefs it might have been conjectured to represent a Hittite city. The wide fertile valley in which it is placed, the backing of hills, the open plain stretched out beyond it, combine to make Arslân Tepeh one of the typical sites chosen by the old people, and excavation might prove it to be the mother-city of the townships, represented by mounds, which were scattered over the lower ground. From Arslân Tepeh we rode for fifty minutes to Old Malaṭiyah, which has moved rapidly towards complete decay since it was deserted seventy years ago (Fig. 214). The walls and bastions are dropping piecemeal into the poppy-fields that fill the moat; of the streets little or nothing remains: the ruined mosques and tall

[1] Melitene does not appear to have been in existence in Strabo's time, for he says that there were no towns in the fruitful plain, but only strongholds upon the mountains (Bk. XII. ii. 6). Procopius states that it was raised by Trajan to the dignity of a city, whereas before it had been nothing but a square fortification on low ground (Palestine Pilgrims' Text Society Edition, p. 82). Diocletian made it the capital of Armenia Secunda (Ramsay: *Historical Geography*, p. 313); it was the centre of the military roads guarding the frontiers of the Roman empire towards the Euphrates, and the standing camp of the XII Legion, Fulminata (*id.* p. 55). With this increase of importance it outgrew, according to Procopius, its former limits, so that the people built over the plain "their churches, the dwellings of their magistrates, the market-place and the shops of their merchants, the streets, porticoes, baths and theatres, and all the other ornaments of a large city." Melitene was thus composed mostly of suburbs until Justinian surrounded it with a wall. There must, however, have been cities in the plain, of which Strabo knew nothing, long before Trajan's time, as is proved by existing mounds, and Pliny seems to have preserved a dim memory of these when he speaks of Melitene as having been founded by Semiramis (Bk. VI. ch. iii.).

minarets rise out of a sea of silvery poppy flowers. The Ulu Jâmi' is still used for prayer, but its door was locked and the key was not to be procured. I climbed by its carved and half-ruined gateway on to the roof, and peering through the windows of the dome, saw that the interior was beautifully decorated with tiles and inscriptions. A rich store of fine Mohammadan work remains to be studied there.

It was a five hours' ride across the plain to Elemenjik, where our camp was pitched.[1] Elemenjik is a great breeding farm, the property of the late Sultan, who owned most of the pasture lands about Malaṭiyah. The population were in some distress at the prospect of a change of masters and the abolition of the privileges attached to a royal estate, and the government was confronted with a difficult problem with regard to the disposition of these domains. Few private persons could afford to pay the full price for the large breeding stables on the Sultan's farms, and the properties will lose much of their value when they lose the military guard that watched over the security of the royal mares. The solitude that will be a drawback when Elemenjik comes into the market, was a delightful advantage to our camping-ground, and the people of Kharpût must have been at their prayers again, for the rain fell in refreshing torrents and, clearing away, left the broad plain and the unexplored peaks of the Dersîm mountains shining in the sunset.

Next morning we passed by another of the Sultan's farms, nestled among poplar-trees in the midst of carefully hedged fields, and in three hours we came to Arga, where we called a halt while we changed zaptiehs. I was well pleased at the delay, for it gave me opportunity to examine some elementary excavations which had been carried out by the Turkish

[1] Malaṭiyah Eskishehr, 9.45; Khâtûnyeh (a quarter of a mile to the left), 10.20; a chiflik (name unknown), 11.45–12.15; Saman Keuï, a village near a big mound, 12.55. In a graveyard near here I noticed two fragments of round columns. At 1.25 we crossed a deep valley and saw the village of Shehna Khân about half-a-mile to the right; Elemenjik, 3.10. Not all these villages are marked in Kiepert and some are wrongly placed. There is cultivation round each village, but the plain between is usually untilled.

government. They had uncovered the foundations of a church with a tesselated marble pavement, fragments of round columns and moulded bases of excellent workmanship; that it was indeed a church I took on trust from the zaptieh, who acted as showman, for the aims of the excavators had not included the revelation of a plan; but the slabs carved with crosses bore out the official view.[1] When he had exhibited all that was to be seen, he handed me over to one of his colleagues, who was to accompany us to Derendeh, with the parting injunction that he was to guide me to every ruin in the hills. "This khânum," he observed, "likes ruins."

"Effendim, olour," replied his interlocutor, "it shall be."

But it was not. Perhaps there are no ruins where we crossed the Akcheh Dâgh, or perhaps in the excitement of the road the zaptieh forgot them as completely as I did. Our path would have done credit to the most sensational of journeys. It led us over wild and rocky hills and down into gorges incredibly deep and narrow, and when we stopped to draw breath at the bottom of one of these breakneck descents,

[1] Arga has been identified with Arca, where there was a Roman station (Arca was also the seat of a bishopric: Ramsay, *Hist. Geog.*, p. 314), and with Ptolemy's Arcala (ed. Müller, p. 888). The great road mentioned by Strabo which led from Babylon to Ephesus, crossing the Euphrates at Tomisa-Iz Oglu, passed through Arca (according to Sir W. Ramsay's suggestion, *op. cit.*, p. 273) and ran through Dandaxina and Osdara to Arabissus and thence through the mountains to Cæsarea. Kiepert places Dandaxina immediately to the south of the Tokhma Su and Osdara in the same latitude; Ramsay puts both places further south, and Sterritt's evidence supports Ramsay's conclusions. Between Arga and Ekrek my route did not touch the Roman road as laid down by Ramsay, but ran further to the north, and where I crossed the mountains, between Osmandedeli and 'Azîzîyeh, I saw no trace of an ancient road, nor can I think that wheeled traffic can ever have followed that line. Ainsworth travelled down the Tokhma Su from Görün to Derendeh, but he came over the Akcheh Dâgh between Derendeh and Arga, whereas I crossed it further east from Arga to Ozan. Ainsworth observes that there were never more than two roads from Derendeh to Malaṭiyah, one following the line he took, and one the valley of the Tokhma Su down to the plain (*Travels and Researches*, Vol. I. p. 247). I do not feel inclined to dispute that opinion, for though I found a third way from Malaṭiyah to Derendeh, it cannot be called a road. The mouldings and capitals which I saw at Arga pointed to a date not later than the sixth century.

we saw the track in front of us climbing mercilessly up the opposite precipice. We came to the bottom of the first valley at 11.45, about an hour from Arga; Deveh Deresi is its name. At the top of the next ridge the splendid gorge of the Levandi Chai opened at our feet. With many warning cries to the baggage animals and much tugging at the taut bridles of our own mounts (for these passages had to be performed on foot) we reached the stream at 1.20 near to the Kurdish village of Levandiler. A steep climb brought us in another hour to the high village of Chaṭagh; a quarter of an hour beyond it we topped the pass and rode down by easy gradients to Levent. Here, surrounded by magnificent rocky hills, we pitched camp. Our hosts were men of the Kizil Bâsh, a sect whose head-quarters are in the Dersîm. Their creed, which is much contemned by the Moslems—and not in words alone—is said to waver between Paganism, Christianity, Manichæanism and Shî'ism, touched with some memories of ancient Anatolian cults. I did not attempt to unravel these mysteries during the evening I spent at Levent, but contented myself with inviting the headmen of the village to a coffee-party, on which simple human basis relations of the most cordial nature were established. The night was sharply cold, and we set out next morning, with numb fingers, to scramble down into the valley below Levent and up to the opposite ridge, which we reached in one hour. Above us towered the rocky plateau of the Ḳal'ah Dâgh, flanked on every side by cliffs, and below lay the wide and fertile valley of the Tokhma Su (Fig. 215). The caravan pursued its way westward, but I turned east, by Kurd Keui and Saman, and touched the river at Ozan, four hours from Levent, where my zaptieh had promised me a ruin. "Ishté bu," said the headman of the village, pointing across the poppy-fields, "here it is;" and he turned away to gather us a dish of ripe mulberries, while I stood in amazement before the Ionic columns and carved garlands of a little tomb that might have graced the Appian Way (Figs. 216 and 217). There are no inscriptions upon it, nor anything to tell whose bones were laid within the vaulted chamber; I sent a greeting across the ages to the shade of him who had brought

FIG. 218.—THE GORGE AT DERENDEH.

FIG. 219.—TOMB NEAR YAZI KEUI.

FIG. 220.—TOMARZA, CHURCH OF THE PANAGIA FROM SOUTH-EAST.

FIG. 221.—TOMARZA, CHURCH OF THE PANAGIA, SETTING OF DOME.

into this remote and inaccessible valley the arts of the West, and journeyed on.

In four hours' ride, by an easy path up the right bank of the Tokhma Su, we reached our camp, pitched near the village of Kötü Ḳal'ah, which takes its name from a small ruined fort on the rock above it,[1] and another four hours brought us next morning to Derendeh.[2] The town is scattered among gardens for close upon an hour's ride along the valley. Towards the upper end a ruined castle stands upon a bold promontory of rock overhanging the stream.[3] A staircase, hewn in the precipice, gave the defenders access to the water; on the further side the hill slopes down more gently, and the ruins of a former Derendeh lie about its foot. We marched three hours further and camped at Yazi Keui, upon the grassy margin of the stream. The bare valley, with its ribbon of cultivation along the water's edge, gave us delightful travelling, but of archæological interest there was nothing to be found, and when a native of Yazi Keui brought us informa-

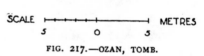

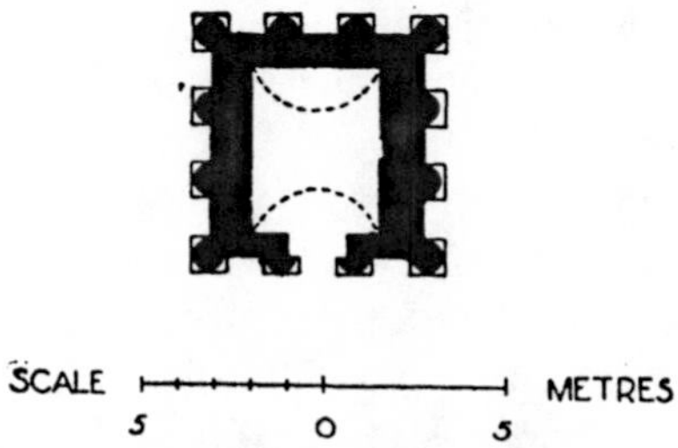

FIG. 217.—OZAN, TOMB.

[1] Ozan, 10.30; Mullah 'Alî Shehr, 11.5–40; Polat Ushagha, 12.35; Tozeli, some distance to the left, 12.55; a ruined khân marked by Kiepert, 1.20. Here we saw up a valley to the north the village of Palanga, marked by Kiepert. Above the khân the river flows through a gorge, and on the rocks above it are the ruins of a small fort, which we reached at 2.20; Kötü Ḳal'ah village, 2.45.

[2] We passed upon the way only one village, Mügdeh, where we crossed the Tokhma Su. Kiepert has suggested that Derendeh may represent the site of ancient Dalanda; for objections to this view, see Ramsay, *op. cit.*, p. 309.

[3] The existing ruins are probably mediæval. Ainsworth (*Travels and Researches*, Vol. I. p. 246) reports an illegible inscription, presumably Arabic or Turkish, over the gate. I do not remember to have seen it. The fortress of Ṭarandah is mentioned as early as the year A.D. 702, when it was in the hands of a Moslem garrison. In the ninth century it was held by the Paulicians, a sect of Eastern Christians whose beliefs were mingled with Manichæanism. (Le Strange: *Lands of the Eastern Caliphate*, p. 120.)

tion of ruins at some distance from our path, I engaged him joyfully to conduct us thither on the following morning. He led us into the hills to the north of the river by a fairly good road (it is the direct caravan road from Sivâs to Albistân, and much frequented) and on to a wide pasturage, an hour and a half from Yazi Keui. The snows of Nurshak Dagh, south-east of Albistân, were visible from the huts of this alpine yaila. At its northern end we found a considerable quantity of shapeless ruins, mere heaps of unsquared stones, and among them three small tombs, half-buried in the earth (Fig. 219). They varied from 2 to 2·50 m. in length, by 1·20 to 2·20 m. in width, and were built of carefully dressed stones. Each had a door in one of the short sides, and each had been covered by a stone vault. In another hour and a half we came down to the Tokhma valley opposite the village of Tikmin; we passed through Telin and reached the khân of Görün in two hours more. There we halted to pick up fresh zaptiehs, and were greeted by the news that the zaptiehs were not ready and that the caravan had gone on unescorted. I had no mind to be parted from my tents upon an unknown road, and, abandoning my intention of visiting a Hittite inscription in the gorge above Görün, I posted after the muleteers with Jûsef at my heels. The path leaves the valley here and crosses some high ground, upon which, after an hour's hard riding, we caught up the caravan and were ourselves caught up, while we paused to lunch, by the zaptiehs. After we had passed a large chiflik belonging to the Sultan, we descended once more into the valley of the Tokhma Su at Osmândedelî.[1] We pitched camp above the village in a flowery meadow, through which hurried the Tokhma Su, a tiny flashing brook. On a rocky point above us were the ruins of a fort with a Greek cross in a wreath cut upon the fallen lintel of its door.

We had now before us the roughest stage of our journey, for we had reached the hills that part the waters tributary to the Euphrates, from those that are tributary to the Saiḥûn—

[1] Görün, 12; summit of hill, 1.15 (but we had ridden considerably faster than our usual pace); Kevak Euren, to the left, 3.10; chiflik, 4.30; Osmândedelî, 5.

the Persian Gulf from the Mediterranean. I cannot recommend the way we took across them, except for the beauty of the high and desolate pass.[1] As soon as we had climbed out of the valley of Osmândedelî we found ourselves on a wide upland, swept by cold airs and ringed about with mountains. The wheat was scarcely up, the grass sodden with newly melted snow, the peaks all white. In the midst of these fields lay Küpek Euren, a small hamlet near a mound which was covered with the building stones of an earlier time, while upon the slopes that closed the western end of the plateau was the village of Bey Punar. Having passed the latter, we climbed into the hills by a shallow gorge down which flowed the head-waters of the Tokhma Su. Our way was decked with flowers. Daphne and androsace, veronica and dianthus grew among the rocks, and purple primulas edged the channel of the stream. The gullies were still full of snow. So we came to the water parting, 2,040 to 2,070 metres above sea-level, according to Kiepert, and bidding farewell to the last source of the Mesopotamian rivers, rode down into the basin of the Mediterranean. The long gently-sloping meadows were rich in grass, but no flocks grazed there, and no summer villages were to be seen among the juniper-bushes. The lonely beauty of these alpine pastures, where nature spreads out her fairest bounty, *e beata si gode*, fell upon us like a benison, and once again I offered up praise to all mountains. The water-runnels gathered together into a small clear stream which rippled away from its birthplace in the green hollows and plunged, we following it, into a pine-clad valley. The path grew steeper and more rocky as we descended, the valley narrower, until there was no place left free from pine and berberis and juniper but the boulder-strewn bed of the river. At length we were able to pull our horses up an exceedingly steep track through the pine-woods, by which we emerged on to a grassy hill-side. Here by good fortune we found a party of Cir-

[1] Osmândedelî, 6.25; Kaindîjeh, 7.10; there is a better road from here, but it makes a long circuit by Günesh and Parenk, and I declined to take it. Küpek Euren, 8.20; Bey Punar, 9.45; water parting, 11.10; Boran Dereh Keui, 5.10.

cassians, who were hauling their bullock wagons, heavily loaded with timber, over ways which we reckoned to be hard going even for our baggage animals. They directed us to Boran Dereh Keui. Before we had gone far we rounded a spur and the snowy peaks of Mount Argæus swam into our ken, set in the midst of the Anatolian plateau.

Boran Dereh Keui is a Muhâjir village, that is to say, it is peopled by Circassian immigrants from the Caucasus. They have filled the valley of the Zamantî Su, and though they are not liked by the indigenous population, their coming has raised very sensibly the level of civilization. Forty years ago the Zamantî valley was innocent of any settled habitation; the nomad Avshars drove their flocks up to it in the summer, sowed scanty crops, and left before the first winter snows. Now it is all under the plough, and the Circassian villages, with their osier beds and neat vegetable gardens, are scattered thickly along it. Nomad life dies out in a cultivated country, and the Avshars are settling into villages, though their houses are not so well built, nor their gardens so well kept as those of the Circassians. The chief town of the district is 'Azîzîyeh. There we changed zaptiehs, and I sat in the konak while the necessary arrangements were being made and drank coffee with the officials. Presently there appeared one who was half a negro and told me his tale in the strong, guttural Arabic of the desert. He was a native of the Ḥejâz; he had wandered up into this country before there were any villages in it and had remained as a merchant.

"It is very beautiful here," said I.

"Yes," said he, "but the desert is different. I have not seen it for forty years." And I understood what was in his heart.

Behind the konak a plentiful spring bursts out from under the cliffs. I walked up to it and saw men digging up old walls in quest of cut stones. Fragments of columns and rude mouldings pointed to the former presence of a church, and perhaps an earlier shrine hallowed, in true Anatolian fashion, the abundant source.[1] From 'Azîzîyeh we turned our faces to

[1] 'Azîzîyeh is the ancient Ariarathia and its foundation dates from the second or third century B.C.: Ramsay, *op. cit.*, p. 310.

Mount Argæus and travelled along a well-laid road to Ekrek.[1] Among the hills at some distance to the right of the road stands the castle of Maḥmûd Ghâzî, magnificently placed upon a peak. My zaptieh told me that in spite of its name it was a Christian fortress, for he had seen crosses carved upon the lintels, and only the distaste for further excursions that follows upon long stages of mountain travel, prevented me from going up to it. I have a shrewd suspicion that it must be the Tsamandos of the Byzantine historians.[2] Ekrek, where we pitched camp, is built in the bottom of one of the deep valleys which are typical of the district about Argæus. The lava with which the plain is covered forms a sharp cliff on either lip of these gorges, and in places the formation of the volcanic beds is so distinct that the lava can be seen lying like a solid pavement upon the soil, broken off at the edges of the valley and scattered down the slopes in huge slabs. Before I got into camp I turned off to see a small ruined church of no very great interest, and within the town there are several larger churches, all remodelled by the Armenian inhabitants.[3] The early Christian architecture of the eastern side of Cappadocia was unknown to me except from books, and finding myself in St. Basil's own country, I seized the opportunity of visiting some of the buildings which sprang up with the monastic impulse which he implanted. Instead of making straight for Cæsarea I rode next day under the slopes of the Köleteh Dâgh to the ruins of the Panagia above the village of Köpekli,[4] and so to Tomarza, where there is one of the finest

[1] 'Azîzîyeh, 10; Emergal, an Avshar village on the left, 12; Takhtalî, on the right across the river, 12.20; Ḳizil Khân, 1.35. (See Ramsay, *op. cit.*, p. 298. It is perhaps Strabo's Erpa "on the road to Melitene.") Bazaar Euren, 2.25. Between Ḳizil Khân and Bazaar Euren there is a small khân with ruins near to it, among them a carved door. jamb. Ekrek, 5.

[2] Ramsay, *op. cit.*, p. 289, places Tsamandos at 'Azîzîyeh, but he had not seen Maḥmûd Ghâzî when he wrote.

[3] The Armenians of this district are Muhâjir, immigrants, no less than the Circassians, though their coming dates from an earlier time. They were forced out of northern Armenia in the tenth century by the Seljuks, who drove them southward into what was then still the Byzantine empire.

[4] Kavak was the name I heard given to the site of the church; Rott

of the Cappadocian ruins (Fig. 220). Both these buildings exhibit the Anatolian type of the domed cruciform, which was already familiar to me, but the decorative details, the engaged pilasters upon the outer walls, the elaborate mouldings, the string-courses carved over doors and windows, are not to be found in the churches that lie further to the west. I sat that night in the Armenian monastery where I was lodged, and pondered over the artistic tradition which these things revealed, and the mingling of occidental with oriental themes which they implied. Not far to the south-east of Tomarza stands among the hills the famous shrine of Comana, sacred to the goddess Ma. With its ancient Asiatic cult and its temples constructed or reconstructed in the Imperial period, Comana was one of the great meeting-places of the culture of East and West; its buildings must have exercised a strong influence over the architecture of eastern Cappadocia, and I determined to seek among its ruins evidences of the age that had preceded the early Christian.

The Armenian priest, whose guest I was, was eager to relate to me the anxieties through which he and his congregation had passed during the last two months. Tomarza lay just beyond the zone of the recent outbreak, but at Shahr, the village which occupies the site of Comana, there had been a "masaleh" (an incident), though he did not enter into particulars as to its character. It was evident that he regarded my interest in antiquities as a mere cloak wherewith to cover a political purpose, and since I was not at the pains to undeceive him—if indeed it had been possible to make my aims clear to him—the announcement of my intention to visit Comana gave him yet stronger grounds for his conviction. By all Tomarza I was regarded as an itinerant missionary collecting evidence with regard to the massacre. The proximity of missionary schools was attested in varying degrees by the acquirements of the population. As I walked through

---

has published it under the name of the Panagia of Busluk Ferek (*Keinasiatische Denkmäler*, p. 188). He has also published Tomarza, p. 183.

FIG. 222.—TOMARZA, WEST DOOR OF NAVE, CHURCH OF THE PANAGIA.

FIG. 223.—SHAHR, DOORWAY OF SMALL TEMPLE.

FIG. 224.—FATTÛḤ.

FIG. 225.—ON THE ROAD TO SHAHR.

the streets I was met by a young man who accosted me in French.

"Vous parlez français?" said he.

"Mais oui," said I.

"Vous parlez bien?" he continued.

"Très bien," I answered unblushingly, and he was obliged to take my word for it, for when I inquired whether he were a native of Tomarza, he could not understand until I repeated the question in Turkish.

My next interlocutor was a boy who spoke English, which he had learnt, and learnt well, in an American college where he had taken his degree. He asked if he might know my name, and when I had obliged him in this particular, he begged that he might be told my object in coming to Tomarza. But I, being at the moment too busy with the ruins of the church to answer so many questions, replied that I had no object, and reduced him to a discomfited silence. The springs of action are different in American colleges.

We left Tomarza at ten o'clock and journeyed into the hills by way of Suvagen, which we reached at 12.40. Almost immediately after we had left the village, we entered a gorge, and our path climbed up through the pine-woods to Kokur Ḳayâ, a small yaila near the top of the pass known as Ḳara Bel. Here we pitched camp at five in the afternoon, close under the snow-wreaths that clung to the northern side of a rocky chain of peaks. Until sunset the clear fresh notes of a cuckoo filled the alp, and all that he had to say was worth hearing; but I wondered whether he enjoyed the society of his brother the kite, whose thin rippling cry dropped down from the rocks above him. I did not take my camp over the pass to Comana, but set out next day with Fattûḥ and a zaptieh and such simple provisions as might enable us to spend a night away from our tents if we found it necessary. Before we started I covenanted with the zaptieh, who was unusually pious, that prayers should be suspended for the day, the previous day's journey having been seriously upset by the occurrence of the 'aṣr (the hour of afternoon prayer), though every one knows that there is a special dispensation with regard to travellers.

The long grassy pass opens on to a confused prospect of desolate mountains and hardly less deserted valleys; the gnarled and twisted pine-woods clinging to the rocks, the flowering hawthorn and regiments of yellow mullein that lined the lower course of the stream, gave to our road a memorable beauty, and if the going was not so good as might have been desired, why, we had seen worse. In the midst of these wild solitudes, five hours from Kokur Ḳayâ, we came upon a ruined shrine. It was a temple-mausoleum, and in this respect the true forerunner of the memorial churches of the Anatolian plateau (Fig. 226); nor did the connection between the Christian and the Pagan work cease here. The shallow engaged pilasters, broken by a moulding into two storeys, which are found in the churches, were present in the temple; if the string-courses did not yet form a continuous band over the window arches, it was easy to see how obvious the transition to the later type would be, and the character of the profiles was the same here as in the churches (Fig. 227). The lower part of the temple contained a vault filled with loculi; the eastern end of the upper floor was ruined and overgrown with thick brushwood, but I have no doubt that it could be disengaged and planned without difficulty. Some clearing away of earth and shrubs would be required before it would be possible to make out the nature of a building, indicated by masses of dressed stones and broken columns, which was placed immediately to the south of the temple, but the ruins standing above ground were an exceedingly instructive link in the chain of Cappadocian architecture, and I rode down to Shahr full of hope. The village lies in the heart of a valley cut out by the Gök Su, a tributary of the Saiḥûn. Its sheltered fields were covered with corn, its

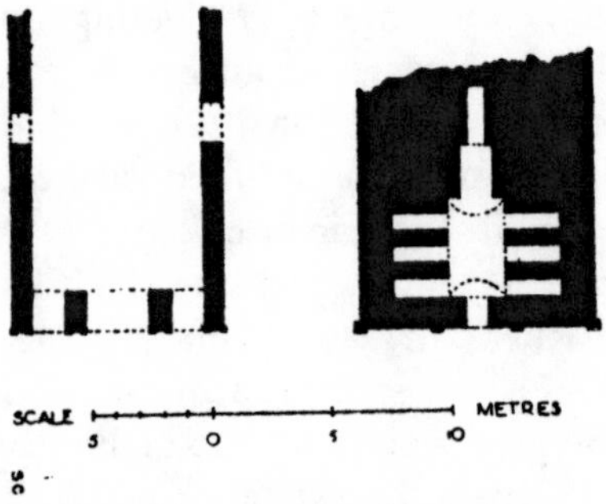

FIG. 226.—SHAHR, TEMPLE-MAUSOLEUM, UPPER AND LOWER STOREYS.

FIG. 227.—SHAHR, TEMPLE-MAUSOLEUM.

FIG. 228.—SHAHR, THE CHURCH ON THE BLUFF.

FIG. 229.—AVSHAR ENCAMPMENT.

FIG. 230.—ḲAIṢARÎYEH, THE CITADEL.

gardens planted with fruit-trees, but the streets and houses were no less ruined than the temples of the Great Goddess. The hot breath of massacre had passed down the smiling vale and left Shahr a heap of ashes. I found the inhabitants huddled together on a bluff where half-a-dozen of their dwellings had escaped destruction. A young school-master from the American college of Tarsus told me the story in my own tongue. He was himself a native of Shahr, and chance had brought him back to his home shortly before the outbreak at Adana and Tarsus. Of this disaster, which began upon April 14, the people of Shahr had received no information until, on April 20, the Kurds, Turks and Circassians from the neighbouring Moslem villages appeared in arms and announced that they did not intend to leave a single Christian alive. The villagers of Shahr had eighty rifles among them. Thus armed they defended the bluff, on which stand the ruins of the chief shrine of Ma, for nine days, at the end of which time tardy help arrived from 'Azîzîyeh. They had not lost a life, but they had been powerless to prevent the destruction of the village in the valley. Every house was looted and burnt; of the bazaars nothing remained but blackened foundations; the charred beams of the bridge had fallen into the stream, and the only wall that yet stood in the low ground was a splendid fragment of ancient masonry facing the river.

"Why," said I, gazing upon the ruin heaps that had once been the school-master's house, "did they spare the fruit-trees and the corn?"

"They thought that we should be dead before the corn was ripe," he answered, "and they meant to reap it for themselves. Also the fruit-trees they looked on as their own. Besides these we have nothing left, and we are so much troubled by hunger."

They were as much troubled by the thought that they could not offer me a fitting hospitality. The oda (the village guest-chamber) was in ashes, and the few houses on the bluff were crowded with women and children. But there was nothing to detain me. The ancient buildings had suffered with the modern; the inscribed stones and acanthus capitals, relics of a golden past, which had decked the streets of the bazaar, lay blackened and half buried among the ruins, and after I had made a brief survey of the site, I handed over to the schoolmaster the little money that was in my purse, and turned back across the hills.[1] The dusk gathered about us as we climbed up to the pass, but the road that we had followed so gaily in the morning was full of darker shadows than those of night. "Nature, red in tooth and claw with ravine," cried out from riven crag and blasted pine; mountain and valley joined in her

[1] In the low ground there are remains of a theatre, a fine bit of stone wall decorated with good mouldings, and part of a vaulted brick building, possibly a gymnasium. All these are upon the left bank of the stream. The temple upon the bluff was converted at an early date into a church, which has long since fallen into decay, though it has been patched up in recent times by the Armenians (Fig. 228). Along the edge of the bluff there are remains of a columned portico. In the ruined bazaar I saw a couple of beautiful funnel capitals, cracked and broken by fire. They should probably be dated in the early sixth century. At the entrance of the valley that leads up to the Kara Bel are the ruins of a small temple with a finely carved doorway (Fig. 223).

Mr. Hogarth sends me the following note:—

Miss Bell has submitted to me five inscriptions found on a temple site at Comana Capp. They are, she thinks, unpublished, and certainly were not seen by me on either of my visits to Comana in 1890 or 1891. Miss Bell sent me good photographs of nos. 1 and 2; but for the others, I have only her hand-copies to go upon.

No. 1 is a commonplace epitaph, intended to be hexametrical; but the necessary proper names would not accommodate themselves to the metre, and the versifier has had to leave ll. 1 and 3 partly prose. In l. 2 he or the lapicide has made the mistake of leaving the ε before ἠδ' unelided. The most interesting point in the inscription, the second name of the dedicator, is, unfortunately, obscured by a breakage of the surface. The lettering is very clear on the photograph except on the right edge.

No. 2 is broken top and right, and the names of the son and mother cannot be restored.

No. 3, the epitaph of a slave set up by his master, offers an instance of the distinction of slaves by the name of the master with a Roman gentile prefix. Either Αὐρ. or Αἰλι. is concealed in Miss Bell's copy of l. 2. Another slave seems to have appropriated the grave afterwards for his wife, and added a note to that effect.

No. 4 is without points of interest. No. 5 adds to other Oriental names found at Comana *Pharnaces* and the name of his father, which, in Miss Bell's copy, reads *Giris*.

1. Altar-stela with wreaths in relief on the front and sides. The inscription is in careful lettering of about the 4th cent. A.D. Words are in some cases divided by points. Square and round forms are

chorus, strophe to antistrophe. Mercilessly she creates and destroys; the fury of the storm, the sharp blade of the frost, the senseless passions of mankind, are alike of her ordering.

---

used indifferently, and ligature is frequent. Worn badly on right edge :—

.ΝΗΜΑΤΟΔΕ·ΤΕΥ////
.Υ·ΤΥΧΗϹ·ΤΑΥΡ////.
ΜΩϹ·ΑΥΤΩΤΕΗΔΑΛ////.
ΠΡΩΤΗΝΚΑΤΕΘΗΚ////
ΝΑΙΚΑ·ΕΥΦΗΜΙΑΙ//Α///
ΘΗΝΚΑΤΑΘΥΜΙΟΝΗ·///
ΑΓΑΠΗΤΗΝ·ΟΦΡΑΘΑΝΟΝ
ΤΙΓΕΝΗΚΟΙΝΟϹΤΑΦΟϹ
ΑΝΦΟΤΕΡΟΙϹΙΚΑΙϹΤΗ
ΛΗΚΟΙΝΗΤΑΔΕϹΗΜΑΙ
ΝΟΥϹΑΦΙΛΟΙϹΙ·

M]νῆμα τόδε τεῦ[ξεν E]ὐτύχης Ταυρα . . . μως
Aὐτῷ τ⟨ε⟩ ἠδ' ἀλ[όχῳ]: πρώτην κατέθηκα [γυ]ναῖκα
Eὐφημία[ν] ἀ[γα]θὴν καταθύμιον ἠ[δ'] ἀγαπητὴν,
Ὄφρα θανόντι γενῇ κοινὸς τάφος ἀνφοτέροισι
Kαὶ στήλη κοινὴ τάδε σημαίνουσα φίλοισι.

2. Altar-stela with wreath in relief below the inscription. Broken top and right top. Finely-cut lettering of 3rd cent. A.D. :—

ΝΛΑΙ	. . . . . .
ϹΕΙϹΗ	. . . [τὸ μνῆ-
ΜΑΤΗ/	μα τῇ [ἀσυν-
ΚΡΙΤΩΜΗΤΡΙ	κρίτῳ μητρί.

Ἀσύνκριτος: for the use of this epithet at Comana see *J. H. S.* xviii. p. 318, no. 29, and also no. 4 below.

3. Altar-stela :—

ΗΛΙΟΔΩΡΟϹ	Ἡλιόδωρος
ΗΛΕΙΗΛΟΔΩ	? Aὐρ. } Ἡλ[ι]οδώ- / ? Aἰλι. }
ΡΩΘΡΕΠΤΩ	ρῳ θρεπτῷ
ΜΝΗΜΗϹΧΑΡΙΝ	μνήμης χάριν.
ΑVΡΗΛ.ΟΔ	Aὐρ. Ἡλ[ι]όδ[ω-
ΡΘΟ////ΑΚΑ////	ρος . . . .
ΑΙΕ	. . . . . .
ΓΥΝΕΚ	γυνεκ[ι

The ruins of Shahr were the sole evidence which I saw with my own eyes of the far-reaching havoc wrought by the outbreak at Adana, but before I reached Konia I had opportunity to judge of its lasting effect. In Cæsarea trade was paralyzed by the economic annihilation of the rich province of Cilicia, as well as by the fear of further disturbances. The massacres had struck terror into the heart of Moslem and of Christian; they extinguished for a time the new-born hopes of peace, and roused once more the hatred between creed and creed which the authors of the constitution had undertaken to allay. Every section of the community suffered from a destruction of confidence which is even more disastrous than the destruction of wealth, though the Armenians suffered incomparably the most. But the fact that they bore a penalty out of proportion to their fault does not acquit them of blame. They had helped to bring upon themselves the calamity that overwhelmed them; by wild oratory they had laid themselves open to the accusations of conspiracy which were brought against them; they had kindled the flames of discord by preaching in their churches the obligation of revenge. The criminal folly of their utterances stirred up vague alarms in the breasts of an ignorant and fanatical population, and from whatever side came the incitement to outrage, it came to ears sharpened by anxiety. But it must be remembered that in several instances catastrophe was averted by the prompt action of the officials who controlled the threatened districts. In Cæsarea the Mutesarrif, rather than allow a repetition of the Adana tragedy, ordered his soldiers to fire upon the Moslem crowd, who

---

The lines 6-8 may conceal the name Βαιβία borne by the wife of Aur. Heliodorus in an epitaph of Comana published by Waddington from copies by Clayton and Ramsay, *Bull. Corr. Hell.*, vii. p. 137, no. 19.

4. On the rock inside tomb:—

ΣΤΛΙΛΝΟΣ	Στ[υ]λι(α)νός.

5. On a small stone with rude pediment:—

ΦΑΡΝΑΚΗΣΓΕΙ	Φαρνάκης Γ(ε)ι-
ΡΕΟΥΣΤΑΥΡΙΣ	ρέους ? Ταυρίσ-
ΚΩΙΤΩΙΥΩΙ	κῳ τῷ υ(ἱ)ῷ.

clamoured about the serai for arms on the plea that their lives were in danger from the Christians, and his uncompromising attitude brought the town to order; the Ḳâimmaḳâm of Eregli patrolled the streets night after night during a week of panic; the Mutesarrif of Kozan drove back the armed bands of Circassians who had marched down from the mountains bent on slaughter. Wherever it became evident that the government was not on the side of disorder, disorder was nipped in the bud, and I heard of one example where a handful of Turkish soldiers held in check many hundreds of Kurds, and the Christian village which they had assembled to destroy escaped untouched. I believe that no great massacre has taken place in Turkey without the encouragement of the central authority, or a passivity which amounts to connivance on the part of the local officials; a strong Vâlî backed by an enlightened government would keep peace in the most fanatical province of the empire.

On our way back to Tomarza we passed a large encampment of Avshars. The tents of these Turkish nomads are of a pattern which is common to nearly all the tribes of central Asia, but entirely different from that of the Arabs (Fig. 229). They are round, with a domed roof of felt supported on bent withes, and the sides are of plaited rushes over which a woollen curtain is hung when the nights are cold.[1] We did not sleep a second night at Tomarza, but marched a couple of hours further upon the road to Cæsarea, and camped at the village of Mardîn, which lies in a cleft of the lava beds under the twin peaks of Mount Argæus. Next day we skirted the flanks of the great volcano, passing by the ruined Sarî Khân and under the small peak of 'Alî Dâgh, which is (so I was credibly informed by my zaptieh) nothing but a stray boulder dropped by 'Alî ibn abi Tâlib when he was engaged in helping the Prophet to pile up the huge mass of Argæus.[2] Not only the geographical features of the land, but also the

[1] "Their houses are circular," says Marco Polo of the Tartars of inner Asia, "and are made of wands covered with felts": Yule's edition, Vol. I. p. 252.

[2] Mârdin, 6.30; Yamachlî, to right, 7.30; Sarî Khân, 8.45; Ispileh, to right, 10.30; Talas, 11.30.

physical and moral qualities of the inhabitants of Cæsarea came under our consideration as we rode.

"If a serpent bites a man of Ḳaiṣarîyeh," observed Fattûḥ, "the serpent dies."

"Jânum!" exclaimed the zaptieh (who was not a Cæsarean). "My soul! they can outwit the devil himself. Have you not heard the tale?"

"I have not heard," said Fattûḥ.

"This it is," said the zaptieh. "Upon a day the devil came to Ḳaiṣarîyeh. 'Khush geldi,' said the people, 'a fair welcome,' and they showed him the streets and the bazaars of the city, the mosques and the khâns, all of them. When he was hungry they set food before him till he was well satisfied, but when he rose to depart, he looked for his cloak and belt and they were gone. The devil is not safe from the thieves of Ḳaiṣarîyeh."

"God made them rogues," said Fattûḥ.

"What can we do?" observed the zaptieh philosophically. "Dunya bîr, jânum—the world is all one."

"Great travelling they make," continued Fattûḥ. "In every city you meet them."

The zaptieh was ready with historic evidence on this head also.

"There was a man," said he, "who lived some time in Cæsarea, and having had experience of the people, he found them to be all pigs. Therefore he resolved to journey to the furthest end of the earth, that he might escape from them. And he went to Baghdâd, which is a long road."

"It is long," admitted Fattûḥ.

"And then he entered the bath and demanded a good ḥammâmjî to knead the weariness out of his bones. And the owner of the bath called out: 'Bring the lame Cæsarean!' Then said the traveller: 'A Cæsarean here and he lame!' and he fled from Baghdâd."

Fattûḥ is innocent of any sense of humour. "Oh Merciful," said he gravely.

I do not know whether it was the effect produced by these

FIG. 231.—MOUNT ARGAEUS FROM NORTH-WEST.

FIG. 233.—NIGDEH, TOMB OF HAVANDA.

FIG. 234.—NIGDEH, TOMB OF HAVANDA, DETAIL OF WINDOW.

tales which prevented me from lodging in Ḳaiṣarîyeh, or whether the prospect of two days spent in the society of people of my own speech and civilization would not have proved too strong a temptation, even if the Cæsareans had shone with every virtue; at any rate I went no further than Talas, and there remained as a guest in the hospital of the American missionaries. And if I saw little of the famous city of Cæsarea, I passed many hours in the hospital garden at the feet of men and women whose words were instinct with a wise tolerance and weighted by a profound experience of every aspect of Oriental life.

Ḳaiṣarîyeh was the end of the caravan journey. In two days we had sold our horses ("One for us to sell and one for them to buy," said Fattûḥ), and packed our belongings into the carts which were to take us to the railway at Ereglî. I rode down from Talas to conclude these arrangements and to visit the citadel which stands on Justinian's foundations. The interior is now packed with narrow streets, the houses being built partly of ancient materials (Fig. 230). The fragments of columns and the weather-worn capitals which are imbedded in the walls of the houses were derived either from the early Christian town which occupied the site of modern Ḳaiṣarîyeh, or from ancient Cæsarea, which lay upon the lower slopes of Mount Argæus. A few foundations outside the limits of the present town are all that remain of the churches that adorned the greatest ecclesiastical centre of the Anatolian plateau, the birthplace of St. Basil, but the memory of the Seljuk conquerors, who gave it a fresh glory during the Middle Ages, is still preserved in many a decaying mosque and school.

We set out from Ḳaiṣarîyeh a diminished party, Ḥâjj 'Amr and Selîm having found work with a caravan of muleteers and returned with them across the mountains to Aleppo. The first day's drive took us round the foot of Argæus to Yeni Khân, a solitary inn, not marked in Kiepert, which lies two hours to the north of Ḳaraḥiṣâr. The mighty buttresses of Argæus, rising out of the immense flats of the Anatolian plateau, are as imposing as the flanks of Etna rising from the sea, and its height, over 13,000 feet, is scarcely less from base to summit than that of the Sicilian volcano.[1] The second day brought us to a khân by the roadside, half-an-hour from the village of Andaval; upon the following morning we reached, after three-quarters of an hour's drive, the church of Constantine, of which the foundation is attributed by legend to the Empress Helena,[2] and in two hours more we came to Nigdeh, where I halted for a few hours to see the Seljuk mosques and tombs for which the town is famed. Of these the most beautiful is the so-called mausoleum of Havanda, the wife of 'Ala ed Din.[3] It is in ground plan an octagon, but above the windows the number of faces is doubled, the additional angles being built over projecting brackets, finely worked with stalactite ornaments (Figs. 232 and 233). The spandrils above the windows are decorated with pairs of sphinxes (Fig. 234), and the door is framed in a delicate tracery of lace-like patterns. Beyond Bor we came into a well-known country dominated by the twin peaks of Ḥassan Dâgh, the Lesser Argæus, which I greeted with a respect mingled with the familiarity born of an intimate acquaintance with its rocks. Three hours from Nigdeh we reached Emîr Chiflik, where there is a khân unnamed by Kiepert, and next morning we drove into Bulgurlû, the present terminus of the Baghdâd railway. But the art of modern travel accords ill with the habits of the East; the

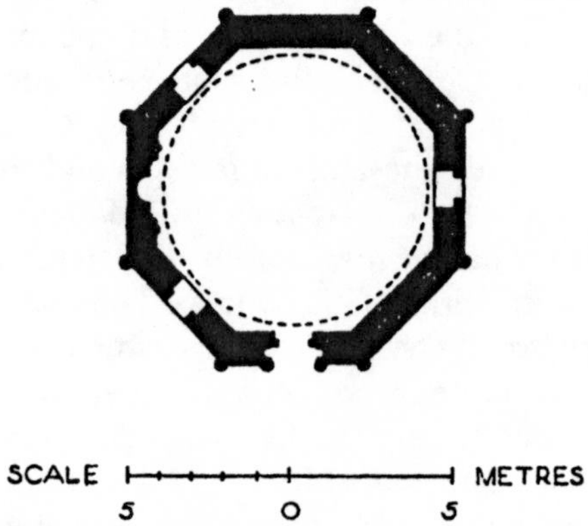

FIG. 232.—TOMB OF HAVANDA.

[1] The plateau is here about 3,500 feet above sea level.

[2] It has been well published by Rott: *Kleinasiatische Denkmäler*, p. 103.

[3] 'Ala ed Din reigned from 1219 to 1236, but the tomb is dated by an inscription in the year 1344.

baggage wagon missed the daily train and we were obliged to wait for it at Ereglî.

"Your Excellency does not wish to see the pictures of the Benî Hît?" said Fattûḥ suspiciously as we stepped out upon the platform. We had never before passed through Ereglî without visiting the great Hittite relief in the gorge of Ivrîz. But I reassured him: we had seen enough.

One more expedition lay, however, between us and Konia. It was to be accomplished in light order; indeed, we might have ridden up to the Ḳara Dâgh without possessions, for there was no man in all the mountain who would not have been proud to offer us a lodging. Fattûḥ and I shone there with a reflected glory that radiated from the Chelabî, whose fame is not confined to the Ḳara Dâgh, though few perhaps of his colleagues in the Scottish Academe which he adorns would recognize him under his Anatolian title. Had we not spent weeks under his direction in grubbing among old stones, to the delight and profit of all beholders? Had we not consumed innumerable hares and partridges at twopence a head, and offered a sure market for yaourt and eggs? And when the regretted hour of departure arrived, what store of empty tins and battered cooking pots was left behind to keep our memory green! Our renown extended even to Ḳaramân, where we alighted from the train on the following evening. The khânjî was a trusted friend, the shopkeepers pressed gifts of rose jam upon us, and when the hiring of horses presented a difficulty, I had only to step out into the streets and explain our needs to the first acquaintance whom I met. He happened to be a ḥammâl (a porter) who had done a couple of days' work for us in the Ḳara Dâgh, and he was intimate with an arabajî (a carriage driver), who would without doubt place his horses at our disposal; and if I would come in and drink a cup of coffee the matter should be settled. I accepted the invitation and was introduced triumphantly to the ḥammâl's wife: "This is the maid I told you about—she who worked with the Chelabî." On our way back to the khân we chanced to pass by the exquisite Khâtûnyeh Medresseh,[1] and

[1] It was built in 1381–2 by the wife of 'Ala ed Dîn, Prince of Ḳaramân. See Sarre: *Denkmäler Persischer Baukunst*, p. 135.

since the mullah was standing under the carved gateway, I stopped to bid him a good-evening. In the tomb chamber that opens out of the cloistered courtyard I remembered to have seen fragments of a fine inscription of blue tiles: scarcely a tile was left upon the walls and I knew how they had vanished, for I had found one of them in the hands of a Konia dealer and bought it from him. This incident I related to the mullah.

"You did very wrong," said he. "You have stolen one of our tiles and carried it away."

"I did not steal it," I pleaded weakly. "I found it at Konia."

"It is all one," he replied. "You should give it back."

But as we went out through the cloister I noticed that the columns which supported it were double columns of a type peculiar to Christian architecture. They had in all probability been removed from a church.

"Mullah Effendi," said I, "we are equal. I have taken a tile out of your Moslem tomb, and you the columns from our Christian church."

The mullah's indignation vanished in a flash. "Âferîn!" he cried, with a jolly laugh. "Bravo!" and he clapped me on the back.

The ḥammâl's confidence in the arabajî had not been misplaced; we set out next morning for the Ḳara Dâgh, and every mile was full of delightful reminiscence. The yellow roses dropped their petals in familiar fashion over the mountain path, mullein and borage spread their annual carpet of blue and gold between the ruins, and the peak of Mahalech, on which I had found a Hittite inscription and a Christian monastery, stood guardian, as of old, over the green cup wherein had lain an ancient city. The sturdy Yuruks came striding down from their high yailas to bid us a joyful coming and a slow departure; many were the greetings that passed round the camp fire, and it was well that Fattûḥ had laid in a good provision of coffee at Ḳaramân.

So on a hot morning we struck our last camp and rode down the northern slopes of the mountain to rejoin the railway by which we were to travel to Konia. And as we crossed the level plain Fattûḥ observed with satisfaction :

"The cornland has increased since two years ago. Effendim, there is twice as much sown ground."

"Praise God!" said I. "It is the doing of the railway."

"Wherever it passes the corn springs up," said Fattûḥ. "Mâshallah! Konia will become a great city."

"It has grown in our knowledge," said I. "But this year we shall find it much changed, for all our friends have left."

"Where have they gone?" inquired Fattûh.

"Riza Beg is in Salonica," said I, mentioning one who had eaten out his heart in exile for ten weary years. "He has gone back to his wife and child."

"He would make haste to join them," assented Fattûḥ.

"And Meḥmet Pasha is in Constantinople. I saw his name among those who helped to depose the Sultan."

"He has risen to high honour," said Fattûh. Meḥmet Pasha was another of the proscribed.

"And Suleimân Effendi is deputy for Konia, where he was so long in exile. Oh Fattûḥ, we shall be strangers there now that our friends have gone."

"Your Excellency will meet them in other cities," said Fattûḥ. "And they will be free men."

INDEX

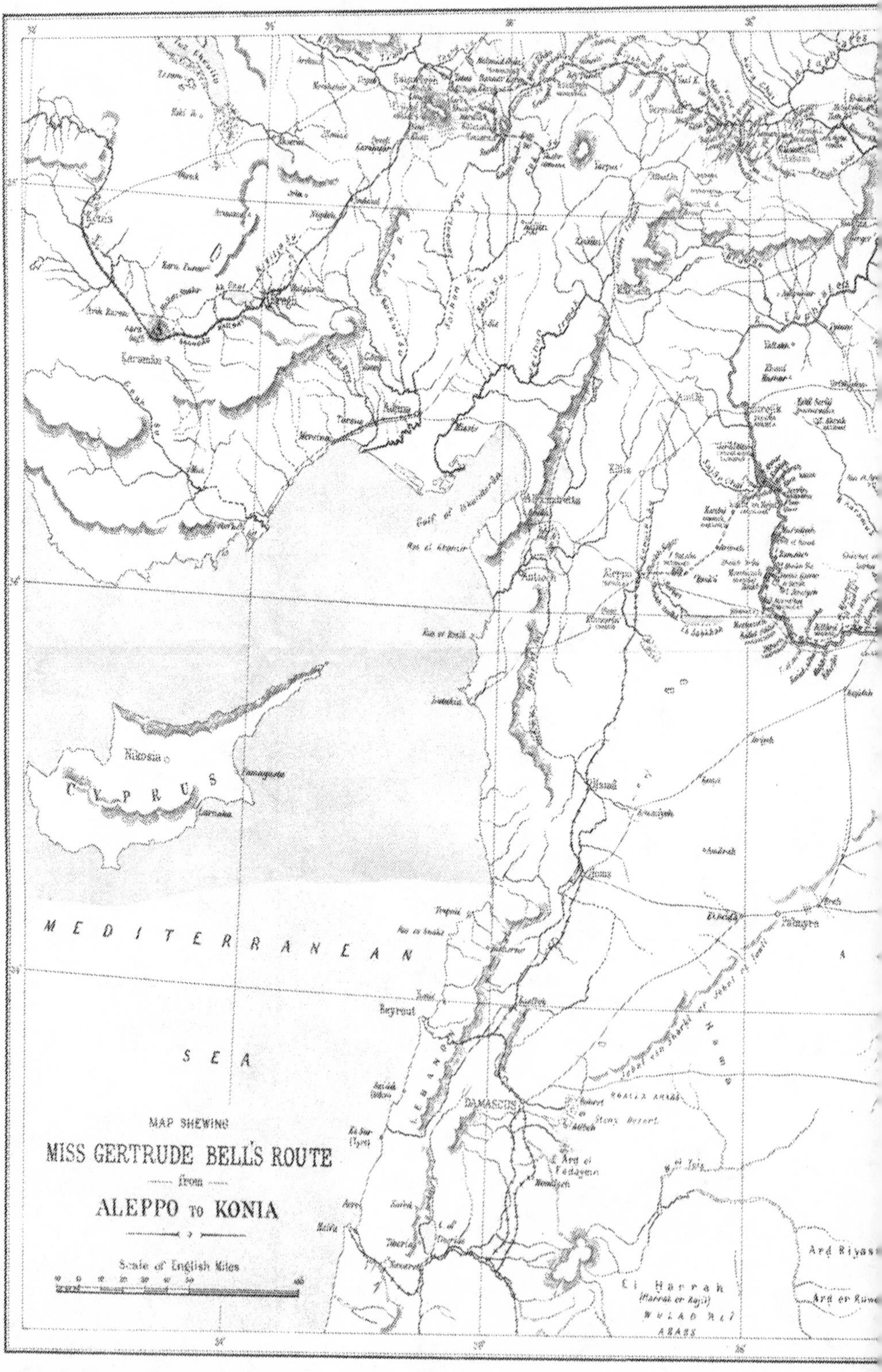
MAP SHEWING
MISS GERTRUDE BELL'S ROUTE
from
ALEPPO to KONIA
Scale of English Miles
MEDITERRANEAN
SEA
CYPRUS
Nikosia
Famagusta
Larnaka
Gulf of Iskanderun
Aleppo
Antioch
Adana
Tarsus
Mersina
Karaman
Konia
Eregli
Hama
Homs
Palmyra
Tripoli
Beyrout
Baalbek
DAMASCUS
Stony Desert
Tiberias
Haifa
Acre
Es Sur (Tyre)
Saida (Sidon)
El Harrah
Ard Riyas
Ard er Ruwe

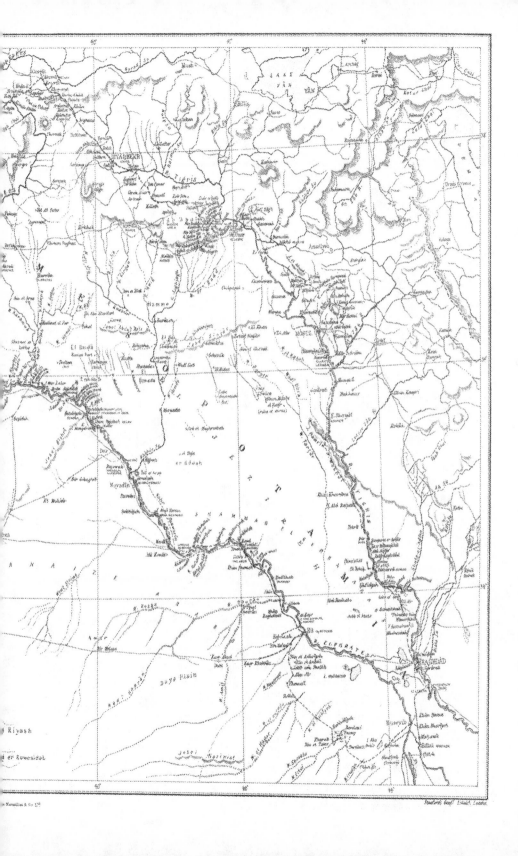

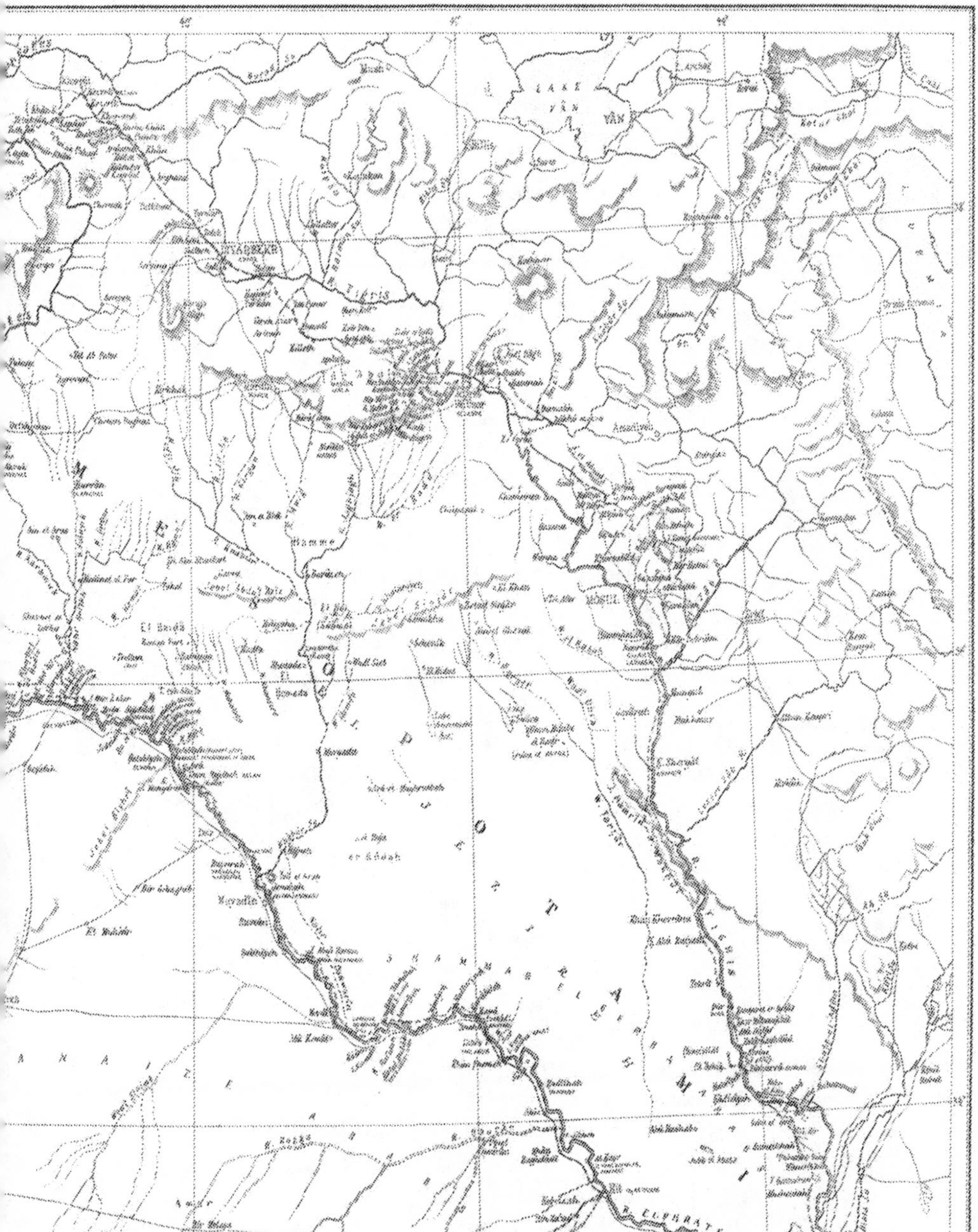

Macmillan & Co Ltd

Stanford's Geogl. Estabt, London

GORGIAS REPRINT SERIES

1. J. B. Segal, *Edessa 'The Blessed City'* (2001, based on the 1970 edition).
2. J. Hamlyn Hill, *The Earliest Life of Christ: The Diatessaron of Tatian* (2001, based on the 1910 2nd abridged edition).
3. Joseph Knanishu, *About Persia and Its People* (2001, based on the 1899 edition).
4. Robert Curzon, *Ancient Monasteries of the East, Or The Monasteries of the Levant* (2001, based on the 1849 edition).
5. William Wright, *A Short History of Syriac Literature* (2001, based on the 1894 edition).
6. Frits Holm, *My Nestorian Adventure in China, A Popular Account of the Holm-Nestorian Expedition to Sian-Fu and Its Results* (2001, based on the 1924 edition).
7. Austen Henry Layard, *Nineveh and Its Remains: an account of a visit to the Chaldean Christians of Kurdistan, and the Yezidis, or devil-worshipers; and an inquiry into the manners and arts of the ancient Assyrians*, Vol. 1 (2001, based on the 1850 5th edition).
8. Austen Henry Layard, *Nineveh and Its Remains*, Vol. 2 (2001, based on the 1850 5th edition).
9. Margaret Gibson, *How the Codex Was Found, A Narrative of Two Visits to Sinai From Mrs. Lewis's Journals 1892-1893* (2001, based on the 1893 edition).
10. Richard Davey, *The Sultan and His Subjects* (2001, based on the 1907 edition).
11. Adrian Fortescue, *Eastern Churches Trilogy: The Orthodox Eastern Church* (2001, based on the 1929 edition).
12. Adrian Fortescue, *Eastern Churches Trilogy: The Lesser*

Eastern Churches (2001, based on the 1913 edition).

13. Adrian Fortescue, *Eastern Churches Trilogy: The Uniate Eastern Churches: the Byzantine Rite in Italy, Sicily, Syria and Egypt* (2001, based on the 1923 edition).
14. A. V. Williams Jackson, *From Constantinople to the Home of Omar Khayyam: Travels in Transcaucasia and Northern Persia for Historic and Literary Research* (2001, based on the 1911 edition).
15. Demetra Vaka, *The Unveiled Ladies of Stamboul* (2001, based on the 1923 edition).
16. Oswald H. Parry, *Six Months in a Syrian Monastery: Being the Record of a Visit to the Head Quarters of the Syrian Church in Mesopotamia with Some Account of the Yazidis or Devil Worshipers of Mosul and El Jilwah, Their Sacred Book* (2001, based on the 1895 edition).
17. B. T. A. Evetts, *The Churches and Monasteries of Egypt and Some Neighbouring Countries, Attribted to Abû Sâlih the Armenian* (2001, based on the 1895 edition).
18. James Murdock, *The New Testament, Or the Book of the Holy Gospel of Our Lord and Our God Jesus the Messiah, A Literal Translation from the Syriac Peshita Version* (2001, based on the 1851 edition).
19. Gertrude Lowthian Bell, *Amurath to Amurath: A Five Month Journey Along the Banks of the Euphrates* (2001, based on the 1924 second edition).
20. Smith, George. *Assyrian Discoveries: An Account of Explorations and Discoveries on the Site of Nineveh, During 1873 and 1874* (2002, based on the 1876 edition).
21. Dalley, *Stephanie. Mari and Karana, Two Old Babylonian Cities* (2002, first US paperback edition).
22. Grant, *Asahel. The Nestorians or the Lost Tribe* (2002, based on the 1841 edition).
23. O'Leary, De Lacy. *The Syriac Church and Fathers* (2002, based on the 1909 edition).
24. Burkitt, F. C. *Early Christianity Outside the Roman Empire* (2002, based on the 1909 edition).
25. Wigram, W. A. *The Assyrians and Their Neighbours*

(2002, based on the 1929 edition).

26. Kiraz, George. *Lexical Tools to the Syriac New Testament* (2002, first US edition).
27. Margoliouth, G. *Descriptive List of Syriac and Karshuni Manuscripts in the British Museum Acquired Since 1873* (2002, based on the 1899 edition).
28. Wright, William. *Lectures on the Comparative Grammar of the Semitic Languages, With a General Survey of the Semitic Languages and Their Diffusion and of the Semitic Alphabet, Origin and Writing.* Edited with a Preface and Additional Notes by William Robertson Smith (2002, based on the 1890 edition).

Printed in the United States
104310LV00005B/184/A

9 780971 598690